An Introduction to Forensic Phonetics and Forensic Linguistics

This textbook provides a practical introduction to the fields of forensic phonetics and forensic linguistics. Addressing how these fields are both distinct yet closely related, the book demonstrates how experts from both fields can work together to investigate and deliver justice in complex legal situations.

With pedagogical features including real-life case studies, exercises, and links to further reading, topics covered include:

- Profiling from spoken and written texts;
- Disputed meaning and how meaning is made and evolves;
- Interviewing techniques, including working around those who might be considered linguistically vulnerable;
- Author and speaker determination;
- Audio enhancement and authentication of recordings;
- Language analysis in the asylum procedure (LAAP).

Accompanied by online audio and video resources as well as signposting readers to freely available software to aid their studies, this book is the ideal springboard for students beginning work in forensic phonetics, forensic speech science, forensic linguistics, and law and language.

Adrian Leemann is Professor of German Sociolinguistics at the University of Bern, Switzerland.

Ria Perkins works as a civil servant for the Ministry of Defence, and is an Honorary Research Fellow at the Aston Institute for Forensic Linguistics in Birmingham, UK.

Grace Sullivan Buker is a Lecturer in Forensic Linguistics and Cross-Cultural Communication at Northeastern University, USA.

Paul Foulkes is Professor of Linguistics and Phonetics at the University of York, UK.

LEARNING ABOUT LANGUAGE

Series Editors:
Brian Walker, Queen's University Belfast, UK; **Willem Hollmann**, Lancaster University, UK; and the late **Geoffrey Leech**, Lancaster University, UK

Series Consultant:
Mick Short, Lancaster University, UK

Learning about Language is an exciting and ambitious series of introductions to fundamental topics in language, linguistics and related areas. The books are designed for students of linguistics and those who are studying language as part of a wider course.

Also in this series:

The History of Early English
An Activity-based Approach
Keith Johnson

An Introduction to Foreign Language Learning and Teaching, Revised Third Edition
Keith Johnson

The History of Late Modern Englishes
An Activity-based Approach
Keith Johnson

Analysing Sentences
An Introduction to English Syntax, Fifth Edition
Noel Burton-Roberts

An Introduction to Sociolinguistics, Sixth Edition
Janet Holmes and Nick Wilson

Critical Discourse Analysis
A Practical Introduction to Power in Language
Simon Statham

Introducing Linguistics
Edited by Jonathan Culpeper, Beth Malory, Claire Nance, Daniel Van Olmen, Dimitrinka Atanasova, Sam Kirkham, and Aina Casaponsa

Discourse Analysis
A Practical Introduction
Patricia Canning and Brian Walker

An Introduction to Forensic Phonetics and Forensic Linguistics
Adrian Leemann, Ria Perkins, Grace Sullivan Buker, and Paul Foulkes

For more information about this series please visit: www.routledge.com/series/PEALAL

An Introduction to Forensic Phonetics and Forensic Linguistics

ADRIAN LEEMANN, RIA PERKINS,
GRACE SULLIVAN BUKER, AND PAUL FOULKES

Routledge
Taylor & Francis Group

LONDON AND NEW YORK

Designed cover image: © Getty Images | Ole_CNX

First published 2025
by Routledge
4 Park Square, Milton Park, Abingdon, Oxon, OX14 4RN

and by Routledge
605 Third Avenue, New York, NY 10158

Routledge is an imprint of the Taylor & Francis Group, an informa business

© 2025 Adrian Leemann, Ria Perkins, Grace Sullivan Buker, and Paul Foulkes

The right of Adrian Leemann, Ria Perkins, Grace Sullivan Buker, and Paul Foulkes
to be identified as authors of this work has been asserted in accordance with
sections 77 and 78 of the Copyright, Designs and Patents Act 1988.

Every effort has been made to contact copyright-holders. Please advise the publisher
of any errors or omissions, and these will be corrected in subsequent editions.

British Library Cataloguing-in-Publication Data
A catalogue record for this book is available from the British Library

ISBN: 978-0-367-61658-8 (hbk)
ISBN: 978-0-367-61657-1 (pbk)
ISBN: 978-0-367-61659-5 (ebk)

DOI: 10.4324/9780367616595

Typeset in Sabon
by Newgen Publishing UK

Access the Support Material: www.routledge.com/9780367616571

Contents

About the authors

Adrian Leemann is Professor of German Sociolinguistics at the University of Bern, Switzerland. He holds an MA and PhD degree from the University of Bern and a Habilitation from the University of Zürich. He has expertise in phonetics, sociodialectology, and a strong passion for the advancement of innovative data collection and analysis methods. Within the field of forensic speech science, his research delves into the investigation of how speech rhythm and intonation can convey distinctive speaker-specific information that holds relevance for forensic applications. His contributions to dialectology shed light on the identification of regional accents – particularly in German-speaking Europe as well as the United Kingdom – augmenting our comprehension of how speakers' linguistic origins can be discerned.

Ria Perkins works as a civil servant for the Ministry of Defence, and is an Honorary Research Fellow at the Aston Institute for Forensic Linguistics in Birmingham, UK. She holds a BA from Royal Holloway University of London, and an MA and PhD from Aston University, Birmingham, UK. Her casework speciality is authorship profiling, and her research interests include the language of persuasion and power, and Other Language Influence Detection (OLID).

Grace Sullivan Buker is a Lecturer in Forensic Linguistics and Cross-Cultural Communication at Northeastern University, USA. Her PhD is from Georgetown University, Washington DC. Her research focuses on racial and social injustices of institutions, particularly the criminal justice system of the United States. To reach a wider audience on the issues of Forensic Linguistics and Cross-Cultural Communications, Dr Buker established the consulting company, Cadence Advising, which has held workshops and training courses around the world.

Paul Foulkes is Professor of Linguistics and Phonetics at the University of York, UK. He holds the degrees of MA, MPhil, and PhD from the University of Cambridge (Churchill College). His background is in phonetics, phonology, sociolinguistics, and dialectology, mostly dealing with British English. He has undertaken casework in forensic phonetics since 1999, with a focus on speaker comparison, speaker profiling, and forensic transcription. He has worked as an expert witness in over 200 cases, mainly from the UK but also from Australia, New Zealand, Ghana, and Sweden. He conducts research on speaker comparison, earwitness evidence, and language in the asylum procedure (LAAP). He has also provided training and consultancy on forensic phonetics for the FBI, US Secret Service, and a number of national governments and forensic laboratories.

Acknowledgements

We thank the following friends and colleagues who have provided valuable advice on drafts of chapters in this book: Tallulah Buckley, Tina Cambier-Langeveld, Martin Duckworth, Ben Gibb-Reid, Tammy Gales, Amelia Gully, Hannah Hedegard, Jim Hoskin, Priska Hubbuch, Vincent Hughes, Thomas Kettig, Olaf Köster, Karoline Marko, Kirsty McDougall, Chloe Patman, Richard Rhodes, Emily Shepherdson, Heidy Suter, Bruce Wang, and Jessica Wormald.

We are also grateful to a number of people who helped with particular questions, or who kindly gave permission to use figures and other data from their work. Thanks to: Tamsin Blaxter, Abigail Boucher, Almut Braun, Qasim Chaudhari, Annina Heini, Haytham Fayek, Jodie Fox, Stefan Goetze, Deepthi Gopal, Philip Harrison, Finnian Kelly, Ghada Khattab, Katharina Klug, Jonas Lindh, Belén Lowrey-Kinberg, Nancy Niedzielski, Francis Nolan, Richard Ogden, Tae-Hyun Oh, Ulrich Reubold, James Tompkinson, and David Willis.

Copyright credits

Figures and sound files were produced by the authors unless otherwise stated.

Chapter 2

Figure 2.1: courtesy of Amelia Gully

Figures 2.2 and 2.3:

IPA Chart, www.internationalphoneticassociation.org/content/ipa-chart, available under a Creative Commons Attribution-Sharealike 3.0 Unported License. Copyright © 2018 International Phonetic Association.

Figure 2.5:

User:Presto, Public domain, via Wikimedia Commons

https://commons.wikimedia.org/wiki/File:Arytenoid_cartilage.png

Figure 2.6:

User:Presto, Public domain, via Wikimedia Commons

https://commons.wikimedia.org/wiki/File:Glottis_positions.png

Figure 2.9:

Reproduced with permission from https://wirelesspi.com/the-concept-of-freque ncy

Rainbow.wav – provided courtesy of the PASR project (Person-specific automatic speaker recognition: understanding the behaviour of individuals for applications of Automatic Speaker Recognition, University of York. Funded by the UK Economic and Social Research Council, grant ES/W001241/1).

Chapter 3

Figure 3.1: reproduced from Hedegard et al. (2023), with permission of the authors

Figures 3.2 and 3.3: reproduced with permission of the Tweetolectology project – Tamsin Blaxter, Deepthi Gopal, Adrian Leemann, and David Willis

Figure 3.4: adapted by the authors from Labov (1964)

Figure 3.5: adapted by the authors from Reubold, Harrington, & Kleber (2010)

Figure 3.6: reproduced from https://speech2face.github.io/ with permission of Tae-Hyun Oh

Chapter 4

Figure 4.3: adapted by the authors from Thaitechawat and Foulkes (2011)

Figure 4.4: adapted by the authors from Laver (1980) and San Segundo et al. (2019)

Figure 4.5: reproduced from Hedegard et al. (2023), with permission of the authors

Figure 4.6: reproduced with permission from Haytham Fayek https://haythamfayek.com/2016/04/21/speech-processing-for-machine-learning. html

Figure 4.7: adapted by the authors from AFSP (2009)

Chapter 5

Figure 5.1: Public domain, via Wikimedia Commons https://commons.wikimedia.org/wiki/File:Charles_Lindbergh_and_the_Spirit_ of_Saint_Louis_(Crisco_restoration,_with_wings).jpg https://commons.wikimedia.org/wiki/File:Lindbergh_baby_poster.jpg

Figure 5.2: created by the authors, based on Taswegian Words blog

Figure 5.3: © Corinne Lanthemann, reproduced with permission

Figure 5.4: adapted from Nolan et al. (2013), with permission of the authors

Chapter 6

Figure 6.4: reproduced with permission from Goetze (2013)

Figure 6.5: reproduced with permission from Braun (© Equinox Publishing Ltd 1994)

Figures 6.9 and 6.10: reproduced from Morrison et al. (2014) with permission of Jonas Lindh and Elsevier

Chapter 7

Figure 7.1: The logo shown is not authentic. It has been adapted from the actual logo. The crowned portcullis is taken from https://commons.wikimedia.org/ wiki/File:Crowned_Portcullis_redesign_2018.svg, and is understood to be in the public domain.

1 Introduction to the book

This book provides a general overview of forensic phonetics and forensic linguistics. We expect that most readers will have a prior background in linguistics and/or phonetics and will be familiar with basic terms (e.g., *phoneme*, *feature*). However, this textbook also provides a brief introduction to key concepts and methods in phonetics (Chapter 2) and linguistics (Chapter 8) that underpin both forensic research and casework. In a book this size, we have inevitably covered only a selection of the activities of forensic speech and language analysts, reflecting our own experience and expertise.

Despite the similarity of their names, forensic phonetics and forensic linguistics are often regarded as separate. Very few forensic practitioners deal with cases or research in both phonetics and linguistics. Moreover, most practitioners also have specialisms within their field. Casework therefore often involves teams of people working together, combining their expertise. However, there are certain types of casework that draw on both forensic phonetics and forensic linguistics, for example Language analysis in the asylum procedure (LAAP). The principles of record keeping, report writing, and acting as an expert witness are also common to both fields (as they are to all forensic sciences). We hope the book serves to highlight the similarities and areas of mutual interest so that there is more communication between different types of expert.

About the book – how to use it

This book is divided into two core sections: the first (Chapters 2–6) focuses on forensic phonetics, the second (Chapters 8–12) on forensic linguistics. Chapter 7, on language analysis in the asylum procedure (LAAP), involves both phoneticians and linguists and is thus situated as a transition between the two main sections. The final chapter (13) considers both forensic phonetics and linguistics in the context of legal systems and courts. At the end of each chapter you will find suggestions for further reading.

There are exercises at various stages throughout the book, which are intended to enhance understanding of the theories and methodologies. These exercises can be tackled individually, or used as the basis for class activities. It is virtually impossible to learn through reading alone, as some aspects need to be

DOI: 10.4324/9780367616595-1

experienced first-hand as an analyst. Furthermore, in forensic practice it is important to understand that there is often no 'correct' answer. The key value of these exercises is to help you to understand and experience the methodologies used to analyse forensic speech and language data. The exercises are often simplified or reduced versions of what we might experience in casework situations. In a genuine casework situation, the questions sometimes have more complex dimensions, and require a more extensive analysis and response from the practitioner. Nonetheless the exercises will help you gather important insights, so we encourage you not to skip them or to just read the answers.

Each chapter includes references to forensic cases, and to websites for further information. Some of the case discussions have been altered due to their sensitive nature. However, the core details remain true to real-life situations as far as possible. Real names and information are used where permissions have been given, or the information is already available in the public domain. The support material website for the book (www.routledge.com/9780367616571) contains clickable links to allow you to go directly to the sources (these are indicated by the support material icon in the print text). The support material website also provides colour versions of some of the figures shown in the book, and other data files.

This book is designed to be used as a step towards further studies. **This book alone will not train you to be a forensic linguist or a forensic phonetician.** Both require years of further study at postgraduate level, and training via experience in established forensic labs. However, the book will provide a solid grounding and an initial introduction to guide you on your journey.

About forensic phonetics and forensic linguistics

The analysis of language is not a modern phenomenon. In fact, people analyse language frequently in everyday circumstances. When you answer the telephone, for example, you (usually subconsciously) analyse the opening words in order to establish whose voice it is. Is it someone you know, or a stranger? Does the voice match the name shown on your telephone screen? Furthermore, the idea of language analysis being used for legal, or quasi-legal, purposes is also not new. For example, in a well-known Bible story, the Gileadites undertake a basic form of speaker profiling based on the phonetic elements of migrants' speech. The Ephraimites pronounced /s/ in words where Gileadites had /ʃ/. The punishment was death if the person was deemed to be an Ephraimite:

> And the Gileadites took the passages of Jordan before the Ephraimites: and it was so, that when those Ephraimites which were escaped said, Let me go over; that the men of Gilead said unto him, Art thou an Ephraimite? If he said, Nay; Then said they unto him, Say now Shibboleth: and he said Sibboleth: for he could not frame to pronounce it right. Then they took him and slew him

at the passages of Jordan: and there fell at that time of the Ephraimites forty and two thousand.

Judges 12:5–6 King James Bible

The example in the story, *shibboleth* (meaning 'ear of corn'), has passed into general usage to refer to words that signal membership of a particular group. More recent examples of shibboleths have been evidenced from the war in Ukraine, with the word паляниця (palyanitsa/palyanytsya, a kind of bread) allegedly being used to identify potential undercover Russian saboteurs, as it is believed that this is a hard word for Russians to pronounce (Hyde 2022). Chapter 3 discusses the methodology behind phonetic profiling, while Chapter 11 looks at authorship profiling. (Unsurprisingly, we do not suggest that the pronunciation of one word is enough to determine with any certainty where someone is from, or that it should be used as evidence leading to serious legal outcomes.)

Beware the CSI effect

You might have seen forensic speech or language analysis in movies and on television. Forensic experts in drama often possess an enormous array of analytic skills. They collect samples from crime scenes, interview suspects and witnesses, analyse materials in impressive-looking laboratories with state-of-the-art software and hardware systems, and deliver their results in a matter of seconds. (And all while coping with everyday traumas in their private lives, and maintaining perfect hair.) The results are often presented confidently as a 'match' or 'mismatch', supported by some impressive sounding statistics ('99.4% certainty!'). Some dramas also involve automatic systems, for example to control entry to top security areas. We see characters speak into devices, and a visual image which shows their 'voiceprint' matching perfectly with some sample the machine has already stored. The outcomes of these forensic analyses are then often critical for the development of the plot.

Exciting though such scenes are, they bear little resemblance to the reality of forensic speech and language work. First, the work might take days rather than seconds. Second, real forensic scientists rarely if ever report their results in binary terms like match/mismatch. This is because forensic analysis is unlikely to give a black or white conclusion: there is almost always some doubt. The general principles of objectivity and transparency are absolutely vital in forensic science. This is true even in cases people tend to think are straightforward, like DNA analysis. A scientist might analyse a DNA sample from a crime scene, and show that it contains identical DNA to that of the suspect accused of committing the crime. This does not mean, however, that the suspect must be the criminal: it means he *could* be the criminal. But so could other people who share that DNA profile – and there can be thousands of candidates. Furthermore, information beyond the DNA is crucial to establishing whether the suspect was in the vicinity of the scene, had a motive, and so on. Such information is available to the court (judge and jury), but it is not available to the forensic scientist, whose role is limited to providing an informed, expert opinion on some question relating to the forensic evidence. Things can get very complicated with speech and language analysis, because no two samples of speech or writing are ever identical. Forensic speech and language analysis can therefore only discuss similarities and differences, the balance between the two, and the overall likelihood of the evidence supporting either the prosecution proposition (that the evidential materials come from the same source) or the defence proposition (that the materials come from a different source). We discuss these issues in more detail in Chapters 4 and 13.

Personal and social implications of working with forensic language data

There is considerable variety in the data that might be encountered in forensic phonetics and linguistics. Many cases involve work with data that might be considered mundane (e.g., phone calls dealing with financial transactions), but many other cases involve materials that could potentially be traumatising. Either way it is wise to remember that either the data itself, or the context surrounding it, might be triggering or disturbing (to you or others). There has been a significant amount of work that looks at vicarious trauma in other professions (particularly among therapists), and while this has not been extensively considered with relation to forensic phonetics and linguistics, it is still relevant. There is a growing recognition within the fields of the need for a proactive approach to mental health and resilience. This can be seen, for example, in the work of Giménez, Elstein, and Queralt (2020), who conducted interviews with forensic linguists to understand how they managed wellbeing during the pandemic.

It is important to look after your mental health. Based on our experiences, we recommend that you take time to respect that the work and material can be tough, and they can affect you. The apparent seriousness of a crime does not equate to the difficulty in analysis, nor how much it impacts you as a scientist. We are all individuals and will find different things difficult at different times. It is always ok to set boundaries, to step away for a break, or to only look at cases/material that you feel able to cope with at that time. Do not suffer in silence; most professional institutions offer various kinds of support. It is strong and wise to seek this out.

Focus on perpetrators

While a lot of the cases that we work on are civil rather than criminal, some of the cases discussed in this book are of a violent and disturbing nature. It is worth recognising the social as well as personal implications of this. When we talk about murders, kidnappings, and rapes, these are real people who have gone through this trauma. It is sometimes easy to forget that when we focus on the academic aspects of the evidence.

One issue of particular social significance is the emphasis on the attackers rather than the victims. Many people are familiar with the names of Ted Bundy, Peter Sutcliffe (the Yorkshire Ripper), and Ted Kaczynski (the Unabomber). Fewer people are familiar with the names of their victims – Karen Sparks, Wilma Mary McCann, Hugh Scrutton, David Arthur Faraday, Betty Lou Jensen, and many others. This further robs victims of their agency, diminishes the perceived impact of the crime, and allows the perpetrators to gain notoriety. For that reason, the former Prime Minister of New Zealand, Jacinda Ardern, refused to name the terrorist who attacked mosques in Christchurch in 2019. Throughout this book we often focus on determining more about the creator of a piece of language or communication, and this regularly (though not always) corresponds to the perpetrators. We encourage you as reader not to lose sight of the wider context, or of the many individuals that have been harmed (directly or indirectly) by the cases.

It is also very important to remember that how we talk about such cases matters. We have tried to use the most sensitive language that we have at our disposal, but awareness around this is constantly evolving, and we, like you, are constantly learning. We would encourage you to consider the language you use and the implicit power it might hold. Related issues around power and institutional framing are discussed further in Chapter 10. However, we also ask you to keep questioning if the language you use to discuss such things is consistent with the values you hold. This is particularly important when we are discussing cases that have had significant impact on those involved. Dark humour might be a coping mechanism when dealing with difficult material. However, you never know when you might be sitting next to a victim or offender's family member.

Ethics

For both casework and research it is important to be aware of, and adhere to, relevant ethical frameworks and codes of conduct (discussed further in Chapter 13). One vital ethical principle of forensic work is to know the boundaries of your expertise and the limitations of your methods. Forensic experts should never be tempted to comment on issues outside their specialisms, and should always present a realistic picture of what their analysis can and cannot do. Most professional institutions have robust ethical guidelines and procedures. We encourage you to seek out such information in your own organisation.

It is crucial that forensic scientists understand their obligations to be objective – to tell 'the truth, the whole truth, and nothing but the truth', as the oath for witnesses across many jurisdictions has it. There should be no motivation to push a conclusion to be any more or less confident than the analysis merits, or to try to help any particular party in a legal case. A person who is accused of a crime should be assumed innocent until proven guilty. Forensic evidence serves to assist a court in establishing the likelihood of guilt; if the evidence reveals doubt, then the court must be made aware of that doubt. Remaining objective and impartial is perhaps the most difficult skill to master for a forensic scientist. This is something that cannot easily be taught in a book such as this. Instead it requires experience and training under the tutelage of established forensic scientists with expertise in the relevant area. Perhaps such a future lies ahead for you. We hope this book inspires you to try.

Resources

Aston Institute for Forensic Linguistics. University website, including links to publicly available recorded lectures.
www.aston.ac.uk/research/forensic-linguistics/events/past-events

Bunn, S., & Foxen, S. (2015). *Forensic Language Analysis*. POST Note 509, Parliamentary Office of Science and Technology, UK. A briefing produced for the UK Parliament to outline forensic phonetics and linguistics.

En Clair podcast and website. *A Casebook of Forensic Linguistic Cases, Literary Detection, and Language Mysteries.* https://wp.lancs.ac.uk/enclair/

Forensic Transcription Australia. Helen Fraser's website on issues in transcription, which includes sound files and commentary on forensic cases. https://forensictranscription.com.au/

International Association for Forensic Phonetics and Acoustics (IAFPA). Website for the main international community involved in forensic phonetics and speech science. www.iafpa.net

International Association for Forensic and Legal Linguistics (IAFLL). Website for the main international community involved in forensic linguistics. https://iafll.org/

There are also several other podcasts (varying from academic to non-academic) that introduce complex linguistic topics in accessible ways. A list is included on the support material website.

Extensive discussions of the fields are provided in:

Coulthard, M., May A., & Sousa-Silva, R. (eds.) (2020). *The Routledge Handbook of Forensic Linguistics*. Routledge.

Nolan, F., McDougall, K., & Hudson, T. (eds.) (2025). *Oxford Handbook of Forensic Phonetics*. Oxford University Press.

Picornell, I., Perkins, R., & Coulthard, C., (eds.) (2022). *Methodologies and Challenges in Forensic Linguistic Casework*. Wiley.

Tiersma, P., & Solan, L. (eds.) (2012). *Oxford Handbook of Language and Law*. Oxford University Press.

Detailed research studies and legal case reports are published in key journals:

International Journal of Speech, Language, and the Law (IJSLL). https://journal.equinoxpub.com/IJSLL

Language and Law/Linguagem e Direito. https://ojs.letras.up.pt/index.php/LLLD

International Journal of Legal Discourse. www.degruyter.com/journal/key/ijld/html

Useful links combining forensic linguistic resources and/or data:

International Bibliography of Language and the Law. https://legal-linguistics.net/bibliography/

Tools for corpus analysis. https://corpus-analysis.com/

The Forensic Linguistic Databank (FoLD). Website maintained by the Aston Institute for Forensic Linguistics at Aston University, UK. https://fold.aston.ac.uk/

Forensic linguistic resources. Website maintained by Tammy Gales at Hofstra University, New York, USA. https://forensicling.com/

The Cambridge Elements series are short publications on different aspects of forensic linguistics. www.cambridge.org/core/publications/elements/forensic-linguistics

References

Giménez, R., Elstein, S., & Queralt, S. (2020). The pandemic and the forensic linguistics caseworker's wellbeing: effects and recommendations. *International Journal of Speech, Language & the Law*, 27(2), 1–22.

Hyde, L. (2022). Saboteurs spark suspicion and solidarity in Kyiv. *Politico*, 26 February.

2 Introduction to phonetic analysis

In 1983 a telephone caller placed a series of bomb threats to Pan American Airlines. Some of the calls were recorded. The police arrested a suspect, Paul Prinzivalli, and eventually charged him. He agreed to record a version of the calls for his defence team. The recordings were sent to a sociolinguist, William Labov, who demonstrated through acoustic and auditory phonetic analysis that Prinzivalli had a different accent from that of the caller. Of particular importance was the pronunciation of the vowels in the words *bomb* and *off*. The caller, who had a Boston accent, used a very similar vowel in the two words. The suspect, however, used different vowels, which is a characteristic of his New York accent. Prinzivalli was subsequently acquitted, with the judge citing the phonetic evidence as a crucial factor in establishing reasonable doubt about his guilt.

This case is one of the earliest documented examples of expert *speaker* (or *voice*) *comparison* (Labov 1988). It illustrates how a comparison is made between a questioned sample (i.e., we do not know who the speaker is) and a known sample (i.e., the recording is from a speaker whose identity we know). Voice comparisons are the most common type of case in forensic phonetics. Acoustic, auditory, and sometimes computer-automated approaches are used to extract and compare information from the recordings. An analysis is made of particular speech sounds, such as the vowels illustrated in the Prinzivalli case, and other phonetic features of the voice such as intonation and voice quality. This chapter introduces you to the range of phonetic features and analysis types used in forensic casework.

Aim

In this chapter we introduce you to a variety of phonetic features which are often analysed in forensic phonetic casework. We will familiarise you with the fundamentals of **speech production** (Section 2.1) and **acoustic analysis** (Section 2.2) to give you a broad understanding of the **phonetic features** discussed in the rest of this book, especially in Chapters 3–7. In this chapter, we will focus on features which are particularly significant in forensic phonetic analysis. This chapter, then, provides a general introduction to phonetics, and will be useful to you especially if you have not studied this subject before.

DOI: 10.4324/9780367616595-2

2.1 Fundamentals of speech production

First, we need to talk about how speech is produced. At the core of speech production is the **source-filter model**. In this understanding of speech, the source is air that is pushed upwards from the lungs (an egressive pulmonic airstream), initiating vibration in the vocal folds (also known as vocal cords). Vocal fold vibration happens at the glottis, which is shown at the bottom of Figure 2.1. This **source signal** is then **filtered** by articulators in the oral and nasal tracts (see further section 2.1.1), producing a wide variety of different sounds. Moving the articulators – the lips and tongue, for example – changes the shape of the oral tract and thus its resonance characteristics. For example, if your tongue is raised and fronted and your lips are spread, you produce an [i] sound. This is similar to the vowel in standard British English *see*, German *sieben* 'seven', or French *six* 'six'. If your tongue is backed and lowered and your lips are spread, you produce an [ɑ] sound, like in standard British English *palm*. The filter modifies the source signal, i.e., the sound produced by the vibrating vocal folds, in different ways

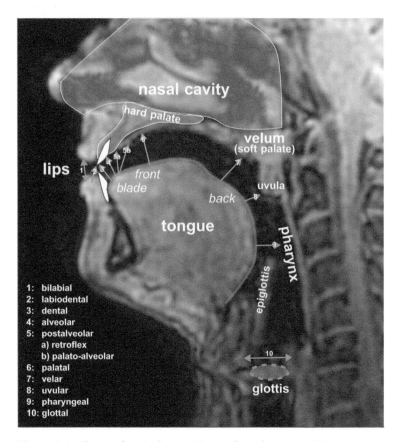

Figure 2.1 Places of articulation. (Image based on an MRI scan, courtesy of Amelia Gully).

depending on its shape and associated resonance characteristics after moving the articulators. In turn this results in the production of a particular sound. The vocal tract performs a filter function like the equaliser of a stereo – for instance, you can set it so it boosts bass frequencies and dampens higher frequencies. Note that when we talk about sounds in general, we transcribe them with symbols from the International Phonetic Alphabet (IPA) and put them between square brackets, [x]. When we refer to sounds in a specific language we put the IPA symbols between slashes, /x/, and when we talk about written/orthographic letters, we show them in *italics* or put them between angle brackets, <x>.

Not all sounds in the world's languages are produced by air that is flowing out of the mouth (i.e., an **egressive** airstream). There are also sounds that are produced by air flowing inwards (i.e., an **ingressive** airstream) such as **click** consonants. Clicks include the sounds that you make when clucking a disapproving *tut tut* or *tsk tsk*. If you pay careful attention when producing these sounds, you realise that air is flowing inwards, not outwards. In English these sounds have no linguistic role, but they act as regular consonants in some African languages, such as Xhosa.

In speech production we distinguish between *segments* and *prosody*:

- **Segments** are individual vowels and consonants (see section 2.1.1).
- **Prosody** – or suprasegmental information – operates 'above' segments, affecting more than one individual sound: e.g., stress, intonation, rhythm, speaking rate, tone, and voice quality (see section 2.1.2).

2.1.1 Segments: consonants and vowels

Segments are the individual speech sounds that together make up words. All languages use two basic sound categories, consonants and vowels. Note that the use of these terms in phonetics is different from popular usage referring to orthographic symbols. Consonants are sounds that are made with a close constriction in the vocal tract, while vowels involve a more open articulation.

Consonants are defined by three parameters:

- Voicing (or phonation)
- Place of articulation
- Manner of articulation

This may sound complex; however, this three-way distinction is helpful when it comes to understanding consonants in the world's languages. First, let's look at the **voicing** (or phonation) parameter, which is relatively straightforward: the vocal folds are either made to vibrate or they are not. Vocal fold vibration is a highly complex physical process. For adult men, who have relatively large vocal tracts, vocal fold vibration may typically happen around 100–125 times per second (indicated in Hertz, i.e., 100–125 Hz); adult women, who have smaller vocal tracts, may produce more rapid vocal fold vibrations at around 180–220 Hz, while children typically phonate above 300 Hz. The vocal fold vibration rate is called the fundamental frequency, abbreviated f0 (see further section 2.1.2). Through vocal fold vibration we produce sounds that are classified as voiced, like the /z/ in 'zebra'. Voiceless sounds, on the other hand, are produced without such vibration, like the /s/ in 'super'. If you hold your fingers at your larynx (voice box) and say 'fussy' and 'fuzzy' several times, you should feel the vocal fold vibration in <zz> but not in <ss>.

Let's move on to **place of articulation**, the second defining feature of consonants. Articulation happens using active and passive articulators. The active articulator, most often the tongue, moves toward the passive articulator (e.g., the hard or the soft palate; see Figure 2.1). The name of the place of articulation is determined by the location of the passive articulator. For instance, if the tongue front (the active articulator) moves toward the hard palate (the passive articulator), then this place of articulation is called 'palatal'. There are eleven recognised places of articulation, from bilabial (at the lips) to glottal (at the glottis or vocal folds). The following list indicates the active and passive articulators involved in each place of articulation, with the active and passive articulators separated by a semicolon.

- **Bilabial**: upper and lower lips; no passive articulator
- **Labiodental**: lower lip; upper front teeth
- **Dental**: tongue tip or blade; upper front teeth
- **Alveolar**: tongue tip or blade; alveolar ridge
- **Postalveolar**: tongue tip or blade; rear of alveolar ridge
- **Retroflex**: tongue tip; hard palate
- **Palatal**: tongue front; hard palate
- **Velar**: tongue back; soft palate
- **Uvular**: tongue back; uvula
- **Pharyngeal**: tongue root; rear wall of pharynx
- **Glottal**: vocal folds; no passive articulator

The places of articulation are shown in Figure 2.1, which is an MRI scan of the final author's vocal tract. (In this scan the speaker was producing the vowel [ə], in which the vocal tract is in a neutral position.) In terms of the source-filter model, the place of articulation is the location of the obstruction that is the main influence on the filter.

We now come to **manner of articulation**. We typically distinguish between sounds produced with a fully blocked or turbulent airstream – **obstruents** – and sounds produced with an air stream that can escape easily – **sonorants**. Figure 2.2 shows pulmonic consonants as they occur in the languages of the world – pulmonic meaning that they are produced via air coming from the lungs (cf. pulmonary, relating to the lungs). Place of articulation is shown horizontally in columns, while manner of articulation is indicated vertically in rows; whenever there are two sounds in a box, the one on the right is voiced, while the one on the left is voiceless. Each symbol indicates one specific sound. You can listen to the sounds online at the IPA website. (Clickable links are provided on the book's website.)

CONSONANTS (PULMONIC)

	Bilabial	Labiodental	Dental	Alveolar	Postalveolar	Retroflex	Palatal	Velar	Uvular	Pharyngeal	Glottal
Plosive	p b			t d		ʈ ɖ	c ɟ	k ɡ	q ɢ		ʔ
Nasal	m	ɱ		n		ɳ	ɲ	ŋ	ɴ		
Trill	ʙ			r					ʀ		
Tap or Flap		ⱱ		ɾ		ɽ					
Fricative	ɸ β	f v	θ ð	s z	ʃ ʒ	ʂ ʐ	ç ʝ	x ɣ	χ ʁ	ħ ʕ	h ɦ
Lateral fricative				ɬ ɮ							
Approximant		ʋ		ɹ		ɻ	j	ɰ			
Lateral approximant				l		ɭ	ʎ	ʟ			

Symbols to the right in a cell are voiced, to the left are voiceless. Shaded areas denote articulations judged impossible.

Figure 2.2 Pulmonic consonants shown in the table of the International Phonetic Alphabet (IPA).

Obstruents include plosives (also called stops), affricates, and fricatives. Sonorants include nasals, approximants, trills, taps, and flaps as well as all vowels. Let's look at each sound type in turn.

Plosives: Plosives (or stops) are produced with a full oral and nasal closure. For all plosives, the velum is raised so that air cannot pass into the nasal cavity. In terms of the oral tract, plosives can be made with a complete closure at most places of articulation (as you can see from Figure 2.2). For example, if you make a voiceless bilabial plosive [p] (i.e., with no voicing, both upper and lower lips coming together for a full oral closure) in the sequence [ɑpɑ], you will notice that no sound escapes while producing the [p]. If you produce the [p] very slowly (and it might help to look in a mirror while you do so), you can distinguish between an approach phase (upper and lower lips approaching each other), a closure phase (upper and lower lips touching each other), and a release phase (upper and lower lips moving away from each other).

Fricatives: Fricatives are produced by an air stream that is made turbulent by narrow or close constriction between the active and passive articulators. When you produce the voiceless alveolar fricative [s], for instance in the sequence [ɑsɑ], you can hear a hissing sound as air flows through the narrow constriction between the tongue tip and the alveolar ridge or teeth. If you add voicing to [ɑsɑ] you will get [ɑzɑ], i.e., a voiced alveolar fricative. There are some fricatives, called lateral fricatives, in which air flows across one or both sides of the tongue rather than centrally. Fricatives are the only manner of articulation that can be produced at all places of articulation (see Figure 2.2).

Affricates: Affricates, such as the /t͡ʃ/ in English /biːt͡ʃ/ 'beach', have plosive as well as fricative characteristics. Affricates are created by first forming a short closure between the active and passive articulators (the plosive part) and then releasing the closure relatively slowly, causing the air to form turbulence between the articulators (the fricative part). In /biːt͡ʃ/, after forming a short alveolar closure (/t/), the tongue tip slowly moves away from the alveolar ridge to produce a fricative much like the initial sound in 'shoe' (/ʃ/).

Nasals: Nasals are produced when there is an oral closure but the velum is lowered, allowing air to escape through the nasal tract (note that Figure 2.1 shows the velum in a raised position). The type of nasal is determined by where in the vocal tract the oral closure occurs. In a voiced alveolar nasal, for example, the tip of the tongue forms a closure with the alveolar ridge, the velum is lowered, and air escapes through the nose, resulting in the sound [n]. Say the sequence [ɑnɑ]. Now try to produce that sound while pinching your nose. You will notice that it is impossible to produce a nasal sound with the nose closed, since the air needs to escape through the nasal cavity.

Approximants: As the name suggests, approximants are a class of sounds in which the articulators approach each other (i.e., they approximate each other), but not closely enough for the air to become turbulent or blocked (which is why approximants are sonorants). We differentiate between lateral approximants, such as the /l/ in English 'love', and central approximants, like the /ɹ/ in English 'read'. In lateral approximants, the air flows sideways around the tongue, while in central approximants, the air flows across the centre of the tongue. If you produce [l] and [ɹ] in turn, you should notice a difference in where the air flows.

Trills, taps, and flaps: Trills, taps, and flaps are all similar to plosives. However, the closure between active and passive articulators is not held long enough for air pressure to build up, which is why these sounds are considered sonorants. With **trills**, the active articulators vibrate towards the passive articulators multiple times, as in /r/, the sound in Spanish *perro* 'dog'. To make a **tap**, such as in Spanish *pero* 'but', the tongue tip touches the alveolar ridge only once and very briefly. The same sound is used as a variant of /t/ between vowels in American or Australian English, for example in 'city'. With **flaps**, the tongue first curls backward and then moves forward again, touching the tip briefly on the hard palate. Punjabi is an example of a language which has the voiced retroflex flap /ɽ/.

So far, we have introduced you to consonants, which can be distinguished by their voicing, and place and manner of articulation (or VPM). For example, /z/ is a voiced alveolar fricative, meaning that it is voiced, with an alveolar place and fricative manner of articulation.

Vowels are also determined by three parameters:

- Tongue position
- Tongue height
- Lip position

Figure 2.3 shows the vowels of the world's languages in the International Phonetic Alphabet.

VOWELS

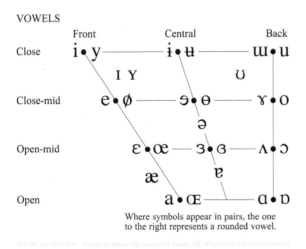

Where symbols appear in pairs, the one
to the right represents a rounded vowel.

Figure 2.3 Vowels shown in the International Phonetic Alphabet (IPA).

Produce the vowel [i], as in standard English *see*, German *sieben*, or French *six*. Pay close attention to how your tongue is positioned. The front of your tongue should be raised quite high, close to your hard palate. In contrast, if you produce the [ɑ] vowel, as in standard English *palm*, the tongue and jaw are lowered, and the tongue's highest point is toward the back of the mouth. If you add lip rounding to [i], you get [y], a sound that English doesn't have but which you can hear in French *rue* 'street' or German *grün* 'green'. If you add lip rounding to [ɑ], you get [ɒ], found in standard British English *lot*.

In Figure 2.3, the highest point of the tongue is indicated on the y-axis. Another way to think of this dimension is in terms of how open or closed the jaw is, which is why Figure 2.3 contains the labels open (sometimes called low), open-mid, close-mid, and close (sometimes called high). Tongue advancement is shown on the x-axis, with the labels front, central, and back. When vowels are shown in pairs in Figure 2.3, the vowel on the right is articulated with rounded lips. Vowel parameters are typically described in terms of whether or not they involve lip rounding, the height of the tongue, and the position of the tongue. Thus [i] is an unrounded close front vowel. The vowels described so far are **monophthongs**, or vowels that consist of a single vocalic element. There are also vowels made up of two elements, such as in English *nine*, /naɪn/, which are called **diphthongs**.

When we talk about vowels in a particular language, we often use sample words that contain the target vowel. For example, the word *nine* has the phonological structure /naɪn/. This word usually patterns in the same way as all words that contain the vowel /aɪ/, such as *guide, might, price, refine, shining*. The actual pronunciation of vowels can vary widely across accents, but most words in a group are affected in the same way. This set of words containing /aɪ/ as the

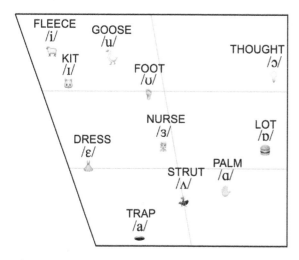

Figure 2.4 Lexical sets shown as emojis on a vowel trapezoid.

stressed vowel is often labelled with the keyword PRICE (keywords are shown in small capitals). Thus, phoneticians talk about 'PRICE words' or 'words with the PRICE vowel'. The keyword system was devised by John Wells for his survey of English accents (Wells 1982). An advantage of referring to vowels via the keyword system is that it works equally well for most accents. The phonological transcription given in slashes, like /naɪn/ can be misleading, as it implies a particular pronunciation that might not apply in all accents. Invariably the symbols used in the phonological form represent the standard accent, such as Received Pronunciation (RP) in the UK.

Figure 2.4 shows Wells' lexical sets for monophthongs as emojis (just for illustration purposes). The positions are based on an acoustic study of standard British English and illustrate the approximate qualities of word sets for young RP speakers (Hawkins & Midgley 2005). The figure also indicates the phonemic symbols that are usually used in discussions of English. Note, however, that the GOOSE vowel is much fronter than implied by the traditional phoneme symbol / u/. This is because this vowel has changed quite dramatically in RP over the last century. The FOOT vowel has also fronted and lowered for younger speakers. Note, in line with what we have said above about lexical sets, that all words in a lexical set are affected by the change – not only *goose* but also *lose, refuse, youth*, and so on. (By contrast, in some other accents, including Nigerian accents and some Yorkshire accents, words in the GOOSE set retain a back pronunciation, close to [u].)

Up to this point, we have discussed individual segments: consonants and vowels. A vast array of phonetic features are not found at the local segmental level, but exist 'above' them. These features are called **suprasegmentals** or **prosody**, from the Greek *prosodia* 'that which is sung'.

2.1.2 Suprasegmentals

Suprasegmentals include various features such as fundamental frequency (f0) and intonation, voice quality, prominence (stress), speech rhythm, and speech tempo. While segmental features involve individual units of sound, suprasegmental features affect a series of segments.

Fundamental frequency: We have previously introduced the concept of voicing, i.e., vocal fold vibration. The rate at which vocal folds vibrate is called the fundamental frequency, abbreviated f0 ('F zero'). We use the term 'f0' when we talk about measuring fundamental frequency in speech production (e.g., 'He has an average f0 of 88 Hz'.). When we talk about how we perceive f0, we use the term **pitch** (e.g., 'She had a low pitched voice' or 'There was a rise in pitch on the last syllable'). Linguistically speaking, varying pitch can convey different meanings. If you say 'The dog chases the cat' with a falling pitch contour, this is understood as a statement. If you say the same phrase with a rising pitch contour, you convey a question. The linguistic meaning of varying pitch is called **intonation**. f0 is also the main component of linguistic **tone**. Tone refers to different f0 patterns that are used to create contrasts between words. Many languages use tone, including Mandarin, Thai, and Yoruba. In Thai, for example, the syllable /kʰa/ spoken with a high level tone (i.e., high and steady f0) means 'to trade'. The same syllable with a falling tone means 'to kill', and with a rising tone means 'leg'.

Voice quality: Voice quality refers to the different **timbres** of a person's voice. To describe this in more detail, we need to look at how the voice is produced in the larynx. Figure 2.5 shows the main physiological components involved in voice production, looking downwards onto the vocal folds).

Figure 2.5 shows the glottis, which is made up of vocal folds (or vocal cords) that are attached to the thyroid cartilage on the front end (top of Figure 2.5; the thyroid cartilage is what you can feel as your Adam's apple) and to the arytenoid cartilages at the back end (bottom of Figure 2.5). What is particularly important is that the arytenoid cartilages can rotate, thereby modifying the shape of the glottis by moving the end points of the vocal folds. When we speak, air is pushed

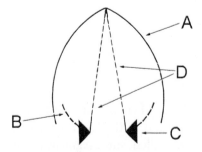

Figure 2.5 Physiology of the glottis. A: Thyroid cartilage; B: Cricoid cartilage; C: Arytenoid cartilage; D: vocal folds. (Source: Wikimedia)

up from the lungs, initiating vocal fold vibration as the air pressure forces apart the closed vocal folds. For voiced sounds, the vibration comprises a continuous back-and-forth between glottis positions A and B seen in Figure 2.6 (looking downwards onto the folds): a fast alternation between closing and opening the vocal folds while the arytenoid cartilages are held together closely. For voiceless sounds, the glottis position is as shown in position E in Figure 2.6: the glottis is open and relaxed. To produce whispered speech, air is made turbulent by flowing through a small triangle created by the arytenoid cartilage folding inwards, shown in position C. To produce breathy voice, the arytenoids are folded outwards to open up the glottis slightly more (position D).

The deep-breathing position of the glottis (position F in Figure 2.6) is used, for example, when you're exercising and your blood needs more oxygen. To produce glottalised or 'creaky' voice (not depicted in Figure 2.6), only the outermost edges of the vocal folds vibrate while the glottis is in phonation position; this can result in a crackling sound, reminiscent of sliding a stick against railings. Note that voice qualities like creak can result from natural effects of a speaker's anatomy and physiology, but they also vary. To some extent people can control aspects of voice quality, for example to signal attitude, while voice quality also varies because of changes in health and emotional state.

Prominence (stress): Syllables (groups of segments) can be made more perceptually prominent if the speaker adjusts certain parameters. Take, for instance, the difference between English *IMport* (noun) and *imPORT* (verb). Typically, prominent syllables are louder, longer in duration, and higher in pitch. These three parameters do not necessarily have to coincide, however – their interplay is often language- or even dialect-specific. Syllables can sometimes be made more prominent by decreasing their volume, duration, or pitch: if a syllable is markedly different from adjacent ones, then it stands out.

Speech rhythm: What is speech rhythm? There is no easy answer. On an abstract level, **rhythm** denotes a repetitive pattern of some sort. The units that make up these patterns can vary, though, depending on how rhythm is defined. Traditionally, linguists have distinguished between 'stress-timed' and 'syllable-timed' rhythms. Stress-timed languages have repeating, regular units of stressed

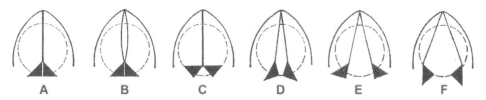

Figure 2.6 Different positions of the glottis. A: closed; B: modal voice; C: whisper; D: breathiness; E–F: breathing (voiceless, full airstream). Triangles represent the arytenoid cartilages. (Source: Wikimedia)

(or prominent) syllables; this rhythm has been likened to the short and long units of Morse code. In a phrase such as 'I don't think we can walk up the hill in this way', the prominent syllables 'I', 'think', 'walk', 'hill', and 'way' appear at about equidistant time intervals despite the varying numbers of syllables between each prominence; the unstressed syllables get shortened in order to fit the metre. Thus in most dialects of English, rhythm is timed according to stressed syllables. Many Germanic languages have been said to lean towards stress timing. In contrast, in European French, it is syllable durations that govern speech rhythm. In the phrase *Les participants avaient besoin de plus d'information sur la loi* ('Participants needed more information about the law'), each syllable is about equal in duration (though there is still some variation in syllable durations). French thus tends towards syllable-timing, a rhythm that has been compared to the regular staccato of a machine gun. However, these are only broad categories, and no language fits perfectly into one or the other; rhythm is more of a continuum.

Speech tempo: We all know people who talk fast and some who speak very slowly. Speech tempo can be measured in different ways. In measuring tempo, one typically distinguishes between **articulation rate** and **speaking rate**. Articulation rate looks at the tempo of speech while excluding pauses from consideration; speaking rate includes pauses. Analysis of speech tempo involves measuring a unit of speech and how often it is realised per second. Most commonly, this unit is syllables per second. Somebody who talks quickly in standard English, for example, realises 7–8 syllables per second. (The world record for fastest rap MC is held by the Spanish rapper El Chojin, who rapped 921 syllables in a minute, i.e., a rate of 15.35 syllables per second.) Somebody who talks slowly only produces around 3–4 syllables per second. Note that this measure can depend on the phonotactics (i.e., the segmental make-up) of a language. If we classify segments as C (consonants) or V (vowels), we can classify the syllable shapes that are permitted in a given language. A language like Japanese, which mostly has CV syllables (with a single consonant and a single vowel), will likely exhibit a higher average syllable per second rate when compared to Polish, for example, where syllables such as CCVCC (with consonant clusters) are common.

2.2 Acoustic analysis

Since the advent of personal computers, linguists have been able to analyse speech signals easily in very close detail. The principal computer program in use today by students of phonetics, professional phoneticians, and forensic phonetic experts is Praat (Dutch for 'talk'). Praat is a free signal analysis program developed by Paul Boersma and David Weenink at the University of Amsterdam. It is extremely powerful and allows for various analyses of the speech signal, e.g., analyses of f0, formants (acoustic features involved in determining the quality of a vowel), loudness, and voice quality. Praat further allows users to add time-aligned labels to audio files and to create figures and graphs of the speech signal, to name just a few of its functionalities. A series of short tutorials, produced by Richard Ogden at the University of York, provides a brief introduction to the basics of how to use Praat.

In the following section we introduce you to the fundamentals of acoustics. We will also give you a practical introduction on how to measure the acoustics of vowels, consonants, and suprasegmentals.

2.2.1 A primer in acoustics

To begin, we must return to the source-filter theory mentioned in section 2.1. Remember that speech production usually involves air being pushed upwards by the lungs (a pulmonic egressive airstream), thereby initiating vocal fold vibration in the larynx. These vibrations constitute the source signal. After the signal is filtered by the oral and/or nasal tracts, sound pressure variations are transmitted through the air by dispersing air molecules. When they arrive at our eardrums, we perceive these variations in air pressure as the speech signal. Similarly, when air pressure variations arrive at the membrane of a microphone, the speech signal can be captured and made visible. Figure 2.7 shows the air pressure variations of an unvoiced sound [s] followed by a voiced sound [ʊ].

The voiceless sound [s] is characterised by an **aperiodic signal**, i.e., there is no pattern that repeats itself. The following [ʊ] shows a repetitive, periodic pattern which stems from the vocal fold vibrations. This is the primary acoustic distinction between voiceless and voiced sounds. Figure 2.7 is an example of a type

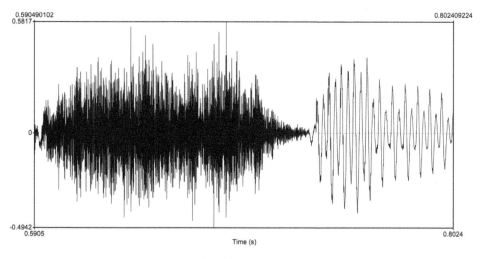

Figure 2.7 Air pressure variations of a voiceless sound followed by a voiced sound, i.e., [s] followed by [ʊ].

of diagram called a waveform. **Waveforms** show time on the x-axis and amplitude (i.e., loudness) on the y-axis, giving us a rough idea of how loud a sound is over time. However, for us to be able to better distinguish between sounds, we also need information about their frequency components – information that waveforms do not contain. An [i] and an [ɑ] look very similar in a waveform, but they are made up of different frequencies. We can see these differences in another type of visualisation called a **spectrogram**. To talk about spectrograms, however, we first need to introduce what is referred to as the **Fourier transform.**

If you look at Figure 2.8, which is a close-up of the waveform of the [ʊ] vowel shown in Figure 2.7, you see the overall repetitive pattern – evidence that the sound is voiced – but you can also notice little bumps and spikes, and you may note that the peaks and troughs do not appear in perfectly equidistant intervals.

If the peaks and troughs occurred in perfectly timed intervals and if there were no bumps and spikes in the signal, you would get a sine wave, which sounds like a whistle or beep. In the early nineteenth century, Joseph Fourier, a French mathematician, was able to show that every complex periodic signal (like the one in Figure 2.8) can be split up into sinusoidal (sine wave) subcomponents. Figure 2.9 shows how a complex periodic signal is made up of individual subcomponents. The x-axis shows the time domain, the y-axis shows amplitude, and the z-axis denotes frequency. The largest sine wave on the x-axis is the fundamental frequency, the base frequency at which the signal repeats. This is also called the first harmonic (H1). The second harmonic (H2), the second largest sine wave, is double the fundamental frequency (i.e., double the H1 in Hz); the third harmonic (H3), the third largest sine wave, is triple the fundamental frequency, etc. Note that harmonics become less loud the higher their frequency. If you add up all harmonics you get the resulting thick line on the x-axis, a complex periodic signal like the one in Figure 2.8.

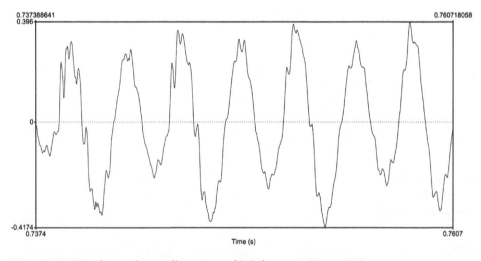

Figure 2.8 Waveform of a small portion of [ʊ] shown in Figure 2.7.

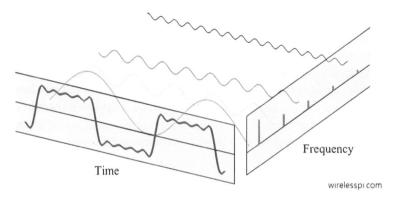

Figure 2.9 Composition of a complex periodic signal. (Source: Wireless Pi)

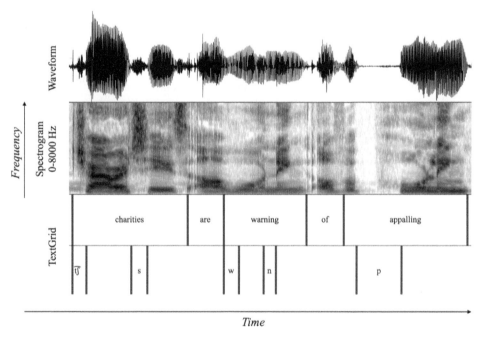

Figure 2.10 Waveform (top), spectrogram (centre), and Annotation Grid (TextGrid, bottom) of the words 'charities are warning of appalling…'.

Having elaborated on this, we can now talk about spectrograms. An example is shown in Figure 2.10, which shows the waveform (air pressure variations; top panel), spectrogram (centre), and annotation grid (TextGrid; bottom). Each vertical line in the spectrogram represents one opening and closing of the glottis (or 'glottal pulse'). These are very clear at the start of the words *are* and *of* (in fact because the speaker uses creaky voice here), but you can also make out the vertical structures in all of the vowels. The spectrogram further shows frequency on the y-axis and amplitude on the z-axis (here represented by the degree of

21

darkness – darker sections are louder). The source signal is modulated by the vocal tract across time, which is why the spectrogram looks different as time passes; it shows the acoustic stamp of the vocal tract over a stretch of time. Vowels and consonants look very different from each other in the spectrogram because the vocal tract configuration keeps changing, such that some frequencies pass through while others are damped (as in the equaliser analogy introduced earlier). This changing of the filter leads to different resonances, which are manifested differently in the spectrogram. If you use Google Chrome, you can try out a real-time spectrogram viewer.

Having given you this primer in acoustics, let's look at some of the different acoustic features of vowels and consonants.

2.2.2 Acoustic analysis of vowels and consonants

Figure 2.10 showed that a short, two-second stretch of speech contains lots of different filter characteristics which are reflected in the spectrogram. Let's look at these in more detail – we'll begin with plosives.

From an acoustic perspective, **plosives** are special because they consist of a series of visually salient phases, illustrated in the bilabial plosive [p] (as in *appalling*) in Figure 2.10: a closure phase, shown as silence in the waveform and spectrogram and a release phase, shown as relatively strong acoustic energy in the signal.

Fricatives, on the other hand, manifest as longer periods of noise in the waveform and the spectrogram, shown in Figure 2.10 in the alveolar fricative [s] (in *charities*, which is phonologically /z/ but here produced without voicing). Remember that in fricatives air is made turbulent to create a hissing sound. Voiceless fricatives are characterised by aperiodic (i.e., non-regular) perturbations in the waveform and spectrogram, like white noise. If the fricative is voiced, as in [z], the hissing sound is accompanied by periodicity stemming from vocal fold vibration.

Affricates are a mix of two manners of articulation: a plosive followed by a fricative, shown in the affricate [t͡ʃ] (in *charities*) in Figure 2.10. Remember that the release of the plosive happens relatively slowly, creating a small opening through which air can rush through to create a hissing sound. Acoustically, we thus find plosive and fricative characteristics in an affricate: at first, there is the closure phase of the plosive, shown as a flat line in the waveform. This is followed by the release of the plosive, shown as a small, brief burst of energy, and then aperiodic noise as air rushing out creates turbulence.

Nasals are produced by a complete oral closure with the velum lowered, allowing air to flow through the nose. Because the nasal cavity is made up of soft tissue, the sound is heavily damped compared to vowels, and the nasal tract itself adds extra resonance characteristics to the filtered sound. This translates to lower energy shown in spectrograms of nasals, along with wider and less well-defined formants. This is evident in the alveolar nasal [n] (as in *war<u>n</u>ing*) in Figure 2.10; you can see a white band of low amplitude energy between 3000 and 4000 Hz.

Approximants are produced by the articulators approaching each other, but not producing enough closure for the air to become turbulent (fricatives) or fully blocked (plosives and nasals). This characteristic makes approximants acoustically very similar to vowels. Figure 2.10 shows the labio-velar approximant [w] (as in *<u>w</u>arning*). In this specific sound, both lips 'approximate' each other and – at the same time – the back part of the tongue 'approximates' the velum so as not to allow air to become turbulent or blocked, causing the production of the [w] sound.

Finally, **trills and taps** are produced with short closures between the active and passive articulators – so close that air pressure does not build up. This is reflected in the waveform and the spectrogram. You find a tap, for example, in the American or Australian English articulation of *city*, [sɪɾi]. In producing the tap [ɾ], there is a single closure of the active articulator (the tongue tip) against the passive articulator (the alveolar ridge), but air pressure does not have much time to build up. The alveolar trill [r] involves repeated closures and looks like a sequence of taps, i.e., short interruptions of the air stream.

Before we move on to vowels, we need to discuss the vocal tract and the concept of resonance in more detail.

2.2.3 Resonance and formants

Resonance denotes the vibration properties of an object. More specifically, it is the body of air trapped in a specific object that creates resonance. Imagine you tap a glass – you get a very particular sound. This sound is characterised by the shape of the glass, and how full it is (i.e., how much air it contains). If you take a different glass with a different shape or containing a different amount of liquid (and air), you get a different sound when you tap it. The vocal tract functions much the same way. If your tract is configured to make an [ɑ] (without actually producing it) and you flick your larynx, you will get one sort of sound; do the same while your tract is configured for [i], and you get a different sound. This is because each of these configurations reshapes the vocal tract and the bodies of air it contains. The vocal tract has different resonances depending on its shape, making the air vibrate in different ways. The acoustic energy maxima of these resonances at a given frequency are called **formants**. They are shown as dark, often black, horizontal bands in a spectrogram (look back to Figure 2.10). The two lowest-frequency formants on a spectrogram, referred to as F1 and F2 (i.e., the first formant and second formant), are closely related to the quality of the vowel (i.e., whether you produce an [i] or an [ɑ] sound). Vowel height is reflected in F1 and vowel backness is reflected in F2, as shown in Figure 2.11.

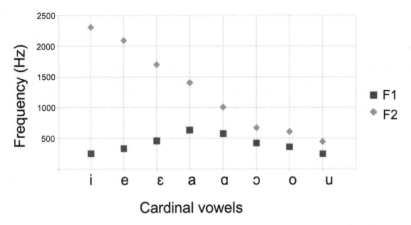

Figure 2.11 Typical F1 and F2 values of cardinal vowels as spoken by an adult male.

Figure 2.11 depicts typical formant values for the cardinal vowels. These are not vowels as they are used in real language, but reference vowels used by phoneticians for which the tongue is in extreme positions (the symbols appear around the edges of the vowel diagram in Figure 2.3). For example, as we noted earlier, [i] is similar to German *sieben* and French *six*, but in its cardinal form the tongue is as high and front as it can be, and the lips as spread as they can be, without these articulations generating frication (since otherwise the sound would be a fricative rather than a vowel). F1 and vowel height stand in an inverse relationship: the closer the vowel, the lower the F1; the more open the vowel, the higher the F1. F2 relates to how far front the mass of the tongue is within the vocal tract. The more fronted the vowel, the higher the F2; the more backed the vowel, the lower the F2. Higher formants are indicative of lip rounding (F3) and often carry speaker-specific information (F4). Note that when we refer to 'high' or 'low' formants we are speaking in relative terms. The vocal tracts of men are generally larger than those of women, adults have larger vocal tracts than children, and individuals vary too. Larger vocal tracts generate lower resonances (in the same way that larger wine glasses generate lower notes than smaller glasses). So, a man's [i] will typically have much lower F1 and F2 values than a child's [i]. But [i] will have a relatively high F2 and low F1 compared to other vowels produced by the same speaker. If we were to show a similar plot to that in Figure 2.11 based on a child's voice, we would see much higher frequencies on the y axis, but the relative spacing of the formants across the vowels would be very similar.

2.2.4 Acoustic analysis of prosody

Here we discuss how features of prosody can be analysed, particularly f0, voice quality, prominence, speech rhythm, and speech tempo.

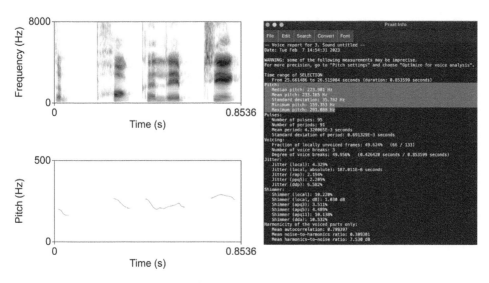

Figure 2.12 A spectrogram (top left), tracked f0 contour (bottom left), and voice report (right) as output in Praat.

f0 is probably the most straightforward feature of prosody to measure. Remember that f0 denotes the number of times per second the vocal folds vibrate. It is possible to measure a speaker's average f0 over a specific time, how much their f0 varies, and what their overall f0 range is. Praat can be used to perform all of these analyses. Figure 2.12 shows a stretch of speech (top left), the tracked f0 contour (bottom left), and a voice report (right).

Among other information, the voice report shows the median, mean, and standard deviation (average variability) of pitch values in the selected portion of speech, as well as minimum and maximum pitch. The latter two values can be used to calculate pitch span (pitch maximum minus pitch minimum), which gives an overall impression of a speaker's pitch range. Keep in mind that measurements of f0 in software such as Praat are estimates and can sometimes be inaccurate. It is worth checking your data if you think some values might be causing incorrect results. For example, if we judge a speaker's pitch to be relatively normal (depending on whether they are male or female, adult or child, speaking at a quiet conversational level), we can predict their typical f0 values. An adult male speaking at conversational level and with a normal pitch should give us f0 values around 100–130 Hz. If we see values at 200 Hz we should therefore be wary: they could be correct, but such values would imply the speaker has shifted into a very high register, possibly even falsetto. However, they could also reflect errors in the way the software program has analysed the pitch. This does happen from time to time, especially with unusual voice qualities or problematic recordings of the sort that are often encountered in forensic work (e.g., because of interference from background noise).

f0 is of course intimately related to intonation, the linguistic function of pitch variation. Numerous theoretical models have attempted to describe the different functions of intonation. The most prominent model among intonation researchers at the moment captures intonation as a series of high (H) and low (L) tones and how these tones align with strong, or prominent, syllables (see Ladefoged & Johnson 2015 for further details).

Voice quality: Analysing voice quality is somewhat trickier than measuring f0. Differences in voice quality manifest in numerous changes to the acoustic signal, such as **jitter, shimmer,** and the **harmonics-to-noise ratio** (all three of which are displayed in Praat's voice report, as shown in the bottom right half of Figure 2.12). Other harmonic-based measures like H1–H2 can also be taken into consideration. Let's introduce these main measures of voice quality in more detail.

Jitter and shimmer are both measures of the regularity of vocal fold vibration: jitter relates to the variation in frequency between individual periods (a period is one cycle of vibration). Typically, healthy young adults have jitter values between 0.5% and 1.0%. These values tell us that the frequency of vocal fold vibration is very consistent. An unhealthy larynx (such as when you have a cold and your vocal folds cannot vibrate normally) leads to more variation in the vibration rate and therefore higher jitter values. Shimmer measures the regularity of cycle amplitudes rather than frequencies, capturing variation in the loudness of the sound generated by the vibration. The harmonics-to-noise ratio (HNR) refers to the ratio between periodic and aperiodic components in a measured vowel, expressed in decibels (dB). The lower this ratio, the more noise is in the signal. HNRs under 7 – that is, with substantial noise in the voice – typically indicate some form of vocal pathology (e.g., irregularity in the form of disease or injury). Lower HNR is often caused by poor adduction (closure) of the vocal folds, allowing air to escape during vibration. Low HNR gives the auditory impression of hoarseness, breathiness, and roughness. Another measure, H1–H2, concerns the amplitude difference between the fundamental frequency and the second harmonic. This is a measure of breathiness and creakiness.

Prominence: Prominence can be captured by measuring the pitch, duration, and loudness of syllables. Consider again the example of *IMport* (noun) vs. *imPORT* (verb). Suppose we measure the pitch, duration, and amplitude of <IM> in a recording of the noun and compare that to the values of <port> in the same word. We would probably find that <IM> is higher in pitch than <port>, that its vowel is comparatively long (since typically we only measure the duration of vowels in a syllable), and that <IM> is louder than <port>. The reverse would apply to the verb *imPORT*. By acoustically marking certain syllables in all or some of these ways, speakers make them stand out, i.e., become prominent.

We mentioned earlier that **speech rhythm** is a rather elusive concept. Accordingly, there are several ways to measure rhythm. The core rhythmic

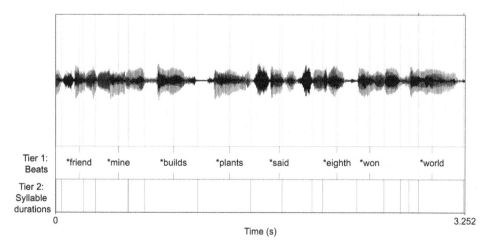

| Tier 1:
Beats | *friend | *mine | *builds | *plants | *said | *eighth | *won | *world |

Tier 2:
Syllable
durations

0   3.252

Time (s)

Figure 2.13 Stress and syllable timing in Donald Trump's speech.

difference among languages is, as mentioned earlier, that some synchronise speech according to stressed syllables (stressed syllables occur at relatively equal intervals), while others do so by sticking to relatively similar syllable durations. Figure 2.13 shows a short section from an online recording of Donald Trump, an excerpt of the first presidential debate between Hillary Clinton and Donald Trump in 2016.

Underneath the waveform in Figure 2.13 is an annotated tier (tier 1) with the main beats of the signal labelled. Trump really emphasises these syllables. Below these labels, in tier 2, we have placed a boundary between each syllable. These syllables are (roughly): *a.frien.dof.mine.who.builds.plants.said.it's. the.eighth.won.der.of.the.world*. To determine whether Trump is more stress- or syllable-timed, we would measure the variability between the durations of stressed syllables (tier 1) and also the variability of all syllable durations (tier 2). We would then compare these measures: the one showing less variability indicates the type of rhythm the speaker tends to gravitate towards. Just from visual inspection, you may notice that the stressed syllables shown in tier 1 are more equal in duration to each other than if we compare all syllables together, including unstressed ones. This means that in this stretch of speech, Trump's speech is more stress-timed, typical for his variety of English as well as English more generally. Contemporary research also quantitatively analyses speech rhythm by looking at the role of vocalic or consonantal intervals and how they stand in relation to each other (see White & Mattys 2007).

Compared to other prosodic measures, capturing **speech tempo** is relatively straightforward. When measuring how fast someone talks, one typically looks at the number of syllables produced per second of speaking time. So if you look at a speech signal of, say, 6.2 seconds and you then remove all the pauses from the signal, you may end up with a stretch of speech of 4.79 seconds; if you then count 28 syllables uttered in that span, you simply divide that by the time, obtaining the numbers of syllables per second: 28 syllables/4.79 sec = 5.8 syllables/sec. In the example shown in Figure 2.13, you can count the number of syllables articulated by the speaker (N=16, in this case) and look at the total duration of the stretch of speech (3.25 seconds), which gives you 16 syllables/ 3.25 sec = 4.9 syllables/sec. This is the calculation of **articulation rate** – the raw tempo of speech, excluding pauses from consideration. If you leave the pauses in and then calculate speech tempo you calculate **speaking rate.**

Counting syllables is not always straightforward, especially in a language like English where speakers often reduce or omit whole syllables when speaking quickly compared to speaking carefully. For example, *library* has three syllables in careful speech (/laɪ.bɹə.ɹi/), but most speakers say the word with only two syllables: /laɪ.bɹi/, with the middle vowel omitted and just one /ɹ/. Of course words like this would change the syllable count, depending on whether you count the actual number of syllables spoken, or the theoretical maximum number of syllables in the word. It is usually much easier to take the latter approach, so that we don't need to listen and judge every syllable in the speech sample.

2.3 Which features are analysed in forensic phonetic analysis?

Recent surveys have asked forensic phoneticians around the world which features they most routinely analyse in forensic phonetic casework (Gold & French 2011, 2019).

- In terms of segments, almost all practitioners report measuring vowel formants. F2 is the most measured formant, followed by F1 and F3. (As we will explain in Chapter 4, F1 is often affected by the technical quality of the recording, especially in telephone transmission.) Most experts measure frequencies at the midpoint (centre) of vowels (and in the case of diphthongs, formant trajectories). Most experts also examine consonants, either auditorily, or with acoustic measurements of frequencies and durations. Fricatives and plosives are the most frequently investigated.
- In terms of prosody, all experts report examining fundamental frequency. In particular, they usually measure means, medians, modes, and standard deviations. The linguistic function of f0 – intonation – is examined by about 85% of respondents.
- The majority of forensic phoneticians take into consideration voice quality (in large part auditorily).
- Most experts report analysing speech tempo, usually applying a formal measure such as articulation rate.
- Around three quarters of respondents consider speech rhythm.

- Aside from strictly phonetic features, experts may also examine discourse markers (also discussed in Chapter 8), turn-taking behaviour, and lexical choices. They might also consider filled pauses, tongue clicking, breathing behaviour, throat clearing, and even laughter.

Experts have also been asked which phonetic feature they find carries the most speaker-specific diagnostic information. Voice quality is cited most commonly, followed by dialect and accent variation as well as vowel formants. These features are then followed by speech tempo, f0, rhythm, lexical and grammatical variants, and fluency. Note, though, that many experts say that it is not one particular feature that makes a speaker distinct, but rather a combination of features – as discussed at the beginning of this chapter – which is why it is important to provide as comprehensive as possible a picture of a speaker when examining their voice.

Conclusion

This chapter has given you a brief introduction to the production of speech. We have shown that speech consists of segments (vowels and consonants) and prosody (intonation, speech tempo, voice quality, etc.), and we have provided a brief introduction to how speech is represented and can be measured acoustically. This is fundamental information for the five chapters to follow on forensic phonetics.

Further reading

For more extensive introductions to the field of phonetics:

Ladefoged, P., & Disner, S. F. (2012). *Vowels and Consonants*. Wiley.
Ladefoged, P., & Johnson, K. (2014). *A Course in Phonetics*, 7th edition. Wadsworth Cengage Learning.
Practical guides to using Praat. www.york.ac.uk/language/current/resources/praat/

Works cited

Gold, E., & French, P. (2011). International practices in forensic speaker comparison. *International Journal of Speech, Language & the Law*, 18(2): 293–307.
Gold, E., & French, P. (2019). International practices in forensic speaker comparisons: Second survey. *International Journal of Speech, Language & the Law*, 26(1): 1–20.

Hawkins, S., & Midgley, J. (2005). Formant frequencies of RP monophthongs in four age groups of speakers. *Journal of the International Phonetic Association*, 35(2): 183–199.

Labov, W. (1988). The judicial testing of linguistic theory. In D. Tannen (ed.) *Linguistics in Context: Connecting Observation and Understanding*. Ablex, pp. 159–182.

Wells, J. C. (1982). *Accents of English* (3 volumes). Cambridge University Press.

White, L., & Mattys, S. L. (2007). Calibrating rhythm: First language and second language studies. *Journal of Phonetics*, 35(4): 501–522.

Activity section

Activity 2A – Annotating a sound file

In this first activity, you will attempt to annotate a speech signal sound-by-sound. As a first step, download Praat. Watch tutorials 1–5 in Richard Ogden's Praat tutorial series. Then open the file rainbow.wav (provided on the book's website of support material). This is a short extract of a British English-speaking man reading the following text:

> *When the sunlight strikes raindrops in the air, they act as a prism and form a rainbow.*

Annotate a selection of sounds in the file using a text grid. Watch tutorial 10 in Richard Ogden's series to show you how. You do not have to label each one, just the sounds you can recognise. You can copy and paste IPA symbols from the IPA website or an online IPA keyboard.

Answer 2A

You can find our annotations as a TextGrid file on the book's website of support material. It is not always easy to label individual sounds. For example, the first two words, *When the*, are unstressed and spoken rather quickly. The boundaries between the sounds are not particularly clear, as is often the case when sonorant sounds occur in combination. In phonetic analysis we have to make decisions which parts of a recording we can analyse with confidence. It is not necessary or advisable to try to measure everything. We have therefore only labelled and annotated sections where the acoustic events are clearly defined.

You will note that the speaker does a number of things that at first glance might appear unusual, though in fact they are quite typical in fluent speech.

- /ɹ/ is produced in different ways in different words: [ɹ] in *rainbow*, but devoiced [ɹ̥] when it follows the /t/ of *strikes* and /p/ of *prism*, and a voiced fricative after the /d/ of *drops*.

- The speaker produces a glottal stop [ʔ] for the /t/ of *sunlight*, which is very common in British accents. He also produces [ʔ] for the /p/ of *raindrops* and the /k/ of *strikes*.
- The /n/ of *rainbow* is produced as [m], because the place of articulation of the nasal is assimilated to that of the following /b/ (i.e., it is bilabial instead of alveolar).

Activity 2B – Formant estimates

In this second activity, you will perform formant measurements. Watch tutorial 6 in Richard Ogden's series. Perform a mid-point measurement of F1, F2, and F3 for the first seven monophthong vowels in the file you just annotated in Activity 1. Copy and paste the values into a spreadsheet.

Answer 2B

Here are the measurements of F1, F2, and F3 for the first six monophthongs in the file. We measured the formants at the approximate centre of each vowel, judged by eye.

Vowel	Word	Time (sec)	F1 (Hz)	F2 (Hz)	F3 (Hz)
/ʌ/	sun	0.463256	543	1211	2822
/ɒ/	drops	1.532834	546	980	2429
/ɪ/	in	1.736431	363	1500	2474
/ɛː/	air	2.071956	653	1625	2577
/a/	act	2.533059	772	1481	2561
/ɪ/	prism	3.091632	400	1586	2578

There is likely to be some variation between analysts here depending on where exactly the measurement was taken and which settings are used in Praat. We have reported the formant values to the nearest integer, which is standard practice. We have also used the standard settings of five formants in 5.5 kHz (you can change the settings via the Formant menu). The standard settings work well for this file, but it is important to check that the formant tracker function places the estimates (usually shown as red dots) in the middle of the dark formant bands. If it doesn't, change the settings or estimate the values using the cursor. In fact these settings do make some small errors, for example around the F3 of the /ɪ/ of *prism*.

Note how close vowels such as /ɪ/ have a low F1 (363 and 400 Hz) and open vowels like /a/ have a high F1 (772 Hz). Similarly, note how front vowels like /ɛː/ have a high F2 (1625 Hz) and back vowels like /ɒ/ have a low F2 (980 Hz).

Activity 2C – Articulation rate

Perform an articulation rate measurement for the rainbow.wav file. Delete all the pauses, count the number of syllables spoken, and look at the duration of the entire stretch of speech (the number at the bottom-most bar in Praat). Divide the total number of syllables by the duration of the entire stretch of speech to obtain your articulation rate measurement. Do you judge the speaker to be fast, slow or average? Articulation rate data are shown in Figure 4.1 in Chapter 4. Compare your results with the data shown there. Does your AR measurement support your impressionistic judgement?

Answer 2C

Having deleted all pauses, the remaining stretch of speech is 4.061187 sec, or the raw articulation duration. In those 4 seconds, the speaker articulates 21 syllables. He therefore has an articulation rate of roughly 5.17 syllables/sec (=21/ 4.06), which is typical for English spoken relatively carefully.

3 Speaker profiling

This chapter considers the types of information we can ascertain about a speaker from their voice. When people speak, they do so to convey information about a given topic. They do so largely via their choices of words and syntax. At the same time, however, a voice also conveys a lot of indexical – i.e., social and personal – information. For example, the sociolinguist Peter Trudgill (1974) observed that if two Englishmen engage in a conversation on a train about the weather, they are likely to find out not just their thoughts on the weather but they can also deduce the speaker's regional origin or social class. Similarly, when we receive an (unwanted) call from a call centre representative, we may wonder who the person behind the voice is: 'He sounds American, maybe 40 years old, educated, from the Midwest'.

While we encounter such situations on a regular basis, attributions of this type of indexical information based on speech alone can carry substantial weight in the context of forensic phonetics. Consider the situation we described at the start of Chapter 2, in which a company receives a telephoned bomb threat. In such cases, a recording of the call might be available thanks to the routine process of recording all incoming calls to the company. The person who had received the threatening phone call would be interviewed by the police about the incident, and might be asked to describe the voice they had heard on the phone. The police also listen to the voice on the call. Using the witness's description and their own observations, the police would try to construct a speaker profile, based on which they will look for suspects. These profiles may include information about the speaker's regional and educational background, approximate age, etc. The relevant details of the voice might be fairly obvious, such that the police themselves might be able to construct a workable profile. However, in many cases they are not so obvious, and the police might therefore commission an expert report from a forensic phonetician. A copy of the recorded call would be sent to the phonetician, who would then analyse the voice.

Aims

The aim of this chapter is to introduce you to the **types of information that are typically considered in speaker profiling**. We will consider **information that is almost always extracted** when experts create a speaker profile (e.g., regional background), information which is **sometimes extracted** (e.g., speech pathologies), and information derived from the speech signal which deserves **strong caution** (e.g., biometric information like speaker height). When going through these sections, keep in mind that recordings of unknown speakers – such as ransom calls – are often short, and depending on the quantity and quality of the material provided, not all types of information can always be derived.

3.1 Introduction

Typically, speaker profiles are constructed in cases where police have recordings of an unknown speaker, but no suspects have yet been identified. This includes cases such as:

- ransom demands in kidnappings
- telephone threats
- masked robberies (where the perpetrator is on camera but their face is disguised)
- instances where a speaker was not seen due to darkness, poor image quality, or being outside the camera frame
- child abuse videos (where the perpetrator's voice is recorded but the speaker is off camera)
- surveillance recordings from 'bugged' buildings or cars
- cases of questioned identity, where an individual refuses to provide legitimate documentation to confirm their identity.

Profiling is also crucial to other forensic tasks, such as transcription (cf. Chapter 6 on speech content determination), setting up reference populations in speaker comparison cases (cf. Chapter 4), and LAAP (cf. Chapter 7). There is also a similar approach in forensic linguistics, where analysts construct profiles of authors (or sometimes speakers) based on their language use (see Chapter 11).

In profiling cases, experts analyse a recording to gather as much information as possible about the unknown speaker. The aim of the profile is usually to narrow down the field of suspects and therefore to assist the police with the investigation. Sometimes the audio samples in question may even be released to see if someone in the general public recognises the speaker's voice. Experts are often under severe pressures due to the time sensitivity of such cases: during kidnapping or extortion crises, profiles need to be constructed in a matter of hours because lives may be in danger.

Experts are not called upon to construct speaker profiles very often, however, and profiling has not been documented in much detail in forensic phonetics. At the former British lab JP French Associates, for example, only about 2–5 cases per year were profiling cases (out of a total of 100–150); at the German Bundeskriminalamt (BKA, the German state forensic lab) they make up about 10–20% of casework. This number is higher for the BKA because they also do investigative work, with kidnapping cases and child abuse videos being the most frequent type.

In principle, forensic phoneticians distinguish between three types of information that can be derived in speaker profiling:

Key information

- speaker sex/gender
- regional background
- social background
- language(s) spoken and L2 influence
- speaking style: spontaneous or read
- environment, time, and date (information derived from non-speech information in the recording).

Information that may additionally be derived

- speech disorder or pathology
- influence of drugs/alcohol.

Information that deserves strong caution

- age
- biometrics: weight, height, and facial features
- psychological state.

Where profiles are created, they can vary greatly in terms of how much information is extracted by the analyst. It would be highly unusual to find that a speech sample in any given case would contain sufficient features for the linguist to make determinations in respect of all of the dimensions listed above. There can also be considerable differences in the degree of confidence that can be attributed to a given observation: some **indexical** properties are easier to identify than others. ('Indexical' is used as a term in sociolinguistics to refer to features of speech or language that are linked to some social, regional, or stylistic factor.) Various factors affect what can be concluded in a profile. The most important of these include the quantity and quality of the recorded material to be analysed, the availability of documentary information on the indexical properties of the language or dialect, and the individual experience of the caseworker in performing the analysis.

3.2 Key information in speaker profiling

A number of social and regional features can be analysed in most recordings. In this section we address each in turn.

3.2.1 Sex and gender

Most speakers in forensic casework are men. In England and Wales in 2019, for example, 85% of arrests and 73% of convictions were of men, while men made up 95% of the prison population. It is widely assumed that the attribution of speaker sex is relatively straightforward. The primary acoustic indicator of differences in sex is **fundamental frequency**. f0 is (typically) considerably lower in adult males than it is in adult females: as we explained in Chapter 2, men tend to have longer and larger vocal folds, which vibrate more slowly than shorter ones.

Figure 3.1 shows the fundamental frequency distribution of 500 males and 500 females speaking Swiss German – spontaneously (dashed line) and read (full line). This was collected in an experiment exploring population distributions of f0 and articulation rate (Hedegard et al. 2023). On average, men speak with f0 at 125 Hz in read speech and 129 Hz in spontaneous speech. Women had an f0 of 201 Hz in read speech and 198 Hz in spontaneous speech. There is some overlap between men and women, particularly between 150 and 170 Hz. This overlap between the ranges gives a clue why male speakers are sometimes perceived as females and female speakers are perceived as males. Biological sex intersects closely with social gender. Speakers can consciously (or unconsciously) increase or decrease pitch as a means of portraying more feminine or more masculine identities, but only within limits imposed by their anatomy and physiology (note, though, that perception of sex and gender also comes down to modifying other speech features, such as formant values).

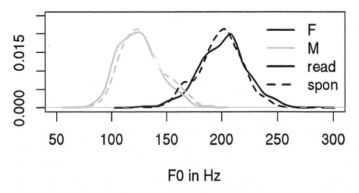

Figure 3.1 Fundamental frequencies of 500 males and 500 females speaking Swiss German in read and spontaneous (spon) speech.

As Figure 3.1 shows, f0 alone does not separate all men from all women. f0 is also affected by many factors, including health, intoxication, and heightened stress or emotion. One such case is documented in Boss (1996), in which a man perpetrated an armed robbery at a service station. He was clearly agitated and his voice affected by his emotional state. In the criminal recording his f0 was recorded at 228 Hz. Note that this value lies towards the higher end of the female range in Figure 3.1.

Speakers of different languages also often have different average f0s. For example, cross-linguistic differences have been found between Japanese and American women, in that Japanese women typically exhibit higher average f0s than their American counterparts. It has been suggested that these differences may stem from cultural differences regarding gender and its relationship to physical and psychological power (Hanley et al. 1966). On a side note, speech technologists have been working to create 'genderless' voices. Online you can hear an example voice that was created so that it speaks with an f0 of 145– 175 Hz, which roughly corresponds to the area of overlap between males and females in Figure 3.1.

3.2.2 Regional background

In profiling cases, analysis of a speaker's regional background is often very useful, as this helps police narrow down a potential suspect population geographically. Discerning where a speaker is from depends on (a) the degree of regional variation present in the country where the language is spoken, (b) the degree of mobility experienced by the target speakers and the communities in question, and (c) the amount of research on regional variation that is available to experts. In the US, UK, Germany, France, the Netherlands, Switzerland, and several other countries in Europe, there is a rich tradition of dialectology. Regional variation in these countries has been studied extensively since the second half of the nineteenth century. In the UK, for example, the most famous work on regional variation is the *Survey of English Dialects* (SED). In the 1950s, researchers collected data particularly from older rural speakers across more than 300 localities in England, Wales, and the Isle of Man. They asked participants more than a thousand questions in the phonetic, lexical, and grammatical domains, and their findings were illustrated through hundreds of maps. Figure 3.2 shows variation in the STRUT vowel (in words like *duck, rubbish*), as captured by the SED.

The map shows a relatively clear north–south divide, with the southeast and southwest realising the vowel predominantly as [ʌ] (dark in Figure 3.2; green in the colour version) while much of the north realises it as [ʊ] (light/yellow). In the light-coded regions, FOOT and STRUT rhyme (a pattern also referred to as 'no FOOT–STRUT split'), meaning that *look* and *luck* are pronounced identically. In the dark-coded regions, FOOT and STRUT have different vowels (i.e., we can say there is a 'FOOT–STRUT split'). Dialect maps stemming from atlases like

37

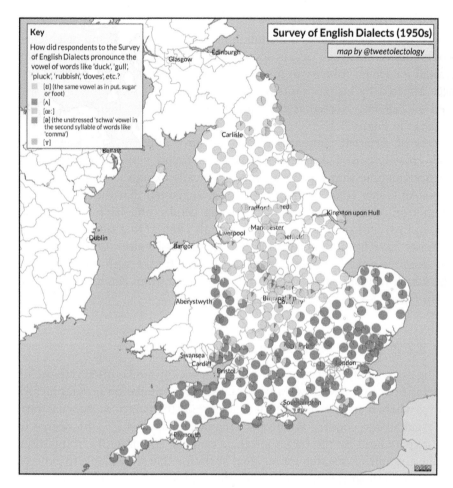

Figure 3.2 Realisation of the STRUT vowel in the SED. (Published with permission)

the SED are often consulted by forensic phoneticians in speaker profiling cases. There is one obvious issue with these maps, however: much of the material is outdated and overgeneralised. Figure 3.2, for instance, reflects the state of language in England in the 1950s. Studies have shown that dialects and accents have changed substantially since then due to migration, speaker mobility, dialect contact, and other social upheavals. There are other problems with the SED, too. For example, the speakers were mostly older men in rural areas, and most locations were represented by a single informant. To get a more up-to-date and comprehensive picture, experts also seek out contemporary material, if available. Figure 3.3, for example, shows geographic differences in the realisation of the STRUT vowel – just as in Figure 3.2 – in a more contemporary dataset (the English Dialects App) from 2016. Note that the project that generated the data also included respondents from Ireland and Scotland, and allowed for variation in responses within a location.

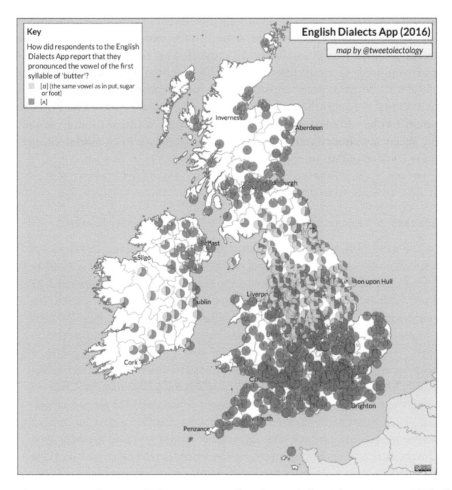

Figure 3.3 Realisation of the STRUT vowel in the English Dialects App. (Published with permission)

This newer data shows that the typical northern feature of no FOOT–STRUT split (light/yellow) appears to be receding. The dialect boundary is shifting northwards, and many people living in the north appear to be moving towards having a FOOT–STRUT split (dark/green). Highly granular, up-to-date maps such as Figure 3.3 enable us to look up pronunciations in very specific localities. Even where such information is available, experts must also use their knowledge and experience to narrow down the likely regional background of the speaker. Experts might also supplement their analyses with reference recordings from areas of interest, and may have a suspect's recording played to 'native' listeners from a particular region to elicit judgments regarding their accent.

Depending on the region and language, forensic speech experts have been shown to perform well in speaker localisation tasks. In one study (Köster et al. 2012), 15 forensic experts in Germany were asked to judge the regional accent of several voices in a mock speaker profiling case. Twenty samples of one-minute spontaneous speech recordings were presented to the experts, who were told to analyse them as quickly as possible. Results revealed an error rate of only 15%; for comparison, naïve German listeners have been shown to have error rates of around 50–70%. Most experts consulted previously existing audio databases, and some combed through the dialectology literature and atlases. The time the experts spent on the samples varied dramatically; some claimed to analyse each sample in about a minute (acting as real-time processors of 'regional accent') while others took about an hour per sample.

Example case for regional speaker profiling: the Yorkshire Ripper hoaxer

There is one particularly famous instance of speaker profiling in which an expert was able to tell where someone was from with a very high degree of accuracy: the Yorkshire Ripper hoax case, also known as Wearside Jack. In the 1970s, a man committed 13 murders in Yorkshire, in the north of England. In the course of their investigations, the police received letters and a recording that claimed to be from the perpetrator. Clips of the original recording can be heard online. The police contacted the phonetician and dialectologist Stanley Ellis and asked him to conduct a speaker profile, in particular to establish where the caller might be from. Ellis consulted dialect atlases (such as the SED, for which he had been a fieldworker) and narrowed the geographical region down to the north east of England, specifically the city of Sunderland. The alleged perpetrator also sent in letters that originated from Sunderland. Ellis then visited Sunderland, made further recordings (as experts often do, as noted above), and tried to pinpoint the alleged perpetrator on an even closer level. He concluded that the caller grew up in the suburbs of Southwick or Castletown. The police began searching for potential suspects in that region with a matching accent. However, no suspect was found even after the recording was played widely on the television and in football grounds – and the murders continued. The police eventually concluded that the caller was most likely a hoaxer. In 1981, the real murderer, Peter Sutcliffe, was arrested in West Yorkshire (further south and west than Sunderland) and was sentenced to life in prison. He was himself from Yorkshire, and had a Yorkshire accent. The identity of the hoaxer remained unknown until 2005, when the police performed DNA analyses on the hoax letters and established a match on a DNA database.

The hoaxer, John Samuel Humble, was convicted for attempting to pervert the course of justice. Because of his hoax tape and letters, the investigation was derailed, and authorities undertook a search for suspects in the wrong place and with the wrong profile. They had even questioned Sutcliffe earlier in the investigation but released him because his accent was not north-eastern. Humble was sentenced to eight years in prison. What is striking about this case from a forensic phonetic point of view is that Humble, the hoaxer, grew up one mile away from the area Ellis had suggested the speaker came from.

It is rare that an analyst would get to such a level of geographical accuracy as Ellis managed in the Yorkshire Ripper hoax case (see box). Nowadays, at least in a UK context, it is more common to report general accent areas, narrowed down depending on whether the material contains specific regional features. It might only be possible to say with confidence, for example, that the speaker comes from northern England, although certain segmental features might enable us to specify the north-east, Merseyside, or West Yorkshire, and so on. In the case of Australia or New Zealand, however, there are few regional accent differences and it might not be possible to reduce the geographical possibilities beyond the national level.

Most speaker profiling cases are currently conducted by humans using auditory and acoustic analysis methods. This stands in contrast to forensic speaker comparison cases, where many analyses are now conducted with the help of computer-automated systems (see the next chapter). However, recent research (e.g., Brown & Wormald 2017) suggests that automatic systems may be on the rise for speaker profiling, too, especially regarding accent localisation. These systems work particularly well if there is sufficient high-quality material available to run them on. However, case recordings are often relatively short and poor in technical quality, which strongly affects the performance of automatic systems. Some automatic measures need at least three minutes of speech per speaker for an automatic accent classification. The question thus arises as to how useful these automatic technologies may be in forensic casework.

In some countries, there are apps that allow you to test how accurate software can be at identifying your regional accent. For example, UK speakers can download the English Dialects App (iOS and Android), which analyses words, pronunciation, and grammatical features to estimate where in the UK a speaker is from.

3.2.3 Social background

Speakers often vary not just geographically, but also along various social dimensions. This information can also be used to profile an unknown speaker. The UK, for example, has traditionally had a well-established class system that is reflected in language use (although class-based differences are much less marked now than they were a few decades ago: even the younger members of the royal family use some non-standard features). The US also shows class stratification in language, but to a lesser degree than in the UK. There are countries where variation is particularly prevalent geographically but somewhat less pronounced socially, as in Norway and German-speaking Switzerland. Still others, such as Australia and New Zealand, have socially-based variation but not very much regional variation.

Social class stratification in the phonetic domain can take many different forms. Segments are the most common features to be included in stratification studies. One of the most famous studies of social stratification in language was carried out in New York City (Labov 1964). (Labov's expertise in the accents of the US led to him acting as an expert witness in the Prinzivalli case, mentioned in Chapter 2.) Labov knew that different department stores attracted different clienteles, and hypothesised that social variation in language could be investigated in these environments. He went to Saks (which attracted upper-class customers), Macy's (which attracted middle-class customers), and S. Klein (which attracted working-class customers). Labov was interested in the articulation of /r/, suspecting that r-fulness (pronouncing /r/) or r-lessness (dropping /r/) would be strongly linked to speakers' social class. In each store he asked employees for directions to an item which he knew was located on the fourth floor, thus triggering each person to respond with an answer that included the term 'fourth floor'. He repeated his question, pretending he did not hear the answer the first time around; he then discreetly noted how that employee had articulated /r/ in these tokens (i.e., auditory coding). Figure 3.4 shows what he found.

The x-axis in Figure 3.4 shows the different department stores examined, and the y-axis indicates the percentage of r-fulness in the speakers' articulations. The white bars represent the /r/ in the word 'fourth' and the grey bars represent /r/ in the word 'floor'. Roman numeral I indicates employees' first iterations of the phrase 'fourth floor', and II indicates their repetitions of the phrase. Several interesting trends are evident from Figure 3.4: firstly, employees at the upper-class store (Saks) used the highest rates of /r/, followed by those at the middle-class

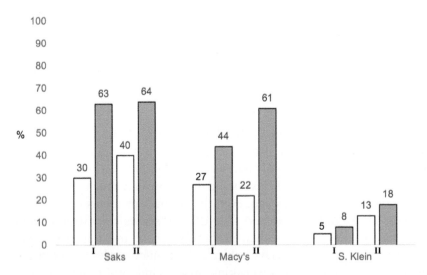

Figure 3.4 Social stratification of /r/ in New York City Department Stores. (Adapted from Labov 1964)

(Macy's) and working-class (Klein) stores. Secondly, in casual speech (i.e., the first iteration), r-lessness was more prevalent; upon being asked for clarification in the second repetition, r-fulness increased. Thirdly, productions of 'fourth' (white bars) showed substantially more r-lessness than 'floor' (grey bars), indicating that the articulation of /r/ was dependent on the phonological context. The employees were all of the same social class. So, regardless of the employees' class, the employees can 'borrow prestige' from the context that surrounds them if necessary. This was one of the first studies that showed how language can vary systematically in the social domain. (Note that social class is now recognised as a complex issue, and appropriate definitions and social class categories are not universally agreed upon. See further section 11.6.4.)

3.2.4 Language(s) spoken and L2 influence

An issue that is sometimes addressed in profiling cases is that of what language is being spoken. While this is often obvious, it might not be clear if the language is not a mainstream one such as English. Next time you hear a language you do not understand, for example on the television or spoken by people you pass in the street, see how easy you find it to identify what language is being spoken. Furthermore, the majority of the world's population speaks more than one language, and people often switch between languages within a conversation (a phenomenon called **code-switching**). Experts might therefore be called upon to identify the language(s) being spoken. Confirming the language often involves working with a consultant who is a native speaker of the suspected language. Many terrorist cases in the early 2000s were at first assumed by investigators to involve Arabic, but closer inspection by linguists revealed them to be more usually in Pashto, Sylheti, or Urdu.

Bear in mind also that many mainstream languages have more speakers who are 'non-native' speakers than 'native'. Linguists tend to classify people as first language (L1) speakers and second language (L2) speakers depending on whether they acquired a language in childhood or later. English, for example, has around 373 million L1 speakers and over a billion L2 speakers. The figures for French are around 80m versus 194m, for Urdu 70m versus 161m, and Swahili 16m versus 55m (data from Ethnologue 2022). It is therefore not surprising to find a forensic recording in which features of speech indicate an L2 speaker.

The expert's first task might be to establish whether the speaker is L1 or L2. If the conclusion is L2, then a follow-up question is whether we can establish the speaker's likely L1. In principle this is possible, especially where the observed features are stereotypical. When we speak in a foreign language we usually leave traces of our first language. When French or German people speak English, they stereotypically replace English /θ/ and /ð/ with [s] and [z]; French and German do not have interdental fricatives, so speakers may replace those sounds with ones which are articulatorily (and often perceptually) relatively similar. In turn, English speakers struggle with unfamiliar sounds in other languages, like the uvular form of /r/ (pronounced [ʁ]) in standard German and French, or the trilled /r/ in Spanish or Arabic. People are relatively good at determining whether someone is an L1 speaker of their own language or whether someone sounds foreign-accented. However, aside from stereotypical features such as those illustrated above, establishing someone's L1 from their L2 is much harder. Moreover, even if we can identify the likely L1, it might not be possible to infer anything about the speaker's regional or social background in the way that can be done with L1 speakers. For example, it might be possible to tell that someone is an L1 speaker of Arabic from a recording of that person speaking L2 English, but Arabic is an official language in 22 states and is spoken by over 400 million people. It would be very difficult to pinpoint which country or region the speaker comes from. For related forensic linguistic analysis see Chapter 11, particularly section 11.7.1 on other language influence detection (OLID).

3.2.5 Speaking style

Assessing speaking style in a ransom call, for instance, is important because it can indicate whether a text was prepared ahead of time: if a text was prepared carefully and then read, this may point to a more serious criminal intent than if the call was not premeditated. The two speaking styles of spontaneous and read speech are very different from each other. Spontaneous speech is optimised for human-to-human communication and has been shown to exhibit greater variability in both segmental and prosodic domains. In this style, segmental realisations can be less precise and exhibit a greater degree of reduction (e.g., vowels becoming centralised). This package of acoustic features enables experts to tell (relatively accurately) whether a sentence or a passage has been produced spontaneously or whether it has been read. There are also distinctive linguistic properties of particular style, for example, in terms of the syntactic complexity of sentences, and the number and type of pauses used.

In the Yorkshire Ripper hoax recording it is very noticeable that the speaker leaves long silent pauses, and the speech delivery is in general slow and lacks any of the disfluencies typical of spontaneous speech (such as false starts, repetitions, filled pauses, or discourse markers – *uh, um, sort of, you know*). It thus appears clear that the text had been prepared in advance and was not spontaneous. The message ends with the phrase 'hope you like the catchy tune at the end', which is followed by an excerpt of the song *Thank You for Being a Friend* by Andrew Gold (which was used as the theme tune in the TV comedy series *The Golden Girls*). Technical analysis of the tape showed that the hoax message was made up of four separate recordings, and that the music had been recorded onto the cassette prior to the hoax message (French et al. 2007). The hoaxer must have known that the music was already present on the tape, which suggests considerable planning.

3.2.6 Environment, time, and date

In some cases, information about a speaker's environment can be extracted from the recording. Perhaps a train station's loudspeaker system is audible in the background or church bells with specific ringing characteristics may be heard; there may be reverb on the recording or the noises of cars, buses, or trams passing by. These sounds can be analysed auditorily and acoustically, and might give some indication of the whereabouts of the speaker and the time the recording was made. For instance, in the movie *The Fugitive,* starring Harrison Ford, location spotting is performed via the Chicago overhead railway that is heard in the background of a recorded message. In a real case in Germany, an expert was involved listening to the feeding of young birds in the background. With the help of an ornithologist the expert was then able to establish the rough time of day and location of the recording. Whether the recording took place indoors or outdoors may provide further useful information about the speaker. Acoustic analyses can even be performed for the purposes of so-called 'room printing': based on the way sound reflects off walls, a reconstruction of the room in which the recording took place can be performed to some degree (Moore et al. 2014).

Further, for some digital recordings, Electrical Network Frequency (ENF) analyses can be performed. ENF is like a digital watermark that is left on the signal – the 'hum' from the electrical supply. ENF varies randomly over time, but the variation is stable across a specific electrical network (such as the national grid in the UK). Provided reference recordings of the ENF are available, the ENF frequency can help experts determine the time and location a recording was made, and whether there are signs it has been edited. ENF analysis is discussed by Amelia Gully on Tom Scott's YouTube channel.

3.3 Information that may be considered in speaker profiling

In this section we consider types of information that are extracted less frequently than those covered in section 3.2, or which are analysed with considerable caution.

3.3.1 Speech disorders and pathologies

Potential speech disorders that the speaker exhibits may also be helpful for forensic experts. Disorders and pathologies do not occur very frequently in forensic casework, but if they do, they can be considered a lucky strike. Phoneticians would consult with speech pathologists to classify a disorder. Given their low frequency, they are often highly diagnostic, and – if the speaker has sought treatment – the patient might even be on record with a clinic or speech pathologist. Medical records may thus be a useful resource when trying to narrow down a suspect population. Speech disorders can manifest in different ways: they may have physical causes (e.g., cleft palate, prevalence of ca. 0.06% in the US population), neuro-motor causes (e.g., stuttering, prevalence of ca. 1% in the US population), or they may be functional (e.g., lisp, prevalence of ca. 20–25% in the US population). Each of these disorders leaves different traces in the speech signal. Note that speech disfluencies such as hesitations, filled pauses, lengthening of speech sounds, and restarting (which can pathologically manifest in stuttering) are not themselves pathological, but can still be some of the most valuable features to identify. In Chapter 4 we talk more about speech disfluencies and how they can be helpful in forensic casework.

3.3.2   Influence of drugs

Whether or not the speaker in the recording may be under the influence of a drug can also help to narrow down a potential suspect population. The effects of illegal drugs on speech have not been investigated by many studies for obvious ethical reasons. One typically distinguishes between four types of drugs: depressants, which slow down brain function (e.g., alcohol); stimulants, which increase the activity of the central nervous system, potentially elevating mood (e.g., cocaine or methamphetamines); hallucinogens, which alter people's perception of reality (e.g., LSD); and opiates, which are often used as painkillers and at the same time can make people feel euphoric (e.g., heroin). Let's have a look at some of the effects of different types of drugs on speech.

Alcohol, a depressant, has been the most thoroughly researched. It is known to affect reaction times, reflexes, coordination, and nerve transmission. Given that speech articulation is at its core a series of muscle movements, it is not surprising that alcohol affects such movement. In the segmental domain, for example, it has been shown that apical consonants (i.e., consonants that are produced with the apex, or tip, of the tongue) are particularly affected by alcohol intake due to the paralysing effect of alcohol on muscle tension. Words such as *check* or *jump* which are typically produced as [tʃɛk] or [dʒʌmp] are frequently articulated as [ʃɛk] or [ʒʌmp] when under the influence of alcohol, a process called deaffrication (i.e., affricates are no longer produced as affricates but as simple fricatives instead). In the suprasegmental domain, research on alcohol's effect on f0 has produced somewhat conflicting results. Most studies indicate an increase in average f0 with alcohol consumption. Speaking rate, too, can be affected, with people who are intoxicated showing slower rates due to decreased cognitive function. Disfluencies (e.g., false starts) increase in alcohol-intoxicated individuals. However, while we might be able to imagine a stereotypical 'drunk' voice, it is in fact difficult to generalise about the effects of alcohol on speech. Effects vary depending on how much alcohol has been ingested, and the effects also interact with changes of mood that can be induced by alcohol. The same level of alcohol intake could lead one speaker to be morose but make another person very animated. The first person's speech might become relatively slow and monotonous, with low f0, while the second person might speak in a 'lively' way with higher than usual f0 and a lot of f0 modulation.

When we look at cannabis, research suggests that it does not fit neatly into any of the categories of drugs mentioned earlier. It can depress the nervous system, but it can also excite or impair it. To further complicate things, cannabis has been shown to have varied effects on people. In terms of speech production, speakers high on cannabis have been shown to exhibit more variation in voice onset time (VOT, i.e., the temporal duration from the beginning of the plosive to the onset of voicing) as a result of the drug affecting the motor timing between the larynx (which holds the vocal folds) and lip movement. While interesting, the question is, of course, whether this variability in VOT is observable in poor or noisy recording conditions such as when speech is transmitted over a telephone line. A speaker high on cannabis may further exhibit a reduced range and flatter trajectories of f0, as well as a decrease in shimmer (i.e., the amplitude regularity of vocal fold vibration).

Stimulants such as methamphetamines (e.g., ecstasy), can make people become more fluent and talkative, with shorter pauses. These effects are consistent with how stimulants may affect cognitive function in other domains (e.g., a general increase in 'wakefulness'). The effects of hallucinogens such as LSD are somewhat different from those of depressants or stimulants. LSD typically does not affect reaction times or affect speech fluency, but rather seems to affect semantics: speakers may, for example, make errors such as saying 'butterfly' when describing a picture that shows a bee. Finally, opioids like heroin can have a similar effect on speech production as depressants (e.g., deaffrication or difficulties with apical consonants). Long-term addicts may manifest withdrawal symptoms when they have not taken heroin in a while (a state sometimes called 'rattling'). Vocally this can lead to high variation in f0 and voice quality, and an increase in disfluency.

How is this all relevant to speaker profiling? The acoustic cues just mentioned may be indicators as to whether a perpetrator was under the influence of a drug when they made a ransom call, for example. The acoustic cues may also help when the question is not 'who was speaking?' but rather 'what state was the known person in at the time?' A real case involved the *Exxon Valdez* oil spill, when a tanker ran aground in Alaska in 1989 causing huge environmental damage. It was alleged that the ship's captain had been drunk at the time of the accident. His speech, which had been recorded via radio transmissions, was analysed for evidence of intoxication (albeit with inconclusive results; Hollien 1993).

There is one major conundrum in profiling cases involving potential intoxication, though: we usually do not know whether the speaker always talks like that or whether they really were under the influence of a drug. Caution is therefore required when assessing the potential influence of a drug.

3.4 Information which deserves strong caution

In this section we consider a further set of indexical categories, evidence for which might occasionally be available in a profile case. However, it is particularly difficult to link these indexical features to phonetic features. Analysis and interpretation therefore require strong caution.

3.4.1 Age

Age estimations are potentially useful in speaker profiling, as they can substantially narrow down a suspect population. However, estimating age is much more difficult than it might appear. Listen to a selection of voices on the radio: how narrowly could you estimate the speakers' ages? There are indeed some very clear signs of age, for example if you compare the voice of a five-year-old with that of a fifty-year-old. However, there are no vocal cues that relate neatly to age across the whole lifespan, or which can be generalised across a population. The effects of ageing vary enormously between individuals. As a consequence, it can be very difficult to establish whether a speaker is 20, 40, or 60 based on their voice alone.

Voices do vary across time, of course, and forensic cases almost never involve recordings that are made contemporaneously. Some investigations may even extend across many years; the Yorkshire Ripper hoax case mentioned earlier, for example, involved a delay of 26 years between the first recording and the hoaxer's arrest. Male voices are known to typically 'break' at around 15 years of age (when the larynx and vocal folds experience sudden growth, leading to lower f0). f0 decreases until about age 40, then remains stable until about age 60, and then increases slightly in old age. Women tend to exhibit a different pattern: f0 decreases upon menarche (first period), then remains stable, and then decreases again after menopause. Changes in f0 across the lifespan have been studied using the speech of Queen Elizabeth II, for example (see Figure 3.5). Importantly, though, fundamental frequency also changes over the course of the day, with many people having lower f0 in the morning. This complicates the use of f0 as a diagnostic for age.

Voice quality is another feature that changes across the lifespan. From adulthood to old age, the perceived harshness of a voice often increases. Voice quality may further vary across the lifespan due to damage to the vocal folds, such as from prolonged smoking. However, just like f0, voice quality can vary depending on time of day; if you're exhausted at the end of the day, you tend to creak more and sound hoarser (especially after talking a lot). Studies have also shown that speaking rate can be affected by age, with older speakers typically talking more slowly than younger speakers (Bóna 2014).

To make accurate predictions about an unknown speaker's age, one would need longitudinal data for that person in order to present a fuller picture of their age at the time of recording. Such data is, obviously, nearly never available in

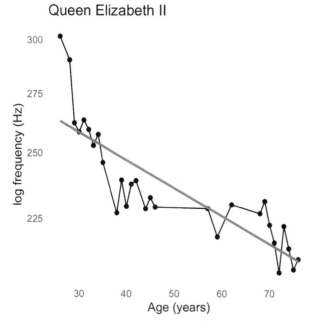

Queen Elizabeth II

Figure 3.5 Changes in f0 across the lifespan, illustrated with the voice of Queen Elizabeth II. (Adapted from Reubold, Harrington & Kleber 2010)

criminal forensic work. Because of this wide variation in vocal parameters, automatic systems and naïve listeners perform relatively poorly when it comes to estimating age. Both automatic systems and humans typically have an error rate of around plus/minus ten years, meaning that age estimations need to be taken with a large pinch of salt.

3.4.2 Biometrics: weight, height, and facial features

Intuitively, many people believe that they are relatively good at envisioning the physical traits of a speaker from their speech alone. This is because we tend to have a stereotyped view of how voices and physical traits relate to one another. Picture a heavyweight boxer and a jockey. Which do you expect has the lower pitched voice? Most people would say the boxer, because his much larger overall size implies his vocal folds might also be larger, and thus give him a low f0. But in reality such stereotypes are just that – stereotypes. It is easy to find counter-examples, and the overall correlations of body size and phonetic features are weak at best. Research has shown that accurate assessments of such biometric information are almost impossible, which is why features such as these are typically not mentioned in reliable forensic reports.

Along similar lines, there has been research looking at the link between vocal characteristics and faces. Studies have shown that listeners can match dynamic

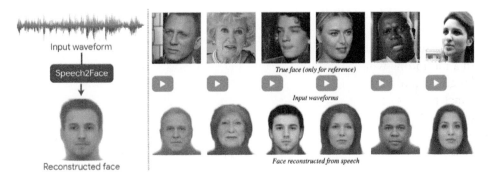

Figure 3.6 Faces reconstructed from the speech signal using artificial intelligence. (Adapted and reproduced with permission, from Oh et al. 2019)

images to voices (Smith et al. 2016). In most speaker profiling cases, however, only the voice is heard and the speaker is not seen. The question thus becomes more about whether humans can create an image in their heads based on a speaker's voice, which can then be used to create a photofit or e-fit (i.e., a facial composite sketch) of a potential suspect. Recent research (Oh et al. 2019) studies precisely this question. Using artificial intelligence, systems attempt to reconstruct a speaker's likeness based on the speech signal alone. An algorithm can be applied to millions of YouTube clips, creating a neural network that associates vocal attributes with facial features. The algorithm appears to estimate age, gender, and ethnicity relatively successfully (see Figure 3.6). However, the system is rather opaque. It is not possible to fully interrogate what acoustic features influence the decision for a specific speaker. Such systems are therefore at present of limited use forensically.

3.4.3 Psychological states

Intuitively, we may also think we can deduce whether someone is lying or telling the truth based on speech alone. This could be useful in speaker profiling cases such as ransom calls. Research has shown, however, that human listeners (as well as automatic systems) are not capable of telling whether someone is lying above chance level. Why do we think we are good at making such judgments? Perhaps it is because humans tend to be good in everyday circumstances at reading the emotional state of a speaker based on vocal features. To achieve this, we process prosodic markers that are indicative of different emotional states; for instance, higher overall pitch, more pitch fluctuation, and upwards pitch inflections indicate excitement, while relatively high, monotonous pitch alongside downward pitch inflections and slow articulation rate indicate sadness. Such prosodic cues to emotional involvement are currently being harnessed in voice assistants like Apple's Siri, Amazon's Alexa, and Google Assistant. Amazon, for instance, is focusing its current research on detecting when users are frustrated. Evidence from this strain of research suggests that machines are catching up with humans in detecting emotion. However, the problem here again is that stereotypical features are not universal. Not all speakers sound lively when excited, or speak in a monotone when bored or disengaged. It is also clear that some cues vary by language and community. Using vocal cues to infer emotion is thus a far from exact process, and it is not clear that experts are any better placed than non-experts to judge emotion.

Even more difficult is the detection of psychological or cognitive states. Many crime TV shows and movies try to make the audience believe that truthfulness can be gathered from acoustic analysis of the voice. TV chat shows regularly employ 'lie detector' devices to address family disputes, while dramas often include scenes in which a speaker's voice and physical reactions are analysed to establish whether or not they are telling the truth (one example occurs in *Mission Impossible – Rogue Nation*). This does not only occur in fiction and provocative TV shows, though: there are police forces, insurance companies, and even airport security systems that use techniques like 'voice stress analysis' (probably a euphemism for 'lie detector') or 'layered voice analysis' (LVA). Independent research by academics (rather than in-house research by manufacturers) has shown that such systems only operate at chance level, and the underlying principles have been heavily criticised (see e.g., Damphousse et al. 2007). Forensic phoneticians do not regard such systems as having any validity.

A problem for speaker profiling and comparison: voice disguise and spoofing

Of course, perpetrators usually don't want to be identified from their voice when making a call. For this reason, kidnappers and other criminals often try to change their voice to conceal their identity. The technical term for this phenomenon is 'voice disguise' – a deliberate attempt to change the voice to hide one's identity. There is a link between the type of crime committed and whether voice disguise occurs. Disguising happens particularly often in blackmail and kidnapping cases, and thus is more likely to occur in countries where such crimes are frequent. Precise statistics as to the overall prevalence of voice disguise are difficult to retrieve. The German BKA claims that about 15–25% of all profiling and speaker comparison cases (covered in the next chapter) involve some form of voice disguise.

There are different ways of disguising one's voice, including electronic voice changers. Though these are easy to obtain through smartphone apps, they are (perhaps surprisingly, and contra what you might see in the movies) hardly ever used in criminal recordings. This might be because such apps do not (yet) allow for spontaneous communication or real-time changes when making a threat call, for example. Speakers can also voluntarily change their voice source characteristics (e.g., raising pitch or whispering), change their resonance features (e.g., speaking with a nasal voice, or trapping a pen between the teeth to minimise jaw movement), or try to change their language or accent/dialect. If a perpetrator attempts to disguise their voice, these disguises can cause substantial within-speaker variability, which may impinge on experts' attempts to narrow down suspect populations. Different types of disguises affect the speech signal differently. Covering the face with a piece of cloth, for example, dampens higher frequencies (like some fricative frequencies) and thus makes certain features that contribute to a speaker's vocal uniqueness more difficult to detect. On a side note, this is exactly what happens with people's voices when they wear protective hygiene masks at a hospital or during a pandemic: higher frequencies are dampened.

The disguise methods mentioned here have been shown to be relatively effective: whispering, for example, has been found to reduce the identification rates in voice line-ups (cf. Chapter 5, e.g., if the perpetrator was heard whispering on the phone but later was heard in regular phonation in a voice line-up; Orchard & Yarmey 1995). Changing one's accent can also be very effective: in some studies, correct identification has been found to fall to almost chance level (Sjöström et al. 2006). The sophistication of imitation is affected by the talent of the imitator as well as the length of the speech material: the more the person says, the more likely they are to slip up and make errors in their dialect imitation.

Well-trained forensic speech experts can tell relatively well whether an accent is authentic or not. Sociolinguists have found that variation is typically patterned and systematic, so if a speaker does not imitate certain features consistently, experts may pick up on this issue. It is very rare for experts to encounter incredibly good imitators. In a case one of us worked on, for example, the perpetrator of abusive phone calls maintained a consistent but clearly fake foreign accent of English. He nevertheless had some very unusual features in his natural voice, including a tendency to pronounce /v/ as [f] (e.g., *very* was pronounced [fɛɹi]). He was not able to disguise these unusual features, which therefore surfaced in his fake accent too.

Another (potentially) growing problem for speaker profiling and speaker comparison is spoofing: i.e., the use of speech and video technology to create fake voices and videos. Fraudsters may use so-called deepfake technology to make phone calls to banks where they claim to be the account holder. One such case occurred in the UK in 2019, for example, when fraudsters tricked a manager into transferring €220,000 using a fake voice. It is likely that such spoofing technology will become increasingly more sophisticated and will eventually find its way into forensic casework. Research is now underway to establish how to separate fake voices from real ones (for example, Kirchhübel & Brown 2022).

Conclusion

In this chapter we have presented different types of information that can be derived from the speech signal in speaker profiling cases – that is, when a recording of a crime exists but there are no suspects yet. The information that experts deduce from voices can be separated into three categories: information that is almost always analysed (e.g., regional background), information that may sometimes be analysed but needs to be treated with caution (e.g., drug intake), and information which bears theoretical interest but needs to be treated with strong caution and is thus typically not mentioned in case reports (e.g., biometric information like height and weight). We have shown that voice disguise – the voluntary act of changing the voice to conceal one's identity – can be an effective identity-masking tool for many perpetrators.

Expert phoneticians are generally more reliable at profiling than lay people. They have a more extensive knowledge of the distribution of indexical features, and a greater appreciation of the confounding factors that must be considered when inferring social or demographic information from the voice. They are also trained to express appropriate degrees of caution in their conclusions. This is discussed further in Chapter 13.

Further reading

For detailed discussions of speaker profiling:

Jessen, M. (2020). Speaker profiling and forensic voice comparison. In M. Coulthard, A. May, & R. Sousa-Silva (eds.) *The Routledge Handbook of Forensic Linguistics*. Routledge, pp. 382–399.

Schilling, N., & Marsters, A. (2015). Unmasking identity: Speaker profiling for forensic linguistic purposes. *Annual Review of Applied Linguistics*, 35: 195–214.

For discussions of the Yorkshire Ripper hoaxer case:

Ellis, S. (1994). The Yorkshire Ripper enquiry: Part I. *Forensic Linguistics: The International Journal of Speech, Language and the Law*, 1(2): 197–206.

French, P., Harrison, P., & Windsor Lewis, J. (2007). R v John Samuel Humble: The Yorkshire Ripper hoaxer trial. *International Journal of Speech Language and the Law*, 13(2): 255–273.

References

Bóna, J. (2014). Temporal characteristics of speech: The effect of age and speech style. *Journal of the Acoustical Society of America*, 136(2): EL116–EL121.

Boss, D. (1996). The problem of F0 and real-life speaker identification: A case study. *Forensic Linguistics: The International Journal of Speech, Language and the Law*, 3: 155–159.

Brown, G., & Wormald, J. (2017). Automatic sociophonetics: Exploring corpora using a forensic accent recognition system. *Journal of the Acoustical Society of America*, 142(1): 422–433.

Damphousse, K. R., Pointon, L., Upchurch, D., & Moore, R. K. (2007). *Assessing the Validity of Voice Stress Analysis Tools in a Jail Setting.* US Department of Justice, National Criminal Justice Reference Service.

Ethnologue (2022). *Languages of the World.* www.ethnologue.com

Hanley, T. D., Snidecor, J. C., & Ringel, R. L. (1966). Some acoustic differences among languages. *Phonetica*, 14(2): 97–107.

Hedegard, H., Fröhlich, A., Tomaschek, F., Steiner, C., & Leemann, A. (2023). Filling the population statistics gap: Swiss German reference data on F0 and speech tempo for forensic contexts. *Proceedings of Interspeech 2023*, 2558–2562.

Hollien, H. (1993). An oilspill, alcohol and the captain: a possible misapplication of forensic science. *Forensic Science International*, 60(1–2): 97–105.

Huber, M. (2008). Ghanaian English: Phonology. In R. Mesthrie (ed.), *Varieties of English, Volume 4: Africa, South and Southeast Asia.* Mouton de Gruyter, pp. 67–92.

Kirchhübel, C., & Brown, G. (2022). Spoofed speech from the perspective of a forensic phonetician. *Proceedings of Interspeech 2022*, 1308–1312. Incheon, Korea.

Köster, O., Kehrein, R., Masthoff, K., & Boubaker, Y. H. (2012). The tell-tale accent: Identification of regionally marked speech in German telephone conversations by forensic phoneticians. *International Journal of Speech, Language & the Law*, 19(2): 51–71.

Labov, W. (1964). *The Social Stratification of English in New York City.* Center for Applied Linguistics.

Moore, A. H., Brookes, M., & Naylor, P. A. (2014). Room identification using roomprints. *Audio Engineering Society Conference: 54th International Conference: Audio Forensics.* Audio Engineering Society.

Oh, T. H., Dekel, T., Kim, C., Mosseri, I., Freeman, W. T., Rubinstein, M., & Matusik, W. (2019). Speech2face: Learning the face behind a voice. *Proceedings of the IEEE/CVF Conference on Computer Vision and Pattern Recognition*, 7539–7548. Long Beach, California.

Orchard, T. L., & Yarmey, A. D. (1995). The effects of whispers, voice-sample duration, and voice distinctiveness on criminal speaker identification. *Applied Cognitive Psychology*, 9(3): 249–260.

Reubold, U., Harrington, J., & Kleber, F. (2010). Vocal aging effects on F0 and the first formant: A longitudinal analysis in adult speakers. *Speech Communication*, 52(7–8): 638–651.

Sjöström, M., Eriksson, E. J., Zetterholm, E., & Sullivan, K. P. (2006). A switch of dialect as disguise. *Proceedings of Fonetik, Lund University Working Papers*, 52, 113–116.

Smith, H. M., Dunn, A. K., Baguley, T., & Stacey, P. C. (2016). Matching novel face and voice identity using static and dynamic facial images. *Attention, Perception, & Psychophysics*, 78: 868–879.

Trudgill, P. (1974). *The Social Differentiation of English in Norwich*. Cambridge University Press.

Activity section

Activity 3A – Speaker profiling

This activity is best conducted with assistance – do it in class or with a colleague. Ask your instructor or colleague to play about two minutes of any voice sample. (Note: numerous examples can be accessed at www.dialectsarchive.com). Here is an excerpt of the text that you will hear.

> *Well, here's a story for you: Sarah Perry was a veterinary nurse who had been working daily at an old zoo in a deserted district of the territory, so she was very happy to start a new job at a superb private practice in North Square near the Duke Street Tower. That area was much nearer for her and more to her liking. Even so, on her first morning, she felt stressed. She ate a bowl of porridge, checked herself in the mirror and washed her face in a hurry. Then she put on a plain yellow dress and a fleece jacket, picked up her kit and headed for work. When she got there, there was a woman with a goose waiting for her. The woman gave Sarah an official letter from the vet. The letter implied that the animal could be suffering from a rare form of foot and mouth disease, which was surprising, because normally you would only expect to see it in a dog or a goat. Sarah was sentimental, so this made her feel sorry for the beautiful bird* (© 2000 Douglas N. Honorof, Jill McCullough & Barbara Somerville.)

Construct a simple speaker profile for the voice you heard. Where is the speaker from? How old are they? Can you say something about the speaker's educational background? Is the recording spontaneous or read speech? What evidence do you have to back up your claims? Complete this task based on auditory analysis alone.

Answer 3A

Note that the following profile is based on www.dialectsarchive.com/ghana-2. According to the Dialects Archive website, this person speaks Ghanaian English. He was 40 years old at the time of recording and has a PhD. The highly mobile speaker has lived in Malaysia and Canada, and currently resides in the United States. The recording is based on read speech. There is some evidence for the speaker coming from Ghana, such as his more syllable-timed rhythm, his non-rhoticity (i.e., postvocalic /r/s like in 'here' are not articulated), and his replacement of interdental fricatives with alveolar plosives (e.g., /ðæt/ is pronounced [d̥æt]). There is also evidence of his international mobility. Ghanaian English typically merges the FLEECE and KIT vowels, so words like 'fleece' become a shorter [flis] rather than a longer [fliːs]. This speaker, however, does not say [flis] but [fliːs], which may be indicative of time spent in North America, where FLEECE and KIT are typically unmerged. He also articulates 'Duke' as [duːk] rather than [djuːk]; this yod-dropping (i.e., not pronouncing /j/ before /uː/ in some words) may be further evidence of his US residence, though Ghanaian English also has variable yod-dropping for some speakers (Huber 2008). As previously discussed in this chapter, estimating someone's age based on their speech can be difficult. His educational background may be evident in his strong reading ability and reading fluency. The sentences are grammatically standard, with few false starts, and are spoken at a relatively slow articulation rate. These observations may indicate that the speaker is reading from a prepared text rather than speaking spontaneously.

It's unlikely you would have been able to identify Ghana itself, but you might have steered towards an African variety. What matters most is spotting the phonetic and linguistic features that could potentially be useful diagnostics of some regional or demographic feature. Establishing precisely what they indicate can be very difficult, and is often a team effort.

Activity 3B – 'Lord Buckingham'

In 2005, Charles Stopford was arrested trying to enter the UK at Dover using a fake passport and fake name: Lord Christopher Edward Robert Buckingham. He was sentenced to 21 months in prison for providing false information about his identity. Stopford claimed that he was educated at Harrow (a prestigious private school) and Cambridge. Oddly, he was also in possession of letters addressing him as Alexei Romanoff, which garnered lots of media attention and suspicion that he could be an Eastern European spy. It was further speculated (for unknown reasons) that he may have had South African or Australian origins. A TV company approached forensic speech experts in the UK to provide an analysis of Stopford's true origins based on his police interview. Imagine you were a forensic speech expert: how would you go about verifying whether he had South African, Eastern European, or Australian linguistic influences? More generally, how would you explore Stopford's linguistic biography using the police interview as material? What features of speech might you expect for a Harrow and Cambridge educated man?

Answer 3B

Experts conducted auditory and acoustic analyses of the available material, consulted existing literature on these varieties of English, and – perhaps most importantly – consulted with native speakers to check whether they believed him to be a native speaker of their variety. The question of whether native speakers should be consulted in cases such as this one will crop up again in Chapter 7 on language analysis in the asylum procedure (LAAP). Findings revealed that the speaker overall showed many features typically found in standard southern British English. However, there were some striking features such as several examples of postvocalic /r/ articulation, yod-dropping, and his articulation of his own alleged name 'Buckingham' as ['bʌkɪŋˌhʌm] as opposed to ['bʌkɪŋəm] that pointed to American English influence. Yet other features were found that are not typical of either British or American accents, such as strong devoicing of final stops. With the help of native speakers and linguists who specialise in these varieties, speech experts concluded that the variety spoken was neither Australian nor South African English (neither of which is rhotic, for example). They also ruled out an Eastern European origin due to an overall lack of non-native traces. It seemed that he was speaking British English peppered with American English features. In the end, soon after his case was publicised, the perpetrator's sister identified his photograph and outed his identity as Charles Stopford III, which was later confirmed by fingerprints. It turned out that he had been convicted in 1983 for the possession of explosives and disappeared after a short jail term in Florida. His alleged name (Buckingham), his alleged education (Harrow and Cambridge), and the letters addressed to him as Alexei Romanoff had been created to construct a false identity. In retrospect, the combination of British and American features might appear obvious, but at the time of the original case a large team of experts found it difficult to reach a clear consensus because of the mixture of the accent features, and also because there were features that were not characteristic of either British or American English. Even with well-documented language varieties like these, profiling is rarely an easy task.

Activity 3C – 'Jihadi John'

In 2014 and 2015, a man dubbed 'Jihadi John' was seen in several videos published by the Islamic State of Iraq and Syria (ISIS). He reportedly beheaded seven western journalists and aid workers as well as more than 20 unknown Syrian soldiers. The audio heard in the video clips indicated that the speaker came from an English-speaking country, specifically the UK. As a member of a four-man group of active ISIS militants, western media outlets soon dubbed him 'John' after John Lennon, one of the four Beatles musicians. Many were shocked to hear a native English speaker as a leading ISIS representative. Listen to the audio file on *The Guardian* newspaper's website. This is an extract from an ISIS video published in 2015, featuring Jihadi John. His voice was typically distorted in the videos, but *The Guardian* used speech software to try to alleviate this distortion. In the audio file you hear, Jihadi John addresses the Japanese government and Japanese hostages.

Listen to the file very carefully. What can you tell about the speaker's geographical origins and upbringing? What can you say about the variety of English he speaks? Be sure to mention concrete examples, using auditory and perhaps also acoustic analysis.

Answer 3C

Jihadi John's rather syllable-timed rhythm (i.e., resembling that of French rather than English) was hypothesised to stem from a foreign language background; studies have shown that dialect and language contact can lead to such influences in rhythmic patterns. Some features in the signal point to what is referred to as Multicultural London English (MLE). MLE is spoken by people from diverse backgrounds, mostly working-class, in multicultural parts of London, although research suggests that the variety is also starting to emerge in culturally diverse neighbourhoods in Manchester (in the north of England) and Birmingham (in the Midlands). One feature of MLE is GOOSE fronting. For example, the word 'you' is pronounced [jʏː], at 29.582 s. TH-stopping (where the fricative is realised as a plosive) is another feature of MLE, also evident in this signal at 7.799 s, where 'the' is pronounced [də]. It turned out that Jihadi John's real identity was Mohammed Emwazi, a Kuwaiti-born British national who grew up in West London and who received a degree in computer programming from a British university. Allegedly, he left the UK to travel to Syria in 2012. As this analysis shows, some phonetic indicators in the speech signal indeed pointed to the regional and social origin of the speaker in this case.

4 Speaker comparison

Forensic speaker comparison (FSC, also sometimes called forensic voice comparison) is the main task of forensic speech scientists, making up about 70% of caseloads. In the UK, FSC was first brought in evidence in 1967, and is nowadays applied in around 500 cases a year. Several high-profile criminal cases have involved FSC. In the UK these include the trials of Abu Hamza al-Masri (for inciting racial hatred, 2005–6) and David Bieber (for murder, 2004). FSC is also becoming more common around the world, for example in Ghana (a drugs trial, 2007), Egypt (relating to the deposition of President Morsi, 2015), and at the International Criminal Tribunal into war crimes perpetrated by Radislav Krstic (2001) and Slobodan Milošević (2003–6).

In FSC, experts compare speech patterns found in **questioned recordings** (so called because the identity of the speaker is in question or dispute) with one or more recordings of a known suspect. The case concerning Paul Prinzivalli, outlined at the start of Chapter 2, is a typical example. In the UK, the suspect recordings, also referred to as **known or reference recordings**, are usually from police interviews. Some examples of questioned recordings include those of kidnappers making ransom demands, drug dealers arranging illegal transactions, and stalkers leaving voice messages. Note that this task is different from profiling (discussed in Chapter 3), in which only unknown recordings are available and suspects have not yet been found. Usually, speaker comparisons are performed 'manually' by experts (i.e., using auditory and acoustic analyses), but in recent years automatic procedures involving speaker recognition technology have also been used to complement 'manual' analyses. Questioned and suspect recordings are compared with respect to several linguistic-phonetic and signal processing features, many of which we will discuss in this chapter. Once a comparison has been performed, experts report their scientifically motivated conclusions and state the strength of the evidence assuming the samples are (i) from the same speaker or (ii) from different speakers.

DOI: 10.4324/9780367616595-4

Aim

In this chapter we will discuss **different approaches to FSC** (section 4.1) and general **problems in conducting FSC** (4.2). We then describe **'ideal' phonetic features** for FSC (4.3), and survey the **features that are typically analysed** in an FSC task (4.4). Finally, we delve into what is probably the most complex part of this half of the book: the **expression of conclusions** (4.5), which includes the expression of probabilities via **likelihood ratios (LRs)** (4.6).

4.1 Approaches to FSC

There are various ways that recordings are handled in FSC. We can distinguish between three main approaches:

- **Auditory and acoustic analysis,** where experts use a combination of standard methods from phonetics: (1) listening carefully and repeatedly to speech samples using high-quality equipment and attending to segmental and suprasegmental features; and (2) analysing and quantifying aspects of the speech signal using specialist software.
- **Analysis by automatic speaker recognition (ASR),** using software that calculates degrees of similarity and typicality (see section 4.2) based on statistical models of acoustic features which are extracted from the recordings.
- **ASR with human assistance,** a combination of ASR and phonetics-based analyses.

Agencies and jurisdictions differ in the approaches they use. The first approach is the most labour-intensive since it requires preparation and analysis of speech material. However, this approach is still used most often. In recent years, ASR-based analyses in combination with human assistance have been on the rise worldwide.

A note on 'voiceprinting'

The forensic laboratory has analyzed the mystery voice. Although the voice is disguised, there is an essential speech pattern, a voiceprint of the stalker. And I obtained an interview Petrocelli gave on television recently. The laboratory is analyzing that. If the voices match, then we have our man.

Murder, She Wrote (1995)

Between the 1960s and 1980s, there was some hope for an approach called voiceprinting, a term explicitly coined as a parallel to fingerprinting. The Federal Bureau of Investigation

(FBI, the intelligence service of the United States) employed the technique for many years, and was still using it as recently as 2007. The idea was that acoustic images of speech – for example the spectrogram in Figure 2.10 – could be examined visually for patterns that were unique to individuals, rather like the manual examination of fingerprints. You still hear this term regularly in fictionalised accounts of speech analysis, as illustrated by the extract above from the crime drama *Murder, She Wrote*. Speech scientists, however, quickly dismissed the approach as invalid. The voice simply varies far too much for visual inspection alone to be viable, and technical differences in recordings can also have huge effects on acoustic patterns. Even proponents of the technique admitted that it could not be applied in almost two thirds of all cases (Koenig 1986). No reputable labs use this approach nowadays. That is not to say that acoustic analysis itself is not valid: most practitioners use acoustic analysis software to make measurements of speech features. However, in doing so they compare overall patterns averaged across many examples and make careful measurements of specific acoustic features rather than conducting a holistic visual inspection. They also make allowances for known sources of difference between recordings (such as the effect of phone transmission).

4.2   Problems in FSC

From everyday experience you will probably agree that people have different voices, and that therefore the voice can act as a marker of personal identity. You might, for example, have heard a voice in a crowd, and realised that a friend is unexpectedly nearby. Voice acts as a **biometric** – something that can be used to identify a person. However, unlike other biometrics such as fingerprints, voice is an *imperfect* biometric. Despite what you see in the movies, there is no such thing as a 'voiceprint', in the sense of something unique and permanent (see the box above). Voices are indeed characteristic, but what makes them recognisable is a very large set of features occurring in combination. Every feature is variable, and is present only some of the time a person speaks. For example, as we explained earlier, fundamental frequency (f0) varies constantly as we speak, and f0 is not present at all when a speaker produces voiceless sounds, or speaks in a whisper. It is a fact that no two samples of speech are identical even if they are made by the same speaker. Speech is a complex and dynamic process, generated by complex movements of several articulators that shape airflow. It is not possible for a person to make exactly the same set of physical and aerodynamic changes more than once. In that sense, every speech event is unique.

To fully understand this, it might help to draw a parallel with another dynamic process: handwriting. Signatures are used as markers of personal identity, but no two examples of a signature are ever identical because a writer's hand movements vary slightly every time they write. In the same way, no two recordings contain identical speech features. This is true of any sort of recording, but the difficulty of FSC work is further exacerbated by a number of factors that are typical of forensic recordings. Some of these factors relate to speaker behaviour, and others to technical issues. For example, questioned recordings often involve people experiencing high levels of emotion, or who are intoxicated. By contrast, police interviews tend to be formal, and some suspects are morose and taciturn. Recordings of voices are further affected by technical differences. There may be background noise (like music, or cars passing by), signal distortions (for instance, if the material is transmitted over a telephone line and information is lost at certain frequencies), or reverberation from room acoustics. Sometimes, questioned samples like a ransom demand call are very short (perhaps only a few seconds). Furthermore, it is common for many of these factors to vary even within a given recording. For example, the speaking mode might start calm, but then the speaker might become more agitated over time, and the background noise may also vary in type and intensity as the speech unfolds.

These facts present major problems for forensic speaker comparison no matter what method is adopted. FSC is therefore not a matter of seeking unique and matching (or mismatching) features in different recordings. It is inevitable there will be differences between the recordings (since no two samples of speech are identical) but also some similarities (almost certainly the same language, and voices similar enough that police officers believe the recordings were produced by the same person). Forensic speech analysts therefore do not assume there will be a 'match' or 'mismatch' at the end of a speaker comparison. The analyst needs to consider the differences between the samples – the technical quality, emotional state of the speaker, and so on – and make a careful analysis of a range of features that are expected to serve as good diagnostics of speaker identity. FSC conclusions, as we will discuss in section 4.6, are therefore usually presented on a scale rather than as a binary match/mismatch decision. In the next section we discuss the types of features that are regularly analysed in FSC, and some of the difficulties presented by variation in recordings.

4.3 What are 'ideal' phonetic features?

You may wonder how speaker comparison is even possible given all the factors that may be present in a crime recording! For the reasons outlined below, forensic speech experts are particularly interested in the features that best withstand these types of confounds. Such features can be considered 'ideal' phonetic features. By this we mean that they are relatively common, easy to measure, and not too badly affected by the sorts of variation we described in the last section. To talk further about these ideal features, we need to introduce some fundamental concepts in FSC: inter-speaker and intra-speaker variation, similarity and typicality, robustness to transmission, and robustness to disguise and mimicry.

Inter- and intra-speaker variation: Ideal features for the purposes of FSC demonstrate high **inter-speaker** (or between-speaker) variation. This means features by which speakers differ from each other substantially. At the same time, these features should also have low **intra-speaker** (or within-speaker) variation. In other words, the features should not be subject to much variation within a speaker, for instance over the course of the day or because of changes in health.

Similarity and typicality: When conducting FSC, forensic experts assess the similarity and typicality of features in the questioned and known samples. **Similarity** between recordings is a pretty straightforward concept: for instance, two samples might show similar f0 patterns or articulation rates. If the speech samples are very similar in respect of lots of features, then this increases the likelihood that they were produced by the same speaker. **Typicality** refers to the frequency with which certain features are distributed within a relevant population. A 'relevant population' here generally refers to all other speakers who share the same demographic and linguistic characteristics as the person in the questioned sample. For instance, if the speaker in the questioned sample appears to be a male speaker aged between 20 and 50 with a New Zealand accent, then the relevant population might be all male New Zealanders aged between 20 and 50. Note that defining the relevant population is itself a potentially difficult task, as it has to be based on the questioned sample. Of course, there is a problem here: the identity of the speaker is not known for certain – that is, after all, what the court is trying to decide – and therefore neither is the population the speaker comes from. The forensic analyst usually has to make a judgment of the most likely population. In effect, this means they have to construct a speaker profile of the person in the questioned recording (see Chapter 3). Sometimes, however, the relevant population has been agreed by all parties in the case. For example, the questioned material might have been recorded covertly in a car, and CCTV footage shows that three people were in the car at the time. The relevant population for comparison with the suspect would therefore just be the other two people.

Low typicality means that the feature examined is not very frequent in that relevant population, while **high typicality** means that the feature is frequent. If a particular phonetic feature that occurs in both the questioned and the known samples has low typicality in the relevant population, then this increases the likelihood that the samples come from the same speaker. However, comparison is also likely to reveal lots of features that have high typicality, i.e., many people in the population share those features. The observed similarity is therefore not very helpful in reaching a conclusion on whether we have the same speaker or not.

We can illustrate how similarity and typicality affect a conclusion. Figure 4.1 shows the distribution of articulation rate (AR) for Swiss German. The histogram represents data from a study of AR in 500 men. The overall average value for this population is around 4.4 syllables per second (syll/s). Most speakers in the study cluster in the middle of the figure, between 4 and 5 syll/s. Only a few

SPEAKER COMPARISON

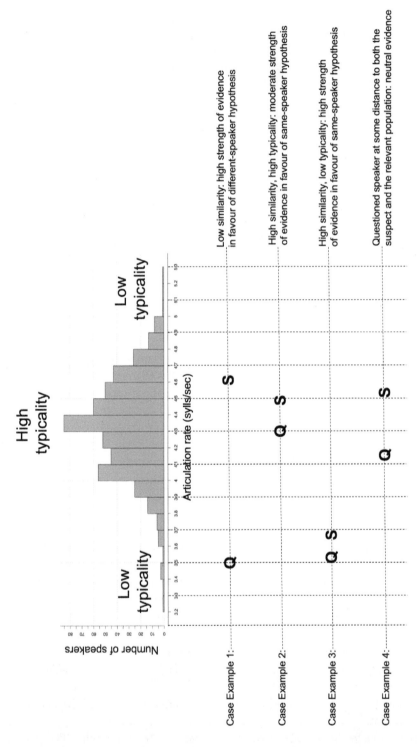

Figure 4.1 Histogram of spontaneous speech articulation rate in a population of 500 male Swiss German speakers, illustrating different cases with high- and low-typicality and similarity. Q = questioned sample, S = suspect sample (adapted from Jessen 2018).

64

speakers spoke very slowly (note the speakers on the far left whose AR values were lower than 3.7 syll/s) or very fast (the speakers on the far right with an AR over 5 syll/s). Below the histogram are four hypothetical case examples. The Q in each case refers to a hypothetical AR value from the questioned sample, while the S represents AR from the suspect sample. In Case Example 1 the Q value is low and the S value is high relative to the population data in the histogram. Both values are relatively atypical, but at opposite ends of the scale (one fast, one slow). The two values are therefore neither similar nor typical. This observation would probably contribute to a conclusion that there are different speakers in the recordings (though the final conclusion would depend on observations of many other features too). In Case Example 2, both Q and S values are close to the average of the population. The observations are similar but also typical. The AR data therefore offer some evidence in favour of the idea we have the same speaker in the recordings, but it is not strong evidence because many people use this sort of AR. By contrast, Case Example 3 shows high similarity and low typicality. This is relatively strong evidence that we have the same speaker. Case Example 4 shows relatively low similarity, with Q at the lower end of the typical range of the population distribution and S towards the middle of it. This does not provide strong evidence in either direction.

Transmission robustness: The features being analysed should be robust to different kinds of signal degradation. Forensic case material often involves speech transmitted via telephone. Consequently, the signal gets degraded. You will recognise this from everyday experience. Put more technically, there is a band-pass transmission of around 300–3400 Hz over landlines. Speech frequencies outside that range are filtered out or weakened by the transmission. Figure 4.2 illustrates the telephone transmission effect. The two spectrograms show exactly the same spoken material. The top panel is taken from a studio recording and the lower panel shows the same speech sample filtered through a mobile telephone (the text is: *When the sunlight strikes raindrops in the air*). Note especially how the high frequencies are damaged in the lower panel.

Mobile phone-transmitted speech can vary even more in transmission quality and the effects of band-pass filtering. These effects compromise the reliability of acoustic measures that are heavily reliant on frequency information, such as measures of formants and voice quality. For instance, telephone transmission tends to raise the estimate of F1. Studies show an average rise in F1 of 14% in landline speech (Künzel 2001) and 29% in mobile phone speech (Byrne & Foulkes 2004) compared to a baseline of unfiltered speech. This is because some low-frequency harmonics (under around 300 Hz) are filtered out by the telephone transmission and are thus invisible to acoustic analysis software. Figure 4.2 shows this effect – note the weaker energy (shown as lighter grey) in the lowest frequencies in the bottom panel. Formant estimates can only be generated from the available information, and therefore tend to be artificially raised relative to the speech actually produced by the talker because only the

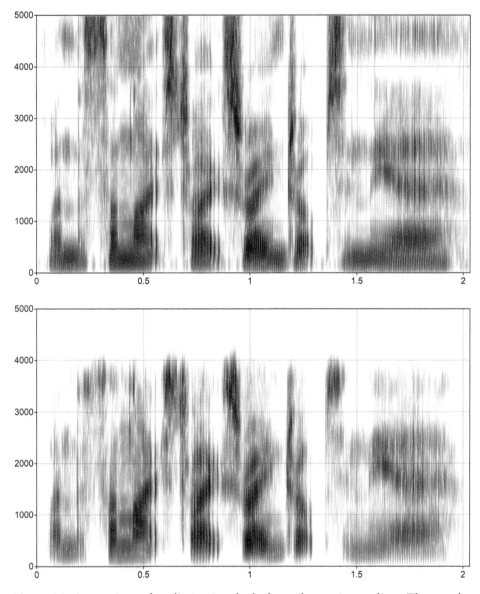

Figure 4.2 Comparison of studio (top) and telephone (bottom) recordings. The speech sample is identical in the two spectrograms (*When the sunlight strikes raindrops in the air*).

higher frequency components survive the telephone transmission. Fricatives like [s] and [ʃ] are also badly affected, because they contain a lot of energy at frequencies higher than 3400 Hz (that is why you have to spell out unusual words when speaking on the phone – fricatives can easily be mistaken for one another if the important high-frequency components are removed). The tricky thing for speaker comparison is that speech signals from suspect recordings are typically higher in quality than questioned recordings. So, ideal acoustic features should withstand variation due to different types of signal degradation.

***Disguise and mimicry robustness*:** The features to be analysed should withstand attempts at disguise or mimicry. Imagine that a perpetrator imitates a different accent from his own in a bomb threat call. When recorded at the police station, it is unlikely that they will again disguise their voice in a similar way. Ideal acoustic features should capture speaker-specificity in both recordings, regardless of whether the speaker has attempted to disguise their voice or not.

4.4   Features typically analysed

Forensic speaker comparison exploits what is referred to as the 'componentiality of speech'. **Componentiality** means that speech can be broken down into different components or layers such as segments (consonants, vowels, connected speech processes), suprasegmentals (voice quality, intonation, pitch, speech rate, rhythm, tone), and higher-level linguistic features (morphology, syntax, lexicon, discourse features, disfluencies, pausing behaviour, etc.). To a large extent these components are independent of one another. In FSC cases, experts generally try to analyse a good sample of different features to obtain a picture of the speakers that is as complete as possible. The range of features analysed in practice depends on various factors, including the length of the material, the language or dialect of the recording, and analyst preference. Methods of analysis also differ for similar reasons. Sometimes auditory analysis is sufficient and may be useful to counter problems for detailed acoustic analysis. In this section, we present some findings and insights from research on FSC regarding speaker individuality in different features. We will discuss these features in terms of whether, in principle, they show high between-speaker and low within-speaker variation, transmission robustness, and robustness to disguise and mimicry.

4.4.1 Vowels

Almost all analysts examine a selection of vowels in any given case. Vowels are assumed to be fairly speaker-specific, as they are heavily dependent on a speaker's biology: longer vocal tracts typically mean lower formant frequencies. In many languages vowel qualities also depend on regional and social accent, and can therefore vary substantially between speakers. Vowel formants are usually well-defined acoustically, even with poorer quality recordings. They are therefore relatively easy to measure and interpret. Some analysts take single measures close to the centre of the vowel, where the speaker has made the most extreme articulatory movement to produce the sound. Analysts can also measure vowels at multiple points rather than just one in order to probe how their

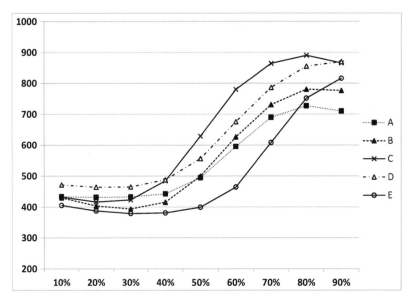

Figure 4.3 Time-normalised F1 frequencies (y-axis) for five Thai speakers over nine measurement points (x-axis). Average measurements for /ia ua ɯa/. (Adapted from Thaitechawat & Foulkes 2011)

acoustic energy changes over time; these are called **formant trajectories** or **vowel dynamics**. Research suggests that the dynamic features of vowels exhibit substantial between-speaker variation (e.g., McDougall 2006). Just as humans walk, jump, and throw in individual ways, articulation is also a form of movement which is highly individualised as it is affected by differences in tongue size, palate shape, and many other aspects of physiology. Figure 4.3 shows such speaker specificity in vowel dynamics. Here, F1 measurements are shown for five male speakers of Thai. The measurements are averaged across 600 tokens per speaker and three different vowels: /ia ua ɯa/. All three vowels are diphthongs in which the first element is a close vowel and the second element is the open vowel /a/. Hence, we expect the F1 to start low, as befits a close vowel, before rising into the open vowel.

Speakers have individual ways of moving from target to target across the sounds in the sequence. Speaker E, for example, starts with a lower F1 than the other speakers, and his F1 remains lower than the others until the final 20% of the sequence. His F1 rise also starts later. Speaker C's F1 is in the middle of the range at the start, but rises sharply and early, and remains high until the end. This example illustrates how, in the articulation process, speakers can take different routes moving from sound to sound, leaving individual temporal and frequency traces in the speech signal.

An important issue with vowel measures, however, is that they are affected by telephone transmission. As we have already mentioned, F1 is artificially raised over landlines and mobile phones, though F2 and F3 are relatively immune to these effects. Differences in speaking style can also affect vowels, as formants are raised in louder speech and shouting. What this means is that we cannot simply measure vowel formants and expect a 'match' – very similar values – in different recordings. The analyst has to interpret the data and make allowances for known sources of difference such as the telephone effect.

4.4.2 Consonants

Consonantal features are often analysed auditorily, with acoustic analysis used mainly to confirm auditory judgments. In British English consonants vary a great deal regionally and socially. In British cases it is therefore common to analyse the following:

- /h/ (does the speaker use '/h/-dropping', pronouncing *head* as [ɛd]?)
- /θ/ and /ð/ (does the speaker use standard variants, or [f] and [v] – *another thing* as [ənʌvə fɪŋ], or stops – [ənʌdə tɪŋ]?)
- /t/ between vowels in words such as *better* (options include [t], [ɾ], and [ʔ])
- /ŋ/ in polysyllabic words (*swimming* can be [swɪmɪŋ], [swɪmɪn] or [swɪmɪŋg])
- /l/, which varies between alveolar [l] and velarised [ɫ], and is sometimes pronounced as a vowel rather than a lateral, e.g., [bou] for *ball*)
- /r/ (does the speaker pronounce /r/ at all in words like *car* and *arm*? And when /r/ is produced, what phonetic form is used? Options include [ɹ], [ɾ], [r], [ʋ], [ɻ], and [ʁ]).

The David Bieber case

The David Bieber case provides a good example of how useful auditory analysis can be. Bieber was an American citizen who lived under a false identity in Yorkshire, in the north of England, for some years. He was convicted of murdering a police officer and injuring two others. He had been apprehended in a car with false registration plates, and the police officers had asked him to sit in the back of their police car. He drew a gun and fired several shots before escaping. The questioned sample was captured by a camera placed on the dashboard of the police car (so the speaker was not visible in the footage). Bieber spoke very little in police interviews after he had been caught, but the police were able to obtain known samples of his voice from telephone betting companies. Comparison of the recordings revealed a number of unusual features. Most important of all was that the speaker in both recordings had a mixed accent, consisting of both American and Yorkshire characteristics. Most strikingly, the questioned and known recordings both exhibited what dialectologists call *rhotic* accents, i.e., /r/ was pronounced in all word positions (for example, in the questioned sample in *right, recovery, pardon,* and in the known sample in *road, worries, third*). That pattern is typical for speakers with North American accents.

However, it is not found for most accents in England, and certainly not those from Yorkshire. These accents are *non-rhotic*, which means /r/ is only pronounced when it is followed by a vowel. Non-rhotic speakers do not pronounce the /r/ in *pardon* or *third*. Despite the American accent, the speaker also produced typical Yorkshire variants of the FACE and GOAT vowels (*mate* as [mɛːʔ], *road* as [ɹɔːd]) and Yorkshire terms of address like *mate* and *love*. Those features are not used in US dialects. The key diagnostic features were all easily amenable to auditory analysis and judged to be highly unusual for the broader population. Peter French who carried out the analysis, referred to it as 'one of the most clear-cut cases' he had worked on.

Research has also explored the speaker-specificity of acoustic properties of consonants. Fricatives in particular show considerable variation between speakers. In addition, there may be a degree of socially-learned differentiation in fricative production. For instance, in Glaswegian English (spoken in Glasgow, Scotland), some working-class speakers exhibit a more retracted /s/ than speakers of higher social classes (Stuart-Smith 2007). A commonly analysed acoustic property is the so-called **centre of gravity** (COG). The COG is a frequency value which balances the relative amplitude of energy in the signal: half the energy is above the COG value and half below it. /s/ has a higher COG than /ʃ/, for example. However, as we noted earlier, relying on fricatives in FSC is difficult in the case of telephone-transmitted speech because telephone band-pass filters cut off higher frequencies, making some fricatives difficult to distinguish over landlines. Nasals also carry substantial speaker-specific information, in particular the bilabial nasal [m]. Nasal cavities are complex and exhibit large anatomical variability among humans, ultimately contributing to variation among voices. Here too, analysis of COG works fairly well for the discrimination of individual speakers.

4.4.3 Connected speech processes

Connected Speech Processes, CSPs, are phonological processes that occur in fluent speech in order to make speech flow more naturally. Here are some examples:

- **Assimilation:** sounds assimilate (become more similar) to each other, e.g., *handbag* /handbag/ is pronounced ['ham̩bag]. Here the alveolar nasal /n/ is produced as the bilabial [m], to match the bilabial place of articulation of the following /b/.
- **Elisions:** sounds or syllables are deleted, e.g., *camera* /kamərə/ is pronounced ['kʰamɹə], *library* /laɪbɹəɹi/ as ['laɪbɹi].
- **Epenthesis:** sounds are inserted, e.g., *hamster* /hamstə(ɹ)/ is pronounced ['hampstə(ɹ)].

One might also call these shortcuts that speakers take. Some speakers may use these shortcuts frequently, while others may not use them as frequently. Some speakers may have (unconscious) preferences for specific CSPs and not for others. The types of CSPs used and the frequency with which they are used vary by accent and by speaker. They can therefore be diagnostic of a speaker's identity and useful for FSC.

4.4.4 Voice quality

Most experts consider **voice quality** in FSC. One framework that is often used is **Vocal Profile Analysis (VPA)**, first proposed for analysis of disordered or pathological speech (Laver 1980). VPA is an auditory analysis of a speaker's vocal settings and vocal characteristics. Researchers have adapted and simplified Laver's complex VPA protocol in various ways, such as the protocol shown in Figure 4.4. In this version the analyst decides whether a feature of speech is 'neutral' or not, and then rates any non-neutral features on a three-point scale: 'slight', 'marked', and 'extreme' (but non-pathological).

VPA focuses on three general types of vocal characteristics: **vocal tract features** (e.g., lip rounding and jaw opening), **muscular tension** (e.g., tenseness of the larynx and vocal tract), and **specific phonation features** (e.g., creakiness and breathiness). There are a few issues with this type of analysis, however. First, it requires substantial training to be able to do the coding reliably. Second, it is based on perceptual judgment (although some observations can be supported via acoustic analysis). Third, to do a proper analysis of voice quality, a substantial amount of material is required: ideally, experts should have access to at least 40 seconds of speech to be able to perform a reliable analysis. Finally, a major caveat is that phonation features in particular (shown under C in Figure 4.4) are influenced by factors such as stress, exhaustion, alcohol intake, and emotional state. Ultimately, this means that differences in phonation features between the questioned and known samples do not necessarily point to different speakers, because they could be caused by substantial within-speaker variation.

4.4.5 Fundamental frequency

Fundamental frequency (f0) – the main physical correlate of perceived pitch – is one of the principal characteristics analysed by forensic speech experts. Most experts study f0 **averages**, **ranges** (i.e., differences between f0 maximum and minimum), and **standard deviations** (i.e., average fluctuations in f0 over time). This array of metrics begs the question of how much material is sufficient to determine representative f0 values for a particular speaker. Around one minute of continuous speech is needed to obtain representativeness. Figure 4.5 displays population data for f0. It is based on analysis of speech from 500 male speakers of spontaneously produced Swiss German (from Hedegard et al. 2023). Note

	FIRST PASS		SECOND PASS				
	Neutral	Non-neutral	SETTING	Slight	Marked	Extreme	Notes
				1	2	3	
A. VOCAL TRACT FEATURES							
Labial			lip rounding/protrusion				
			lip spreading				
			labiodentalisation				
			extensive labial range				
			minimised labial range				
Mandibular			close jaw				
			open jaw				
			extensive mandibular range				
			minimised mandibular range				
Lingual tip/ blade			advanced tongue tip/blade				
			retracted tongue tip/blade				
Lingual body			fronted/raised tongue body				
			lowered/backed tongue body				
			extensive lingual range				
			minimised lingual range				
Pharynx			pharyngeal constriction				
			pharyngeal expansion				
Velopharyngeal			nasal				
			denasal				
Larynx height			raised larynx				
			lowered larynx				
B. OVERALL MUSCULAR TENSION							
Vocal tract tension			tense vocal tract				
			lax vocal tract				
Laryngeal tension			tense larynx				
			lax larynx				
C. PHONATION FEATURES							
Voicing type			falsetto				
			creaky				
			whispery				
			breathy				
			murmur				
			harsh				
			tremor				

Figure 4.4 Example protocol for VPA. (Adapted from Laver 1980 and San Segundo et al. 2019)

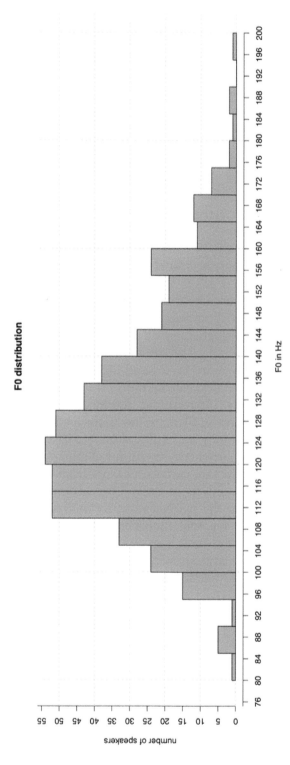

Figure 4.5 Distribution of 500 male Swiss German speakers' f0 mean values in spontaneous speech. (Adapted from Hedegard et al. 2023)

that the distribution, like that for AR shown in Figure 4.1, is statistically normal. That means that most data points cluster in the middle of the distribution, with fewer towards the tails (the high and low end). For this Swiss data, there is a median of 126 Hz (the middle value when all 500 of the Hz values are sorted in ascending or descending order). The minimum value is 81 Hz, and the maximum is 197 Hz. Data like this helps us judge typicality.

f0 comes with several advantages for FSC. You can detect f0 quite well even with substantial background noise present, which is useful given that audio quality in FSC can be poor. In telephone-transmitted speech, too, f0 remains detectable. You might wonder how, given the low frequency cutoff issue referred to earlier: frequencies below 300 Hz are impaired or removed altogether by phone transmission. This is rather complicated, but worth mentioning. Despite the cutoff, f0 can still be detected both by the human perceptual system and by acoustic software, because it can be reconstructed from the harmonics in the spectrum. For example, if harmonics can be detected at 500, 600, 700, and 800 Hz, the underlying f0 must be 100 Hz because harmonics occur at integral multiples of the f0.

Using f0 in FSC is tricky because f0 is subject to substantial within-speaker variation. In terms of style, f0 rises when we speak louder, as we usually do on the phone. f0 also tends to be higher in read speech than in spontaneous speech. In addition, speakers may exhibit lower f0 in the morning than in the evening, and may show substantially more varied and higher f0 in agitated compared to non-agitated emotional states. Furthermore, smokers tend to have lower f0 means than non-smokers. Interestingly, despite the fact that virtually all experts conduct measurements of f0, many say that substantial within-speaker variability means that it is rarely a useful feature in a case. It appears that f0 as a feature used in FSC is particularly useful for eliminating suspects (that is, experts may confidently eliminate certain speakers from consideration based on f0 analysis early in the analysis process). One advantage of analysing f0, however, is that members of the public can easily understand what it means and can judge pitch – the perceptual equivalent of f0 – fairly well. Presenting information about f0 is thus a good way to explain the general principles of FSC in court: what a vocal feature is, why analysis by software can be helpful, the concept of population statistics, and how and why vocal features vary.

4.4.6 Intonation and tone

Intonation refers to f0 changes that carry linguistic meaning. For instance, in English and many other languages, a general fall in f0 over the course of a phrase can denote a statement, while an increase in f0 at the end of a phrase may denote a question. Some speakers exhibit certain f0 fluctuations that may be forensically relevant. Measures that have been shown to carry speaker-specific information in some languages include f0 declination (the degree to which someone's f0 declines over the course of an utterance) and the relative timing of f0 rises relative to stressed syllables. These measures are relatively robust to variation in speaking style (e.g., spontaneous vs. read speech; see Leemann et al. 2014a). Properties of tones (see section 2.1.2 in Chapter 2) also vary between individuals and between dialects of the same language.

4.4.7 Speaking rate and articulation rate

As mentioned in Chapter 2, **speaking rate** (the number of syllables per second including pauses) is distinct from **articulation rate** (the number of syllables per second without pauses). Research shows that the former tends to exhibit more within-speaker variability, caused, for example, by changes in speaking style and emotional state. Articulation rate, on the other hand, exhibits somewhat less within-speaker variation, which is favourable for FSC. We showed population data for AR in Figure 4.1. AR does vary stylistically, with read speech usually a little slower. Studies have further uncovered patterns in articulation rate based on various demographic factors. Elderly speakers, for instance, tend to talk more slowly due to general cognitive decline. Furthermore, there can be regional variation in AR within a language.

However, bear in mind that data for research is often gathered from highly educated speakers such as university students. Students do not adequately represent the wider population, for example, in that they are highly educated and generally in a relatively narrow age range. People who appear in real forensic case data might show quite different patterns. For example, speaking rate might be rather slower in some forensic materials than in research data. In UK police interviews, suspects sometimes decline to answer police questions, but agree to read a statement that is prepared by their legal team. The prepared text is often stylistically different from spontaneous speech, being written in a formal style and containing phrasing that is unfamiliar in ordinary conversation. (See also Chapter 8, where cases such as that of Derek Bentley reveal disparity in written versus spoken style.) An example of a read statement, adapted from a real case, is shown below:

The investigating officer has said that I am suspected of being the getaway driver. I was not involved in that capacity or at all. On the evening of the fourteenth of the seventh two thousand and twenty I was indoors at 7 Acacia Avenue, my home address, watching international football on the television, after which I remained indoors until the next day. With regard to certain unsolicited comments that I am said to have made, I have no recollection of making them.

Less well-educated suspects often find the task of reading such statements quite difficult, both because of the unusual form and also because they might not be fluent readers. As a result, these read statements tend to be slower not only than research data, but also than the suspects' spontaneous speech. They are also likely to contain many hesitations and disfluencies. The forensic phonetician needs to understand the reasons for such differences, and make allowances for them in an analysis.

4.4.8 Rhythm

Relatively little attention has been paid to speech rhythm features and how they can be useful for FSC. This is perhaps because rhythm is a difficult concept to measure, as discussed in section 2.1.2. Researchers explore rhythm by annotating various kinds of duration intervals in the signal, following the assumption that recurring duration patterns are the main acoustic feature that determines rhythm. Measurements capture variation in consonant and vowel durations, syllable durations, and the durations of voiced and voiceless intervals. Based on these measurements, one can calculate various rhythm metrics. This type of annotation has also been used to explore speaker-level idiosyncrasies in speech rhythm. Even speakers of one particular dialect of a language, articulating the same read material, exhibit substantial variation in some rhythm metrics. Variation in speaking style – i.e., read versus spontaneous speech – shows relatively little variation, however. In particular, the %V metric – the total percentage of vocalic (vowel) portions in the signal – exhibits high speaker-specificity that seems robust to variation in style (Leemann et al. 2014b).

4.4.9 Higher-level and non-linguistic features

Aside from purely phonetic features, experts occasionally also examine higher-level features such as silent and filled pauses, and word choices. Pausing behaviour appears both speaker-specific and exhibits relatively little within-speaker variation (Kolly et al. 2015). Filled pauses are also useful in FSC. **Filled pauses** are non-silent events such as word prolongations, hesitation markers such as *uh* and *um*, and the repetition of phrases, words, or parts of words. Pragmatically speaking, filled pauses help speakers plan ahead when talking, and help listeners comprehend when an interlocutor is holding the floor to continue speaking. Filled pauses such as *uh* and *um* are speaker-specific, in that one speaker may use them much more than another. The acoustic qualities of *uh/um* can also be analysed in the same way as vowels, and filled pauses perform better than lexical vowels in speaker discrimination experiments (Hughes et al. 2016).

Other higher-level features that may be idiosyncratic include how speakers make use of their language variety's morphology, syntax, and lexicon. For instance, some speakers use sentence-final tag questions like *innit?* (UK) or *right?* (US) more frequently than other speakers, and individuals differ in their use of non-standard grammatical features. Some speakers have specific ways of greeting others or answering the telephone, and some may use specific discourse patterns in conversation (e.g., the discourse marker *like*). Taken together, such features can provide a relatively comprehensive picture of individuals' voices and speaking behaviours. What is particularly interesting about these higher-level features is that they probably operate below the level of consciousness; speakers are likely not aware, for example, that they pause or say *um* or *like* a lot. Non-linguistic features can also carry speaker-specific information that may be used in FSC, for instance breathing (e.g., type and frequency), tongue clicking, laughing, and throat-clearing behaviours. However, the study of these non-linguistic features is often difficult in FSC because material can be very limited and may not include such features due to the nature of the evidence.

4.5   Use of automatic speaker recognition in FSC

Over the past decade, a growing number of labs have begun to use automatic speaker recognition (ASR) technology to support FSC. There are several stages involved in ASR:

(a) Pre-processing
(b) Feature extraction
(c) Speaker modelling
(d) Speaker comparison
(e) Score interpretation

Stage (a), **pre-processing**, includes a number of steps that are taken to make the working files ready for ASR. This step might involve re-sampling of sound files to make them compatible with ASR system requirements. Pre-processing usually also includes voice activity detection (VAD), a process by which the software detects the speech signal within the recording and separates the speech from silence and noise. Once the materials have been pre-processed, **feature extraction** can take place – stage (b). The ASR system extracts acoustic features from the recordings. These acoustic features are usually different from the ones discussed so far. They are not properties of specific phonetic or phonological features like f0 or vowel formant frequencies (although some ASR systems can be tailored to work on a subset of speech sounds such as a specific vowel). Instead, they are more abstract features that capture spectral properties of the voice across a whole recording. ASR systems typically extract MFCCs (Mel Frequency Cepstral Coefficients). The Mel scale is an alternative way of representing the frequency scale in speech. Spectrograms of speech, like the example in Figure 4.1, usually show a linear scale on the y axis, measured in Hertz (i.e., there are equal distances between equal frequency values). The Mel scale warps the frequency scale to mirror the human perceptual system, which is better at distinguishing low frequencies than high frequencies. MFCCs are compact representations taken from a short extract of speech (usually around 20–30 milliseconds) that capture the overall acoustic characteristics of the vocal tract, particularly those related to resonance characteristics generated above the larynx. Cepstral analysis represents the whole frequency range: not only peaks in energy (like formants do) but also troughs, or low points of energy. Further, it does this throughout the whole signal rather than only for specific vowels (as is typically done in formant analysis). Between 10 and 20 MFCCs are usually taken every 10 milliseconds or so. A long recording might therefore generate many thousands of MFCCs. These mathematical coefficients capture the properties of the acoustic signal across the whole sample. The coefficients are then subjected to statistical **modelling** to generate a speaker or voice model. This is stage (c) of the process. Nowadays state-of-the-art systems do this in the form of so-called x-vectors, generated via Deep Neural Networks (DNNs). (Sometimes, perhaps unfortunately, the speaker model is called a *voiceprint* in ASR. Note that the term has a very different meaning from the voiceprints discussed in section 4.1.)

Figure 4.6 illustrates the transformation of a waveform into MFCCs. Colours represent the strength of energy.

Stage (d) is the **comparison** of speaker models. The model for the questioned sample is compared with the model for the known sample. The same process underlies experimental research to test ASR systems. The models are compared and assessed for similarity and typicality to produce a numerical score. The last stage, (e), is the **score interpretation**. This step converts the ASR scores into likelihood ratios (LRs; see further section 4.6), which involves further statistical processing and adjustment (a process called calibration, which is based on findings derived from a separate set of training data). The ASR system compares the questioned speaker model to other models representing the relevant population,

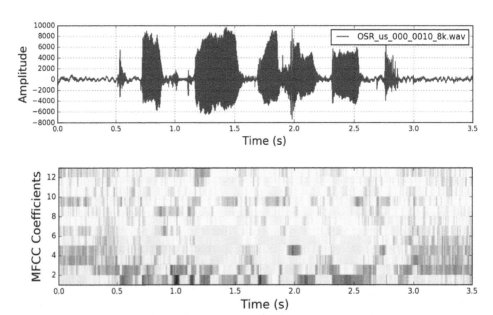

Figure 4.6 Conversion from acoustic signal to MFCCs. (Reproduced with permission from haythamfayek.com)

to find out how typical the features found in the questioned sample are within that population (see the illustration in Figure 4.8). This stage therefore involves assessing the likelihood of the score assuming it is the same speaker versus the likelihood of the score assuming it is a different speaker. The relevant population model must be tailored to the facts of the case so that the result is interpretable in the context of the case. For example, the speakers chosen for comparison should be limited to a demographically-defined set of people based on the speaker in the questioned sample, such as adult men who speak with an Australian accent. It could be narrower still if a specific reference population has been identified in the case – just the other passengers in the car, for example, in the scenario outlined earlier. Such decisions depend on the facts of the case and whether the suspect's legal team have a specific line of defence. The final outcome of the ASR analysis is then reported in the form of a likelihood ratio.

In a 2019 survey over 40% of FSC practitioners indicated that they use ASR systems, a substantial increase from a survey done eight years previously (Gold & French 2019). There are some obvious advantages to using ASR systems in forensic speaker comparison. Most importantly, to some extent they take the human analyst out of the equation and thus make analyses more objective. However, keep in mind that the human analyst still makes plenty of vital decisions, including choices of recording samples, software settings, and population models. In addition to their objectivity, ASR-based analyses also enable replicability, which is highly desired in FSC and any scientific work: one expert can analyse the same material with the same software and parameter settings as another expert and obtain the same results. Further, automated analyses are very fast: ASR systems can conduct numerous comparisons in a matter of seconds that would take human analysts several hours to complete.

There are also drawbacks to ASR, however. First, in order to work reliably, systems generally need a minimum of about ten seconds of speech from both the questioned and known samples. That means ten seconds of usable (or 'net') speech after the removal of silences, repetitions, noisy sections, and so on. Results improve with more material, and at least 30 seconds net is ideal. Until recently, ASR systems also needed audio of a fairly high technical quality. Systems must cope with **channel mismatch**. This term refers to the difference in general technical quality found in typical forensic comparisons. For example, forensic materials often involve a telephone recording being compared with a recording made in a police interview suite, with better quality equipment but a poorer quality environment with sound reflected off hard surfaces. The gross acoustic effects of technical quality of course affect the MFCCs, since these capture the features of the acoustic signal throughout the recording. Adjustments therefore need to be made to the ASR processing to compensate for such effects. ASR technology is improving rapidly, however. A number of laboratories took part in a study to see how well ASR systems performed with realistic forensic case data (Morrison & Enzinger 2019). The results of the better systems were very impressive. The latest x-vector systems are also much better at dealing with channel mismatch, largely because they are trained with a wider variety of recording types.

A further issue with ASR systems is that they remain 'black boxes' (this is similar to the problem of fully automated attempts at comparative authorship analysis, as discussed in Chapter 12). That is, they lack transparency with respect to how their results translate to definable properties of the voice. With manual or computationally assisted analysis of phonetic features such as vowel formants and f0 it is possible to explain to a court what it is about the speaker's voice that is being analysed and interpreted. This includes the ways in which the voice in the questioned sample is similar to, and different from, the voice of the suspect, and whether the observed features are typical or atypical in the broader population. With ASR speaker models, by contrast, there is generally no clear relationship with features the court might be expected to understand, such as pitch or regional accent. This in turn raises questions for how a court can evaluate ASR analysis. A core principle of justice is that there should be transparent evidence against the person accused of a crime or misdemeanour. A 2022 report by the UK Parliament identified transparency in technology as an area of concern for the delivery of justice.

At the time of writing, ASR has not yet been admitted in evidence in UK courts, although it is used elsewhere in the world. Most reputable labs combine ASR analysis with phonetic analysis (i.e., a human–machine team approach) in order to get the best of both approaches, and to ensure the human analyst can check that the ASR results do not miss phonetically clear patterns such as differences in accent. The forensic scientist must also make a range of vital decisions about how to design the analysis: framing the specific question to be answered, defining the relevant population, choosing materials from the recordings, etc. ASR should only be used by practitioners with training in how the systems work, as well as a thorough understanding of their limitations.

4.6   Expressing conclusions

Whether using ASR or auditory-acoustic phonetic methods, once the questioned and known samples have been analysed, experts must reach an overall view of their observations. If analyses were undertaken auditorily, experts work with categories. For example, if they have analysed /h/-dropping in an English language case, they might have concluded that the suspect had 20% /h/-dropping, while the speaker in the questioned sample had 50%. If acoustic measures were used, then the gradient measurements can be plotted and judged for similarity, with allowances made for any known confounding factors like telephone transmission.

When observations from the questioned sample are consistent with those from the known sample, experts can say that there is similarity between the samples. Allowances need to be made for differences between the recordings, e.g., in respect of technical acoustic quality and the emotional state of the speaker. However, remember that experts not only assess similarity of features, but also typicality of features. Typicality is assessed based on relevant population data such as measurements from speech corpora (see Figure 4.1 for an example). Unfortunately, general population data in phonetics is hard to come by and, as of today, exists only for some language varieties and for just a few features such as f0, articulation rate, and formant frequencies. If no relevant population data is available, experts can either create one (but this takes time), or they can offer estimates about typicality based on previous research and/or prior experience. Note, though, that experience-based judgments are inevitably more subjective than judgments based on relevant population data.

Once speaker comparison has been conducted, the results are translated into a conclusion that captures the strength of evidence. This is a very important but delicate step (for discussion about wider aspects of report writing see Chapter 13). Before the 1990s, conclusions regarding speaker identity were often expressed in a binary fashion, for example: *the speaker in the questioned sample is (or is not) the same as the speaker in the known sample.* Some analysts still do this, but it is now widely accepted that binary formulations are inappropriate. One reason for this is that no speech features are unique or invariant, as we explained earlier. It is therefore almost impossible to perform FSC and reach a conclusion that only one person in an entire population could have produced the speech sample. (The exception would be where there is a small set of possible candidates, and this is agreed by all parties in a case.) As a result, most practitioners have now shifted towards expressing their conclusions in terms of **likelihood ratios** (usually abbreviated to **LRs**). ASR systems also report their results as LRs. In fact, this is a change that has affected most forensic sciences, such that it is now recommended by official bodies such as the Association of Forensic Science Providers in the UK (AFSP 2009).

Likelihood ratios are a measure of the strength of the evidence given two hypotheses, or propositions. In speaker comparison these two hypotheses are usually (i) that the recordings were made by the same speaker, and (ii) that the recordings were made by different speakers. We discuss this further below. LRs are often calculated via statistical analysis and presented as numerical values, but they can also be estimated and expressed verbally.

LRs are not as complicated as they might first appear. First, a ratio is simply a number that compares one thing with another. A likelihood ratio compares likelihoods, or probabilities, of something happening. A LR of 100 means that one thing is 100 times more likely than another. It is worth noting that, in effect, we all compute LRs every day in order to make decisions. LRs are the outcomes of a type of logical thinking, called Bayesian reasoning (named after a statistician, Thomas Bayes). A simple example should help to clarify that LRs in science are simply a formal way of doing something very routine:

> Imagine trying to cross a road. How do you decide whether to cross? In order
> to make the decision, you observe the scenario (presence and type of visible

traffic, the speed and proximity of the traffic, the width of the road, etc.). This is your evidence. You then consider the evidence in respect of two hypotheses: (i) that you can cross safely, versus (ii) that you cannot cross safely. You decide whether the evidence is more likely given hypothesis (i) or hypothesis (ii), as well as judging the relative difference between the two options. Provided (i) sufficiently outweighs (ii) to your satisfaction, you will choose to cross.

Put another way, you have undertaken Bayesian reasoning and computed a LR, and its value is large enough to convince you that the likelihood of (i) is much larger than (ii). Many factors might affect your decision: whether you are in a hurry, how much traffic you can see, how close the traffic is and how fast it appears to be travelling, your previous experience of crossing this road or others like it, and so on (in Bayesian reasoning this part is called the priors). Note that there is always a possibility of both outcomes. Even on a totally clear road something unexpected could happen, like a car suddenly appearing, or you could trip over as you cross. The decision to cross is therefore not a straightforward yes/no decision. Instead, you consider the balance of probabilities in light of the evidence, and update your calculation based on any new information that you become aware of. You do not normally assign specific numerical values when you do this, of course, but in effect this is what you are doing in your mind.

In forensic speaker comparison, we calculate the likelihoods to show whether our evidence favours the prosecution (same speaker hypothesis) or the defence (different speaker hypothesis). We examine the evidence – the observations from the questioned sample – and we consider the likelihood of observing them under (i) the same speaker hypothesis, and (ii) the different speaker hypothesis. The logical formula below captures the two alternatives. The abbreviations are as follows: p = probability, E = evidence (i.e., observations), H = hypothesis, SS = same speaker, DS = different speaker, I = given or assuming. Note that the same formulation works for any scenario. In order to cross the road you make observations of the traffic (that's the evidence part), then compute the probability of the observations given the 'safe crossing' hypothesis relative to the 'not safe crossing' hypothesis.

$$\frac{\text{probability of evidence given same speaker hypothesis}}{\text{probability of evidence given different speaker hypothesis}} = \frac{p(E \mid H_{SS})}{p(E \mid H_{DS})}$$

In some fields, including ASR, the LR is derived numerically through calculations based on specific data, and delivered via the relevant specialist software. In other fields, the LR is estimated by the analyst and expressed on an agreed verbal scale. Phonetic analysis tends to use the verbal LR framework, as it can be problematic to derive specific numerical values for most features that are analysed.

Supported hypothesis	Verbal scale	LR range	$\log_{10}$LR range
The same speaker hypothesis is supported against the different speaker hypothesis	extremely strong	> 100,000	> 5
	very strong	10,000–100,000	4 – 5
	strong	1,000–10,000	3 – 4
	moderately strong	100–1,000	2 – 3
	moderate	10–100	1 – 2
	weak	1–10	0 – 1
inconclusive		1	0
The different speaker hypothesis is supported against the same speaker hypothesis	weak	0.1–1	0 – -1
	moderate	0.01–0.1	-1 – -2
	moderately strong	0.001–0.01	-2 – -3
	strong	0.0001–0.001	-3 – -4
	very strong	0.00001–0.0001	-4 – -5
	extremely strong	< 0.00001	< -5

Figure 4.7 Example verbal LR scale, with numerical equivalents. (Adapted from AFSP 2009)

Figure 4.7 shows a verbal LR framework similar to the one currently used widely in the UK. The two rightmost columns also show the equivalent numerical LR ranges, which we will explain presently. The table has 13 rows, consisting of a neutral or inconclusive point in the middle, and a symmetrical set of six grades of increasing strength. The six at the top capture conclusions that are in favour of the same speaker hypothesis, while those at the bottom reflect the different speaker hypothesis. In carrying out FSC, analysts consider a wide range of features and their similarity and typicality. They then interpret their overall findings with reference to both specific population data, where it is available, and their overall experience, to reach a final opinion. The expert opinion will be selected from the 13 options shown in the table to ensure consistency in approach. The expert's report will then frame the conclusion in the appropriate terms, for example: *The voice evidence lends moderately strong support to the view that the questioned and known speakers are the same person.*

Numerical LRs can be calculated where there are well-defined datasets that are large enough to give reliable estimates of a feature's distribution in the relevant population. The data shown in Figures 4.1 (articulation rate) and 4.5 (f0) are examples of population data that can be used in this way.

A simple example from another forensic science illustrates how numerical LRs are calculated. At a crime scene, investigators find a size 13 shoe print. The suspect has size 13 feet. Thus, the similarity is very high. We can capture that similarity as a value of 1 (this means 100% similarity). Population data on foot size suggests around 5% of men have size 13 feet. The typicality value is therefore 0.05. The LR is the ratio between one value and the other. In this case, the LR would be 1 ÷ 0.05 = 20. This means that the evidence – the size 13 print – is 20 times more likely to have been produced by the suspect than another man drawn at random from the population. What the LR alone does not tell us is whether the suspect did leave the print: it could be many other people instead. The final decision of guilt is up to the court, not the analyst. The court will have access to other sorts of evidence as well as the forensic shoeprint analysis. The LR provided by an expert simply helps the court judge the strength of that single piece of evidence.

Numerical LRs for phonetic data are calculated in the same way. Figure 4.8 illustrates how this is done. Imagine we have analysed some acoustic feature in our questioned and known recordings, and we have data for the same feature from a larger population (e.g., men of a similar age and dialect community). The figure shows two distributions. On the right is the distribution of measurements from the known sample, and on the left those from the overall population. The x axis uses a hypothetical scale for simplicity, while the y axis represents the

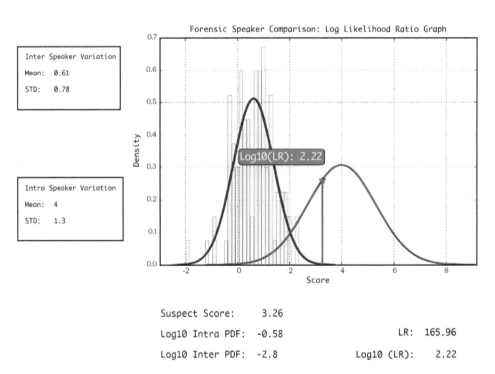

Figure 4.8 Likelihood ratio calculation from hypothetical data. Black (left) curve = population data, grey (right) curve = suspect data, grey line = feature sampled from questioned recording. (Figure by the authors, based on typical ASR system graphic outputs)

probability of finding the data at each value. The curves represent the overall distribution of data, smoothed to a normal distribution (this step assists the statistical calculations). Note that there is overlap between the distributions, but our suspect has higher values on the whole than the population, and is thus relatively atypical for that population. The boxes on the left summarise the mean and standard deviation values for the two curves.

The vertical line near the centre of the figure represents data from one observation in the questioned sample, measured at 3.26 on this hypothetical scale (the same process would be repeated with all observations, but we are just showing one data point here for simplicity). Calculating the LR helps us to decide whether the observation from the questioned recording is more likely under (i) the same speaker hypothesis, or (ii) the different speaker hypothesis. The visual impression from the figure is that the questioned observation is much more likely under (i) than (ii), since it falls fairly close to the middle of the suspect data, but towards the extreme high end of the population data. By using statistical analysis software we can quantify this formally. The probability of finding this observation under the same speaker hypothesis is around 0.265 (you can read this figure off the y axis, where the questioned recording sample meets the curve representing the suspect data), whereas for the population data the probability is very small, in fact around 0.0016. The LR is the first value divided by the second, hence $0.265 \div 0.0016 = 166$ to the nearest integer. In simple terms, then, this data point is 166 times more likely to be found in the suspect data than the population data.

One thing that still remains difficult is interpreting an LR in the context of the case. Is an LR of 166 big or small? There is no simple answer to that. It all depends on other information in the case, and that information is usually not available to the forensic analyst. There is, however, an agreed method of converting numerical LRs onto a verbal scale to assist in interpretation. This is shown in Figure 4.7. If you look at the column entitled LR range, you will notice that there appears to be a difference in the LR values towards the top of the table compared to the bottom. 'Positive' LRs, which favour the same speaker hypothesis are greater than 1, and can be very large. By contrast, 'negative' LRs are smaller than 1 but never smaller than 0 (0 means literally zero chance of something happening). A positive LR of 100 is equivalent in strength to a negative LR of 0.01, while 100,000 is equivalent to 0.00001. Many people find it confusing to compare apparently tiny fractions with large whole numbers. For that reason, forensic scientists convert these LR values to a logarithmic scale. These are shown in the rightmost column in Figure 4.7. The $\log_{10}$LRs, as they are called, mean the same thing as LRs, but they are arranged on a more intuitive symmetrical scale, centred on zero. 100,000 converts to 5 on the $\log_{10}$ scale, while 0.00001 converts to −5. (The $_{10}$ refers to the base 10 system, and $\log_{10}$LR values basically tell you how many powers of ten there are in the raw value.) In our hypothetical example, the LR of 166 equates to a $\log_{10}$LR of 2.22 (shown at the bottom right of Figure 4.8). On the scale shown in Figure 4.7, this value is categorised as 'moderately strong' evidence in favour of the same speaker hypothesis. Of course that is just one measurement in our hypothetical example. This same process would be carried out for all the data being analysed, with an overall average score used as the basis for the final conclusion.

4.6.1   Example case using the LR framework

In 2012–2013, there was a case in Australia in which a caller committed fraud against a financial institution (the case is discussed in Enzinger, Morrison & Ochoa 2016). Calls were recorded and the material was submitted for FSC. A suspect was taken into custody, interviewed, and recorded. Forensic speech scientists used an ASR system to assess the likelihood of the voices in the recordings coming from the same source versus a different source. They calculated numerical likelihood ratios as follows. First, based on the questioned sample, they defined the relevant population as adult male speakers of Australian English. They selected a reference population from a corpus of Australian English, and ASR was used to train a relevant population model. This model gave the experts an indication of the acoustic make-up of the broader population. The questioned sample contained both background noise and reverberation, and had been degraded in channel transmission through a landline telephone. The experts simulated these conditions by manipulating the reference population recordings (which were originally recorded in high quality) to increase the similarity in audio quality. The questioned sample model was then compared with the known speaker model and the relevant population model to calculate likelihood ratios. The probability of finding the evidence given the same speaker hypothesis was found to be to be 3,287 times higher than the likelihood of finding the evidence given the different speaker hypothesis (that equates to 3.52 on the $\log_{10}LR$ scale). Translating this to a verbal likelihood (Figure 4.7), the evidence (i.e., the ASR analysis) provided strong support for the same speaker hypothesis.

Conclusion

In this chapter we have introduced you to forensic speaker comparison, which deals with cases where we have a questioned sample (e.g., a ransom demand call) and a known sample (e.g., a suspect recording). Both samples are analysed for various phonetic and non-phonetic features to see how similar the samples are. At the same time, the features found in the questioned sample are checked for typicality in a relevant population. Experts express their conclusions about the strength of evidence in various ways, but increasingly as likelihood ratios, which assess evidence with regard to same speaker and different speaker hypotheses.

Further reading

For detailed discussions of forensic phonetic methods:

Jessen, M. (2008). Forensic phonetics. *Language & Linguistics Compass*, 2: 671–711.

Jessen, M. (2018). Forensic voice comparison. In J. Visconti (ed. in collab. with M. Rathert), *Handbook of Communication in the Legal Sphere*. Mouton de Gruyter, pp. 219–255.

Morrison G. S., Enzinger E., & Zhang C. (2018). Forensic speech science. In I. Freckelton & H. Selby (eds.), *Expert Evidence* (Ch. 99). Thomson Reuters.

For a historical account of forensic phonetics in the UK:

French, J. P. (2017). A developmental history of forensic speaker comparison in the UK. *English Phonetics*, 21: 271–286.

References

AFSP [Association of Forensic Science Providers] (2009). Standards for the formulation of evaluative forensic science expert opinion. *Science & Justice* 49(3): 161–164.

Byrne, C., & Foulkes, P. (2004). The mobile phone effect on vowel formants. *International Journal of Speech Language and the Law*, 11(1): 83–102.

Enzinger E., Morrison G. S., & Ochoa F. (2016). A demonstration of the application of the new paradigm for the evaluation of forensic evidence under conditions reflecting those of a real forensic-voice-comparison case. *Science & Justice*, 56: 42–57.

Gold, E., & French, P. (2019). International practices in forensic speaker comparisons: Second survey. *International Journal of Speech, Language and the Law*, 26(1): 1–20.

Hedegard, H., Fröhlich, A., Tomaschek, F., Steiner, C., & Leemann, A. (2023). Filling the population statistics gap: Swiss German reference data on F0 and speech tempo for forensic contexts. *Proceedings of Interspeech 2023*, 2558–2562.

Hughes, V., Wood, S., & Foulkes, P. (2016). Strength of forensic voice comparison evidence from the acoustics of filled pauses. *International Journal of Speech, Language and the Law*, 23(1): 99–132.

Koenig, B. E. (1986). Spectrographic voice identification: A forensic survey. *Journal of the Acoustical Society of America*, 79(6): 2088–2090.

Kolly, M. J., Leemann, A., Boula de Mareüil, P., & Dellwo, V. (2015). Speaker-idiosyncrasy in pausing behavior: Evidence from a cross-linguistic study. In The

Scottish Consortium for ICPhS 2015 (ed.), *Proceedings of the 18th International Congress of Phonetic Sciences*. University of Glasgow. Paper number 0294.

Künzel, H. J. (2001). Beware of the 'telephone effect': The influence of telephone transmission on the measurement of formant frequencies. *Forensic Linguistics: the International Journal of Speech Language and the Law*, 8(1): 80–99.

Laver, J. (1980). *The Phonetic Description of Voice Quality*. Cambridge University Press.

Leemann, A., Mixdorff, H., O'Reilly, M., Kolly, M.-J., & Dellwo, V. (2014a). Speaker-individuality in Fujisaki model f0 features: Implications for forensic voice comparison. *International Journal of Speech, Language and the Law*, 21(2): 343–370.

Leemann, A., Kolly, M. J., & Dellwo, V. (2014b). Speaker-individuality in supra-segmental temporal features: Implications for forensic voice comparison. *Forensic Science International*, 238: 59–67.

McDougall, K. (2006). Dynamic features of speech and the characterization of speakers: Toward a new approach using formant frequencies. *International Journal of Speech Language and the Law*, 13(1): 89–126.

Morrison, G. S., & Enzinger, E. (2019). Multi-laboratory evaluation of forensic voice comparison systems under conditions reflecting those of a real forensic case (forensic_eval_01) – Conclusion. *Speech Communication*, 112: 37–39.

San Segundo, E., Foulkes, P., French, P., Harrison, P., Hughes, V., & Kavanagh, C. (2019). The use of the Vocal Profile Analysis for speaker characterization: Methodological proposals. *Journal of the International Phonetic Association*, 49(3): 353–380.

Stuart-Smith, J. (2007). Empirical evidence for gendered speech production: /s/ in Glaswegian. In J. Cole & J. I. Hualde (eds.), *Laboratory Phonology 9*. Mouton de Gruyter, pp. 65–86.

Thaitechawat, S., & Foulkes, P. (2011). Discrimination of speakers using tone and formant dynamics in Thai. *Proceedings of the 17th ICPhS*, Hong Kong, pp. 1978–1981.

Activity section

Activity 4A – f0 and articulation rate

In this first exercise, you will perform a speaker comparison task using f0 and articulation rate measures, only comparing similarities of speakers. On the source materials website you will find two sentences from the unknown speaker (Activity_4A_questioned1.wav, Activity_4A_questioned2.wav) and ten files from five suspect speakers (two sentences per speaker, e.g., Activity_4A_suspect1_1.wav, Activity_4A_suspect1_2.wav, etc.). These audio files were retrieved from the Free ST American English Corpus. In the spreadsheet, you can copy and paste your measured values into the white cells in the topmost table.

- *How to measure pitch values*: Open each .wav file in Praat. Click on Pulses > Show pulses. Highlight the entire signal in the spectrogram. Click on Pulses > Voice report. Copy/paste the values required.

- *How to measure articulation rate*: In Praat, delete silent periods longer than 100 milliseconds (if any) from the signal (highlight portion > Edit > Cut). Save the resulting file under a new and transparent name, such as Activity_4A_suspect1_1_ASR.wav. (Note that these samples each contain a single fluent sentence, so there should not be any silent periods except for the start and end of each file. You will see some acoustic silences, but these are mostly the hold phases of voiceless stops, so you should not delete them.) Count the number of syllables in the words spoken. The easiest way to do this is to calculate the number of phonological syllables if the words were spoken in their most careful form. Look at the bottom-most grey bar to find the duration of the entire signal, below the spectrogram. Enter these values into the spreadsheet.

The top table of the spreadsheet calculates pitch span (green; f0 max minus f0 min) and articulation rate (green; syllables per second) for you. It further calculates averages from the two measurement points (orange). The bottom table compares the average of each suspect to the average of the questioned speaker. This table populates itself once you have copy/pasted your numbers into the top table. A value in the bottom table of (for instance) 10 in the pitch mean cell for Suspect1 means that Suspect1 has on average an f0 that is 10 Hz higher than the questioned speaker. Once all the measurements are complete and you inspect the table at the bottom, answer the following questions:

- Which suspect is most similar to the questioned speaker based on just f0 parameters and articulation rate?
- Is there consistency across the different parameters?

Answer 4A

Look at the key for the measurements we collected. If you inspect the table at the bottom, you will see that in pitch mean and pitch variation, Suspect4 is the closest to the questioned speaker. In speaking rate, Suspect4 is also very close to the questioned speaker; the similarity in pitch span is somewhat lower. This suggests that – just considering these four parameters – Suspect4 is most similar to the unknown speaker. If you wanted to investigate further, you would also look at feature typicality. Suspect4 has an average articulation rate of around 4.5 syllables/second, while the questioned speaker has a rate of roughly 4.8. Both are very typical measures within the relevant population (American English articulation rates are very similar to German rates, cf. Figure 4.1). The fact that the two speakers are similar in articulation rate is thus not helpful as a diagnostic. The same goes for their average f0s: the questioned speaker is at 106 Hz, Suspect4 is at 108 Hz, and both of these are very much in line with typical f0s for male speakers (cf. Figure 4.5). If you were to conduct further analyses of, say, voice quality, formant frequencies, rhythm, and other acoustic parameters, these would probably also indicate that Suspect4 is closest to the questioned speaker. Perhaps you might find similarities in a feature which is not common in the relevant population; this would then increase the likelihood that the recordings are from the same speaker. In fact, the recordings from Suspect4 are indeed from the same speaker as the questioned files.

Activity 4B – Speaker comparison

In this second exercise, you will perform a more comprehensive speaker comparison and write this up as a short report. The questioned sample (QS, Activity_4B_QS_phone.wav) is a (fictitious) intercepted phone call. The known sample (KS, Activity_4B_KS_hifi.wav) is a (fictitious) extract of an interview with a suspect in police custody. The sound files were again retrieved from the Free ST American English Corpus.

Examine the files carefully, and identify any features that might prove useful in a full speaker comparison. Define at least four features carefully. For example, it might be the TRAP vowel (look for /a/ in stressed syllables) or word-initial /h-/. Find each token of the feature. If the feature can be analysed auditorily, classify it using IPA notation. If appropriate, use acoustic measurements such as vowel formants. Use linguistic terminology (and phonetic notation) in your work. Summarise your findings and produce a short report. (See further Chapter 13 for further discussion of expert reports.)

Structure your report as follows: title, materials, software used (e.g., Praat for playback and acoustic measurements), analysis methods (auditory and/or acoustic analysis), analysis results (list at least four features that you found useful in this case and use phonetic notation), and discussion. In the discussion consider whether the observations are similar or different. You might also try to estimate whether they are typical or atypical for the population (if you can determine what that is). In the discussion, you can speculate as to what your formal speaker comparison conclusion would be.

Answer 4B

Here is what your report might look like:

Title: Speaker comparison of QS (Activity_4B_QS_phone.wav) and KS (Activity_4B_KS_hifi.wav)

Materials: The KS is about 12 seconds of speech. In Activity_4B_KS_hifi.wav, the speaker says a few sentences. Recordings were made with a high-quality recording device. No background noise or reverb audible. The QS is about the same length but consists of an intercepted phone call. The speech signal is thus degraded and frequencies >4 kHz and <300 Hz are cut off. There is no background noise or reverb, but there is obvious degradation due to the telephone channel.

Software: We used Praat software (version 6.1.42) for playback and acoustic analyses.

Analysis methods: The FSC was conducted mostly on an auditory basis. To support our auditory impressions we checked a sample of measurements of the signal using Praat.

Analysis results: There were four particular features in the speech signal we thought to be of note:

(1) **Staccato rhythm and pausing**

In both samples, the speaker has a distinctive rhythm which is framed by his frequent pausing (sometimes after every word). This is clearly audible in both samples, regardless of the channel degradation due to telephone transmission in the QS. So there is close similarity in this respect. There is no relevant population data on how speech rhythm is distributed, however. Intuitively, we would assume that these types of rhythmic patterns are not very common in the population; this would speak in favour of the same speaker hypothesis.

(2) **Centre of gravity in alveolar fricatives**

In the KS, at 5.72 s, the speaker exhibits relatively loud frequencies in /s/ at around 8 kHz. The same can be said of the /s/ at 11.32 s. Looking at the QS, it appears that here, too, notably high COGs may be heard/seen. However, telephone transmission cuts off exactly such high frequencies; the /s/ at 8.94 s in the questioned sample has a COG of around 7 kHz. That's right around the cut-off frequency of the telephone filter applied to this signal. COG in alveolar fricatives, then, may seem at first like an interesting feature, but it is not a helpful diagnostic when the signal has been transmitted over a telephone line.

(3) **Creaky voice**

Both samples contain clear examples of creaky voice, but only in the final syllable of each sentence. In the KS there are examples at 1.9 s (*today*), 4.6 s (*shop*), 7.8 s (*brain*), 10.9 s (*altitudes*). In the QS there are similar creaky syllables at 2.0 s (*etching*), 5.5 s (*co-operative*), 8.1 s (*years*), 11.0 s (*Kentucky*). The creaky portions are very clear visually as well as auditorily – you can see widely spaced and sometimes irregular glottal pulses, which show that vocal fold vibration is slowing down abruptly. As for typicality, it is unclear how creaky voice is distributed in a relevant population. Intuitively, we would claim that it is relatively common for young American men. Perhaps, then, this feature is not an especially valuable diagnostic, given its prevalence in the population.

(4) **Unreleased alveolar plosives in word-final position**

In both samples, we notice that the speaker has several unreleased plosives in word-final position, such as [nait̚] at 10.396 s. The KS shows this in [wɛnt̚] at 3.41 s. This similarity speaks in favour of the same speaker hypothesis. However, studies of American English indicate that unreleased syllable-final /t/ is frequent in the population.

Discussion: Based on the analysis performed here, and the short duration of the materials, it is difficult to assess the likelihood of the questioned and known samples being from the same or different speakers. The analysis of rhythm points in the direction of the same speaker hypothesis, as does the analysis of fricative frequencies (though channel degradation in the QS impinges on reliable COG measurements). In both instances, QS and KS are similar, and these acoustic features may not be particularly common in a relevant population. Turn-final creaky voice and unreleased alveolar plosives in word-final position are very similar between QS and KS; however, they are probably widely distributed in the relevant population. Analyses of many more acoustic parameters would be necessary to give a better estimate of the likelihood that the QS and KS come from the same or different speakers.

5 Earwitness evidence

In the previous chapters we have discussed cases where analysis is conducted by experts on recordings of speech. There are cases, however, where no (usable) recording exists, but a voice was heard by a victim or witness. In these situations, the earwitness might be asked to try and identify the perpetrator from among a group of speakers. A (non-exhaustive) list of case types may include the following:

- A person is sexually assaulted and hears the perpetrator but does not see enough to identify them.
- In the course of a masked robbery, witnesses overhear interactions between perpetrators but do not see their faces.
- A person receives abusive or obscene phone calls, but does not record them.

The witnesses mentioned in these cases may be asked to perform a speaker recognition task in which they take part in a **voice line-up** or **voice parade**. In principle, a voice line-up is very similar to a visual identification line-up: witnesses are asked to identify the target speaker from the line-up, but the options are in audio form rather than visual. Phoneticians might be asked to construct the line-up, or to assess the fairness of a line-up designed by someone else (often police officers). This type of evidence is called **earwitness identification evidence**.

Aims

This chapter introduces you to earwitness evidence and will cover three main topics.

The first topic is **voice line-ups**. How are they constructed? How valid are they? The second section addresses **factors that affect listener recognition performance**, such as familiarity with a perpetrator's voice, quality of speech material heard during exposure in the crime scene, and latency (i.e., the time interval between the crime and the voice line-up). Finally, we discuss **example cases** and present an overview of the **legal context for earwitness evidence**.

DOI: 10.4324/9780367616595-5

5.1 Voice line-ups

A high-profile case involving earwitness evidence is that of Charles Lindbergh, the famous American aviator (see Figure 5.1). In March 1932 his 20-month-old child was kidnapped from the nursery; a note was found in the child's room asking for a ransom of $50,000 (for discussion of this note see Chapter 11). After a series of negotiations, the Lindberghs decided to pay the ransom. A month after the incident, Charles Lindbergh drove his negotiator to a cemetery where the money was to be handed over. Lindbergh stayed in the car, 70–100 metres away, and heard someone shout to his negotiator: 'Hey, Doctor! Over here, over here!' Lindbergh did not see the perpetrator but he did hear his voice. One month later, his child was found dead. Almost two and a half years after the kidnapping, authorities claimed to have caught the perpetrator, Bruno Richard Hauptmann. Lindbergh listened to Hauptmann repeat the words spoken at the cemetery, and reported that he was 'certain' that this was the kidnapper. As a result, Hauptmann was charged with the abduction and murder, and subsequently executed.

The case is controversial for several reasons. One reason is the time delay: identification of an alleged perpetrator so long after the criminal act is likely to be severely impaired by decay of memory. Another reason is the very short sample, amounting to just a few words, on which the identification was based. Most importantly, perhaps, Lindbergh's testimony was accepted by the court without

Figure 5.1 Charles Lindbergh. (Source: Wikimedia)

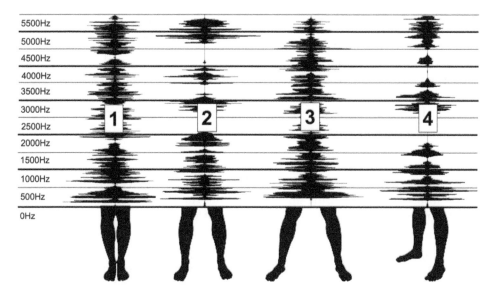

Figure 5.2 Metaphorical illustration of a voice line-up. (Based on Taswegian Words blog)

him having to demonstrate that he could recognise Hauptmann's voice. We will discuss such issues in this chapter.

These days, victims of crimes who have heard the voice of a perpetrator might be asked to take part in a voice line-up (or voice parade). In principle this is a test designed to demonstrate that the witness can indeed identify the voice they claim to have heard at the crime scene. Figure 5.2 shows a metaphorical illustration of a voice line-up; each speaker's upper body is represented by a waveform to represent their voice.

There has been limited research comparing visual and auditory line-ups, but it seems that auditory identification performance tends to be less successful than visual identification performance (Olson et al. 1998). It is assumed that this has to do with the fact that voices are primarily used to communicate content, so listeners typically pay attention mostly to *what* is said, not *how* it is said – that is, people are unaccustomed to studying a speaker's voice closely and deliberately while they speak. Furthermore, until recently there has not been any generally agreed-upon or standardised formal procedure amongst law enforcement agencies regarding how voice line-ups should be conducted. Methods have differed regarding how line-ups are conducted, how many voices are presented, and how similar or different the voices presented should be to optimise accuracy. There is further dispute about the best order for playing the voices. In the following sections, we outline current best practices and indicate their various caveats and pitfalls.

5.1.1 Foil selection

To construct a voice line-up, authorities prepare a suspect's voice recording to play to the witness along with a set of other recorded voices, known as **foils**. Sometimes the line-up is constructed by police officers, but ideally the work should be done by forensic phoneticians (who are impartial to the case). After hearing all of the voices, the witness is then asked whether the voice of the person heard at the crime scene was one of the voices in the line-up. If the answer is 'yes', the witness is asked which one.

Selecting the foil voices can be tricky. Typically, two issues are considered in foil voice selection: witness descriptions of the perpetrator's voice, and resemblance to the suspect's voice. During an investigation, the earwitness will be asked to describe to the authorities what the perpetrator's voice sounded like (e.g., what type of accent, notably high or low pitch, etc.). While this may sound like an easy task, bear in mind that most people are quite bad at describing a person's voice in detail, simply because they lack the experience and technical vocabulary to do so. For example, they may be aware that a speaker had very peculiar articulation of /s/, but they may struggle to describe this – after all, most people do not know about retracted tongue tip positions, centre of gravity measures, or fricative frequencies. Interpreting what a witness says about the voice is therefore also potentially problematic: what did they mean by 'a soft voice' or 'tinny', for example? Even with relatively transparent labels like 'local accent' or 'high pitch' we need to consider the witness's parameters: how narrowly defined is 'local' for this witness, and just how high is 'high pitch'? These difficulties are a further justification for the involvement of forensic phoneticians, who might be better placed than police officers to interpret terminology with appropriate caution. Furthermore, we cannot assume that non-linguists necessarily notice the features that linguists would consider characteristic of an accent or individual. Even if they do spot the key feature, there is no guarantee that they would correctly interpret the indexical properties of that feature. For example, English speakers in England often notice when a speaker is rhotic. Recall that this means /r/ is pronounced in all word positions. Non-rhotic speakers do not pronounce /r/ unless it is followed by a vowel. Words like *farm* and *card* are useful for distinguishing between the two. Rhoticity is a well-known and very salient difference between standard accents in the US (rhotic) and England (non-rhotic). People in England, however, are often quick to jump to the conclusion that a rhotic speaker must be American. They tend not to consider that rhoticity is also found in many other regions (Canada, Ireland, Scotland, the Caribbean, and some parts of England and New Zealand), and is widely used by speakers for whom English is an L2. Descriptions are also strongly influenced by the extent of a witness's familiarity with the perpetrator's accent; if the witness knows the accent well, they tend to be much better at describing it. Witness descriptions are further biased by natural memory processes that may lead to misleading descriptions.

One further problem in this regard is that very few police forces have a protocol for interviewing a witness about voice. In most cases the witness is simply asked to describe the voice as best they can as part of a general witness statement. The Netherlands Forensic Institute does have a protocol for interviews that police officers are advised to work with. It starts with questions about the witness's language background and their experiences at the crime scene. It then asks the witness to describe the voice and speech. This is an open question, to avoid biasing the witness. The protocol then asks more and more detailed questions about regional and foreign accents, speech impediments, slang usage, and a set of dichotomous descriptors which aim to capture key components of the voice (e.g., fast-slow, high-low, young-old).

Given such difficulties, witnesses' descriptions of a perpetrator's voice are considered in selecting foils, but with strong caveats. In practice, the foils are generally matched to the sex, broad accent type, age and ethnicity of the speaker described by the witness.

The other important factor that is considered when selecting foils is the vocal profile of the suspect, which should be matched in the foils. A suspect may have a specific accent, a specific f0, or a specific speech tempo. Using a 'suspect resemblance approach', foil voices are selected that also contain these features. Voice line-ups are sometimes constructed by police officers, but it is generally recommended that the process be handled by independent forensic experts.

Normally, there are between five and eight foils in a voice line-up. A substantial amount of speech is typically presented, usually around 60 seconds per foil (although recent studies suggest that 15–30 seconds may suffice; Smith et al. 2018). The foil samples should be produced in the same speaking style as the recording of the suspect (for instance, read or spontaneously produced; spontaneous samples have been shown to increase witness recognition performance), and all should match the style heard by the witness.

Foil selection is a delicate and difficult matter for various reasons. First, if experts construct voice line-ups with voices that are too similar to that of the suspect, then this increases the difficulty of identification. On the other hand, it is not fair to the suspect (or the wider judicial process) if the foils are too different. Imagine, for example, if a suspect with low f0 were matched with only high f0 foils; the suspect would then stick out too much to a witness based only on pitch. Secondly, foil selection must often be conducted swiftly because witnesses' audio memories of a perpetrator's voice decay rapidly (see below for further discussion). These steps obviously entail substantial work on the part of experts. Recently, automatic speech recognition (ASR) systems (discussed in Chapter 4) have been developed for potential use in foil selection; these systems can assist with similarity assessments (McDougall 2021).

In some cases, forensic phoneticians have been asked to assess the fairness of a line-up. Butcher (1996) discusses an example from South Australia. He compared a range of phonetic features in a 12-speaker line-up to assess how well the foils matched the suspect. Some features, including f0 and articulation rate

(AR), were well matched: the measured values covered a relatively narrow range within the normal distribution for adult men, and the suspect was not an outlier. For example, average AR varied between four and six syllables per second, and the suspect's AR was just over five syllables per second (cf. the AR data discussed in Chapter 4). However, the suspect's sample was the only one to include the non-standard use of [v] for /ð/ (e.g., in *other*). While this is a very common feature in British accents, it is rare in Australia. Butcher therefore concluded that the suspect stood out unfairly from the foils, because the voice sample contained a property that is unusual in the broader population and it might therefore stand out to a non-witness. It also emerged that the witness had in fact referred to this feature in interview. As noted earlier, it is a general principle that all the samples should conform to the witness's description, but in this respect none of the foils did so. The judge agreed with Butcher and ruled the evidence from the line-up to be inadmissible.

5.1.2 Sequential and serial line-ups

Two types of line-up procedures have been proposed: the **sequential approach** ('one-at-a-time') and the **serial approach** ('all-at-once').

Sequential voice line-up: In the sequential setup, several sentences produced by the suspect and several sentences produced by the foils (ca. 20–25 sentences in total) are played to the witness one-by-one. The sentences are presented in a randomised order so as to distribute the suspect's sentences among the foil sentences, and after each sentence the witness answers with a 'yes' or a 'no' to indicate whether the sentence they just heard was the voice of the perpetrator. For each sentence, the witness can thus correctly select the target speaker ('hit'), fail to identify the target speaker ('miss'), identify a foil as the target speaker ('false alarm'), or correctly reject a foil ('correct reject'). The hits and correct rejections are then counted and divided by the total number of sentences presented to the witness to obtain a score. For instance, if 25 sentences are presented and 21 of these are correctly identified as coming from the target or correctly rejected as not coming from the target, this would be counted as a score of 84%; a score of around 85% or higher is usually interpreted as meaning that the earwitness can indeed identify the target (Hollien 2012). Much of the research into the construction of voice line-ups has revolved around this approach. Such research has shown, though, that the repeated presentation of sentences from the suspect and foils causes a learning effect on the part of the earwitness; as the listener becomes more familiar with the voices, they may 'lock in' and falsely select voices as those of the perpetrator.

 Serial voice line-up: The serial approach is currently recommended by the UK Home Office. Here, the witness listens to the voices one after another until all samples are heard. If needed, the witness can then replay some or all of the voices again. At the end of this comprehensive review of samples, the witness comes to a decision and makes a claim about whether a particular voice in the line-up is that of the target speaker; the witness also always has the option of saying that the target speaker was not present. The problem with the serial approach is that it stretches working memory demands, as listening to all samples and then deciding requires substantial cognitive work.

5.1.3 Practical setup

A common setup for how a voice line-up is conducted is illustrated in Figure 5.3. The witness (A) is seated at a desk with a laptop or computer. Typically, the witness has a PowerPoint file in front of them, with one voice per slide. On the final slide, all voices can be replayed if needed. A police officer (B) is supervising the line-up. To avoid any bias, this should not be a police officer who has been involved with the case or the construction of the line-up. The defence solicitor (C), too, is present but may leave the room during the line-up. Their job is to choose the order of the line-up and review the recordings to make sure they have no objection to the selection of voices or material. The witness's reactions and response are video recorded (D).

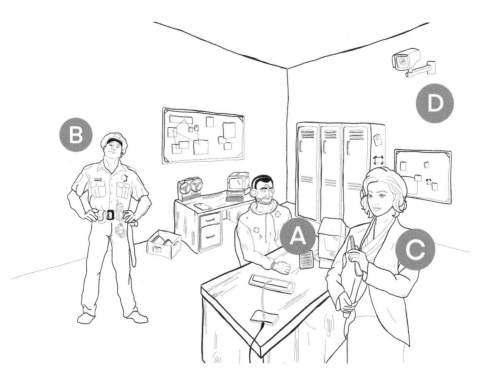

Figure 5.3 Illustration of a voice line-up setup. The witness (A) and a police officer (B) as well as the defence solicitor (C) may be in the room. The reactions and responses of the witness are being video recorded (D). © Corinne Lanthemann

5.2 Listener performance

Several factors potentially affect listener performance – that is, how well listeners can identify the target from a voice line-up. Here, we differentiate between three main types of factors, all of which can lead to significant variation in the identification performance of listeners.

- Factors to do with the perpetrator's voice (e.g., familiarity) (section 5.2.1).
- Factors to do with the material heard and the latency of (or time until) the voice line-up (section 5.2.2).
- Factors to do with earwitness characteristics (e.g., talent, predispositions, etc.) (section 5.2.3).

5.2.1 Factors to do with the perpetrator's voice

Familiarity

Identifying voices that are familiar is easier than identifying voices of people one does not know. This is not surprising: speakers that you are familiar with, like friends and family, have provided you with ample speech material over the years. You intuitively know how they vary their speech depending on the time of day, their emotional state, and their level of intoxication, because you have been familiarised with plenty of within-speaker variation for that voice. This gives you a very complete picture of that voice and allows for high identification rates. Note, though, that even familiar speaker identification is not 100% accurate. Even for highly familiar speakers, all listeners make mistakes. One study found, for example, that even among members of a close social network who had known each other for two years and who currently lived together there can be misidentification (Foulkes & Barron 2000). Peter Ladefoged, a highly-respected phonetician, admitted that he had trouble identifying his own mother on the phone from just a 'hello' and that he needed more material to identify her (Ladefoged & Ladefoged 1980).

Given the large difference in identification performance depending on whether the perpetrator's voice was familiar or unfamiliar to the earwitness, courts routinely take this into consideration when evaluating earwitness testimony. Earwitnesses claiming that the speaker was familiar to them are typically in a more believable position. Voice line-ups are not usually conducted if the witness claims to know the speaker, because the question would be different. Rather than addressing the question of whether the witness can identify the voice they heard at the crime scene, a voice line-up for a familiar voice would test whether the witness can indeed identify the voice of the person they claim to know.

Typicality

Typicality, i.e., whether the perpetrator exhibited speech features that are rare or common in a population, plays a major role in the assessment of earwitness testimony. If the target speaker has very peculiar, atypical features relative to the witness's experience, such as a lisp or an unusual regional accent, he might be identified more easily. If the perpetrator shares many phonetic features with the rest of the population, on the other hand, then earwitnesses will have a much more difficult time identifying them.

Familiarity of accent or language

A perpetrator's accent, dialect, or language can affect earwitness performance. People perform more poorly at identifying voices in samples with foreign accents, unfamiliar dialects, and foreign languages. In one study, for example, monolingual English listeners were shown to be better at identifying native speakers of English than at identifying Spanish speakers talking in Spanish, or Spanish speakers talking in English with a Spanish accent (Thompson 1987). Voice identification performance nearly doubles when a listener understands the language of the samples they are working with. If a speaker talks with an accent that a listener shares (an in-group accent), then the listener is able to pay more attention to speaker-specific cues helpful for voice identification (e.g., pitch, speaking rate, etc.). Speech in foreign accents, unfamiliar dialects, and unknown languages can pull a listener's attention away from cues helpful for voice identification since they are more focused on trying to understand the speaker.

5.2.2 Factors to do with the material and time point of line-up

Quality of speech material

The quality in which speech material is encountered (for instance, transmitted over telephone) also affects earwitness performance. In an experiment by Nolan et al. (2013), speakers were recorded in a studio and over a telephone landline simultaneously. These recordings were then grouped into same-speaker and different-speaker pairings. The pairs were played to a group of listeners who judged how similar or different the speakers sounded in three different conditions:

  (i) in one condition, both recordings of the pair were played in studio quality;
 (ii) in one condition, both recordings were played in telephone-transmitted quality;
(iii) in one condition, one recording was played in studio quality, while the other was played in telephone-transmitted quality.

Figure 5.4 shows the overall results for how listeners judged speaker similarity and difference. The judgments were given on a scale from 1 to 9, with 1 being very similar and 9 being very different. The same-speaker pairs were, as expected, judged to be much more similar than the different-speaker pairs. However, in both cases note the effect of transmission type. When the pairs were heard in studio quality (black bar), they were on average perceived as more different than when pairs were heard in telephone-transmitted quality (grey bar). If one sample of the pair was heard in studio quality and one in telephone quality, then the pair was perceived as most different (white bar).

In both same-speaker pairs (left three bars in Figure 5.4) and different-speaker pairs (right three bars in Figure 5.4), the mixed condition exhibited the highest difference between the voices, while over the telephone, voices sounded most similar. Voices sound more similar over a telephone line because of the cut in bandwidth that occurs when voices are transmitted via telephone (see Chapter 4); the frequencies that are removed or damaged by telephone transmission may carry important, speaker-specific information, so voices that are transmitted over the telephone are perceived as more similar.

Studies such as this one indicate that voice line-up samples should be presented using the same transmission characteristics as the witness's first exposure to the voice – if the witness heard the perpetrator over a landline, then the voice line-up should also use telephone samples. Experiments have further shown that if a perpetrator is originally heard in an emotionally agitated state (e.g., very angry) and subsequently heard in a voice line-up in a non-agitated, 'normal' voice, earwitness identification rates are very low due to high within-speaker variation. It should further be kept in mind that earwitnesses frequently hear a perpetrator's

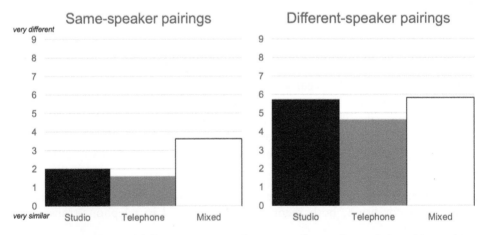

Figure 5.4 Bar chart of difference ratings when pairs of recordings are heard in studio quality (black), over a telephone line (grey), and in mixed conditions (white). Same-speaker pairings on the left, different-speaker pairings on the right. (Adapted from Nolan et al. 2013)

voice alongside background noise such as traffic or the hum of machines. This may further affect identification performance.

Quantity of speech material

Regarding the quantity of the speech material, i.e., the length of time a witness was exposed to a perpetrator's voice, one might assume that the more material the witness hears during the crime, the better their subsequent identification performance. This is only partly true. Some studies have shown superior identification when witnesses have longer exposure (e.g., Cook & Wilding 1997); other studies have found less dramatic effects of exposure time on identification performance (e.g., Künzel 1990). There is no magical tipping point of exposure quantity at which witnesses' identification rates suddenly become very reliable. What is clear, though, is that longer exposures are certainly not detrimental to identification performance. Furthermore, the degree to which a listener has been exposed to within-speaker variability during a crime (e.g., whether the perpetrator was heard in different emotional states) may play a role in identification performance. The more within-speaker variability the witness heard, the fuller their understanding of the voice of the perpetrator, and so the greater may be the chances of successful identification in a line-up.

Complicating our understanding of the importance of speech material quantity, though, is the fact that witnesses often cannot give reliable information about how long their initial exposure was to a voice heard in the course of a crime. One study, for example, found that almost all witnesses overestimated the duration of the voice sample heard during a crime (Orchard & Yarmey 1995). This shows that the duration of voice samples heard (and memorised) by witnesses are overestimated by a substantial margin. Exposure length is often cited by earwitnesses in court as a reason why they are confident it was this particular speaker, because they heard them speak for a long time. The studies presented here underline how courts must be cautious of such claims unless otherwise corroborated.

Finally, another factor that may affect speaker identification rates is whether the witness engaged directly in conversation with the perpetrator, or whether they merely overheard the speaker. People are also better at identifying voices if they have conversed directly with the speaker rather than passively overhearing them (Hammersley & Read 1985).

Voice disguise and speaker distortions

If a perpetrator disguises their voice during a crime (see discussion in Chapter 3), it goes without saying that earwitnesses will have a more difficult time identifying the undisguised target voice in a line-up. Identification rates can drop dramatically in the case of a voice disguise. Keep in mind that it is not only intentional disguises that alter the voice, but also 'natural' causes: for example, if a perpetrator had a severe cold, was very hoarse, or was wearing a mask over his mouth at the time of crime, this would impinge on earwitnesses' subsequent identification performance. In cases where the voice was disguised during the crime it is possible that a voice line-up may be considered unviable and not even be conducted.

Latency

In most cases, there is likely to be a significant delay between the time of crime (when the voice was heard) and the later attempt to identify the perpetrator in a line-up. It takes time to construct a line-up even if the perpetrator has been apprehended quickly. However, as we saw in the Lindbergh case, it might be months or even years before this happens.

The time between the exposure and the voice line-up is obviously critical for identification performance because of the decay of memory: We typically remember things in more detail if they happened a day ago as opposed to a year ago. Intuitively, then, one might assume a negative linear relationship between delay time and identification performance. However, experiments show somewhat mixed results.

The latency period is interesting because this interval is an objective measure which is almost always known with certainty, unlike witnesses' subjective and relatively unreliable claims regarding length of exposure. Most studies indicate a decline of identification performance the more time passes between crime and line-up (e.g., Papcun et al. 1989). Some research, however, has shown a less substantial decline over time (e.g., Van Wallendael et al. 1994). Perhaps results are inconclusive because of between-study differences in the types of voices presented to participants, since some voices are inherently easier to recognise than others. A pioneering study was conducted in light of the Lindbergh case (McGehee 1944). It tested whether listeners could identify a voice they heard five months after the exposure. The target voice was embedded in five foils. Identification rate dropped to 13% after five months; that is, below chance level performance (chance level being 16% when six voices are heard). After a long delay, then, there is reason to doubt the witness's ability to identify the voice. Crucially, the result of a voice identification that takes place shortly after the crime generally has more credibility than an identification that takes place several months later. In a report prepared for a court, this time interval is typically recognised as a (further) indicator regarding the reliability of the earwitness evidence.

5.2.3 Biological, cognitive, and psychological factors on the part of the listener

Gender and age

Experiments reveal evidence of sex/gender effects, such that males are better at identifying other males and females are better at identifying other females based on their voices. This own-sex bias in voice identification has also been found in eyewitness identification performance. However, male voices are generally identified better than female voices regardless of listener gender. In terms of age, even young children can identify speakers above chance based on voice. (In fact, there is evidence that new-born babies can distinguish their mother's voice from other voices.) Identification performance of children starts to match that of adults from about age 10. Further studies have revealed that listeners between 16 and 40 typically perform better at identification than listeners aged 40+.

Confirmation bias

There is a principle in psychology called confirmation bias, which fundamentally claims that our expectations influence our perceptions and interpretations. This also applies to voice line-ups: if a listener expects to hear a very particular voice based on how the voice is stored in their mind, they are likely to identify one of the voices they hear in a line-up as the voice they expect to hear. This is particularly common in familiar voice recognition, in which listeners may identify an unknown voice thinking it is the voice of a known person.

Attention

One aspect which has also been shown to affect listener performance in the cognitive realm is the degree of attention the earwitness paid to the perpetrator's voice during the crime. The victim may be traumatised during the crime and may not specifically focus on the perpetrator's vocal characteristics. Still, if listeners are instructed (for example, in research conditions) to pay particular attention to somebody's voice, they perform better in a subsequent identification task. This is not to say that if a listener pays attention they will automatically identify the target speaker; however, the degree to which a witness did in fact pay attention or not should (if possible) be taken into consideration when evaluating earwitness evidence.

Confidence

Listeners further vary in terms of how certain they are about their identification ability. Intuitively, one might think that a witness who is highly confident in claiming to have identified the target should be more likely to be accurate. Several studies, however, have found little correlation between listener confidence and identification accuracy. Consequently, the degree of certainty expressed by an earwitness should not be taken as an indicator of whether their identification is correct. Some listeners have a tendency to believe that they recognise a speaker in a line-up even when the target is absent (see confirmation bias, above). Others are naturally unsure about their decision, which may reflect a general behavioural tendency. This has consequences for juries, as a confident witness can be comparatively persuasive. There is, perhaps, an exception to this general lack of correlation: studies have shown confidence to be positively linked with iden-tification accuracy in cases of familiar speaker identification (e.g., identifying a friend or sibling; Yarmey et al. 2001).

Ability

Some listeners are simply better than others at identifying voices, holding con-stant all of the factors listed so far. Indeed, as we noted earlier, every experiment includes people who perform well and others who perform badly. It is therefore important not to generalise from average scores in experimental data to predict the likelihood that a witness's testimony is reliable. McGehee (1944) compared a group of listeners trained in speech, a group trained in music, and a group not trained in either field. When presented with five voices and asked which one was most unlike the others, the listeners from the music group outperformed the other groups. The same was true when it came to judging speaker height, weight, and personality traits: the musically trained group outperformed the others. Why might this be the case? Presumably, pitch discrimination – which highly musical people are good at – may be related to speaker identification if an increased sensitivity to pitch variability from musical training translates to better detection of pitch differences in speech. Recent research is exploring whether there are 'super-recognisers' of voices (Schäfer & Foulkes 2023). Previous research has identified super-recognisers of faces. Skills of this sort have been put to use for intelligence purposes, for example by the Metropolitan Police in London.

Auditory and visual predispositions

Relatively little research has been conducted on earwitnesses' general audi-tory and visual skills and how those might be linked to speaker identification. However, blind listeners outperformed sighted listeners in a speaker identifica-tion task when audio was presented in studio quality (Braun 2016). Blind people tend to discriminate pitch better than sighted people, have superior auditory long- and short-term memory, and have higher temporal auditory resolution – that is, they can better detect sudden changes in the speech signal. Blind listeners are also better at the localisation of sound sources in speech in noise. This audi-tory superiority is useful for forensic speech science generally, which is (pre-sumably) why Belgian police have sought out blind listeners for some forensic speech tasks.

5.2.4 Summary of factors affecting earwitnesses

This overview suggests that voice identification by earwitnesses, especially of unfamiliar voices, must be treated very carefully in court. Overall, the following characteristics are likely to increase the reliability of earwitness testimony in court: a high degree of familiarity with the voice in question; substantial exposure to the perpetrator's voice at the time of the crime; experience of direct conversation with the perpetrator; exposure to the perpetrator's voice in good quality conditions and without disguise; familiarity with the speaker's native-like accent; exposure to a variety of speaking styles and substantial within-speaker variation at the time of crime; a short latency period before the line-up; and careful attention to how the perpetrator spoke. Of course, fulfilling all these conditions is virtually impossible, but they comprise the ideal conditions for a witness case.

Finally, one problem in interpreting any experimental data is that it is not possible (nor would it be ethical) to simulate the real event to cater for the stress and emotion that the witness experienced at the time. Experiments are useful in revealing general patterns of behaviour, but we cannot infer directly from experiments to the case at hand. It might be true that memory degrades, and after a few months experimental subjects can only identify voices at chance level. Some people will nevertheless be good at voice recognition even in difficult circumstances or after a long delay. What happens in real cases might well generate much more robust memories for a voice than is evident from an experiment in which nothing is at stake for the listener.

5.3   Legal framework

To begin with, it must be borne in mind that earwitness performance is not infallible. It therefore ought to be used in conjunction with other forms of evidence. Experiments have found identifications (hit rates) to be at chance or below chance level under many circumstances, with false alarm rates often quite high. Furthermore, voice line-ups are not conducted very often, due to the time and labour – and therefore costs – involved, concerns regarding timing constraints, memory decay, and a lack of awareness of such techniques among police officers. Only four of 43 police forces in England and Wales used voice line-ups between 2005 and 2015 (Robson 2017), while fewer than ten cases are known to have been conducted in Australia (Butcher 1996, McGorrery & McMahon 2017). Solan & Tiersma (2003) discuss a small number of cases from the United States.

Legal admissibility of earwitness evidence is thus a delicate matter, and to complicate things, such evidence is treated somewhat differently from country to country. Some courts give earwitness evidence more credence than perhaps it deserves, while other courts have dismissed it completely. Courts in England and Wales, the US, Canada, and Australia have in some cases prosecuted a defendant on the basis of earwitness identification alone. In Australia, there are relatively clear jury directions on aural identification evidence. These directions function as safeguards implemented by the legal system to protect defendants from wrongful convictions based on mistaken identification. The following criteria are typically considered when it comes to trusting earwitness evidence more generally:

- Whether the offender was a stranger to the witness.
- What opportunity the witness had to hear the voice of the person.
- How attentive the witness was when they heard the voice.
- How clearly the witness heard the voice. (Was there disguise?)
- Whether there was anything distinctive about the voice.
- The length and volume of what the witness heard.
- The delay between the offence and the identification.

(McGorrery & McMahon 2017)

As mentioned earlier, most countries do not have official guidelines when it comes to constructing voice line-ups. The UK Home Office provides concrete advice which was developed via collaboration between a police officer, John McFarlane, and a forensic phonetician, Francis Nolan (2003). These are often referred to as the McFarlane guidelines, though they are based on similar guidelines from the Netherlands. The McFarlane guidelines summarise how voice line-ups should be constructed and administered, setting forth standards for foil selection, number of foils, length of material, and other methodological components. It is recommended, for example, that all voice samples should be compiled from police interview recordings, with sentences spliced together from different sections so that the listener focuses on the voice rather than the content. Care must be taken to ensure that the samples do not contain any reference to specific crimes, which could obviously be a source of bias. The McFarlane guidelines also recommend that a voice line-up should be tested in advance with a group of non-witnesses, i.e., people who have no knowledge of the case. The pre-test is designed to show that the line-up is fair: it should elicit a random distribution of responses from the participants, since none of them should have any reason to choose one voice over the others. The full guidelines are available on the internet. Research is ongoing to explore whether speech technology could assist with the construction of voice line-ups, for example by using ASR to select foils that are well matched to the voice of the suspect.

5.4   Example cases

To end this section, we offer three example cases that involved earwitness evidence and we discuss how this evidence was handled in court. The first two cases took place in Australia and are reported on in McGorrery & McMahon (2017).

5.4.1 Case study: *R. v. Golledge*

The victim, a man, was blindfolded, assaulted, and threatened by two other men. The victim claimed he recognised one of the men, while the other was unfamiliar. Twelve days after the incident, he participated in a voice line-up featuring recordings from eleven speakers to identify the unknown assailant. He found one voice somewhat similar to the second attacker's but was not entirely sure. Despite this partial identification, the court ruled his testimony unreliable, as explained further below (selected points below adapted from McGorrery & McMahon 2017):

1. The offender was a stranger to the victim before the offence.
2. The victim did not refer to any distinctive features of the offender's voice when describing the voice.
3. There was a delay of 12 days between offence and identification.
4. The victim had smoked cannabis and taken valium on the morning of the attack.
5. The victim initially told police that the offender had a 'Kiwi' (New Zealand) accent but the voice he identified did not.
6. The victim seemed to have chosen the defendant's voice more by elimination rather than by recognition.
7. The conversation played in the voice identification recording was an unemotional statement, in contrast with the emotional insults and threats he heard during the offence, i.e., there was a mismatch in speaking style.

5.4.2 Case study: *R. v. Burrell 2001* and *2009*

The following case is also discussed by McGorrery & McMahon (2017). A kidnapper named Burrell abducted a woman and later called her husband's office, where he had also worked, to halt the search and media attention. The receptionist who answered described the caller's voice as 'husky' and belonging to an educated man in his 40s. The police suspected Burrell and created a voice line-up using a prior spontaneous recording of him answering a police question. The foils were recordings of police officers reading the same words. The receptionist listened to Burrell's voice and six others, identifying two as possibly matching the kidnapper's voice, one of which was Burrell's. Despite flaws in the line-up's setup, the court accepted this evidence because it was treated as circumstantial and not a key part of the case.

The line-up process had several issues. The foils were only police officers, likely not matched for age, accent, or other characteristics. The sample used from Burrell was brief, and the foils were simply read versions of his words. The main concern was that Burrell's recording was spontaneous, while the foils were scripted readings, creating a mismatch in speaking styles that may have influenced the witness's identification. Burrell's voice was uniquely spontaneous, making it stand out in the line-up.

5.4.3 Case study: *R. v. Assad Khan*

In 2001 a woman, Harbans Johal, died in a house fire in London. Johal's partner, Didar Bains, was arrested on suspicion of arson. The man's lodger claimed that he had heard a conversation in which Bains arranged for another man to carry out the attack. The lodger further claimed to recognise the voice as a gardener who had worked at their house, Assad Khan. The investigating officer, DS John McFarlane, worked with Francis Nolan, Professor of Phonetics at the University of Cambridge, to produce a voice line-up. Nolan points out that this case was one in which the witness was already somewhat familiar with the suspect's voice, and thus the line-up should have been framed to test his ability to recognise the familiar voice rather than the more open question of whether he could recognise the voice he heard on the day in question. Nolan further concedes that Khan's f0 was high relative to the foils. The judge rejected a request from the defence to rule the line-up evidence inadmissible. However, before the jury were asked to consider that evidence, Bains admitted to the plot and both men were convicted of murder. The procedure followed in this case is detailed in Nolan (2003), and subsequently adopted as the general procedure for voice line-ups in England and Wales (the McFarlane guidelines referred to earlier).

Conclusion

This chapter has introduced cases where earwitness evidence may play a major role. We have covered what a voice line-up is, how one can be constructed, and the main factors that affect identification performance in line-ups. We must not forget that earwitness evidence can be unreliable and that it is still an under-researched area, which means that one needs to be cautious and use this type of evidence in conjunction with other types of evidence. What really complicates this field is that there are few standardised protocols on how line-ups should be administered, how foils should be selected, and how much weight earwitness testimony should be given in court. Given the ever-increasing ease of access to electronic means of changing one's voice, including deepfake technologies, there is likely to be an increase in cases where criminals disguise their voices and potentially evade identification by witnesses. Authorities should therefore devise and adopt best practices that will make earwitness evidence more reliable, fairer, and more accurate. Forensic phoneticians are involved in constructing and assessing voice line-ups, and conducting research to better understand earwitness evidence.

Further reading

For a detailed account of one voice line-up, and a summary of UK guidance on line-up construction (the McFarlane guidelines):

Nolan, F. J. (2003). A recent voice line-up. *International Journal of Speech, Language and the Law*, 10(2): 277–291.

For a survey of voice line-ups in specific jurisdictions:

Robson, J. (2017). A fair hearing? The use of voice identification line-ups in criminal investigations in England and Wales. *Criminal Law Review*, 1: 36–50.

McGorrery, P. G., & McMahon, M. (2017). A fair 'hearing': Earwitness identifications and voice identification line-ups. *International Journal of Evidence and Proof*, 21(3): 262–286.

Solan, L. M., & Tiersma, P. M. (2003). Hearing voices: Speaker identification in court. *Hastings Law Journal*, 54(2): 373–435.

References

Braun, A. (2016). *The Speaker Identification Ability of Blind and Sighted Listeners: An Empirical Investigation*. Springer.

Butcher, A. (1996). Getting the voice lineup right: analysis of a multiple auditory confrontation. *Proceedings of the 6th Australian International Conference on Speech Science and Technology*. Flinders University, pp. 97–102.

Cook, S., & Wilding, J. (1997). Earwitness testimony 2: Voices, faces and context. *Applied Cognitive Psychology*, 11: 527–541.

Foulkes, P., & Barron, A. (2000). Telephone speaker recognition amongst members of a close social network. *Forensic Linguistics: The International Journal of Speech, Language and the Law*, 7: 180–198.

Hammersley, R., & Read, J. (1985). The effect of participation in a conversation on recognition and identification of the speakers' voices. *Law & Human Behavior*, 9: 71–81.

Hollien, H. (2012). On earwitness lineups. *Investigative Sciences Journal*, 4(1): 1–17.

Künzel, H. J. (1990). *Phonetische Untersuchungen zur Sprechererkennung durch linguistisch naive Personen*. Franz Steiner.

Ladefoged, P., & Ladefoged, J. (1980). The ability of listeners to identify voices. *UCLA Working Papers in Phonetics*, 49: 43–51.

McDougall, K. (2021). Ear-catching versus eye-catching? Some developments and current challenges in earwitness identification evidence. In C. Bernardasci, D. Dipino, D. Garassino, S. Negrinelli, E. Pellegrino, & S. Schmid (eds.), *L'individualità del parlante nelle scienze fonetiche: applicazioni tecnologiche e forensi* [Speaker individuality in phonetics and speech sciences: speech technology and forensic applications]. *Studi AISV 8*: 33–56. Officinaventuno.

McGehee, F. (1944). An experimental study of voice recognition. *Journal of General Psychology*, 31(1): 53–65.

Nolan, F., McDougall, K., & Hudson, T. (2013). Effects of the telephone on perceived voice similarity: Implications for voice line-ups. *International Journal of Speech Language and the Law*, 20(2): 229–246.

Olson, N., Juslin, P., & Winman, A. (1998). Realism of confidence in earwitness versus eyewitness identification. *Journal of Experimental Psychology*, 4(2): 101–118.

Orchard, T. L., & Yarmey, A. D. (1995). The effects of whispers, voice-sample duration, and voice distinctiveness on criminal speaker identification. *Applied Cognitive Psychology*, 9(3): 249–260.

Papcun, G., Kreiman, J., & Davis, A. (1989). Long-term memory for unfamiliar voices. *Journal of the Acoustical Society of America*, 85: 913–925.

Schäfer, S., & Foulkes, P. (2023). Towards a screening test for earwitnesses: Investigating the individual voice recognition skills of lay listeners. *International Journal of Speech, Language and the Law*, 30(2): 234–267.

Smith, H. M., Bird, K., Roeser, J., Robson, J., Braber, N., Wright, D., & Stacey, P. C. (2020). Voice line-up procedures: Optimising witness performance. *Memory*, 28(1): 2–17.

Thompson, C. P. (1987). A language effect in voice identification. *Applied Cognitive Psychology*, 1: 121–131.

Van Wallendael, L. R., Surace, A. Parsons, D. H., & Brown, M. (1994). "Earwitness" voice recognition: Factors affecting accuracy and impact on jurors. *Applied Cognitive Psychology*, 8: 661–677.

Yarmey, A. D., Yarmey, A. L., Yarmey, M. J., & Parliament, L. (2001). Commonsense beliefs and the identification of familiar voices. *Applied Cognitive Psychology*, 15(3): 283–299.

Activity section

Activity 5A – Familiar speaker identification

In this first exercise, you will conduct an experiment on familiar speaker identification. The question to be explored is: How much material is needed for a listener who is familiar with a speaker's voice to identify that speaker? Pick a famous person (e.g., Barack Obama). You can either download audio from YouTube or try the VoxCeleb database. Open the audio file in Praat (guidance on this software is given in Chapter 2). Now follow the steps outlined below:

(a) Highlight the file in the object window, click on 'View & Edit'.
(b) Highlight the first syllable in the spectrogram.
(c) Click on 'File' > 'Save selected sound (time from 0)'.
(d) This new file now shows up in the Praat object window. In this window, click on the new file, then 'Save' > 'Save as WAV file…' > 1.wav.
(e) Redo steps (a)–(d) until you have six files of the speaker, with the first file containing the first syllable, the second file containing the first two syllables,

the third containing the first three syllables, etc. Make sure to give all your new files sensible names so that you can tell which is which easily.

On your laptop or on your phone, play the first of these files (the first syllable only) to a listener. Can they identify the person? Probably not. Play the second file (i.e., the first two syllables) and see again if they can identify the speaker. Repeat until the speaker is identified, and write down the number of syllables it took for the listeners to identify the speaker. Do this familiar speaker identification experiment with a few more people.

Answer 5A

In this experiment on familiar speaker identification, you probably found results along the following lines: With only a few syllables (e.g., 2–3 syllables) identification was already possible. The more syllables you played, the greater the chance that listeners could correctly identify the speaker. The fact that speaker identification was possible with so few syllables is because listeners knew the speaker very well beforehand; they have been exposed to ample within-speaker variability from this speaker over the course of their lives and are thus very familiar with their voices. If your material contained lots of stressed vowels in the first few syllables, then identification based on just one or two syllables might have been possible since vowels are the main carriers of voice quality and speaker-specific resonance characteristics. Perhaps you found some variation in performance between your listeners – maybe one listener was particularly familiar with the target speaker or one had a particular talent for identifying familiar voices.

Activity 5B – Voice line-up 1

In this second activity, you will conduct an experiment on unfamiliar speaker identification by creating a serial voice line-up. Select six speakers from any corpus of spoken data (for example, OpenSLR). One of these speakers will be your target speaker and the other five will be your foils. Try to pick the foils according to the criteria outlined in section 5.1. Pick a long sentence for each foil (five sentences in total) and a long sentence for the target speaker (one sentence). Pick a different, longer sentence from the target speaker to be your 'criminal' sample (one sentence), which listeners will hear first in your experiment. You should have seven sentences altogether: five sentences (one per foil) plus two sentences from the target speaker.

Proceed as follows:

- Play the 'criminal' sentence to your listeners (without any further instructions).
- Right after playing the sample, tell your listeners that they will now hear six voices, one-by-one, and that they should then tell you which one was the target speaker that they heard at the start of the experiment. Randomise the order so the target appears in an unpredictable place within these six voices.

- At the end of hearing all the voices, ask the listeners to identify the target speaker they heard earlier.

Conduct this experiment with a number of listeners who did not participate in activity 5A. How did they do? With your peers and your instructor, discuss how your listeners responded to this experiment. Did anyone claim it was a target-absent line-up? Were there lots of false alarms?

Answer 5B

It is likely that you found relatively high identification rates because the voice line-up was presented to your listeners right after they heard the target speaker. It is possible, though, that listeners' performance in this unfamiliar speaker identification task depended heavily on your selection of foils. If you picked foils very different from the target (e.g., with much higher pitch, faster speech, a different accent, etc.), then identification performance was probably high. If your foils were much more similar to the target, then identification rates might be lower. Again, you will likely find substantial performance variation between your listeners, depending on whether they paid close attention to the voice, whether they have a talent for identifying voices, whether they are musical, etc.

Activity 5C – Voice line-up 2

In this activity, you will conduct the same experiment as in 5B, but you won't present your listeners with the line-up right away. Rather, you will include a time delay of three days. Proceed as follows:

- Play the 'criminal' sentence to your listeners (without any further instructions).
- Tell them that you will resume the experiment in three days.
- After three days, tell your listeners that they will now hear six voices, one-by-one, and that they should then tell you which one was the target speaker that they heard at the start of the experiment three days prior. Randomise the order so the target appears in an unpredictable place within these six voices.
- At the end of hearing all the voices, ask the listeners to identify the target speaker they heard three days earlier.

Do this experiment with a number of listeners (different from activities 5A and 5B). How did they do? With your peers and your instructor, discuss how your listeners responded to this experiment. Did somebody claim it was a target-absent line-up? Were there lots of false alarms? Most importantly: Did they perform worse than the listeners in Activity 5B? You might also do a version of this experiment with different time delays for different groups of listeners.

Answer 5C

Now, in this task on unfamiliar speaker identification – with a longer retention interval between hearing the target speaker and the voice line-up – listeners probably performed more poorly than in task 5B. Research has shown that identification performance can drop to chance level with a delay of two weeks. Here we introduced a delay of three days. It is possible that some listeners could still perform above chance, but identification rates probably decreased substantially. Again, results here would also depend on your selection of foils as well as the characteristics of your listeners (see answer section 5B).

Activity 5D – Errors in voice identification

Think about your everyday experience recognising people from their voices, or how other people have reacted to your own voice. Can you think of times when you have made a mistake in identifying someone from their voice, or others have made a mistake with your voice? What were the circumstances? What factors might have led to the error? What other types of error might occur?

Answer 5D

There are three main types of error that everyone makes from time to time. (1) You fail to identify a familiar voice. (2) You mistakenly believe you have identified a voice as familiar, when in fact the voice belongs to a stranger. (3) You mistake a familiar voice for that of someone else you know.

In cases of type (1) it might be that you did not expect to hear that voice in the context it was heard, or that the voice was different from usual because of e.g., health issues or poor listening conditions. Type (2) errors occur if the stranger's voice contains similar features to that of someone you know. This is especially likely to happen if it contains something unusual, such as a regional or L2 accent that is uncommon in your entourage. For type (3) cases, it is quite common to mistake family members for one another, although it is probably equally likely to happen with unrelated people who happen to share some phonetic feature.

6 Authentication, enhancement, and speech content determination

In many countries, forensic casework often involves covert audio recordings of people who have been 'bugged'. These recordings may help police bring offenders to trial. However, covert recordings can be problematic because the microphone(s) may be hidden in inconvenient locations. Additionally, speakers may be talking very quietly, or there may be lots of competing noise like car engines or background music, which can result in poor-quality speech signals. The audio may therefore have to be enhanced before experts can begin working on determining speech content – that is, trying to find out what was actually said on the recording. It is also possible that the perpetrators or a third party may have tampered with the audio before investigators obtained it. Audio forensics deals with such steps: checking the authenticity of the audio, enhancing the audio, interpreting what was being said, determining who did the talking, and helping to reconstruct a crime scene. Note that speech content determination is typically conducted by experts with linguistic and phonetic knowledge, whereas enhancement and authentication involve much more technical processing, and are usually conducted by audio technicians or engineers.

Aims

In this chapter, we introduce you to the main subfields of audio forensics: **authentication, enhancement, and speech content determination**. You will learn that experts follow relatively rigid **protocols and guidelines** when it comes to authenticating and enhancing audio. The latter, for example, requires experts to apply various repair mechanisms on the audio signal, the order of which needs to be approached experimentally and documented meticulously. The final section of the chapter deals with **determining what was being said** and **forensic transcription**, which require a good ear, linguistic awareness, and acoustic analysis skills.

Bear in mind that in authentication, enhancement, and speech content determination, there is what is called a **chain of evidence**, which means that every stage of distributing, accessing, and potentially modifying evidence is meticulously documented. This avoids the interference with or editing of evidence whilst in the hands of the police, law experts, or speech scientists.

DOI: 10.4324/9780367616595-6

6.1 Audio authentication

In audio **authentication,** an audio recording is analysed to check whether it has been tampered with (i.e., edited) or whether the audio has been created artificially, which is called spoofing. If a perpetrator has bad intentions and removes incriminating phrases or words from a recording, this might be detected by forensic speech experts. Similar processes might be used where there is not necessarily any malicious intent, for example, to compare different versions of a recording. In what follows, we outline some of the steps typically involved in the process of audio authentication. The steps are not necessarily sequential, or conducted in a specific order. Note also that the steps outlined here are typically labour intensive. If the perpetrator is skilled and has prepared the audio data very carefully, forensic speech experts working under time pressures might not be able to detect evidence of tampering.

(1) **Critical listening:** As with audio enhancement (see further below), audio authentication often begins with a series of critical listening sessions. An expert carefully listens to the audio material several times, accompanied by visual inspection of acoustic representations of the signal, and notes potential anomalies. Anomalies include sudden changes in background noise, transients (clicks and other abrupt sounds), sudden amplitude differences in the signal, oddities in the syntactic structure or flow of discourse, and sudden voice breaks in the speech (which may point towards a synthesised voice). To conduct this step properly, forensic audio experts need to be in a controlled acoustic environment and need to use high-quality equipment to analyse audio files. Sometimes, critical listening may include multiple experts working together to reach a collaborative view about the sound file.

(2) **Inspection with software and hardware:** The audio signal is explored further via software (for digital recordings) or hardware (for analogue recordings). Analogue recordings include those made on cassette or video tape, where the signal is imprinted on the magnetic surface of the tape. Using special equipment it is possible to visualise the magnetic surface, which could therefore reveal physical changes or unusual features. This process was applied in the case of the Yorkshire Ripper hoaxer, John Humble, revealing that the speech sections had been over-recorded onto an existing music recording (see Chapter 3). The process is different with digital recordings, which do not have a physical form as such. With digital recordings, however, it might be possible to inspect the ENF (see section 3.1.6) as one way to establish whether a recording has been edited.

Both digital and analogue recordings can be analysed acoustically. Typically, experts check for level differences (e.g., if voices suddenly become louder) and changes to the noise floor. The noise floor refers to background sound – the overall ambience of a recording – which normally does not change abruptly within a recording. For instance, if the recording was made outside in busy traffic, the noise of cars passing by should be relatively consistent throughout the signal. Should the noise floor change abruptly – perhaps the traffic noise is suddenly absent or significantly amplified or subdued – this could mean the audio file has been manipulated. Such sudden changes in the frequency domain should be audible, and could be further detected by exploring the spectrogram. Figure 6.1 shows sudden changes in the noise floor between 19.488 and 20.021 s (a test recording prepared by the authors).

Experts further look for instances of splicing and mixing – that is, the copying/pasting of certain segments or words to a different place in the signal. Unsophisticated splicing leaves acoustic traces in the signal that can often be detected upon close inspection. For instance, if the splice is made in the middle of a loud portion of the signal and a newer, quieter signal is inserted, this leaves tell-tale discontinuities (see Figure 6.2).

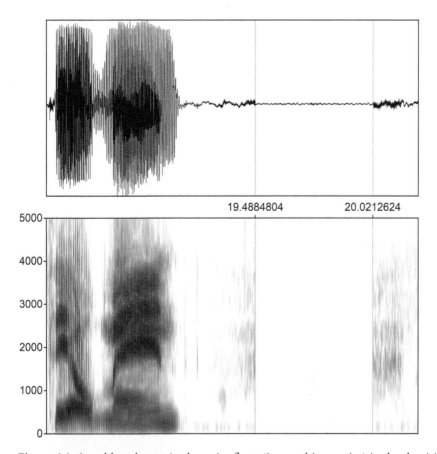

Figure 6.1 A sudden change in the noise floor (i.e., ambient noise) is clearly visible in the waveform, and in the spectrogram as an abrupt change across the frequency domain at 19.488 s. An equally abrupt change can be seen at 20.021 s. (Spectrogram and waveform generated in Praat)

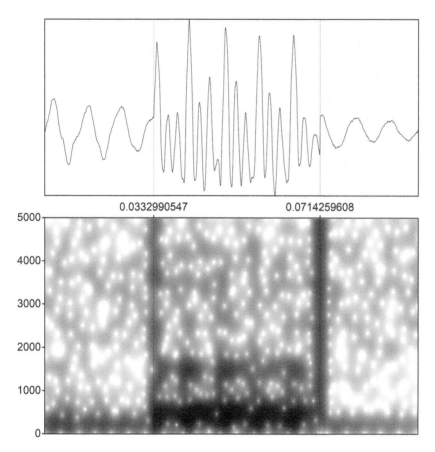

Figure 6.2 Strong zoom on a time interval that contains a splice done carelessly. A waveform discontinuity is visible in both the waveform and spectrogram at 0.033 s and 0.071 s. (Spectrogram and waveform generated in Praat)

The splicing 'error' shown in Figure 6.2 reveals discontinuities in the waveform (top) – note the sudden vertical rises of the waveform disrupting its periodic shape – which are also reflected in the spectrogram (bottom). Auditorily, this careless splicing sounds like very short clicks in the signal.

(3) **Analysis of metadata**: Finally, for some digital signals, metadata can be extracted. Metadata can include technical information on the sampling rate, the number of audio channels, the brand and model of the recording device, the date of recording, and other information about the signal. If the file is authentic, the metadata should straightforwardly reflect the circumstances of the recording. If the recording has been tampered with, then these edits can leave footprints in the metadata file. If examination of the metadata reveals inconsistencies, this could mean that the recording has been electronically modified. Imagine, for example, that a video with accompanying audio of a crime exists. Upon inspection of the file's metadata, you find that the file is in Windows format; however, you also know that the crime was

captured on an iPhone, which typically saves videos as .mp4 or .mov. This could be an indication that after-the-fact file tampering has taken place.

(4) **Overall validity:** Authentication might also involve providing an overall judgment on a recording, to confirm its provenance. This could, for example, involve confirming that the recording was made on a certain type of equipment, in one or more sessions, and on particular dates (see again the discussion of ENF in Chapter 3). This process can involve all of the steps described in this section as well as inspection via various hardware and software systems. An example relating to magnetic tapes is provided in Boss, Gfroerer, & Neoustroev (2003).

Spoofing

One timely issue that experts are currently addressing is spoofing. Perpetrators can now use deepfake technology and artificial intelligence to synthesise voices that can be used, for example, to trick banking bots into transferring money. Some banks now allow e-banking by voice, with clients talking to a virtual assistant. Most commonly, clients can request an account balance through voice; yet the types of transactions that can be voice-activated have expanded recently. One such case is referenced at the end of Chapter 3, in which a large sum of money was obtained fraudulently. In another example, journalists used a voice generated by AI to access sensitive information held by the Australian Taxation Office. The problem with sophisticated audio forging technologies is that the quality has become very good, and it is likely that such cases will become more common. At the moment, some spoofed speech can still be identified by experts using acoustic analysis: the fakes may contain unnatural breathiness or creaky voice, spectrograms may contain formants that lack definition and unnatural glottal striations, which may give the signal a perceptually 'robotic' quality (see Kirchhübel & Brown 2022).

6.2   Audio enhancement

Once authenticity has been determined, audio might in some cases be enhanced before it is possible to interpret what was said and to determine who did the talking. Audio **enhancement** is important in forensic speech science because recordings collected as evidence are typically very different in quality compared to recordings made in a studio. Clandestine surveillance recordings may be made with a hidden microphone, which can lead to poor audio quality. For example, the microphone may be under a shirt or behind an obstacle, leading to a muffled audio signal. Covert recordings are often transmitted via mobile phone technology, and thus also show the characteristic bandwidth limitations of telephone speech (see Chapter 4).

Characteristic	Studio	Forensic
Frequency range	20 Hz – 20+ kHz	Variable (max. 20 kHz)
Signal-to-noise ratio	90 dB+	Negative to 40 dB
Distortion	Negligible	Variable
Equipment operator	Trained technician	Investigator or public
Microphone	Small to large professional	Miniature
	Variation in directivity and frequency response	
Recorder	Professional digital	Inexpensive digital
Quality	Best	Standard
File compression	Usually none	None to highly compressed
Reverberation	Usually dampened	Often high
Speaker distance to mic	Close	Variable
Mic location	Open	Concealed
Transmission system	Usually none	Telephone or radio frequency
Background noise	Minimal	Uncontrolled & variable

Figure 6.3 Typical differences between digital studio audio and covert digital forensic audio recordings. (Adapted from Zjalic 2020: 60)

Figure 6.3 shows some general differences between recordings obtained in a studio and forensic material retrieved from covert operations involving a concealed microphone.

Figure 6.3 shows some of the key differences that are typically encountered between studio and covert recordings. Studio engineers typically work with excellent microphones, room acoustics, and recording equipment, while forensic audio experts must deal with poorer quality recordings that often contain high levels of noise. Enhancement of forensic material is thus crucial because noise can conceal the identity of speakers or words spoken, and disrupt the verification and processing of the speech signal. In principle, the ultimate goal of audio enhancement is to improve intelligibility, or the proportion of words a listener can correctly identify. The golden rule of audio enhancement is thus to maximise intelligibility, even if this decreases the overall quality of the signal. So, for example, if a disturbing masking noise is present in the signal but intelligibility is high, then the noise is not removed through filtering because this may actually cause intelligibility to drop. This is somewhat counterintuitive, so we'll discuss it in more detail later. Most importantly, though, any method of enhancement must be documented in detail for replicability purposes (see section 6.2.4).

Moreover, modified files are usually not used for any acoustic analysis of speech, as the technical changes imposed by the enhancement method might affect the acoustic properties of relevant speech sounds.

Before we look at some audio enhancement techniques, beware that TV shows and movies often give an exaggerated portrayal of what is currently possible in forensic speech science. Public perceptions of audio enhancement techniques are thus frequently warped (sometimes called the 'CSI effect'). If, for example, a recording system simply has not captured an element of a signal due to too much distance between the speaker and the microphone, then this information – no matter how important to an investigation – is simply impossible to recover. Likewise, if a speaking event is completely masked by a truck driving by, then chances of recovery are extremely slim. Even high-quality recordings can present difficulties that are close to impossible to resolve, for example if multiple people speak at the same time.

6.2.1   Step I: Evidence preparation

To preface this section, note that there exist only relatively imprecise official protocols – if any – regarding how audio enhancement should take place (the UK protocols are available online). Here we outline some of the general steps that are typically implemented in the enhancement process applied to poor-quality speech signals.

The first step involves making a copy of the original which specialists then work with, leaving the original untouched. The **sampling rate** (number of measured samples in the time domain) and **quantisation rate** (number of available levels in the amplitude domain) are kept identical in the copy. The expert examines the copy in a sound-treated space by listening to the recording using high-quality headphones with a broad and flat spectrum (meaning that the headphones cover the full audible frequency range and don't dampen or heighten any frequencies); this ensures that what the expert hears mirrors what is on the recording as closely as possible.

6.2.2   Step II: Pre-processing of evidence

Critical listening commences in this step. Experts note problems or issues in as much detail as possible when listening to the recording. Many factors can affect the quality of a recording. The most common issues found in audio evidence involve noise and distortions, both of which can affect the quality and intelligibility of the signal. Noises are undesired acoustic events captured when the recording was made; distortions are changes to the signal introduced by the transmission medium, the recording system, or the recording environment. Typical noises include background sounds such as tones, sirens, engine or machine sounds, hisses, coughs, and the steps of passers-by. Typical distortions found in evidence material include clicks and crackles, clipping (i.e., when the audio signal is too loud for the microphone), bursts (when talking too closely to the microphone), and reverberation.

6.2.3   Step III: Enhancement

We now give a brief overview of some audio enhancement techniques before we introduce two enhancement case studies at the end of this section. Audio enhancement usually takes place in a series of steps. For example, if three steps are involved in a given enhancement (applying a filter, then de-hum, then de-reverberation), the sequencing of these steps must be given close attention because every step creates a new output signal which is then the basis for each subsequent enhancement. Applying the sequence in a different order can affect the quality and intelligibility of the recording in different ways.

De-clicking: Clicks are defined as undesired audible transients. They include, for example, digital errors that can occur in some recordings, or brief noises created by the on/off button of an analogue tape recorder. The problem with clicks is that they can mask speech sounds. Using specialist software, a de-clicking filter can be applied to the signal and unmask affected sounds to some degree. The de-clicking filter samples the signal just before the click and after the click, and interpolates between them to reconstruct the signal minus the click. It is assumed that the resulting effect brings the recording closer to the intended speech sound. There are some downsides to this strategy, though: it can leave audible 'bumps' in the signal, and if the click covers an entire speech sound, that sound might not be recoverable.

De-clipping: Clipping occurs when a signal is so loud that it exceeds the recording threshold of a microphone, making a portion of the signal unintelligible and rendering acoustic measurements less accurate. Clipped regions typically contain at least three consecutive samples (i.e., measurement points) at a maximum loudness level. The section which is clipped can be 'fixed' in that experts resynthesise this portion – they recreate the clipped signal by extrapolating the shape of the waveform based on areas of the signal just before and after it. Note, though, that de-clipping (and de-clicking, above) may be ethically problematic because the section in question is no longer a true representation of the original signal. De-clipping and de-clicking should thus be used with strong caution.

Spectral repair: Spectral repair refers to the precise removal of specific areas of the signal in the time-frequency domain. Here, an unwanted area (such as the frequencies at which birds chirp or dogs bark) is removed in the signal at a particular time point. This area is then replaced with a resynthesis consisting of samples from the surrounding speech signal, just as with de-clipping. This process can also be ethically problematic, because what is done to the signal is something of a 'black box' – little is known about how spectral repair algorithms actually edit the audio.

Reference cancellation: Reference cancellation refers to the isolation of entire elements of the signal in relation to a so-called reference. This may sound abstract, so an example will help. Let's say you have a speech recording, and part way through a fire alarm is set off. The recording therefore contains speech overlaid with the fire alarm signal. In principle it is possible to remove the fire alarm. The acoustic profile of the alarm sound can be identified (in much the same way as we analyse speech sounds themselves), ideally from a section of the recording which contains no speech. That acoustic profile can then be subtracted from the overall signal, hopefully leaving behind any acoustic energy that wasn't part of the alarm signal. This process is easiest to perform when the unwanted signal is periodic or regular, like a recurrent alarm bell, but even then it is difficult to conduct perfectly. More complex and aperiodic (irregular) sounds, such as music, are much harder to isolate and remove because it would be necessary to identify and access the exact version of the music. However, the smartphone application Shazam, which helps users identify unknown songs, does a pretty good job of reference cancellation. Shazam focuses just on whatever background music is playing and isolates that signal for identification purposes even when you're talking to a friend, at a loud shopping centre, or inside a noisy vehicle. In forensic cases, perpetrators who suspect that they are being recorded may switch on a TV or radio to mask what they are saying. In these cases, reference noise – unwanted TV sounds, for example – can be cancelled to some degree using a landmark-based fingerprinting algorithm (providing the original TV audio is available to the investigator). This algorithm essentially analyses the signal to identify the position of the reference noise before removing it from the overall signal.

Equalisation and filtering: Equalisation refers to a process by which the amplitudes of certain frequencies in a recording are adjusted, often to make them more similar to the amplitudes of other frequencies. Generally, this means that one or more filters are applied to a signal in order to attenuate or remove certain frequencies. For example, in cases where the original audio recording happened to dampen higher frequencies, these can be artificially increased to make the recording sound more natural.

Filters can also be applied in cases where there is a disturbing (ideally constant) noise present throughout the recording. Say there is a continuous high-pitched buzz in a signal; you can repair this by applying a low-pass filter that weakens the level of the signal above a particular cut-off frequency. Hissing, for example, can be dampened by filtering out frequencies above 7 kHz while still allowing other frequencies relevant for speech sounds to pass through. Problems with the acoustic signal can occur when an analogue signal is digitised at too low a sampling rate. This effect is called **aliasing**, and results in additional tones being present in the signal. The effect is often clearly audible, sounding a little like bird song (you might notice it sometimes when speaking on a mobile phone). On a spectrogram the additional tones are visible, looking like mirror images of the original signal. The effects of aliasing can be resolved by low-pass filtering to remove affected frequency regions, but any content in the frequency regions affected by aliasing is un-recoverable.

Amplification: Forensic casework recordings are sometimes very quiet. Several forms of amplification (also referred to as gain), or increases in the amplitude of an audio signal, can be applied in such cases. This can be done manually, where the analyst selects regions of an audio file to amplify. It can also be done automatically, using methods such as **dynamic range compression**. Dynamic range is defined as the span between the largest and smallest amplitude values, and dynamic range compression reduces this difference by amplifying quieter sounds and dampening louder sounds in the signal. Any type of gain adjustment must be used with caution as it will also be applied to background noise in the recording.

De-reverberation: Forensic recordings often feature speakers talking in rooms with substantial reverberation, or **reverb**. Reverb can be destructive to speech intelligibility, especially in larger spaces with harder surfaces. (Consider how hard it can be to understand someone talking in a setting like a cafeteria or an indoor swimming pool.) In acoustic terms, the energy of speech sounds in a recording is smeared over time, overlapping with the following sounds (see Figure 6.4).

Figure 6.4 shows the effect of room acoustics on signal quality: The top two panels show the waveform and spectrogram of a recording made in an anechoic chamber (a specialist recording suite treated to remove all reverberation), while the bottom two panels show the same recording from a room with substantial reverb. The smearing of segments is clearly evident in the latter recording, visible as much less well defined acoustic features than those shown in the top panels (a particularly clear example occurs between 1 and 1.2 seconds in both the waveform and spectrogram).

Removing reverb, though, is very complex and often requires working out the frequency response of the room in which a recording was made, as well as the position of the sound source and microphone within the room, since sound waves are reflected and diffused by walls and obstacles. Once such information is available, experts can then try to remove the reverb using a de-reverb filter.

6.2.4 Summary

This has been a short overview of some of the main audio enhancement techniques. Before we move on to some case studies, we want to reiterate an important point: enhancements are applied with the aim of improving the

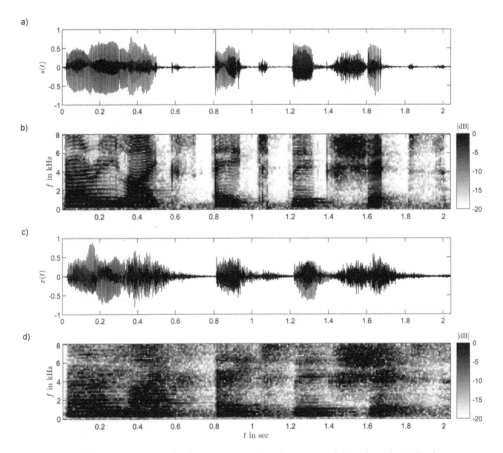

Figure 6.4 The top two panels show a recording in an anechoic chamber; the bottom two panels show the same recording carried out in a chamber with reverb. (Reproduced with permission from Goetze 2013)

overall intelligibility of speech, even if that means signal quality may be adversely affected. This is somewhat counterintuitive, because one would think that a recording that rates high on the intelligibility scale also rates high on the quality scale. However, this is not always the case: a recording which is judged to be of good quality may be rated less intelligible than a recording of poorer quality. It can happen, for example, that a recording that has crackles and hissing noises remains intelligible because fricatives are still clearly audible. If we removed these crackles and hissing noises, this would also remove important information about fricatives since they are predominantly distinguished by the presence of sound in higher-frequency regions. In practical terms, then, this means that experts commonly test out several different filters and enhancements (in different orders) on copies of an audio signal to find which ones render the signal most intelligible. The original recording is always maintained intact, so that its contents remain available to analysts and courts.

6.2.5 Case study: Rodney King

In 1991, a bystander took a video of a Black man, Rodney King, allegedly being beaten by several White Los Angeles policemen. All four officers were charged but later acquitted. Following this, a civil rights trial was conducted which resulted in two officers being sentenced to 30 months in prison. Their conviction was largely based on the visual material in the video recording because the audio was deemed to be too low in quality to admit as evidence. It contained, for example, the noise of a police helicopter overhead. Only later was the audio material analysed further. The forensic phonetician involved in this case, Angelika Braun, was primarily concerned with the following two tasks:

1. To enhance intelligibility and check whether the police officers shouted racial slurs, as alleged by King;
2. To examine whether a taser was activated during the incident.

The use of a taser was examined because King sustained facial injuries resulting from falling. The question was whether he fell because of the taser and then injured his face, or whether his face was beaten by the police officers' batons (or both). To enhance the audio track, Braun proceeded as follows. First, a copy of the video was made. A series of filters was applied to remove as much of the helicopter noise from the audio as possible, which increased intelligibility substantially. Using that cleaned-up audio, she determined that no racial slurs were heard. To assess the presence or absence of taser noise she examined the spectrogram of the audio track. Known samples of taser noise were studied and compared to the evidence recording. Figure 6.5 shows the audio track of the original video.

Figure 6.5 shows vertical striations in the spectrogram, with substantial background noise present from the helicopter overhead. These periodic (i.e., regular and repeated) vertical striations are typical acoustic traces of a taser being used. This led the expert to conclude that a taser was indeed activated at that time, suggesting that this was probably the reason why King fell to the ground and sustained facial injuries.

6.3 Speech content determination

Even when a signal has been enhanced, speech is often still not entirely intelligible in forensic recordings. This is not too surprising, given how regularly misunderstandings arise in everyday speech: Consider the pairs 'thirty' vs. 'thirteen', 'F' vs. 'S', or 'I can do it' vs. 'I can't do it'. Even in normal, non-adverse listening conditions (i.e., without background noise) it can be difficult to perceive these contrasts. This gets even harder when you're speaking over a telephone line, listening to someone who mumbles or talks very quickly, or standing in a location with background noise. Another factor that can complicate intelligibility is

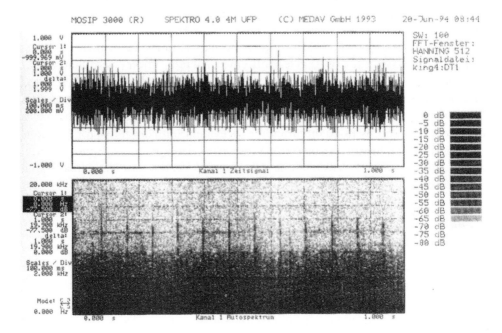

Figure 6.5 A selection of the original audio track from the Rodney King case, clearly showing vertical striations typical of taser noise. (Reproduced with permission from Braun 1994, © Equinox Publishing Ltd)

accent differences. For example, in mainstream British or American English *Kate* is pronounced [kʰeɪt], but as [kʰɐɪt] in Australian English. This pronunciation may be misinterpreted as *kite* by a British or American listener. The task of the forensic phonetician is to best describe what is being said in such questioned utterances. This specific subfield of forensic phonetics, speech content determination, is sometimes also called disputed or questioned utterance/content analysis.

6.3.1 What types of speech content determination tasks are there?

We can differentiate two types of speech content determination tasks:

- An overall transcription of what was being said, typically conducted auditorily.
- A very specific, detailed acoustic analysis that details what was being said at a particularly important point in a recording.

Legal teams might ask forensic speech experts to provide a transcript of what is being said, to assist a court to follow what is being said in an evidential recording. **Forensic transcription** tasks can involve both phoneticians and linguists. The work will be done by listening closely to recordings using high-quality equipment, partially supported by speech analysis software. On a narrow level, lawyers may argue about the identity of a word or phrase. When a very specific section of the signal is in dispute, detailed acoustic analysis may be useful.

6.3.2   Transcription of difficult recordings

The task of writing a transcript may sound easy, but listening to a recording and converting its contents to written form is a subjective event. The listening process is susceptible to cognitive biases and various types of contextual information, including the amount of background an expert knows about a case or even the instructions they are given (see section 6.3.4 on speech content priming). Common difficulties that arise in transcript creation involve speakers who are code-switching between languages, speakers with foreign or unusual regional accents, unclear articulation, as well as recordings of poor technical quality. As a consequence of such factors, different parties may hear different things. Furthermore, the police may want to charge a suspect because they are convinced that the suspect committed a crime, and may therefore produce a transcript that differs from that produced by a forensic speech expert.

Forensic speech experts are typically aware of problems surrounding potential biases and usually have safeguards in place to counter them. For example, the analyst might first attempt the task 'blind' to the purposes of the investigation. Ideally, the case materials are prepared by another expert or assistant, who consults with the client but provides no contextual information to the principal analyst. Any relevant information might be revealed at a later stage to see if it affects the perceived content. This is particularly important if proper names or places are involved, as these types of words are particularly prone to priming (see below). To further reduce bias, a single analyst might transcribe material on several occasions and then compare across transcriptions for consistency, or multiple analysts may be recruited to transcribe speech independently before comparing their results. In some cases, a court of law may reach the conclusion that the speech content is too questionable to be admitted as evidence.

Experienced speech analysts recognise that there is no such thing as a perfect transcript. There are, however, better and worse ones. There are various techniques that are used to assist with transcription. They include:

Taking account of linguistic information: It might be clear from the syntactic context that a difficult word must be a noun or proper name. Consider, for example, the phrase *I was talking last night to a X*. Here X is used to represent a single syllable. Given the context, especially the indefinite article, X is most likely to be a noun, but probably not a proper name (compare *...to a priest* versus *...to a Pete*). Vowels and suprasegmental information like intonation and rhythm tend to be easier to interpret, even in noise, than consonants. Most syllables in most languages contain a vowel, hence it is quite likely that the analyst can detect the number of syllables in a difficult section.

Cross-referencing: Sometimes a word or phrase is used more than once. Some instances might be clearer than others, and can therefore be used as a point of comparison with problematic examples. In this way a transcript might be developed over several stages and in a non-linear fashion. That is, a transcriber will not start with the first word, then the second, the third, and so on in the order of appearance on the recording. They might need to move back and forth in the recording, and return to some sections multiple times.

Consultants: Specialist consultants are often used to help in transcription cases, recruited for their expertise with specific languages or dialects, specialist vocabulary, or to handle cases involving speech disorders.

Decisions need to be taken on the format of the transcript, taking into account its intended audience(s) – jurors, police officers, or other clients, for example. Fluent speech does not resemble the syntactically perfect utterances you might read as reported speech in a novel or as lines in a script for film or theatre. Real speech is full of false starts, repetitions, pauses, incomplete sentences, slang or dialectal terms, and people talking in overlap or against background noise. Do we represent these things in a transcript at all? If so, how do we do it without making it confusing for readers such as jurors? Does the format or content of presentation affect how readers view the individual's personality, background, or truthfulness (see, for example, Tompkinson et al. 2023)? There are no universally agreed answers, but forensic transcripts usually involve some indication of degrees of confidence to show that some parts of the material might be less clear than others. For example, less clear sections might be indicated in brackets, and possible alternatives can be shown to avoid choosing one over the other. Overlapping speech is only indicated where it appears particularly relevant. Words and grammar are usually presented as they are spoken, rather than converted into the standard form of the language (for example, if the speaker says 'he weren't' or 'I ain't never done nothing' these words would not usually be standardised to 'he wasn't' or 'I never did anything'). Spelling, however, usually follows standard norms to avoid becoming confusing. If a speaker of English 'drops' /h/ or uses [f] for /θ/ this would not usually be indicated in a transcript. Finally, bear in mind that the majority of people in the world use more than one language, and a recording might contain multiple languages. How do we represent this? Translating from one language to another presents all sorts of complexities and difficulties that might need to be considered in a legal case.

6.3.3 Case study

Figure 6.6 illustrates a short extract of a forensic transcription produced for a case from Ghana (Foulkes, French & Wilson 2019). This very complex case involved five men apparently discussing a cocaine importation (as well as many other things, since the recording was an hour long). All five men agreed they

Time/line	speaker	Verbatim	English translation
0:03:38			
69	KA	[*laughs*]	[*laughs*]
70	M	(**You know.**)	(You know.)
71	KA	**I like that.**	I like that.
72	KB	**Johnnie Walker** wonya papa deɛ a, ɛyɛ, **but** wei deɛ ɛnyɛ papa.	As for Johnnie Walker, if you get the good quality one that is fine, but as for this one, it is not of a good quality.
73	M	…	…
74	KB	Sɛ woahu enti … na ɛrekɔ.	Have you seen why … It is going.

Figure 6.6 Extract of a transcription. Note that Twi orthography includes special characters based on the IPA, ɛ and ɔ.

were present, and so a key task was determining who said what in order to establish which of them, if any, had knowledge about the drugs. When the case materials were first received by the forensic analysts, a transcription had been provided by the client. However, this transcription was not usable as a means of planning any analysis. It had apparently been produced by a receptionist with no forensic training; it was entirely in standard English; and it covered only a selection of the utterances in the recording. Analysts therefore produced their own transcription as the basis for attributing speech to the five individuals. This was no easy task for several reasons: at least three languages were involved (English, the local language Twi, and occasionally Hausa), the English was spoken with a Ghanaian accent, there was frequent code-switching between languages, the recording had been made outside with lots of background noise, and at times the conversation descended into a heated argument with different people shouting over each other. A linguist from Ghana was recruited to work with the UK team, who collectively produced a transcript consisting of over 120 pages and 1,100 speaking turns.

In the transcription submitted in evidence, two versions of the text were given. First, there was a verbatim transcription which recorded code-switching and separated the different languages (for example, English was highlighted in bold). To facilitate reading, each speaker's turn was presented separately without any indication of overlap. Second, the text was given a literal translation into English, which is the official language of the court. You will also note that some speech was not transcribed at all (shown as …) while other words were not attributed to a particular speaker (hence M in the speaker column, which was used to refer to 'male'). These decisions were taken because the analysts did not always feel confident they could discern what was said, or attribute it definitively to one of the five candidates. Some other sections were transcribed in parentheses to indicate a lower level of confidence than for that shown as regular text. Time points and line numbers were included for reference purposes.

6.3.4 Resolving questioned utterances

Sometimes there may be a question about a specific section of a recording that is potentially of great importance in a case. The questioned utterance could be a phrase, word, syllable, or even a specific consonant or vowel. It could be that there is no clear version presented by any party in the case, or there could be alternative versions. In such instances a forensic phonetician tries to provide an analysis that might resolve the issue. Usually this involves performing acoustic analysis on the questioned utterance. The acoustic properties might help establish which of any alternative versions is the more likely, or it might provide a means to suggest what is said. If possible, the analyst compares features of the questioned utterance with reference material from the same recording. It is also possible to infer interpretations from general knowledge about speech, or based on knowledge about the language and accent in question.

A questioned utterance emerged in a recent murder trial in the US. Alex Murdaugh was on trial for the murder of his wife and son, who had been shot dead in their car. During an interview with police Murdaugh said 'This is so bad, X did [him/it] so bad'. The questioned section, marked X, was interpreted as I by the investigating officers, and thus apparently an admission of guilt. An alternative version was suggested by Murdaugh himself – they. Although the two words differ when spoken carefully – /ðeɪ/ versus /aɪ/ – the speech in the recording is difficult to interpret clearly for several reasons. Murdaugh is very emotional (his f0 reaches well over 400 Hz in this section of the interview), the word in question is spoken quickly, and his southern US accent means that his pronunciation of I tends to be monophthongal, like [æ:] rather than a diphthong. Figure 6.7 shows a spectrogram of the questioned section in context. Some movement in the vowel formants is visible, and there is some evidence for an initial consonant (although it certainly does not resemble a fricative in its usual form). In the case itself, the questioned utterance was not analysed or resolved by an expert on behalf of either prosecution or defence. Instead the section was played in open court, both at normal speed and one third speed, with witnesses simply asked what they heard. We do not consider that to be a valid approach. If an episode of speech is not easily resolved because of its inherent technical quality, it will not be resolved by untrained and potentially biased listeners judging it under poor listening conditions. Ideally, an expert ought to have compared the acoustic properties with non-disputed examples of the same words from the same recording. Two case examples are discussed below to illustrate how this process works in more detail. Murdaugh was found guilty of the murders and

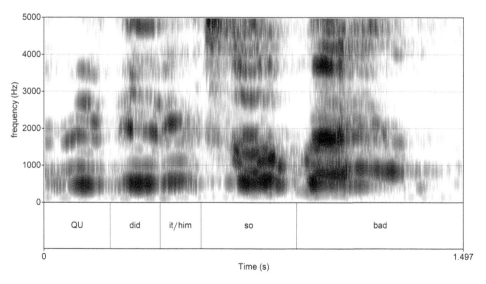

Figure 6.7 Spectrogram of questioned utterance (QU) in Murdaugh case.

sentenced to life imprisonment, although it is not clear whether the questioned utterance contributed to the verdict.

6.3.5 Speech content priming

The perception of a questioned utterance may be affected by the contextual information a listener has about a speaker or a recording. This is called priming. If a jury is asked what they hear in a questioned phrase or utterance, their perception might be influenced by what the prosecution or defence tells them about the speaker they are listening to. The situation becomes even more problematic if listeners are given an (alleged) transcript of a questioned passage. The jury is very likely to 'lock in' to a specific interpretation of the signal, making it harder for them to listen objectively. You can experience the effect of priming very easily. For example, watch the comedy sketch by the British comedian Peter Kay in which he makes fun of misheard lyrics in pop songs. 'Just let me say for the record' is misheard as 'just let me staple the vicar', 'mercy' as 'birdseed', 'but now' as 'pork pie', and so on. It is extremely difficult not to perceive the nonsense versions once primed with them.

To give a serious example where this type of priming was of concern, let us introduce the case of David Bain. In New Zealand in 1994, Bain made an emergency call, after he had discovered his entire family had been shot dead in the family home. Soon after, he was convicted of their murders and sentenced to 16 years in prison. Several parties tried to appeal the decision by the courts in subsequent years. In 2007, there was a retrial during which a detective, listening to the original crisis call from 1994, claimed to hear a confession on the recording (note that there was no such claim at the original trial). Before you read any further you might wish to listen to the audio in the case and determine for yourself what you think was said at the point of the questioned utterance. Beware that the recording is inevitably distressing to listen to. If you do wish to listen to the material it is important to do so before you read the remainder of this section, as any information you read could affect your perception.

Activity 6A – David Bain case

Listen, if you wish, to the questioned section in Bain's emergency call. Bear in mind the speaker is very distressed. The full recording is provided on Helen Fraser's website. The key section occurs between 30 and 35 seconds, and you might focus just on that section. Write down the words you hear, if any. Listen several times and see if your view changes after repeated listening.

After reading the further discussion below, return to this recording and listen again. Now you know the versions suggested by parties in the case, does your perception change? Can you 'hear' more than one version of the words spoken?

For the retrial, both the prosecution and the defence engaged experts to analyse the signal. The defence team were careful not to raise awareness of the questioned utterance in order not to bias their expert witnesses. The dispute was only mentioned later in the process, after transcripts had been submitted. All the experts on both sides agreed that it was not possible to provide a definitive transcript of the questioned utterance. Throughout the recording Bain appeared to be hyper-ventilating or struggling to control his breathing. At times he was speaking with considerable difficulty. At the point of the questioned utterance, some experts had transcribed 'I can't breathe', or parts of that phrase, at least in some drafts of their transcript. All indicated caution over that interpretation, and some marked the section as too difficult to transcribe. None transcribed anything like the apparent confession: the police officer claimed to hear 'I shot the prick'. Both legal teams agreed that the utterance should not be included in any transcript offered to the jury, because of the danger of **priming effects**. Humans have confirmation biases and often 'want to find the criminal': If it had been suggested in a printed transcript distributed that Bain said 'I shot the prick', the jury would have been likely to perceive the disputed signal as such. The defence team went further, and asked for that section to be excised before the recording was played to the jury. This request was initially refused, but eventually agreed by an appeal court, and only the rest of the recording was admitted as evidence for the retrial. It is not clear what impact the recording had, but the retrial jury concluded that Bain was not guilty. Bain's supporters maintain that his original conviction had been a serious miscarriage of justice.

Given the high-profile nature of the case, the entire call was released publicly after the trial ended. Numerous newspaper headlines of 'I shot the prick' were then published. Researchers subsequently ran an experiment on the materials (Fraser, Stevenson & Marks 2011; a version of which is presented by Helen Fraser for the task in Activity 6A). When they played the recording to a group of people without telling them what had been said, almost no one interpreted the utterance as 'I shot the prick'. If, however, it was suggested to the group that it could be 'I shot the prick', 30% of participants claimed to hear just that. Furthermore, even if they were then told that this interpretation was not valid because the signal was too unclear, half of these 30% still claimed to hear 'I shot the prick'. Listen again to the questioned material, and see if you can 'hear' both versions that were suggested: 'I can't breathe' and 'I shot the prick'. This example shows the real dangers of giving listeners transcripts of poor-quality recordings, especially when even experts express doubts about exactly what was said.

6.4   Case studies

In this section, we will introduce three more case studies. The first two involve close listening and acoustic analysis of questioned and non-questioned tokens. The third is a case where investigators were involved in determining what was said in a cockpit recording before a plane crashed.

6.4.1   Case study: *can or can't?*

French (1990) introduced the case of a TV show in the UK which claimed to expose doctors' unethical prescription practices. In one instance, an actor hired by the programme went to a doctor to try and obtain a prescription while posing as a drug addict. The programme broadcast recordings of the exchange between the actor and the doctor. The doctor was an immigrant to the UK from Greece and spoke with a Greek accent. In one instance, the doctor said something that was subtitled on the programme as 'you can inject those things' while referring to the tablet form of a medicine. The General Medical Council (GMC) initiated disciplinary proceedings against the doctor based particularly on this phrase, as injecting the contents of the tablets would be totally contrary to medical guidance. The medical defence union providing legal representation for the doctor then approached a forensic expert to work out what the doctor had really said. The doctor claimed that he had said 'you *can't* inject those things' rather than 'you *can* inject those things'. Figure 6.8 shows the transcript of the questioned phrase made by the expert (Peter French).

Upon initially listening to the recording, the forensic expert was unsure of what the doctor had actually said. French then collected additional data from the doctor and analysed his speech features in detail, paying particular attention

Doctor:	...why are you on the codeine phosphates?
Actor:	Eh?
Doctor:	Why are you on the codeine phosphates for?
Actor:	'Cos like my mother noticed like needle marks, do you know what I mean?
Doctor:	You **can/can't** in- in- inject those things
Actor:	Like I- I don't yeah, but I- I- I don't like telling people
Doctor:	You **can/can't** in- in- inject those things, you know
Actor:	Yeah, but I prefer to take them by mouth.

Figure 6.8 Transcript of the conversation between the doctor and the actor. (Adapted from French 1990)

to how the doctor articulated 'can' and 'can't' at other points in the recording. The 45-minute conversation between the expert and the doctor revealed the following patterns based on auditory impressions of unambiguous tokens:

can

- In unstressed position, the vowel was heavily reduced.

- In stressed position, the vowel was [æ̃] (i.e., nasalised and lowered).

can't

- In both stressed and unstressed positions, the vowel became very similar to [æ̃], perhaps slightly lowered and more retracted.

- The final /t/ was typically fully elided.

This meant that, phonetically, the speaker made little difference between 'can' and 'can't'. The vowel was very similar (whereas it is not in standard British English – /kæn/ versus /kɑːnt/), and the /t/ was reduced or elided altogether. Both instances in the transcript shown in Figure 6.8 exhibited a stressed realisation of the questioned word. Based on auditory impressions, the expert concluded that the questioned words leaned more towards 'can't' as opposed to 'can'. To explore this further, unambiguous tokens were subjected to acoustic analysis. The expert measured the durations of segments and words and found that 'can' and 'can't' were virtually identical. In terms of vowel quality, the expert did find systematic differences based on formant analysis: The 'can't' vowels were lower and further back in the acoustic vowel space than 'can', just as the expert had suspected based on auditory impressions. He then compared the formant values from the questioned words to those of the known samples and found that the questioned words fell within the range established for 'can't' rather than 'can'. These findings, along with a description of the expert's methods, were then reported to the GMC tribunal. It is not clear whether the forensic phonetic analysis contributed to the outcome, but the doctor was struck off the medical register after the disciplinary enquiry for unethical practice in prescribing drugs.

6.4.2 Case study: *dom* or *Tim*?

Another example of an acoustic analysis for speech content determination took place in Sweden in 2008 (Morrison, Lindh and Curran 2014). There was a murder case involving a witness who was interviewed by the police. One word in the interview recording was disputed: it could have been either the pronoun *dom* (English 'they'), typically pronounced [dɔm], or the name *Tim*, typically pronounced [tʰɪm]. The recording contained numerous other unambiguous tokens of *dom* and *Tim* from the same speaker. When the experts asked the witness to take part in additional recordings, she was not cooperative. To figure out whether the disputed token was in fact *dom* or *Tim*, experts conducted measurements on the questioned token as well as on all of the speaker's other known tokens of *dom* and *Tim*. Specifically, they measured voice onset time (VOT, i.e., the time between the burst release and the onset of voicing; see Chapter 2) of the initial plosive as well as the formant frequencies of each word's vowel. In canonical (prototypical) productions of the two words in Swedish, the VOT in *Tim* is much longer than the VOT in *dom*. Likewise, the F1 and F2 of the vowels in *dom* and *Tim* should be quite different, the former having a low back vowel and the latter having a high front vowel. As a safeguard, each measurement was conducted three times and experts subsequently analysed the means of those measurements. Figure 6.9 shows VOTs from the known *dom* tokens (grey) and the known *Tim* tokens (black). The vertical line indicates the measurement taken from the disputed token. The histogram exhibits a very clear separation of *dom* and *Tim* according to VOT, in line with the expected pattern. The VOT of the disputed token (vertical bar) falls within the distribution of *dom*, indicating that it was pronounced with a voiced (or pre-voiced) alveolar plosive.

Figure 6.10 shows a scatterplot of formant measurements of the speaker's known tokens of *dom* and *Tim* in F1/F2 space. The grey dot shows the vowel measurement of the disputed token.

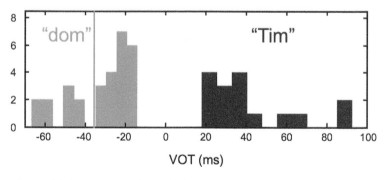

Figure 6.9 Histogram of the VOT measurements for *dom* and *Tim* in the undisputed tokens. The vertical bar indicates the measurement for the disputed token. (Reproduced with permission from Morrison et al. 2014)

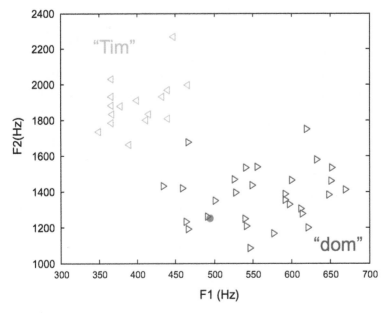

Figure 6.10 Scatterplot of F1 and F2 measurements for the vowels in *dom* and *Tim* in undisputed tokens. The grey dot indicates the F1 and F2 measurements for the disputed token. (Reproduced with permission from Morrison et al. 2014)

In Figure 6.10, the F1 and F2 measured for the vowel in the disputed token (the grey dot) shows a clear overlap with the distribution of *dom* rather than *Tim*. The experts used these data in their analysis to support the conclusion that the witness most likely said *dom* in this specific token.

6.4.3 Case study: cockpit voice recording

The third example involves an analysis of a cockpit voice recording. Cockpit voice recordings (CVRs) typically record a 30-minute loop inside an aircraft's cockpit before overwriting; newer devices that utilise non-volatile solid-state recordings can record up to two hours before overwriting. CVRs capture several channels, including the pilot's headset, the co-pilot's headset, a cockpit area microphone, and communications between the cockpit and cabin crew. The cockpit area microphone can also capture non-speech sounds like engine sounds, vibrations, and warning alarms, which may be important for investigating a crash. In March 2015, Germanwings Flight 9525 took off normally and climbed as planned. About half an hour into the flight, though, the plane began to descend rapidly and the cockpit did not respond to radio calls from air traffic controllers. Ten minutes later, the plane crashed into the French Alps, killing all 115 passengers and crew. The flight recorder was damaged, but the CVR was still intact.

Prior to examining the CVR, there were no surviving witnesses or other communications which could help investigators understand what had actually taken place. However, once the CVR had been analysed by French investigators, it illuminated what had happened. We present this case here not because of a questioned utterance or because it illustrates the type of transcript produced by forensic phoneticians, but as an example of how the crash investigators provided a transcription of what happened on the plane based on closely listening to the CVR, which included voices as well as non-speech noises. Several issues were potentially of relevance to understanding what happened. Were the voices on the recording really those of the pilots? Were voices audible right up to the point of impact? Who was present in the cockpit? Did any alarms indicate that the plane was malfunctioning before it started losing altitude?

Below is a transcript of the signals found on the voice recorder (adapted from the Chicago Tribune):

10:27 a.m.: The aircraft is at 38,000 feet. The captain asks the copilot to prepare the landing. Lubitz [the copilot] replies 'hopefully' and 'we'll see.'

After the check, Lubitz repeats to the captain, 'You can go now.'

There is the sound of a door clicking. The captain goes to the toilet.

10:32 a.m.: Air traffic controllers contact the plane and receive no answer. Around the same time, an alarm in the cockpit: 'Sink rate.'

There follows a bang on the door. The pilot can be heard shouting: 'For God's sake, open the door!' Passengers can be heard screaming.

10:38 a.m.: The plane is at about 13,100 feet. Lubitz can be heard breathing.

10:40 a.m.: The sound of what is believed to be the plane's right wing scraping the mountaintop can be heard. Screams of passengers are the last sounds on the recording.

Based on the transcript provided by the investigators, it became clear what had actually taken place. The captain had excused himself to go to the lavatory and gave controls over to the co-pilot. The co-pilot then intentionally locked the cockpit and took steps to crash the aircraft. The pilot tried to break down the cockpit door, to no avail. There were no mechanical issues – it was a suicidal co-pilot. It turned out later that Lubitz had suffered from deep depressive episodes during his flight training with Lufthansa.

Conclusions

This chapter has provided an overview of audio authentication, speech enhancement, and speech content determination. Audio authentication is a crucial step that involves experts checking evidence material to find out whether it has been tampered with – for instance, whether someone removed parts of the signal or inserted pauses or other sounds. In speech enhancement, experts try to 'clean up' an audio signal in order to increase the intelligibility of speech on the recording. Remember that the basic tenet is to maximise intelligibility even if that means leaving in certain background sounds. Finally, we have introduced you to speech content determination – that is, determining what was said or heard on the signal. Keep in mind that humans have biases, and we sometimes hear what we want to hear. Transcripts of questioned utterances need to be dealt with very carefully and need to undergo substantial cross-checking on the part of experts before a full report can be handed over to legal authorities.

Further reading

For more detailed discussion of authentication and enhancement:

Maher, R. C. (2018). *Principles of Forensic Audio Analysis*. Springer.
Zjalic, J. (2020). *Digital Audio Forensics Fundamentals: From Capture to Courtroom*. Focal Press.

For more detailed discussion of forensic transcription:

Fraser, H. (2020). Forensic transcription: The case for transcription as a dedicated branch of linguistic science. In M. Coulthard, A. May, & R. Sousa-Silva (eds.), *The Routledge Handbook of Forensic Linguistics*. Routledge, pp. 416–431.
Fraser, H. Forensic Transcription Australia [website]. https://forensictranscription.net.au
Fraser, H., Stevenson, B., & Marks, T. (2011). Interpretation of a crisis call: Persistence of a primed perception of a disputed utterance. *International Journal of Speech, Language and the Law*, 18(2): 261–292.

References

Boss, D., Gfroerer, S., & Neoustroev, N. (2003). A new tool for the visualization of magnetic features on audiotapes. *Forensic Linguistics: The International Journal of Speech, Language and the Law*, 10: 255–276.
Braun, A. (1994). The audio going with the video-some observations on the Rodney King case. *Forensic Linguistics: The International Journal of Speech, Language and the Law*, 1(2): 217–222.
Foulkes, P., French, P., & Wilson, K. (2019). LADO as forensic speaker profiling. In P. Patrick, M. Schmid, & K. Zwaan (eds.), *Language Analysis for the Determination of Origin*. Springer, pp. 91–116.
French, J. P. (1990). Analytic procedures for the determination of disputed utterances. In H. Kniffka (ed.), *Texte zu Theorie und Praxis Forensischer Linguistik*. Niemeyer, pp. 201–213.

Goetze, S. (2013). *On the Combination of Systems for Listening-room Compensation and Acoustic Echo Cancellation in Hands-free Teleconference Systems*. PhD thesis, Universität Bremen, Germany.

Kirchhübel, C., & Brown, G. (2022). Spoofed speech from the perspective of a forensic phonetician. *Proceedings of Interspeech 2022*, 1308–1312, Incheon, Korea.

Morrison, G. S., Lindh, J., & Curran, J. M. (2014). Likelihood ratio calculation for a disputed-utterance analysis with limited available data. *Speech Communication*, 58: 81–90.

Tompkinson, J., Haworth, K., Deamer, F., & Richardson, E. (2023). Perceptual instability in police interview records: Examining the effect of pauses and modality on perceptions of an interviewee. *International Journal of Speech, Language and the Law*, 30(1): 22–51.

Activity section

(Activity 6A is provided on page 134)

Activity 6B – Speech content determination

The second exercise is on speech content determination. Produce a transcription of what you hear in the following recordings. The point of this exercise is to explore the detrimental effects of (train) noise on the speech signal and to determine the point at which the speech signal becomes clearer to you. Do this exercise auditorily. If you feel like exploring the signal further, do so by inspecting it in Praat. Follow the steps outlined below:

(a) Open the files Train 1.wav, Train 2.wav, Train 3.wav, Train 4.wav, Train 5.wav, and Train 6.wav in Praat. Play each file repeatedly and write down an orthographic transcription of what you hear. Do this for all six files, in numerical order. In Train 1.wav, the noise is 10 decibels louder than the signal (signal-to-noise ratio/SNR of −10 db). In Train 2.wav, the SNR is −7; in Train 3.wav, the SNR is −3; in Train 4.wav, the SNR is 0 (the signal is as loud as the noise); in Train 5.wav, the SNR is +5 (i.e., the signal is 5 dB louder than the noise), and in Train 6.wav, there is no background noise.

(b) Perform the same task with the files Train 7.wav to Train 12.wav.

How many words did you identify in each condition?

Answer 6B

This exercise demonstrates the detrimental effects of background noise on speech intelligibility. When the background noise is as loud as the signal (Train 4),

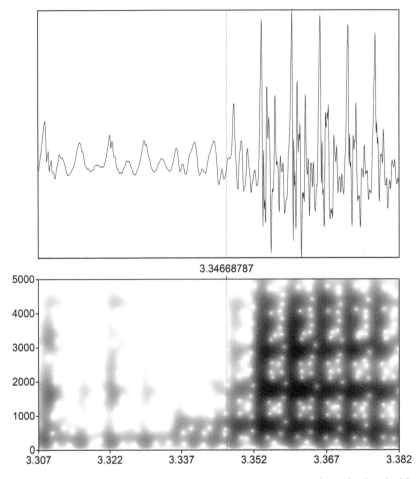

Figure 6.11 Possibly unnatural short pause in the phrase *that I had to hold my hat on and the girls' skirts* (figure shows the end of *on* and start of *and*).

perhaps a few words are intelligible. When the signal is 5 db louder than the noise (as in Train 5 and Train 11), there is an increase in intelligibility, but it's still not at 100%. What's interesting about this example is that, because of telephone transmission, the signal is already degraded to begin with, making it doubly difficult to understand what the person said. So even file Train 6 – without background noise – contains a word that may be difficult to parse without context, namely *third*. Of course, because of the context of being followed by 'class', we can be fairly certain that the word is *third*; however, in general, interdental fricatives [θ, ð] and labiodental fricatives [f, v] become virtually indistinguishable over the telephone.

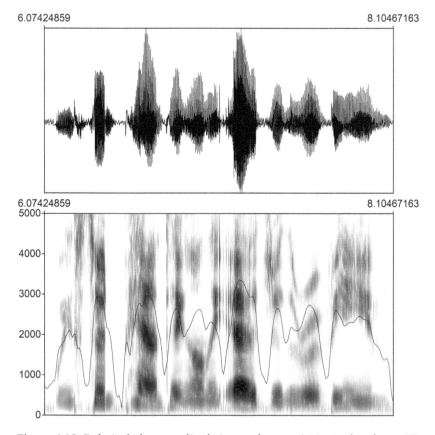

Figure 6.12 Relatively low amplitude in word *we* at 6.11 s in the phrase *We stood panting on the edge of the ravine.*

Activity 6C – Audio authentication

The final exercise is on audio authentication. Listen to 6C Tampered.wav (retrieved from www.openslr.org/12/) and inspect the file in Praat. You will need to zoom in and out to be able to inspect sections of varying duration. Consider the types of issue that can be revealed in authentication tests, and see if you can find any evidence that this file has been tampered with. What type(s) of tampering are evident? Be precise in your description by discussing specific time points of the signal.

Answer 6C

As with any task involving sound files, you should first make a copy of the signal and inspect only the copy. Leave the original untouched. At first, you should

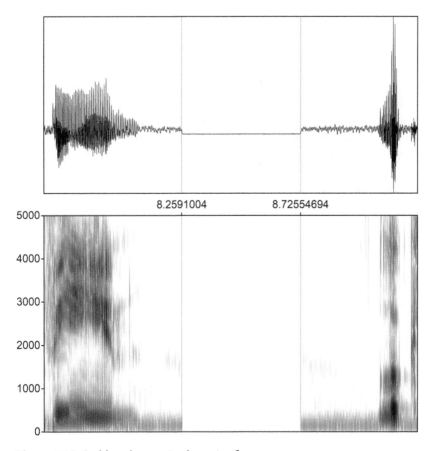

8.2591004   8.72554694

Figure 6.13 Sudden changes in the noise floor.

conduct critical listening. You may note a couple of anomalies. In the phrase *that I had to hold my hat on and the girls skirts* you may notice an unnaturally short pause between *on* and *and* at 3.29 s. See this phrase in Figure 6.11. The auditory impression here is fairly clear – the [n] of *on* appears cut off. Acoustically the effect is not obvious, but there is an unnaturally abrupt turn in the periodic waveform at 3.467 s, where it appears something might have been deleted.

We would expect this pause to be longer, otherwise the phrase sounds quite abrupt. It appears, then, that some form of acoustic deletion may have taken place here. If you explore the signal further, you may notice that the amplitude of the signal is not always the same. In the phrase *We stood panting on the edge of the ravine,* the *we* at 6.11 s is slightly quieter than the rest of the phrase, as can be seen by inspecting the waveform and the intensity curve (yellow line) in Praat (Intensity > show intensity...). See Figure 6.12. There is also a very clear disjuncture in the waveform at 6.247 s. Given these pieces of evidence we would likely conclude that the *we* was taken from another signal with lower amplitude and pasted in at 6.11 s.

Finally, in Figure 6.13 you can see that a silent period from another signal has been copied and pasted into this portion between 8.259 s and 8.726 s. There are obvious changes in the noise floor, visible in both the waveform and spectrogram.

In a further step, you would look for potential anomalies in the metadata of this file to see if the tampering left traces there. We will skip this step because you are unlikely to have access to software that enables such checks to be made.

To sum up: these three examples of potential deletion, word insertion, and intensity manipulation may – taken together – constitute evidence that the audio file has been tampered with.

7 Language analysis in the asylum procedure (LAAP)

Language analysis in the asylum procedure (LAAP) is a form of speaker profiling conducted by forensic speech and language experts in the context of asylum cases. This field is sometimes also referred to as LADO (Language analysis for the determination of origin), LOID (Linguistic origin identification), and LingID (linguistic identification). When asylum seekers do not possess papers to verify their identity, two types of evidence can help establish where they are from: (a) their body, particularly medical evidence that may be related to torture or injury; and (b) their story, especially their language practices, which can function as a 'linguistic passport'. Linguistic experts may therefore analyse the speech of a claimant for specific language, accent, dialect, grammatical, and vocabulary features – as is done in speaker profiling (Chapter 2). The authorities can then combine these pieces of evidence with the asylum seeker's knowledge of the area of origin to establish whether they really are from where they claim. This is a difficult process for many reasons, not least because languages rarely coincide with national borders. Normally, there are three types of cases in which LAAP is applied:

- An asylum seeker arrives in a destination country and there are doubts regarding their origin/place of socialisation.
- A rejected asylum applicant is due to be deported and authorities must determine which country to send them back to.
- A refugee is suspected of having lied about their origin, and an investigation is launched into whether their residence permit ought to be withdrawn.

Aim

In this chapter, we will first introduce you to the **legal context and history of LAAP**. We will then discuss **LAAP interview procedures**, how the linguistic analysis is conducted, and how a report is written. LAAP can be a very complex undertaking because the speakers involved may not be cooperative interviewees with straightforward biographies; this means that both the interview and the analysis processes can be quite difficult, and **it is not always easy to provide a confident conclusion** from the language analysis.

DOI: 10.4324/9780367616595-7

7.1   Asylum - Legal context and numbers

Millions of people are forced to flee their homes due to conflict or to escape persecution. Around one million displaced people currently arrive every year in the European Union alone. In many cases they arrive without documents such as passports to confirm their identity. Governments in the country of arrival therefore need to assess whether there is a right to asylum. This is invariably a politically sensitive issue.

Asylum seekers are people who have applied for refugee status and are in the process of being accepted or denied asylum. **Refugees** are generally people who have successful asylum claims and have received permission to stay in a destination country because they would be at risk if they were to return to their country of origin. Asylum seekers can claim asylum due to persecution on the grounds of religion, race, nationality, sexuality, membership in a particular social group, or political opinion. The UN Refugee Convention of 1951 outlines the rights of asylum seekers. There were 149 signatories of the convention, which is now considered a rule of customary international law. People can claim refugee status if they arrive in countries that have signed the Geneva Convention, can demonstrate that they have been persecuted or are in danger, and that their state of origin has not protected them. Ultimately, this may mean obtaining the right to immigrate to that country.

7.2   Language analysis in asylum cases

In asylum cases, the burden of proof lies with the asylum seeker. That is, the asylum seeker must demonstrate their right to claim asylum. People seeking asylum first have a hearing with the authorities in which they can state their motives, where they are fleeing from, and on what grounds. If they lack documentation or if inconsistencies arise, such as if the person says that they don't remember the route they took out of their home country, or if they change their reasons for leaving their country, this can raise suspicions. In these cases, some countries then ask the applicant to undertake another interview. This interview is recorded and can be analysed by language experts to assess whether or not the claimant really speaks the language or dialect that would be expected for someone who comes from the claimed country or region. The process of language analysis is what is referred to as LAAP. In a sense, LAAP is similar to a speaker profiling task. As we saw in Chapter 3, a person's speech and language provide clues to their regional and social background.

LAAP first appeared in the 1990s in Sweden and Switzerland because a growing number of asylum seekers lacked proof of identity, and authorities doubted many of the claims. Language analysis agencies were therefore established. Some governments now contract out LAAP interviews and analyses to external commercial firms and academics, while the Dutch, Swiss, and German authorities have their own LAAP bureaux (called OCILA, LINGUA, and BAMF, respectively). Based on analysis of the recorded interview, analysts write a report outlining their conclusions as to whether or not the applicant is making accurate claims about their place of socialisation (i.e., where they grew up), or whether it still remains unclear. Alongside other evidence, legal authorities take this report into account when deciding on the asylum claim.

In the Netherlands, LAAP is conducted in about 10% of all asylum cases (on average about 1,500–2,000 yearly out of a total of 18,000 claims). In 2008, 43% of these language analyses had a negative outcome, i.e., the LAAP report concluded that the asylum seeker's claimed origin did not match their actual origin. In Switzerland, LINGUA oversees between 600 and 1,000 interviews per year; in about half of the cases, reports conclude that an asylum seeker's claimed origin does not align with their actual origin. Acceptance rates are much higher in the UK, with around 95% of reports supporting the asylum seeker's claim (Hoskin 2022: 49).

After legal authorities have come to a decision, the asylum seeker can sometimes view the report. If the claim is rejected they may have the right to request that the report be assessed by an independent 'counter-expert'. This is possible in the Netherlands and the UK, for example. The 'counter-expert', who works on behalf of the asylum seeker, aims to provide independent evidence based on the linguistic data the authorities have analysed. They might also make new recordings with the claimant. Immigration judges only really take counter-evidence into consideration if the independent expert can claim with a high degree of confidence that there is doubt about the reliability of the original LAAP report. In 2014, significant errors in LAAP analyses occurred in the case of Somali asylum claims that the UK government had outsourced to the firm Språkab. A warning was therefore issued that reports from Språkab should be treated with caution. As a result the UK was prompted to move its LAAP contracts to a different company, Verified AB.

LAAP is still a relatively new practice and field of research. It is also controversial, receiving a number of critical reports both in academic publications and newspapers. In 2012, there were fewer than 100 academic publications on LAAP in existence; since then, research has increased to some degree. Much of the literature revolves around individual case studies, as well as discussions of how countries and agencies conduct LAAP differently and how LAAP evidence is treated in legal terms. There is a substantial gap in terms of independent studies that could lead to improvements in the field, such as large-scale studies on the role of native-speaker analysts (see section 7.5). There are also no universally agreed guidelines on how to best conduct a LAAP interview or how to most appropriately write up a report.

7.3   Interview and analysis

7.3.1   General guidelines for conducting LAAP interviews and analyses

At the time of writing, and as with processes surrounding earwitness evidence, LAAP lacks fixed, widely agreed on protocols on how interviews and analyses should be conducted. Relatively little documentation is available regarding how different countries and agencies handle LAAP, although a number of publications have outlined the processes different agencies use (e.g., Baltisberger & Hubbuch 2010, Cambier-Langeveld 2010, Prokofyeva 2018, Verrips 2010; a thorough critical review is provided by Hoskin 2022). In 2004, 19 linguists from the US, Europe, and Australia drew up general *Guidelines for the use of language analysis in relation to questions of national origin in refugee cases* (LNOG 2004). A few of the key points of these guidelines are summarised below:

(1) In principle, linguists play an advisory role in which they provide evidence for specific LAAP cases; governments then make decisions based on this evidence along with other pieces of evidence.
(2) Linguists should assess socialisation rather than attempting to determine national origin. Nationality is a political and administrative category that has no direct link with language. A person's socialisation – where and how they live – is what influences their language, not their passport. Take third-generation Italians living in Switzerland, for example: They speak like other Swiss people and perhaps don't even speak Italian any more, but may still hold an Italian passport.
(3) LAAP should be carried out by a qualified and trained linguist, i.e., someone who possesses up-to-date expertise in linguistic theory, methods, and approaches, has access to appropriate data collection tools, and conducts work according to generally accepted scientific standards. Native speakers of the asylum claimant's language should not conduct LAAP cases as experts, even if they have expertise in translation or interpreting.
(4) When doing LAAP, linguists should always be able to express degrees of certainty rather than offer a binary (yes or no) conclusion. Evidence provided by linguists should always be considered in conjunction with other evidence from the case.

These guidelines have since been endorsed by many international professional bodies concerned with language and linguistics (such as the International Association for Forensic and Legal Linguistics, IAFLL). However, the guidelines have also been criticised because the points listed do not contain protocols on how to conduct an interview, how to conduct a valid and thorough analysis, or how to formulate a report. Nor do they specify what kinds of linguistic expertise are required.

7.3.2 Conducting the interview

LAAP interviews are conducted in different ways depending on the agencies and countries involved. In the UK, asylum seekers are screened in an initial in-person interview. If an immigration officer is suspicious of an asylum seeker's claim of origin, perhaps due to inconsistencies that crop up during this initial hearing, they can request a LAAP interview for the purposes of establishing speaker origin. A letter is sent to the asylum seeker asking them for another interview (see Figure 7.1).

Home Office

UK Visas and Immigration
Asylum Team
Sandford House
41 Homer Road
Solihull
B91 3QJ

Tel 0121 XXX XXXX
Our Ref XXX
Date 06 January 2015
Syria-Arab Republic 01 January 1993

You are required to attend the above address on Thursday 15th January 2016 at 09:30. Travel tickets are enclosed to enable you to attend. The appointment will take approximately one hour.

I have arranged for you to talk on the telephone in your own language with a person who is an expert in your language and your country. This will give you the opportunity to demonstrate that you are from the country or area of that country as you have claimed. **You will not be asked your name, or your reasons for seeking asylum.**

The person you speak to will provide the Home Office with a written report, detailing their opinion on where you come from, which may be used to help decide your asylum claim. This information may be shared with other parts of the Home Office, or if you are a child, with the local authority responsible for your care (social services).

You do not have to talk to the language expert, but if you refuse to and cannot provide a reasonable explanation for refusing, it will be taken into account in considering whether you have assisted in establishing the facts of your claim, and could harm your application.

If you are unable to attend this appointment, please call 0121 XXX XXXX as soon as possible.

Yours sincerely,

Figure 7.1 Sample invitation letter for a LAAP interview (adapted from Patrick 2019).

The interview is contracted out to a specialist company (currently Verified AB, based in Sweden). The interview is conducted over a secure telephone line or video link, with an interpreter present. The interviewer asks open questions to prompt answers from the interviewee; analysts then assess the applicant's speech and language based on a recording of the interview.

In Switzerland, where LAAP is conducted by the government unit LINGUA, interviews are also conducted over a telephone line to shield the identities of both the interviewer and the interviewee. Interviews are conducted by either linguists or by native speakers of the claimant's language who have received specific training. There are no interpreters present, avoiding a back-and-forth exchange among the interviewer, the interpreter, and the applicant. Conducting interviews by telephone makes sense because many of the experts involved do not reside in Switzerland, and asylum seekers may be based in various locations across the country. In order to avoid bias during the interview, the interviewer has no access to the asylum files and does not know about the applicant's motivations for asylum. In the Swiss context, interviewers attempt to hold a natural conversation with the applicant to avoid an 'interrogation' style of interview. One of the main rules is that the interviewer should build trust and rapport with the interviewee and assume that everything the subject says is true. Interviewers

I	I'm not going to ask you about the reasons which, uhm, (..) the reasons which brought you to Switzerland. This conversation is recorded and afterwards you will be informed of the results. Can you hear and understand me?
C	I do, I do, but who are you?
I	Well, how shall I put this... (...) I am an independent expert.
C	And where are you?
I	It doesn't matter.
C	Mhm. Yes it does.
I	I am an independent expert, that should be enough for you.
C	Mhm. (.) Got it.
I	Let's start, ok?
C	What, what?
I	Let's start talking.
C	Ya, let's go.

Figure 7.2 Extract of LAAP interview. (Adapted from Hubbuch 2019)

attempt to show genuine interest in the applicant and what they say, and they try not to let the real purpose – and the consequences of a possible invalidation – affect the interview itself. Figure 7.2 shows a translated transcript of the early stages of an interview at LINGUA, where the interviewer (I) introduces himself to the claimant (C). The example illustrates how awkward such a conversation can be, although in this case it did result in a successful interview.

On average, the duration of an interview at LINGUA is between 45 and 90 minutes. To further supplement the conversational data they gather, interviewers at LINGUA may also use word lists or picture tasks to elicit specific linguistic material. The content of the interview involves topics considered relevant to daily life as well as conversations about the interviewee's childhood, culture, education, family background, language contact history, religion, and employment history. Interviewers may also ask about currency denominations or political developments in the region. All this information helps the interviewer understand the socialisation of the asylum seeker. The experts then scrutinise the recording and provide an opinion about the claimant's place of socialisation based on their speech and language patterns and knowledge of the claimed area of origin.

7.3.3 Linguistic analysis and report writing

After the interview, analysts write a report expressing their conclusions with regard to a claimant's origin. A LAAP report includes some detail of the applicant's speech patterns (e.g., phonetics, phonology, lexicon, syntax, vocabulary, etc.) as well as a comprehensive assessment of how accurately and broadly they elaborated on details about their place of socialisation.

For cases handled in the UK, reports generally follow these core tenets:

- The report should cite the literature that analysts consulted and should describe the general tools (e.g., transcriptions, acoustic analysis) used.
- The report should detail who was present during the interview and who conducted the analysis. The LAAP qualifications of the analysts should be listed. (Note: In other countries and agencies this is handled differently, with this information listed in separate documents.)
- The analyst should state openly if they were unsure about certain facts (perhaps because the analysis had to be conducted under time pressure), given that this report forms a core basis for the legal decision of whether to grant asylum.
- The report should be written for non-linguists, so the language cannot be too technical; if some technical detail is necessary, terms should be explained.

Unfortunately, not all agencies and countries adhere to these core tenets of report writing. In some reports, it can be unclear exactly how the parties involved conducted the interview and arrived at their conclusions. Some analysts report their conclusions in *ad hoc* ways, rather than using a standard scale. Steps are being taken to develop an internationally standardised set of guidelines for forensic reports of all kinds (using the verbal likelihood ratio framework discussed in Chapter 4, see Figure 4.7), and LAAP reports should eventually conform to these standards. The establishment as standard of peer review or some other kind of validation process could also enhance the quality of reports. There is a general drive towards transparency and reproducibility in forensic phonetics and linguistics today. However, in practice, various data protection laws constrain the principles of reproducibility when working in immigration. Sending audio recordings to another analyst to validate results, for example, raises a number of data protection issues, especially if the analyst is based in another jurisdiction. Chapter 13 outlines wider considerations in being a language expert, many of which apply here, and report writing considerations.

7.3.4 Case studies

Let us take a closer look at two case studies to illustrate how the findings of LAAP can inform an asylum tribunal. The first case concerns an asylum seeker who had arrived in the UK and claimed to be from Daraa, a city in southern Syria (Matras 2018). The man claimed to have left Daraa at age 16 (his age at the time of analysis is not specified). His main language was clearly Arabic, but there were questions over which variety. His speech undeniably showed some mixture of Syrian and Egyptian features. His initial claim for asylum was rejected after a language analysis, which concluded that there were too many inconsistencies given what would be expected of a Syrian Arabic speaker from Daraa. However, he subsequently won an appeal on the basis of an alternative language analysis. The appeal report attributed the Egyptian features to the man's exposure to urban varieties, where Egyptian features permeate other regional dialects. Figure 7.3 compares some features of the claimant's speech with known samples from Syria and Egypt.

English phrase	Applicant	Syria (Daraa)	Egypt (Cairo)
here	[hoːn]	/hoːn/	/henaː/
don't go	[laː truħ]	/laː truħ/	/maː tiruħ/
two sons and a daughter	[waladeːn uː binit]	/waladeːn uː binit/	/waladiːn wa bint/
like this	[heːk] ~ [kida]	/heːk/	/kida/
teacher (f.)	[mudarrísa]	/mudárrisa/	/mudarrísa/

Figure 7.3 Comparison of asylum claimant's speech against Syrian and Egyptian norms (adapted from Matras 2018, using standard IPA notation). Note that the key difference in respect of 'teacher' is word stress, indicated by the accent. The Syrian version was added by the authors.

English gloss	French	Applicant	Sango
head	tête	[sətok]	/li/
fish	poisson	[gwɛk]	/susu/
I	je	[ɲi]	/mbi/
dog	chien	[gwi]	/mbo/

Figure 7.4 Word production by asylum applicant claiming to speak Sango. (From Cambier-Langeveld 2018)

The second case concerns an applicant who claimed to come from the Central African Republic (Cambier-Langeveld 2018). The applicant claimed to speak Sango, Gbaya, and French. There were doubts about the claim, and so the analysts tested his competence in Sango and Gbaya. He was asked to translate (from French) some simple words and to speak spontaneously. It quickly became apparent that he could not speak fluently in those languages. Moreover, his translations did not match wordlists in published sources. Some examples are shown in Figure 7.4.

These observations provided strong evidence against the claim that he was from the Central African Republic. The question then remained: where was he really from? The analysts checked his word productions and established that the language was in fact Moghomo, spoken in Cameroon.

7.4 Issues involved in analysing speech patterns of asylum seekers

Intuitively, figuring out where someone is from based on their speech patterns seems plausible and perhaps even easy to do. (Have you tried out *The New York Times* quiz that guesses your dialect of English? If not, Google it.) We do this naturally all the time: When we meet someone for the first time, we often talk about where they are from, perhaps prompted by clues found in their accents. It makes sense to link accent and origin because everyone's speech is shaped by their biographical history. The way someone speaks can offer powerful insights to their familial and geographic background because language acquisition and socialisation happens within the family and the immediate speech community. Plenty of linguistic literature shows how indexical properties of a speaker's identity, such as geographical origin, are encoded in language (for discussion of linguistic aspects see Chapter 11).

However, it is often very difficult to assess reliably where someone may have been socialised beyond just rough estimates. There are many factors that affect the way someone talks – and being put on the spot in a formal, and possibly intimidating, asylum interview with government officials may also affect someone's speech patterns! This is even more likely if that speaker has not had a positive experience with those in authority, a likely reality for many seeking asylum (for more on power imbalances see Chapter 10). Several linguists have been critical of LAAP, to the point where they question whether it is really fit for purpose at all. We outline some of these criticisms in this section. Specifically, certain confounding factors may hinder LAAP, such as:

- Applicants having multilingual and highly mobile backgrounds (section 7.4.1).
- Applicants – and people in general – changing the way they speak over their lifetimes (section 7.4.2).
- Applicants intentionally (or unintentionally) shifting the way they speak during an interview (section 7.4.3).
- Applicants speaking an under-studied language or variety (section 7.4.4).

7.4.1 Applicants being multilingual and mobile

The assumption that speech carries diagnostic information about geographical origin applies particularly to small, non-mobile populations. For example, if an asylum seeker claims to be from Chechnya, experts might with some confidence assume that the person should probably be able to speak Chechen, the main language spoken in the small, quite ethnically homogeneous Chechen Republic. Somebody who claims to be from Chechnya but in fact is not may only be able to produce a few words of Chechen. In cases such as these, linguistic experts can make relatively straightforward decisions about asylum cases. However, asylum seekers often come from complex multilingual backgrounds. They may mix language codes in their everyday speech, or may come from diglossic societies in which a 'low' variety is spoken in familiar contexts and a (linguistically very different) 'high' variety is spoken in official settings – as exemplified by Arabic-speaking societies. You might experience elements of this in your own life too: for example, you (or those around you) might consciously or subconsciously switch between using more dialectal speech in informal situations, and more standard speech in formal ones. This is called **style-shifting**, or **accommodation** when we adapt our speech to match that of an interlocutor.

Further, linguistic boundaries very rarely align neatly with political boundaries. Languages may not be spoken uniformly within a nation. For instance, the variety of German spoken in Vorarlberg, a region of Austria on the border with Switzerland, is structurally and phonetically very similar to adjacent Swiss German dialects. There is also the process of natural language change over time, which renders any understanding of sociolinguistic patterning ephemeral. Compare, for example, speakers of Standard English in present day England with speakers in old newsreels or early movies. Fine-grained localisation of a speaker can be especially difficult in places with homogeneous standard dialects or supra-regional varieties rather than distinct, salient local dialects. Further, asylum seekers typically come from mobile populations. Asylum seekers may have resided in camps for long periods of time, which may have shaped their dialects or accents in unpredictable ways (see section 7.4.2). All these factors complicate both making precise claims of linguistic origin and finding the right experts (and interpreters) for the linguistic analysis.

7.4.2 Applicants changing the way they speak over time

A further challenge for LAAP is language attrition. **Attrition** refers to the reduction or even loss of native speaker competence when someone resides for an extended period of time in a place where the relevant language, often their L1, is not spoken. An example of a high-profile case that garnered lots of media coverage was that of the American soldier Bowe Bergdahl. He was released by the Taliban in Afghanistan in May 2014 after being held in captivity for five years. His family reported that when he came home he had trouble speaking English. This was picked up by the media with incredulity, the assumption being that native speakers do not simply 'forget' their first language, particularly not after only five years of being away. Many people thought this apparent loss of a language was the hallmark of a traitor. Linguists who spoke to the media on this case predicted that Bergdahl's English would re-emerge quickly, and commented that such alleged change in access to one's L1 can happen even after a short period abroad. Some British footballers and football managers have developed a slight foreign accent after living and working abroad, at least in certain circumstances such as addressing interviewers whose first language is not English. Joey Barton and Steve McLaren, for example, were widely ridiculed as a result by those who did not understand this process.

Attrition can sometimes be a major challenge for LAAP. How can you assess someone's origin if language is so malleable over time? A substantial body of literature shows that proficiency in an L1 is not entirely stable over time, at least for some people. All levels of language can be affected: studies of L1 attrition have documented reductions in vocabulary, rising numbers of disfluencies and hesitations, and instability in morphosyntactic phenomena such as case marking. Taken together, this means that **attriters** (speakers experiencing attrition) are often perceived as less native-like, which has potentially significant consequences for LAAP.

One study explored how a native listener group of Germans rated speakers with varying backgrounds speaking in German (Hopp & Schmid 2013). One group, the control, comprised 20 monolingual German speakers. Another group comprised L1 attriters, originally L1 Germans who had lived in either the Netherlands or Anglophone Canada for at least nine years. The final group comprised English or Dutch L1 speakers who had lived in Germany for at least three years. The native German listeners rated these three groups in terms of 'foreign accentedness' – that is, how native the speakers sounded – on a scale from 1 ('this speaker is definitely a native speaker of German') to 6 ('the speaker is definitely a non-native speaker of German'). Scores 1–3 could thus be associated with 'native-sounding' speakers, and scores 4–6 with 'non-native-sounding' speakers. Overall the response patterns were predictable: the L1 group received the lowest scores, the L2 speakers the highest, and the attriters fell in between. However, there were also several interesting nuances to this general pattern. First, even some of the native speakers were not perceived as fully native, although none of them was perceived as non-native (>4 rating). The L1 attriters clustered toward the native end of the scale, but in some cases were perceived as non-native (>4 rating). The same went for the L2 group: some learners of German passed as natives, while others were clearly judged as non-native.

What this study clearly shows is that nativeness judgements are not categorical, but gradient – i.e., on a continuum. It also shows that people are not all the same: people with similar language histories produce language differently, such that some are rated native-like and others not. This once again underscores the difficult task LAAP experts are confronted with. The fact that quite a few L1 natives who had left their home country were no longer perceived as native speakers of the L1 is critically relevant for LAAP. Asylum seekers often have a history of mobility and may have resided outside of their home country for years before the LAAP interview. Since language attrition can be a significant factor affecting the determination of a person's area of socialisation, the language data collected during the interview must be viewed against the backdrop of the biographical background of the claimant. This means that the analyst must also consider how long a subject has been absent from their country, and where and how they have been living since leaving.

This effect of being perceived as non-native is even more pronounced when we look at the language of emigrant children. In another study, young adults who had been born in Korea but were adopted by French parents when they were between three and nine years old were found to no longer be able to pick out Korean from a set of different languages by ear – their first language had apparently been wiped from their brains, to put it bluntly (Pallier et al. 2003). Other studies have also shown that international adoptees can lose their L1 extremely rapidly, even within the space of months or weeks. To give a practical example, consider the case of a boy who arrived in the Netherlands from Angola at age nine (Schmid 2019). He was fostered by a Dutch family and learned Dutch, but then forgot the Portuguese he had learned as child. At age 17 the authorities attempted to extradite him. The family appealed, one of their grounds being that it would be unethical to deport him to a country where he could not speak the language. However, the authorities took the view that it was not possible that he could have forgotten his language.

Compounding the complexity of natural language attrition is the fact that asylum seekers may have experienced trauma that can affect their L1 competence. There is substantial evidence that emotional factors play a role when it comes to memory formation and recall. This directly impacts somebody's competence in an L1, which may be associated with traumatising episodes. Suppressing these episodes in memory very often also means not wanting to use or maintain the language associated with these episodes. This can create the impression that an applicant may not be a native speaker of their L1 because 'they can't speak the language' – when, in fact, they may have some sort of mental block on speaking the language due to its links with trauma. It is thus crucial that immigration authorities are aware of research findings such as those discussed in this section so that safeguards can be put in place, both to protect the asylum seeker from further trauma and to ensure validity in the findings.

A further complication for LAAP, however, is that some false claimants construct a story to explain why they cannot speak the expected language for their claimed community. Discrepant findings are attributed to migration, influence of TV and radio, and exposure to other languages or dialects in refugee camps or asylum housing. In one case, for example, a woman claimed to be a monolingual speaker of Kurmanji from Syria. A LAAP analysis concluded that her Kurmanji showed non-native characteristics, and thus she could not establish that she came from Syria. She took her case to appeal, at which stage a new analysis was conducted. The analyst agreed that she displayed a foreign accent, but attributed her unexpected features to the possibility she might have spoken another language in childhood. This claim was not made at the time of the original asylum claim, and could have been constructed after the claim was rejected.

Another example illustrates how difficult LAAP can be in the context of a complex life story (whether true or not). This case is similar to the one mentioned earlier in the case studies (see Figure 7.3 and associated text). A 17-year-old Arabic-speaking asylum seeker claimed to have fled from Syria, but language analysis concluded he came from Egypt rather than Syria. The claimant attributed the Egyptian features of his dialect to the fact he had lived for two years in Egypt after leaving Syria at age 13, and had later shared a flat with an Egyptian. It is very difficult for linguists to establish the likelihood that language can change in this way in the apparent circumstances, not least because there is so much individual variation in how attrition and new language/dialect learning takes place. It would be impossible to establish expected norms for such unique contexts via scientific research. For practical and ethical reasons we could not study a group of Syrian teenagers exposed to Egyptian Arabic in an immersive context to see what happens to their language, in order to compare a given asylum case to patterns established through research. Any language analysis in such a case is dependent on the subjective opinion of the analyst, taking into account the claimed circumstances.

7.4.3 Applicants changing their language or speaking style during the interview

The format and formality of the interview themselves present an obstacle to obtaining vernacular (natural, spontaneous) speech. Essentially, applicants find themselves in a very peculiar situation – speaking to an invisible and anonymous interlocutor via a telephone, where they might be asked to speak a rare language or stigmatised dialect out of its usual context (this is referred to as **deterritorialised** language). This situation can lead applicants to change their language, dialect, or speaking style during the interview. They may select what they believe is the language or variety – for example, English or Dutch – that gives them the greatest chances of obtaining asylum. They may also intentionally accommodate their speech patterns to the person conducting the interview. The problem for the linguist is, of course, that this type of material may yield less useful diagnostic cues to the applicant's place of socialisation. In such cases – at the Swiss agency LINGUA, at least – the experts or interviewers conducting the interview explicitly ask the applicant to speak the variety common among their family and peers.

Note, too, that even identifying the relevant language might not be straightforward. If asked 'what is your language?', many people might initially answer with the official language of their country (e.g., Chinese or Bengali). However, the official language might not be the language someone actually speaks. In some societies different languages are classified as dialects and not referred to as 'languages' by their speakers. Dialects are often treated as degenerate or improper forms of a language, not worthy of study and not suitable for use in formal contexts. Some languages have multiple names, such as Uyghur/Turki. Furthermore, use of a particular language might itself have been one reason why someone was persecuted. For example, Welsh and Gaelic were proscribed (forbidden by law) in Great Britain at different times in the past, and people could be punished if they used those languages. Similar histories apply to many other languages, including Basque, Catalan, and Galician in Franco-era Spain, and Tamil in Sri Lanka in the second half of the twentieth century. Asylum seekers might therefore not be comfortable in acknowledging they speak a certain language, even though that fact is crucial to their asylum claim.

7.4.4 Applicants speaking an under-studied language or variety

Another problem is that some of the languages and dialects spoken by asylum seekers are under-studied and/or may not be well-known or spoken by many experts. In the UK, for example, many applicants come from Afghanistan, Burundi, Ethiopia, Eritrea, Iran, Kuwait, Liberia, Palestine, Rwanda, Sierra Leone, Somalia, and Sri Lanka, among other countries. Many of the languages spoken in these regions have been well-studied. There are cases, though, where perhaps only one linguistic expert in the world has done work on a particular variety. For example, Bajuni islanders in Somalia speak a specific variety of Somali that is on the verge of dying out. Documentation on the language might also now be very old. It is difficult for linguists to conduct up-to-date fieldwork on languages that are located in troubled areas of the world. A compounding issue is that that the communities of these speakers might also be very small. This is one reason why agencies tend to maintain interviewer anonymity.

7.5   Who should do the linguistic analysis: Linguists vs. native speaker experts

There has been extensive debate regarding who should be involved in the analysis of the LAAP interview. The main question is whether, aside from linguists, native speaker experts should be present and active in the analysis process. One camp of researchers and practitioners has been in favour of this approach, but another camp has been critical of such practice. Linguists in the latter camp claim that native speakers lack the training and the tools to perform such analyses (e.g., they might not know about language attrition or how and why language varies), do not know the relevant literature, and do not know how to write a report or draw linguistic conclusions. Some countries even require specific qualifications (e.g., a degree in linguistics) in order to conduct a LAAP analysis, so legally, native speaker analysts may be completely excluded in such cases. The pro-native speaker camp uses arguments such as the following in favour of including native speaker experts:

(a) Studies such as Foulkes & Wilson (2011) and Hoskin (2022), among others, have shown that native speakers are on average better at identifying speakers of their language by regional origin than trained linguists who are not native speakers of the language. Research has shown a link between accuracy of dialect identification and familiarity with that dialect. Native speakers also typically give more confident responses than non-natives (though remember from Chapter 5 on earwitness evidence that confidence is not necessarily a good predictor of accuracy).
(b) Native speakers are in many cases able to justify their decisions with relatively precise linguistic terminology, despite not being trained in linguistics. They can also sometimes demonstrate awareness of variation related to regional or social factors.
(c) Probably most importantly: LAAP is not just about analysing language, but also about *judging* language. Keep in mind that applicants are not always 100% cooperative: they may fake an accent, rehearse interview answers in a language other than their L1, present a second language as their first language, etc. Native speakers assisting in LAAP are often more attuned to these kinds of anomalies than linguists are, despite a lack of formal linguistic training.

In 2009, the International Association for Forensic Phonetics and Acoustics (IAFPA) issued a statement to recognise that trained native speakers do potentially have a role to play in LAAP analyses as long as they work under the guidance and supervision of trained linguists. Many linguists therefore do consult native speaker experts (sometimes also called 'informants'), but do not let them do the actual analysis. From a practical standpoint, there are several ways native speakers can be included in LAAP:

1. The linguist can perform the actual analysis, but in close consultation with the native speaker.
2. A trained native speaker can do the analysis, but under the close supervision of the linguist.
3. The trained linguist could also be a native speaker of the language in question – though this type of linguist might be very hard to find.
4. A native speaker could undertake training in linguistics.

Many researchers who support the use of native speaker consultants propose that the consultants should undergo testing to verify their ability to identify specific varieties and draw correct conclusions regarding a person's origins based on linguistic data. Countries handle the inclusion of native speaker experts very differently: In the Netherlands, for example, native speaker analysts are used by the government bureau. In Switzerland, native speakers are often present during interviews in a consultative capacity, but analyses are done entirely by linguists. Ultimately, combining the two perspectives in a reasonable balance probably renders the most comprehensive LAAP analysis.

7.6   Summary and outlook

Having established the pros and cons of whether to include native speakers in LAAP cases, you may also wonder about the specific skills that experts should possess in order to conduct these kinds of interviews. Experts should have thorough training in practical linguistic analysis, particularly sociolinguistics and phonetics. Most importantly, analysts should be aware of how and why language varies – not only geographically and socially, but also with respect to situational constraints (for instance, the unique situation that applicants find themselves in during a high-stakes interview). Experts need to know how to be objective and open to finding evidence which may contradict their original hypotheses (for more discussion on the duties of being an expert, see Chapter 13). In addition to these technical skills, they should also be good interviewers if they are to conduct LAAP interviews themselves (this is not always simple or straightforward, for more on interviewing practices see Chapter 10). We should end by commenting that, despite the difficulties of performing LAAP, the majority of cases are reported to be straightforward and uncontroversial (Hubbuch 2019).

LAAP is a relatively new field, and a number of promising lines of research have emerged in recent years. Experiments have compared the performance of linguists and untrained native speakers in classifying accents, and others have assessed how good different groups are at spotting whether speakers are genuine or fake. Professional LAAP agencies have started to engage in collaborative research, making some cases available for detailed scrutiny. Such work has, for example, revealed issues in how interviews are structured and why interviewers' questions sometimes fail to elicit the desired response. Work is also underway to examine the role of interpreters in both interviews and tribunals. Finally, some researchers are trying to develop new tests that could be used alongside the LAAP interview procedure. For example, speech technology might be adapted to assist with LAAP. Some programs are available that can classify languages and accents of a given language with high accuracy. The German government has apparently started to trial the use of such tools.

Conclusions

In this chapter we have given an overview of when LAAP is used, how an interview is conducted, and how analyses are performed. LAAP is the analysis of an asylum seeker's language to determine their origin in cases where they have little evidence to offer but their linguistic 'proof', so to speak. It is the exception, and not the rule, to perform LAAP in asylum cases. LAAP is a complex task because asylum seekers are sometimes unco-operative with the investigation and often have complex migratory backgrounds, making pinpointing their origin very difficult. Other factors may also impinge on the determin-ation of origin, such as language attrition and lack of recent documentation about relevant languages. Finally, one main debate in the field is whether only linguists or also native speaker experts should be involved in the analysis.

Further reading

For a more detailed overview of LAAP:

Wilson, K., & Foulkes, P. (2014). Borders, variation, and identity: Language ana-lysis for the determination of origin (LADO). In D. Watt & C. Llamas (eds.), *Language, Borders and Identity*. Edinburgh University Press, pp. 218–229.

For studies and commentary on LAAP:

Patrick, P. L., Schmid, M. S., & Zwaan, K. (eds.) (2019). *Language Analysis for the Determination of Origin: Current Perspectives and New Directions*. Springer.

For an introduction to language attrition:

Schmid, M. (2011). *Language Attrition*. Cambridge University Press.

For those interested in decisions relating to asylum appeals, UK decisions on appeals to the Upper Tribunal from the can be found online.

For a recent survey of practices in the European Union:

EUAA [European Union Agency for Asylum] (2022). *Study on Language Assessment for Determination of Origin*. Publications Office of the European Union.

References

Baltisberger, E., & Hubbuch, P. (2010). LADO with specialized linguists – The development of LINGUA's working method. In K. Zwaan, M. Verrips, & P. Muysken (eds.), *Language and Origin – The Role of Language in European Asylum Procedures: Linguistic and Legal Perspectives*. Wolf Legal Publishers, pp. 9–19.

Cambier-Langeveld, T. (2010). The role of linguists and native speakers in language analysis for the determination of speaker origin. *International Journal of Speech, Language & the Law*, 17(1): 67–93.

Cambier-Langeveld, T. (2018). Language analysis in the asylum procedure: Consider the context. In I. M. Nick (ed.), *Forensic Linguistics: Asylumseekers, Refugees and Immigrants*. Vernon Press, pp. 1–21.

Foulkes, P., & Wilson, K. (2011). Language analysis for the determination of origin: an empirical study. *Proceedings of the 17th ICPhS*, Hong Kong, pp. 691–694.

Hopp, H., & Schmid, M. (2013). Perceived foreign accent in first language attrition and second language acquisition: The impact of age of acquisition and bilingualism. *Applied Psycholinguistics*, 34(2): 361–394.

Hoskin, J. (2022). *Shifting the Burden: Towards New Tests for Language Analysis in the Asylum Procedure*. PhD thesis, University of York.

Hubbuch, P. (2019). "We Only Want to Talk…": Lingua interviews for Linguistic Analyses for the Determination of Origin (LADO). In P. Patrick, M. Schmid, & K. Zwaan (eds.) *Language Analysis for the Determination of Origin*. Springer, pp. 41–59.

LNOG (Language and National Origin Group) (2004). Guidelines for the use of language analysis in relation to questions of national origin in refugee cases. *International Journal of Speech, Language and the Law*, 11(2): 261–266.

Matras, Y. (2018). Duly verified? Language analysis in UK asylum applications of Syrian refugees. *International Journal of Speech, Language and the Law*, 25(1): 53–78

Pallier, C., Dehaene, S., Poline, J.-B., LeBihan, D., Argenti, A.-M., Dupoux, E., & Mehler, J. (2003). Brain imaging of language plasticity in adopted adults: Can a second language replace the first? *Cerebral Cortex*, 13(2): 155–161.

Patrick, P. L. (2019). Language analysis for determination of origin (LADO) in Arabic-dominant settings. In E. Al-Wer & U. Horesh (eds.), *The Routledge Handbook of Arabic Sociolinguistics*. Routledge, pp. 314–330

Prokofyeva, T. (2018). Linguistic origin identification in focus: theory and practice in LOID. In I. M. Nick (ed.), *Forensic Linguistics: Asylum-seekers, Refugees and Immigrants*. Vernon Press, pp. 41–55.

Schmid, M. S. (2019). Language attrition as a problem for LADO. In P. Patrick, M. Schmid, & K. Zwaan (eds.), *Language Analysis for the Determination of Origin*. Springer, pp. 155–165.

Verrips, M. (2010). Language analysis and contra-expertise in the Dutch asylum procedure. *International Journal of Speech, Language and the Law*, 17(2): 279–294.

Activity section

Activity 7A – Spotting 'authenticity'

For obvious ethical reasons it is not possible to give you an actual LAAP interview to analyse. Instead, you will conduct a small study that explores the role of native listeners when it comes to determining whether or not someone is an 'authentic' speaker of a variety. Given that you'll be conducting a small study, there is only one exercise for this chapter. Your study will be loosely based on the experiment conducted by Foulkes & Wilson (2011) (see 'Further reading').

Proceed as follows:

(1) Prepare a short reading passage of 5–10 sentences (you can take a passage from an online source).

(2) Record two native speakers of a particular dialect (here we'll call it 'dialect X') reading that passage aloud.

(3) Record two people who are not native speakers of dialect X reading the same passage aloud. Instruct them to try to imitate dialect X instead of speaking in their own dialect.

(4) Find at least six listeners to participate in the experiment: Half should be native listeners of dialect X, while half should be non-native listeners of dialect X. Make sure that none of the listeners know the speakers who provided the samples.

(5) Play the samples one by one to your listeners. After each sample, ask them whether they think the sample they heard was produced by a native speaker of dialect X or a non-native speaker of dialect X. After each response, code the answers as 0 or 1 (0 = not a native speaker, 1 = native speaker). For each rating, the listener should also tell you how certain they are about their response (1 = uncertain, 2 = not sure, 3 = certain).

(6) Count the hits (target present, identified correctly), correct rejections (target absent, rejected correctly), misses (target present, missed), and false alarms (target absent, identified incorrectly) for your three native listeners and three non-native listeners. Also study the degree of certainty the listeners indicated. Put your findings in a table such as the one shown in the answer section, for example in Excel. What patterns did you find when tallying up hits, misses, false alarms, and certainty levels? What do you make of these findings?

Table 7.1 Sample data for activity 7A

		Speaker								
		1 (non-native)		2 (non-native)		3 (native)		4 (native)	
Listener	Type	Response	Confidence	Response	Confidence	Response	Confidence	Response	Confidence
1	native	0, cr	2	0, cr	3	0, ms	2	1, hit	3
2	native	0, cr	1	0, cr	3	1, hit	3	1, hit	2
3	native	0, cr	2	1, fa	2	1, hit	3	1, hit	2
4	non-native	1, fa	1	1, fa	1	1, hit	3	0, ms	1
5	non-native	1, fa	2	1, fa	1	0, ms	2	1, hit	3
6	non-native	0, cr	2	0, cr	1	1, hit	1	0, ms	3

Answer 7A

Table 7.1 shows what your data may look like (based on fictitious data) (cr = correct rejection, fa = false alarm, hit = hit, ms = miss):

Below is a summary of the hits, correct rejections, misses, and false alarms from the native listeners and the non-native listeners:

- Native: Out of 12 ratings in total – 5 hits, 5 correct rejections, 1 miss, 1 false alarm
- Non-native: Out of 12 ratings in total – 3 hits, 2 correct rejections, 3 misses, 4 false alarms

For the native listeners, then, 10/12 samples were identified or rejected correctly, a rate of 83%. Since 50% is chance level (given that listeners took part in a binary forced-choice experiment), native listeners were able to perform the task above chance. For non-native listeners, 5/12 samples were identified or rejected correctly, i.e., 42% – below chance.

In terms of rating confidence, our (fictitious) data shows the following patterns:

- Native: 28 out of 36 points in total (12 stimuli × 3 confidence points maximum)
- Non-native: 21 out of 36 points in total

Native listeners were more confident in their ratings than non-native listeners in this mock data. You may find similar results suggesting that native listeners are better at correctly identifying whether someone is an authentic speaker than non-native listeners.

Overall, native listeners in this mock dataset exhibited a higher identification rate (correctly identifying a speaker as authentic or correctly rejecting a speaker who was imitating), a lower miss rate (thinking that an authentic speaker was an imitator), and a lower false alarm rate (thinking that an imitator was an authentic speaker). These findings could be interpreted as follows. First, they show that native listeners may be better at identifying their peers than non-native listeners are. Second, these findings show that even native listeners make errors in identifying their peers (error rate of 17%). Finally, they show that native listeners tend to be more certain in their answers than non-native listeners.

Note that the results of the study you conduct may show very different patterns – and that's okay! This is a very small-scale study; when scholars conduct such experiments they would typically test at least 20 listeners per group (i.e., 20 native and 20 non-native listeners of dialect X).

8 Grounding theory – Introduction to linguistic analysis

The first section of this book examined forensic phonetics, the study of the sounds and sound systems of communication in a forensic context. This second section focuses on forensic linguistics, and examines language use in written and spoken discourse across the wider forensic context. Forensic linguistics and forensic phonetics are not always considered separate fields. In the United States, for instance, if you pursue a forensic linguistics degree, your studies will include forensic phonetic theory and scholarship as well. Further, given the nature of the data there is the potential for forensic linguists and forensic phoneticians to work closely with each other, both on casework and research.

This chapter takes a closer look at the building blocks of forensic linguistic work and how we approach forensic linguistic analysis. It sets out some of the core linguistic theories upon which forensic linguistic work is grounded. The following chapters look at some of the core areas of forensic linguistics in more depth, developing and applying some of the theories introduced in the latter half of this chapter, as well as discussing theories and approaches that are more specific to each of the topics. Chapter 9 looks at language and meaning, Chapter 10 looks at language in the wider judicial process, Chapters 11 and 12 both focus on authorship analysis, with the first delving into profiling and the latter focusing on comparative authorship analysis.

Aims

This chapter **introduces the field of forensic linguistics**, what it is, how it evolved, and how it can be of benefit in legal cases. It outlines the **core theories of linguistics** that underpin forensic linguistic approaches to analysing data. The chapter also explores a number of **forensic linguistic cases** that demonstrate the benefits of forensic linguistics to the judicial system.

DOI: 10.4324/9780367616595-8

8.1   What is forensic linguistics?

As a starting point, it is worth considering what we mean by *forensic linguistics*. It has been defined in a variety of ways, but one common element is that it is linguistic knowledge, theory, or methodologies applied to contexts that could be considered forensic. Hence, it is a form of applied linguistics. Here *linguistics* is the scientific study of language, as opposed to the learning or speaking of multiple languages.

Linguistics can be applied to any area in which there is language or communication (for some examples see Figure 8.1). The most frequent examples of linguistic knowledge being used in a forensic context are when linguists have helped in criminal investigations, or served as expert witnesses in court cases (of which there are numerous examples over the following chapters). It is also worth noting that there is a group of crimes that can be categorised as **language crimes**, when the communicative act is itself the criminal act (e.g., threats, verbal abuse, ransom notes, etc.).

There are three main pillars to forensic linguistics: casework, training (or language awareness), and research (see Figure 8.1). These pillars all interact and support each other; one cannot exist without the others. The following chapters will introduce you to a range of cases, as well as the relevant research that has informed the work, or evolved because of it. It is not possible (nor would it be wise) to fully isolate casework from research, due to the constantly evolving nature of language. Further, in order to undertake casework, other people need to see the benefit of linguistic analysis and have an awareness of what it can bring. Equally, research needs to be informed by the wider forensic and legal contexts and an awareness of what is needed in casework situations.

Because forensic linguistics is an applied approach to linguistics, it incorporates lots of different research areas, including sociolinguistics, corpus linguistics,

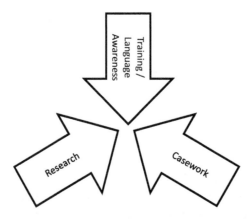

Figure 8.1 Pillars of forensic linguistics.

discourse analysis, and psychology. Therefore, by its nature, forensic linguistics is an interdisciplinary field. It would be far beyond the scope of this book to give an in-depth introduction to all of these fields, as well as how they can be applied in forensic linguistic settings; instead, the following chapters focus on potential applications, and highlight the relevant methodologies. However, it should be emphasised that further learning in these specific areas is encouraged, and in fact necessary, to undertake research and analysis using the methods. Where possible and relevant, we will highlight potential future resources that might aid such continuation of learning, and we would highly encourage you to view this book as a first step towards deepening your understanding of these areas.

Forensic linguistics is the application of linguistic knowledge in a forensic context. A forensic context is anything that involves the law, such as law enforcement, legal settings, and criminal (or civil) investigations.

8.2   History of forensic linguistics

We can see instances of forensic linguistics (though not called this) as far back as biblical texts and before (see Boucher & Perkins 2020, and Picornell & Perkins 2022). In the United States, forensic linguistics as a tool can be traced back to 1920s New York. In 1927, a family received a ransom note from kidnappers demanding money for the return of their daughter. However, the kidnappers addressed the ransom note to the child's uncle, Duncan McLure. Note the spelling of his name; the rest of the family spelled their name McClure, and everyone knew them as such. Police found it odd that the kidnappers would know the nuanced difference in spelling of Duncan McLure's name, and therefore confronted him about it. McLure later confessed to writing the ransom note.

Forensic linguistic applications in the US truly gained momentum in 1963 with the case of Ernesto Miranda, and an investigation into whether he was aware of his rights to an attorney before he made a confession. This case led to the creation of the Miranda Rights, i.e., the standard text read by the police to criminal suspects which advises them of their rights (i.e., *you have the right to remain silent...*). The Miranda case also illustrated the utility of using forensic linguistics on witness questioning rather than police statements (see e.g., McMenamin 2022). Subsequent analyses in the United States then expanded to the legal world of trademarks. For example, the restaurant chain McDonald's asserted its legal claim to the *Mc-* prefix, and sued Quality Inns International for their attempt at opening a chain of hotels called *McSleep* (McDonald's won that case, by the way; *Quality Inns International, Inc. v. McDonald's Corp.*, 695 F. Supp. 198 (D. Md. 1988)).

The term *forensic linguistics* is usually credited as first appearing in 1968 when a linguistics professor at the University of Gothenburg, Jan Svartvik, used it to retroactively investigate a case from England that had taken place in the 1940s. Svartvik was approached by a committee seeking to clear the name of Timothy John Evans, who was suspected of murdering his wife and baby. In 1949, Evans provided statements to the police in London. Based on these statements, Evans was subsequently tried and executed for the crimes. However, nearly 20 years later, Svarvtik found that there were two very different **registers**, or varieties of language that differ based on the interaction or situation, in the statements allegedly provided by Evans. A number of **stylistic** features – as in a person's preference for certain punctuation, spelling, and other flourishes in language – in these statements differed from known writings by Evans and did not match language that would be expected of him, especially given that the prison doctor determined that Evans had a mental age of around 10.5 years. Svarvtik identified a range of features that he considered in keeping with 'such spontaneous speech as might be expected from an illiterate person' (Svartvik 1968: 22) including: grammatical errors in the documents (including language he labelled as 'substandard verb forms'), colloquialisms (such as repeated lexical items, which is more a feature of spoken language), and non-standard language usage (such as double negatives). Examples are shown below. However, Svartvik also noticed many features that were inconsistent with such an author, thus indicating two different styles (including complex grammatical constructions, unusual or formal phrases, and the number of words and clauses per sentence). Svartvik concluded that Evans did not actually write these statements, and instead it was the police that had altered the statements. The analysis therefore questioned the authorship of the statements. In 1966, Evans was posthumously pardoned for the murders, which had been perpetrated by a serial killer, John Christie (two movies have been made of the case, entitled *10 Rillington Place* [1971] and *Rillington Place* [2016]). Svartvik published his work, calling for the application of linguistics to forensic contexts in order to benefit society.

Inconsistent stylistic features in the Evans case (from Svartvik 1968)

Examples of non-standard language used by Evans:

- She asked me where Beryl and the baby **was**. [non-standard verb form]
- I **done** the usual thing. [non-standard verb form]
- He **never** asked **no** money for it. [double negative]

Examples of complex grammar and formal phrasing:

- He handed me the money which I counted **in his presence**.
- She was **incurring** one debt after another.

Sparked by this case, many early forensic linguistics cases in the UK focused on the validity of police interrogations, resulting statements, and disputed confessions, thus bringing linguistic knowledge to support the provision of justice (though sometimes quite late in the process). This was seen in numerous subsequent cases, such as the convictions of Derek Bentley, the Birmingham Six, and the Bridgewater Four (for further discussion see Chi Luu 2017, Coulthard 1994, Coulthard, Johnson, & Wright 2016). In these cases, many forensic linguistic issues focused on the language use and register/stylistic features of witness statements, considering the language of lay people and by officers of the law transcribing witness statements. One example concerned the disputed confession of William Power, one of the Birmingham Six (six Irishmen accused of a series of pub bombings in Birmingham, England, in 1975). In the alleged confession Coulthard identified a feature of what he termed *over-explicitness* in the noun groups, most specifically the frequent occurrence of the pattern [*number*] + *white* + *plastic* + *carrier* + *bag*. Based on what we know about spoken conversation and how language is composed, it is very unlikely that Power would have produced such overly explicit noun groups, let alone multiple times. It is far more likely that it resulted from a series of questions and answers, which were then edited.

Forensic linguistics can be seen entering into American courts in 1979, when a group of poor black families at the Martin Luther King Junior Elementary School in Ann Arbor, Michigan, successfully sued the Ann Arbor School District. Their case was that the School District had failed to take account of the children's home language and its impact on their education. Their home language, African American English (AAE, often referred to at the time as African American Vernacular English, or Ebonics) was shown to be significantly different from the standard English used as the medium of education. The linguist Geneva Smitherman was engaged by the plaintiffs to demonstrate that AAE was a fully-fledged language variety that differed from the standard in systematic ways (see e.g., Labov 1982, Smitherman & Baugh 2002).

In the 1990s, Australian linguists pioneered the application of linguistics and sociolinguistics onto legal issues, thus expanding the field to include the courtroom environment (Eades 1992). These researchers identified the need for more research in the criminal justice system as it relates to racial injustices and dialect variation. For instance, a nuanced investigation into the use of Aboriginal English in the courtroom was performed to highlight that Aboriginal English (like African American English) is a systematic and rule-governed language variety, not just 'wrong English' as many believed at the time (for more on this, see Davis 2022 and work by Diana Eades listed in the recommended reading list at the end of this chapter).

Since the 2000s, there has been considerable growth in the field, with it now being a prolific offshoot of applied linguistics around the world. Forensic linguistics is internationally recognised, with professional associations such as the International Association of Forensic and Legal Linguistics (IAFLL, founded in 1993), dedicated academic journals (such as the *International Journal of Speech, Language and the Law*, and *Language and Law/Linguagem e Direito*), and taught as a major field of study in colleges and universities in Australia, Brazil, the United States, Portugal, Germany, the United Kingdom, and more. Reviews of national practices are available for the United States (Tiersma & Solan

2002), Australia (Eades et al. 2023), and the Philippines (Rañosa-Madrunio & Martin 2023).

8.3 Core forensic linguistic theory

8.3.1 Sociolinguistics and language(s)

The understanding of language as both a social and individual phenomenon is one that informs forensic linguistic analysis and the work within this book. Most forensic linguistic analysis draws on the principles of **sociolinguistics**, which looks at how society and culture influences the way we use language. John Gumperz, a sociolinguist and a pioneer of the field, wrote that sociolinguistics is 'an approach to discourse analysis that has its origin in the search for replicable methods of qualitative analysis that account for our ability to interpret what participants intend to convey in everyday communicative practice' (Gumperz 2001: 215). Similarly, Deborah Schiffrin (1994), another influential sociolinguist, argues that it 'provides an approach to discourse that focuses upon situated meaning' (p. 133).

In other words, sociolinguistics is an approach to analysing language and communication that examines how individuals make sense of the world around them, create identities, and construct relationships through language. Sociolinguistics is also interdisciplinary and in addition to linguistics it incorporates concepts and theories from sociology, psychology, and anthropology. Readers are encouraged to develop their skills and knowledge in the broader area of sociolinguistics. Seminal sociolinguistic texts include those by Goffman (1981) and Gumperz (1982). For the intersection of sociolinguistics and forensic analysis, consider Conley & O'Barr's (1998) integration of sociolinguistics and socio-legal scholarship, Matoesian's (1993) perspectives on structure and agency, and Eades' (2004) discussion of critical sociolinguistics in the courtroom. For broader introductions to sociolinguistics we recommend Wardhaugh & Fuller (2021), Meyerhoff (2018), and Holmes and Wilson (2022).

But the first step is to consider what we actually mean by the term **language**. Historically, language has been defined as 'a system of arbitrary vocal symbols by means of which a social group cooperates' (Block & Trager 1941: 5). This definition draws on early philosophical work and highlights the fact that the noises we make, or even the squiggles on this paper, actually bear no direct relation to real-life objects, or the abstract concepts that we are describing. We now also acknowledge how important it is to include signed languages in our definition of language, which also have syntactic, semantic, morphological, and phonological structures and are fully-fledged languages. Nonetheless there is a clear shared understanding that the noises/symbols/signs we make when speaking, or the little marks on this paper, have shared meaning with other people (and hopefully that includes you, the reader). For this reason, we will be defining language as a shared set of communicative events that are largely mutually intelligible and convey meaning.

Essentially, groups of people come to a collective agreement about meanings and communications (this will be expanded on in Chapter 9 Language and Meaning). This is true when we are looking at the level of national languages (such as French, German, etc.) but also at the level of dialects. In fact, there is very little distinction between a language and a dialect, as summarised by the oft-cited phrase usually attributed to Weinreich: a language is a dialect with an army and navy (or in the original Yiddish: *shprakh iz a dialekt mit an armey un flot*). This highlights the fact that there is not a set linguistic distinction between a dialect and a language. Instead, the difference tends to be whether a particular variant has gained official political recognition (for further discussion of this see Wardhaugh & Fuller 2021). For this reason, linguists will often talk of **codes** or **–lects** to refer to varieties of language(s). **Sociolect** is a variety belonging to a certain social group, a **dialect** belongs to a certain region, and an **idiolect** belongs to a certain individual. **Idiolect** is a core concept to the theory of authorship analysis (Grant & Macleod 2020).

> The linguist approaches the problem of questioned authorship from the theoretical position that every native speaker has their own distinct and individual version of the language they speak and write, their own idiolect, and [...] this idiolect will manifest itself through distinctive and idiosyncratic choices in texts.
>
> Coulthard (2004: 432)

A related term that commonly appears in the media is that of a **linguistic fingerprint.** This term is avoided by the majority of linguists due to its misleading connotations, particularly the implication that language is 100% unique to the individual. If that were the case, we would not be able to understand each other. Instead, our language is a simultaneous push-pull of being socially constructed and individual. Concepts around authorship analysis are discussed further in Chapters 10 and 11.

As is discussed further in Chapter 11, we are conscious that *profiling* can have multiple meanings, often rightly negative. We use the terms **sociolinguistic profiling** or **forensic linguistic profiling** (rather than *linguistic profiling*) to indicate that we are referring to the development of a linguistic profile based on scientific research and analysis and rooted in sociolinguistic theory, as opposed to discrimination or stereotyping of people based on their language.

Language is very closely linked to aspects of identity. An individual will have lots of different aspects of their identity that they can pull on and perform in different ways (for more discussion see Chapter 11). Further, most individuals will produce speech or writing within a range of different registers. The **register** of a text (or spoken utterance) is the variety of language that is being used in a particular context or situation. It is influenced by a variety of factors including the **purpose of communication**, the field, the **tenor**, and the **mode** of communication. The purpose of a communication is somewhat self-explanatory but consider how the different purpose might impact an individual's language when writing a student essay versus a ransom note. In the first they are seeking to impress the marker (this will include using 'correct' grammar and appropriate language), whereas in the latter their aim is to extort money out of the intended audience (they do not need to impress with their grammatical skills; the purpose is different).

Field is the topic or subject of the text or discourse. Certain fields necessitate or accommodate specific technical language and jargon. **Tenor** is the relationship between the people involved. This might be the different speaker(s) and their audience, or it could be between the writer(s) and reader(s). The relationships between the parties, and their social characteristics (such as status, age, and gender), will potentially impact the language used. As a simple example: you talk to your friends differently from how you talk to your doctor. **Mode** refers to the channel or method of communication. Consider how you write versus how you speak, and the differences between WhatsApp and formal letter writing. Different modes have different norms and traits. A nice example of the impact of this is how your language might change when you are emailing a colleague that you happen to be friends with, compared to when you are messaging them through social media. For example, your email would likely be more formally structured, with a greeting and a sign off. Your social media posts might contain more emojis or multimodal content (links and pictures), and more colloquial or informal language (such as pronoun dropping or abbreviations). For more on this, see Tannen & Wallat's (1993) analysis of registers in the medical sphere.

Consider how field, tenor, and mode manifest in the following example, which is the start of a Reddit post (which has been based on elements that are commonly seen in such forum boards). Reddit is a discussion board where people can make multimodal posts (that might contain links, pictures, with or without their own text), and to which other members of the community can reply. Posts are grouped in named sub-reddits or 'communities', which users can be members of. The following two lines exemplify a post a user might make on the board (the bold line being the title, and the second line the start of the core content underneath). Other users might then respond to this post with their verdicts, comments, thoughts, and opinions.

> ***AITA for asking this?***
> *Throwaway account, posting from phone jadda jadda... So last year [...]*

The field is set by AITA, which stands for: *am I the asshole?* We therefore expect that the author is going to outline a situation in which something happened, and they are questioning whether their behaviour was appropriate. The **tenor** is indicated through the fact it is a 'throwaway account'. This term means the author has created a new account and username to distance this post from posts they might make under another username. Essentially, they are setting out that they want the relationship between writer and readers to be anonymous. The mode is not only the obvious fact that they are typing on Reddit, but the manner of how they are doing it, in this case from a phone. This is relevant because it will often account for more (and slightly different) typing errors (typos) than you would get if typing from a laptop or desktop device. For example, one of the authors has several times recently accidentally inserted a crying face emoji into a word when typing on their phone, as it appears as a suggestion directly above their on-screen phone keyboard; this could not happen on a laptop. The Reddit example and (1) the steps that hypothetical author took to anonymise, (2) their language choice with typo inclusion, and (3) emoji usage shows how an author might be aware of the impact of field, tenor, and mode. However, it should be noted that these factors can influence an individual's language whether they are explicitly aware of them or not.

The significance for us now is that language is inherently a social concept and impacted by what Deborah Schiffrin (1994) dubbed **situated meaning,** which suggests the use of a particular language feature changes based on its societal and linguistic context. The participants, topic, culture, physical place of a conversation all changes the 'meaning' of the encounter. It is also worth considering what we mean by **society,** as this will recur as a concept throughout the following chapters. We will adopt a more colloquial understanding of society, such as the one found in the *Oxford English Dictionary*: 'a system of human organisations generating distinctive cultural patterns and institutions'.

8.3.2 Levels of language analysis

Before we delve into the analyses in the next chapters, it is worth considering further what we are actually analysing. The key term that we use is a **language feature** or **variable.** This is essentially any aspect of the language that can be counted or measured. In the chapters on forensic phonetics we saw numerous examples of the variables typically analysed: consonants, vowels, suprasegmental features such as intonation or pitch. In forensic linguistics the variables comprise any linguistic feature, not just those that are classified as phonetic or phonological. When people initially think of linguistic analysis there is a tendency to focus on the words used. While this is certainly part of the analysis, it is far from all of it. A language feature can be a 'lower-level' feature, such as a particularly marked or unusual spelling of a particular term, thus reflecting the phonetics or phonology, or a 'higher-level' structural level feature, such as who introduces a certain topic.

To see an example from our everyday lives, consider the language we use on all our devices: computer-mediated communication (CMC). Linguist and CMC researcher, Susan Herring, introduced a method of analysing CMC using many of the linguistic strategies discussed above in efforts to examining how people adapt their behaviour and their language on the internet. She writes:

> As growing numbers of people interact on a regular basis in chat rooms, web forums, listservs, email, instant messaging environments and the like, social scientists, marketers, and educators look to their behavior in an effort to understand the nature of computer-mediated communication and how it can be optimized in specific contexts of use. This effort is facilitated by the fact that people engage in socially meaningful activities online in a way that typically leaves a textual trace, making the interactions more accessible to scrutiny and reflection than is the case in ephemeral spoken communication, and enabling researchers to employ empirical, micro-level methods to shed light on macro-level phenomena.

> Herring (2004: 1)

She continues with a warning that we, the authors of this textbook, take to heart:

> Internet research often suffers from a premature impulse to label online phenomena in broad terms, for example, all groups of people interacting online are 'communities'; the language of the Internet is a single style or 'genre'. Notions such as community and genre are familiar and evocative, yet notoriously slippery, and unhelpful (or worse) if applied indiscriminately.

> Herring (2004: 1)

This warning can be applied outside the field of CMC and helpful to a forensic linguistic context because not all people from a particular community speak the same way, and in subsequent chapters, we will heed this warning to illustrate the caution needed when making empirical observations that run the risk of generalisation about things like community and genre.

Additionally helpful to the field of forensic linguistics, in this analysis, Herring (2004) identifies four key domains that should be considered in computer-mediated discourse analysis (CMDA). These demonstrate the spread of areas that can and should be considered (as well as what would be missed if we only focused on words). The domains she identified are: **structure, meaning, interaction,** and **social behaviour.** There is also a fifth domain – **participation** – which falls outside the normal bounds of linguistic analysis, but which might still have relevance in a forensic case. Herring's model is very useful for analysis of computer-mediated communication and demonstrates how we can see discourse behaviours indicative of a virtual community across all the domains. This includes: the use of in-/out-group language, and jargon (which fits under the structural domain), exchange of knowledge (which fits under meaning), threads of conversation and reciprocity (interaction), conflict management and the evolution of norms (social behaviour), and frequent regular activity (participation).

A similar model can be considered, which is less restricted to computer-mediated communication, and can be applied to any language or communicative

Figure 8.2 Stop sign UK.   **Figure 8.3** Stop sign USA.

event. This is summarised in Table 8.1 and can be visualised as in Figure 8.4. Table 8.1 shows the different language levels that we often focus on in forensic linguistic analysis, along with a description and a worked example of how this might manifest in a STOP sign (see Figures 8.2 and 8.3). ❷ While a STOP sign might not initially seem to fall into the realms of forensic linguistics, it nicely exemplifies the type of data that is not itself inherently forensic but could be in certain situations (for example, if there were a car crash, and the case revolved around whether the stop sign adequately communicated to drivers what was required from them).

A useful visualisation to remember this is that of an inverse triangle (see Figure 8.4). The levels of the triangle show the narrow features (word-level/lexical, and sub-word-level or morphological) below the wider, broader syntactic, pragmatic, and discourse features. The phonetic and semiotic features are crosscut the other levels of features, not fitting into the hierarchy, but remaining nonetheless important.

When analysing language, we are looking across all levels of language as outlined in Table 8.1. Throughout this book you will often see as you use the word **text**, or we might refer to **language data**. It is worth noting how broad this term can be when used by linguists. Text could be anything from a shopping list, to a text message, to an online manifesto. Further, as indicated by Table 8.1, we do not analyse texts or language data in isolation. For example, if we are analysing a series of online instant message conversations, we are likely to want to understand the order in which the conversations took place (i.e., the pragmatic or discourse levels). These language levels and their application are discussed further with relation to forensic linguistic analysis in Chapter 12.

Table 8.1 Levels of language

	Level description	Meaning	Worked Stop sign example
Discourse	Larger units of language, interaction, text or document level and above	Communicative purpose. Meaning beyond the wider context of the text Topic introduction	A stop sign at an intersection
Pragmatic	Paragraph and text level	Speech acts, implicit meaning	A stop sign contains a directive
Syntactic	Clause level, structure of sentences, phrases, and clauses	Grammatical features of clauses including errors, or rare grammar usage	'Stop' is a one-word imperative as opposed to a full sentence 'you must stop now'
Semantic/ lexical	Clause level, vocabulary or words used, alone and in combination	Meaning in that specific context, within relation to the words and phrases close by Hapax legomenon (words that only appear once in the text), misspellings, unusual collocations	Using a commonly used word like 'stop' rather than a less common word with different meanings like 'halt'
Morphological	Internal structure of words and morpheme elements	Features that relate to prefixes or suffixes	In English we do not need a morphological element to indicate who should stop – whereas in some other languages this would be needed as part of the word
Semiotics	Relationship between textual and visual	Including colours, images, fonts, etc.	A stop sign having a red background in most western countries
Phonological	Relating to the sound patterns and phonetic properties	Spelling items how they might sound in a specific variant of a language. From phoneme level up to phonetic aspects of the code/variety of language	How do you pronounce 'stop': [stɔp], [stɒp], or [stɑp]

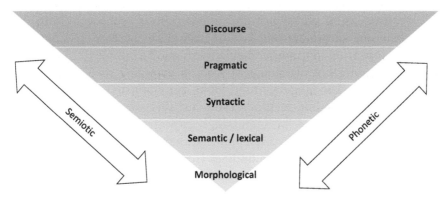

Figure 8.4 Levels of language.

8.3.3 Forensic linguistic data

In forensic linguistics, the data that we are asked to analyse can vary from scrawled graffiti on a wall, a meticulously written manifesto, or comments left on a blog. At the beginning of the internet age, the general consensus was that we were completely anonymous and things like gender expression and identity were completely invisible. However, recent literature finds that claim to be false. In work by Susan Herring and Sharon Stoerger (2014), the claim that computer-mediated communication (CMC) is inherently anonymous was tested. According to the researchers, CMC use on the internet had been claimed to have a level of anonymity that allowed the gender of communicators to be fairly invisible. CMC thus 'allows women and men to participate (and be recognised for their contributions) equally' (p. 586). The researchers examined CMC published between 1989 and 2013 from a number of platforms, including multimodal (e.g., YouTube), textual (e.g., online chat environments), and mobile communications (e.g., SMS texting). They found that the premise of democracy and equal opportunity interactions on the internet was flawed from the outset. The researchers concluded that gender expression was clear via the usage of linguistic features that are found to pattern in face-to-face communication (e.g., written representation of smiling and laughter, degree of interactive engagement, use of profanity). However, these features are exploited in mixed-sex public forums (e.g., Reddit) to encourage consistent harassment of people who utilise them and thus exhibit more 'female' CMC tendencies. As the researchers argue, public forums of CMC often favour assertive 'male' style of speaking over supportive 'female' discourse styles.

We highlight this research because in recent years there has been an increase in computer-mediated communication appearing in forensic linguistic casework. Furthermore, the breadth and variety of types of computer-mediated communication continue to grow too, mirroring our normal life (consider how your communications have changed over the years, from written message, to public messages, to pictures, to voice notes, to videos, etc.).

Due to the increasing prevalence and integration of technology into our daily lives, it is not surprising that we are seeing an increase in computer-mediated data appearing in forensic linguistics. A good example of the importance of understanding how language evolves in emerging media and CMC is the following case. The language used looks quite unusual for how people communicate through online methods now, but this was normal for many people at the time – and hence was increasingly appearing in forensic casework data. The case was undertaken by Malcolm Coulthard in 2005, and detailed by Tim Grant (2020), and supports the findings from Herring & Stoerger (2014) who described the ways in which your identity and idiolect can sneak into your CMC.

The disappearance of Jenny Nicholl

In 2005, 19-year-old Jenny Nicholl of North Yorkshire went missing. She was last seen by her parents leaving her home on the 30th of June. She told them that she would not be home that night, but then her father and friends started receiving suspicious texts supposedly from Jenny. When Jenny had not come home four days later, and her car was found abandoned at an inn on the outskirts of Richmond, her parents reported her to the police as missing. Below you will see a comparison of the texts that Jenny had sent her parents before the night of 30th of June, and the suspicious texts the family received from the 30th onward. All spelling and formatting is shown as it appeared in the original. We have highlighted particularly important elements in bold.

Jenny Nicholl's known Texts:

- Sum black+pink k swiss shoes and all the other **shit** like socks. We r **goin2theindian.Only16quid.**What u doin **x**
- **Shit** is it. fuck **icant2day** ive allready **booked2go** bowling.cant realy pull out. wil **go2shop** and get her sumet soon.**thanx4tdlin** me **x**

Suspicious Texts:

- Thought u wer grassing me up.mite b in trub wiv **me** dad told mum i was lving didnt giv a **shit.been2** kessick camping was great.ave2 go **cya**
- Y do u h8 me i know mum does.told her i was goin.**i aint** cumin back and the pigs wont find me.**i am** happy living up here.every1 h8s me in rich only m8 i got is jak.txt u couple wks tell pigs **i am** nearly 20 **aint** cumin back they can **shite** off

On the 3rd of November 2005, after a massive manhunt lasting five months, Inspector Pete Martin announced that the case had become a murder investigation, although Jenny's body was never found.

Table 8.2 Comparison of text features in Jenny Nicholl case (from Grant 2020). Note that * indicates examples written by Hodgson on request from the police while in custody

	Jenny (known)	Suspicious texts	Hodgson (known)
Abbreviations	ive, im, Im	I am	*I am, *I Am, *i am
Spacing	goin2the Indian, go2shop, have2get 4a while, thanx4tdlin me	ave2 go 4evrything	ave2 hope, *have to go b4 he goes
Possessive	my, myself	meself, me mum, me dad	me pnckets, *my
Swear words	Shit	shite, shit	-
Spelling	Fone	phone	*PhONE
Phonetic representation	have2	ave	has, ave, *have
Negative markers	im not, havnt	aint	aint

Jenny had been in a relationship with 50-year-old David Hodgson. In the investigation, he was one of a small group of potential suspects, and he was eventually convicted of Jenny's murder. It appeared that Hodgson had sent messages using Jenny's phone and had attempted to mirror her style. The investigators obtained some writing samples from Hodgson and contacted Coulthard to provide forensic linguistic expertise on the suspicious text messages. Coulthard identified differences between Hodgson's collected text messages and those received by Jenny's family the day she disappeared. Some examples are shown in Table 8.2.

Although there may have been an attempt from Hodgson to copy Jenny's writing style, Coulthard showed that the disguise was incomplete and that his own idiolect was betrayed in the texts he sent to her family. Coulthard was able to show that the suspicious messages were stylistically close to the known texts (also known as K texts) of Hodgson. Note, for example, the way in which 2 is used to represent 'to' and 4 to represent 'for', and the use of spaces adjacent to them. In texts known to be written by Jenny the number was not separated from the following text by spaces (*going2the Indian, 4a while*). In the suspicious texts, however, 2 was consistently followed by a space (*ave2 go, had 2 lve*). Hodgson's known texts also followed this pattern (*ave2 hope, b4 he goes*), including features like the lack of a space after the digit substitution in items such as *go2shop*, contrasting with *ave 2 go* in Jenny's messages. The whole investigation took three years to come to court, but finally, on the 19th of February 2008, after a four-week trial, Hodgson was found guilty of Jenny's murder and sentenced to life imprisonment. His subsequent appeal was refused. Hodgson still refuses to say what happened to Jenny or where her remains can be found.

8.3.4 Audience design

Another theory that is important in the discussion of forensic linguistics, and is illustrated in the case above, is the theory of **audience design.** Originally coined by Bell (1984), the audience design model addresses the existence of various categories of audiences in an interaction, and the influence that these different audiences have on a speaker or writer. There can be the person you're interacting with (your addressee), perhaps a person walking by (an eavesdropper), or perhaps this interaction is taking place on TV and your interviewer is Oprah Winfrey, and then you understand that you have a wider audience in the public (your auditor). Consider how you text your mom versus how you text your best friend. Do you use more emojis with one than the other? Do you use more swear words? What about abbreviations or inside jokes? That's you unconsciously using audience design, or a way you adapt how you communicate with someone based on the present or assumed audience of your language.

Audience design is also an important concept in forensic contexts. If David Hodgson had only seen messages that Jenny Nicholl had sent to him as a romantic partner, that might have impacted how he wrote any messages from her phone pretending to be her. He had to do some research and work on how to change his own language to that of Jenny Nicholl. The clearest demonstration of this is to consider whether you end messages to your romantic partners the same way that you end messages to friends, colleagues, or family members. Audience design is an important aspect of all forensic linguistic research and casework, because a lot of forensic data is language used in a criminal manner. As such, and due to the perceived potential audience of the authorities, some level of disguise or deception is often present.

Another forensic context in which audience design is particularly pertinent is police interviews. Analysing police interviews, Kate Haworth (2013) applies Bell's audience design to the atypical interaction of a police interview. The formal and potentially stressful context of an interview in police custody presents interactional challenges for citizens, who are not usually used to this type of interactional design. Haworth's analysis shows that interviewers often have a different awareness of audiences that they are considering (and speaking to) in the interview itself (compared to the interviewee). This can be seen with phrases such as 'for the record' and the inclusion of information, or questions to elicit information, that would be of interest to the later potential audience of judge and/or jury. Haworth demonstrates that the law enforcement officer commonly has the institutional know-how and asymmetry in knowledge that this interaction is going to be disseminated to a larger, future audience, and directs their language accordingly. However, the interviewee, the civilian, is rarely found to behave in a way that suggests they are speaking towards this (unaddressed) audience from the future. These civilians are not aware of the asymmetry, thus continuing the power dynamic and interactional disadvantage that exists in the legal system.

A similar asymmetry occurs in the context of interviews in asylum tribunals (for further discussion, see Chapter 7 on language in the asylum procedure). As part of the asylum interview process a person is interviewed, and often encouraged to talk in their native language, mother tongue, or dialect (for more on the problems around the concept or a native language or L1 see Chapter 11). However, if an interviewer with the same language or dialect is not available (e.g., someone who speaks Standard Swedish is interviewing a speaker of a nor- thern Swedish dialect, or an Arabic interviewer uses Modern Standard Arabic to communicate with an asylum seeker from Algeria), then the interviewee might subconsciously accommodate to their interviewer's language variety (see the example discussed in section 7.4). This is compounded by the issues of power asymmetry and lack of familiarity with the institutional processes and contexts surrounding the interview. The outcome is that the interviewee is likely to focus on the interviewer as the primary audience, and to (consciously or subcon- sciously) alter their language accordingly (and therefore likely away from their original variety). This will likely be to their detriment as well as the detriment of the wider fact-finding process. (For more information on power asymmetry in judicial processes see Chapter 10.)

The concept of audience design is central to all communication, and therefore important to keep in mind for the subsequent chapters. The concept of audience design is also relevant for report writing (see Chapter 13), or the dissemination of linguistic knowledge.

8.4 Application

Forensic linguistics, as we have explained, is the application of linguistic theory and knowledge to forensic situations and contexts. The following chapters will demonstrate a range of areas that draw on different sorts of linguistic theory, and methods that are grounded in the concepts introduced.

There is an area of forensic linguistic casework that we can consider as forensic discourse analysis, or context analysis. This is when the question relates not so much as to who wrote the document, but rather, is the apparent context of this document actually accurate? In this area we take knowledge about how language and communication works, and apply it to see if the language of the questioned document matches the context in which it was allegedly produced. An early example of this can be seen in Coulthard's work on the Derek Bentley case. In 1953 Derek Bentley (aged 19) and his friend Chris Craig (aged 16) attempted to burgle a warehouse. Police cornered them on the roof, and Chris Craig shot and killed one of the police officers. Both Craig and Bentley were tried and found guilty of murder, which at the time bore the death penalty. As Craig was a minor he could not be put to death, but after an unsuccessful appeal Bentley was hanged at Wandsworth Prison. His family continued to appeal on his behalf, and even- tually he was posthumously pardoned in 1988. (A movie was also made of the case, *Let Him Have It* [1991].) Linguistic evidence from Coulthard contributed to the court's decision to pardon Bentley. There were a series of core issues in the case: Bentley had a diminished mental capacity and a low mental age; there were also questions over his alleged confession, and what he had meant when he told Craig 'Let him have it, Chris!' Disagreement on this point was whether it was an instruction for Craig to shoot the policeman, or to hand the gun over. While this case has attracted considerable linguistic analysis, it is the second question that we are focusing on here.

Bentley's confession was contained in a statement that the police claimed was a direct, verbatim account of his monologue dictation (three police officers swore under oath that it was produced entirely by unaided monologue dictation). Conversely, Bentley claimed that it was at least in part based on a dialogue: a series of questions and answers that were then edited to appear as a monologue, and containing aspects written by police officers which had no basis in what he said. While this could be confused as an authorship question (who wrote the questioned sections), the question of most importance for the case was actually more straightforward than that: was the text produced in the manner the police claimed (transcribed verbatim monologue) or in line with Bentley's account.

It is well documented that spoken and written language vary significantly. Coulthard identified three things that called into question the police version of how the statement was produced. Two of the findings related to the use of the word *then*. First, it was used regularly in its temporal sense, i.e., to show the relationship between elements in a sequence over time (e.g., *Then I went to the shop*). Second, it was often used as a postponed *then,* where it comes after the pronoun (rather than before), e.g., *I then ran out after them; Chris Craig and I then caught; Chris then jumped over, Chris then climbed up the drainpipe.* Using corpus-based approaches (as will be discussed further in Chapter 11). Coulthard demonstrated that such a high rate of temporal *then* and the use of postponed *then* were both features more commonly found in statements written by police, rather than witness statements written by lay people. Given that Bentley was not a police officer it was unlikely that the text would contain these features if it really were a verbatim record of his monologue dictation. Coulthard further identified that 'several uncalled for denials in the statement did not fit the developing narrative and could have been produced as a result of negative responses to police questions being turned into declarative denials' (Picornell & Coulthard 2022: 115). For instance, the statement contained the following line: *Up to then Chris had not said anything.* It is unusual to document a non-event, and there was no narrative reason why it would be mentioned. This therefore does not match the assertion that the confession was the result of a direct monologue.

Another example can be seen in a statement by Robert Brown, who was convicted of murder. Similar to Bentley, Brown argued that his statement was not the verbatim record that the police claimed but was in fact a monologised version of a dialogue. His statement contained the sentence: 'I was covered in blood, my jeans and a blue parka coat and a shirt were full of blood'. As a monologue this is very unusually phrased and structured. The switch from the pronoun *my* to the indefinite article *a* is not common (unless someone is trying to distinguish items that belonged to them from those that did not, which was not the case here). Coulthard noted that this change could have occurred as a slip when converting a dialogic text into an apparently monologic text. This is strengthened by a record of an earlier interview, where, in response to a question asking what he had been wearing, Brown responded 'I had a blue shirt and a blue parka' (Picornell & Coulthard 2022: 115).

Picornell & Coulthard (2022) also discuss a more recent case looking at an email chain apparently between two financiers. Although Picornell was initially approached with it as an authorship question, it quickly became apparent that the language did not match the context in which the texts were claimed to have been produced. Picornell applied a context analysis toolkit built on established linguistic theories, to show that the language contained did not match the apparent context, and therefore the emails were unlikely to be a genuine set of emails between two people from the finance industry. For example, at the end of a 134-word paragraph detailing Treasury rules and processes (which would not be necessary to explain to someone with experience in the finance industry) the paragraph ends 'We do not need to let this bother us for this transaction'. The question remains then why this paragraph was included, as it is irrelevant. The named addressee would have both known the information given and known that it was not relevant. To put this in linguistic terms, it flouts Grice's maxim of relevance (Grice 1975), which states that in a normal cooperative communication, an individual will seek to include information that is relevant, and only information that is relevant (i.e., exclude irrelevant information). However, if the true intended audience were not the named addressee (with financial experience), but a different individual without financial experience, then the language would match the context. Incorporating principles of audience design analysis, Picornell was able to develop a profile of the likely intended audience: someone concerned about the transactions being discussed, who the author(s) felt needed to be reassured and convinced of one of the authors' expertise, and who was less familiar with the finance industry than the two named people (including financial jargon and processes – which were often described in full).

8.4.1 Disinformation

Context analysis draws heavily on the concept of register, and field, tenor, and mode, as all of these impact any language that is produced. In context analysis you are reverse engineering this to see if the language is consistent with the stated context under which it was produced.

Another good example of this is found in the areas of disinformation and fake news, communicative events that have sparked increasing concern in recent years. It is not for a linguist to determine the veracity of the content (that would require a different skill set). However, they can look at factors like whether the communicative purpose matches the language used. For standard news information, the communicative purpose would be to inform. By contrast, for disinformation the main aim would be to persuade to a certain viewpoint. This is the approach taken by Grieve & Woodfield (2023) in their work on Fake News, focusing on the work of Jayson Blair, a former journalist for The New York Times who fabricated a number of his articles. They demonstrated that there are consistent patterns of differences in the language of his genuine articles compared to his faked ones. The differences include reduced levels of information density (a feature associated with long complex noun phrases) in the faked texts. In the real texts, Blair writes with what Grieve & Woodfield classify as 'greater conviction'. This means that the author adopts a more persuasive and confident stance, through features such as using a greater number of suasive verbs when describing real events and their legal consequences (e.g., *decide, determine, propose*).

Interestingly, work by Sousa-Silva (2022) shows that linguistic patterns that indicate a text is fake news rather than genuine news apply across languages. He analysed overlapping patterns in English and Portuguese, and showed, for example, that fake news makes greater use of words like *truth, truly* and greater use of sentence-initial adverbs (e.g., *disturbingly...*). Defining concepts of fake news or disinformation is notoriously difficult. For example, distinguishing disinformation (where the content is deliberately wrong) from misinformation (where the content is wrong, but the sharer might not know that) is not always clear cut; if someone creates disinformation, and you share it thinking it is real, how should that be classified? What is clear, though, is that it is a communicative event, and hence linguistics can be of benefit. Sousa-Silva (2022) demonstrates that disinformation meets the criteria of being a language crime (language crimes are further discussed in Chapter 9), as:

(a) it can be commissioned both directly and indirectly;
(b) it requires some kind of intent; and
(c) it is committed (primarily) using speech acts (Sousa-Silva 2022: 2421).

8.5   Conclusions

Forensic linguistics is an applied form of linguistics, and draws on a range of theories and methodologies from across linguistics. This chapter and those following introduce the most pertinent key linguistic concepts that underpin work in forensic linguistics. To be a good forensic linguist it is vital to develop your wider linguistic skills, using the signposts in this book and beyond. The recommended reading below (and in the subsequent chapters) provides a good starting point. The following chapters delve deeper into the core areas of forensic linguistics, providing a comprehensive introduction to the value that linguistic theory and methodology can bring to a range of forensic contexts.

Further reading

For an introduction to sociolinguistics:

Meyerhoff, M. (2018). *Introducing Sociolinguistics*. Routledge.
Wardhaugh, R., & Fuller, J. M. (2021). *An Introduction to Sociolinguistics*, 8th edition. Wiley.
Wolfram, W., & Schilling, N. (2016). *American English: Dialects and Variation*, 3rd edition. Wiley-Blackwell.

For seminal work in sociolinguistics and its influence on forensic linguistics, please consider the following scholars:

Goffman, E. (1981). *Forms of Talk*. Blackwell.
Gumperz, J. (2001). Interactional sociolinguistics: A personal perspective. In D. Schiffrin, D. Tannen, & H. E. Hamilton (eds.), *The Handbook of Discourse Analysis*. Blackwell.

For the intersection of sociolinguistics and forensic linguistics:

Eades, D. (2004). Understanding aboriginal English in the legal system: A critical sociolinguistics approach. *Applied Linguistics*, 25(4): 491–512.
Shuy, R. W. (2007). Language in the American courtroom. *Language and Linguistics Compass*, 1(1–2): 100–114.
Solan, L., Tiersma, P., & Gales, T. (2024). *Speaking of Crime: Language of the Criminal Justice System*, 2nd edition. University of Chicago Press.

For an article looking at the representation of forensic linguistics in early literature:

Boucher, A., & Perkins, R. (2020). The case of Sherlock Holmes and linguistic analysis. *English Literature in Transition, 1880–1920*, 63(1): 77–98.

For international perspectives on forensic linguistics:

Eades, D., Fraser, H., & Heydon, G. (2023). *Forensic Linguistics in Australia: Origins, Progress and Prospects*. Elements in Forensic Linguistics. Cambridge University Press.
Rañosa-Madrunio, M., & Martin, I. P. (2023). *Forensic Linguistics in the Philippines: Origins, Developments, and Directions*. Elements in Forensic Linguistics. Cambridge University Press.
Tiersma, P., & Solan, L. M. (2002). The linguist on the witness stand: Forensic linguistics in American courts. *Language*, 78: 221–239.

There are also many podcasts (that vary from academic to non-academic) that introduce complex linguistic topics in accessible ways. A list is included on the website of support material for this book.

Activity section

Note: there are no model answers for these activities, but thinking about them will help you engage with the concepts in a constructive way. We would encourage discussion with your classmates or fellow learners if possible.

Activity 8A - Data types

Use these following research questions as a tool to consider all the information presented in this chapter.

i. When it comes to the theories underpinning forensic linguistics and forensic phonetics, where do the two approaches to analysing data overlap? What concepts or theories would intersect the two?
ii. Choose an area of life or area of work that you are familiar with and think of ways in which sociolinguistic and forensic linguistic research could be relevant, e.g., thinking about the way you and your friends communicate with each other, can you detect idiosyncrasies and person-specific behaviours?
iii. Go to *Lexus Nexus* and search for the term 'forensic linguistics' in newspaper articles to explore how the term is used. Does this accurately represent the breadth of the field of forensic linguistics?

Activity 8B - Language registers

Consider how your language changes in the following situations:

• When chatting informally with your friends in a social situation.
• Giving a presentation on your work.
• Texting with friends.

Try and notice when your language shifts throughout the day. Do you do so consciously? How many of your own distinct registers can you identify?

Activity 8C - Data task

Consider the following:

You are undertaking a research project to determine what features a native Portuguese speaker might demonstrate when writing online for forensic casework situations. You decide to collect data from native Portuguese speakers writing online. What are the advantages and disadvantages for the following two forms of data for your research project? Focus on the theoretical and methodological advantages and disadvantages, rather than questions of ethics.

- Student essays: you have access to electronic versions of computer written essays by students.
- Online forums: you have discovered that there are publicly available forums online in which authors talk about their political views and often reveal their social and linguistic backgrounds.

Discussion 8C

Below are the key advantages and disadvantages of both data types. This is not a definitive list, and there are likely more you can find. It is also worth remembering that your research question, and potential future applications of your findings, will impact the significance of the advantages and disadvantages, and well as the compromises you decide to make.

STUDENT ESSAYS

Advantages

- Depending on how the material was collected you can often be more sure that the linguistic background information you have is correct.
- The format of the essays is often very consistent.
- The monologic nature means that there is very little cross-contamination of features.

Disadvantages

- The communicative purpose is very different from that of genuine standard forensic texts – the students are usually writing in order to satisfy marking criteria and in order to achieve a good grade.
- Students are often explicitly aware that their language will be evaluated and should match a certain prescribed style.

ONLINE FORUMS

Disadvantages

- You cannot be as sure about the background of the individual.
- It might be more time-consuming to collect and clean that data into a con-sistent usable format.

Advantages

- Genuine data – people are writing for a variety of communicative purposes, but not usually to have their language examined.

- More closely representative of what is often encountered in forensic cases.
- Covers broad spectrum of topics, authors, and registers.
- Easily collectible and accessible.
- More likely to include dialect, slang, or taboo terms.

References

Bell, A. (1984). Language style as audience design. *Language in Society*, 13(2): 145–204.

Chi, L. (2017). Sentenced to death (and other tales from the dark side of language. *Lingua Obscura. JSTOR Daily*, 6 September.

Conley, J., & O'Barr, W. (1998). *Just Words: Law, Language and Power*. University of Chicago Press.

Coulthard, M. (2004). Author identification, idiolect, and linguistic uniqueness. *Applied Linguistics*, 25(4): 431–447.

Coulthard, M. (2014). Powerful evidence for the defence: an exercise in forensic discourse analysis. In J. Gibbons (ed.) *Language and the Law*. Routledge, pp. 414–427.

Coulthard, M., Johnson, A., & Wright, D. (2016). *An Introduction to Forensic Linguistics: Language in Evidence*. Routledge.

Davis, S. (2022). Aboriginal English – what isn't it? IndigenousX, 13 January.

Eades, D. (1992). *Aboriginal English and the Law: Communicating with Aboriginal English Speaking Clients: A Handbook for Legal Practitioners*. Queensland Law Society.

Grant, T. (2020). Text messaging forensics revisited: Txt 4n6: Idiolect-free authorship analysis? In M. Coulthard, A. May, & R. Sousa-Silva (eds.), *The Routledge Handbook of Forensic Linguistics*, 2nd edition. Routledge, pp. 558–575.

Grant, T., & MacLeod, N. (2020). *Language and Online Identities: The Undercover Policing of Internet Sexual Crime*. Cambridge University Press.

Grice, P. (1975). Logic and conversation. In P. Cole & J. J. Morgan (eds.), *Syntax and Semantics 3: Speech Acts*. Academic Press, pp. 41–58.

Grieve, J., & Woodfield, H. (2023). *The Language of Fake News*. Cambridge University Press.

Gumperz, J. (1982). Fact and inference in courtroom testimony. In J. Gumperz (ed.), *Language and Social Identity*. Cambridge University Press, pp. 163–195.

Haworth, K. (2013). Audience design in the police interview: The interactional and judicial consequences of audience orientation. *Language in Society*, 42(1): 45–69.

Herring, S. C. (2004). Computer-mediated discourse analysis: An approach to researching online behaviour. In S. A. Barab, R. Kling, & J. H. Gray (eds.),

Designing for Virtual Communities in the Service of Learning. Cambridge University Press, pp. 338–376.

Herring, S.C., & Stoerger, S. (2014). Gender and (a)nonymity in computer-mediated communication. In J. Holmes, M. Meyerhoff, & S. Ehrlich (eds.), *Handbook of Language and Gender*, 2nd edition. Wiley-Blackwell, pp. 567–586.

Holmes, J., & Wilson, N. (2022). *An Introduction to Sociolinguistics.* Routledge.

Labov, W. (1982). Objectivity and commitment in linguistic science: The case of the Black English trial in Ann Arbor. *Language in Society*, 11(2): 165–201.

Matoesian, G. M. (1993). *Reproducing Rape: Domination through Talk in the Courtroom.* University of Chicago Press.

McMenamin, G. R. (2022). Mourning the slow death of Miranda: California v. Ceja. In I. Picornell, R. Perkins, & M. Coulthard (eds.), *Methodologies and Challenges in Forensic Linguistic Casework*. Wiley, pp. 95–113.

Picornell, I., & Coulthard, M. (2022). Detecting faked texts. In I. Picornell, R. Perkins, & M. Coulthard (eds.), *Methodologies and Challenges in Forensic Linguistic Casework*. Wiley, pp. 114–127.

Schiffrin, D. (1994). *Approaches to Discourse.* Blackwell.

Smitherman, G., & Baugh, J. (2002). The shot heard from Ann Arbor: Language research and public policy in African America. *Howard Journal of Communication*, 13(1): 5–24.

Sousa-Silva, R. (2022). Fighting the fake: A forensic linguistic analysis to fake news detection. *International Journal for the Semiotics of Law*, 35(6): 2409–2433.

Svartvik, J. (1968). *The Evans Statements. A Case for Forensic Linguistics.* University of Gothenburg.

Tannen, D., & Wallat, C. (1993). Interactive frames and knowledge schemas in interaction: Examples from a medical examination/interview. In D. Tannen (ed.), *Framing in Discourse*. Oxford University Press, pp. 205–216.

Case

Quality Inns Int'l, Inc. v. McDonald's Corp. – 695 F. Supp. 198 (D. Md. 1988).

9 Language and meaning

9.1 Introduction

The communicative nature of language makes meaning (and its transfer or understanding) an inherent part of discussions around language. This is an area in which forensic linguists are often consulted, with many cases revolving around questions of meaning, directly or indirectly. Cases have included, for example, questions such as: is this utterance or text a threat? Is talking about *duppying* someone talking about killing them? When Person X said *yeah*, were they accepting a bribe? Further, forensic linguists have regularly been called on to analyse whether a warning label was sufficiently clear to inform users of potential danger, or to assess the comprehensibility of the rights that might be read by the police when someone is arrested.

In this chapter we cover theories of how meaning is made and understood (section 9.2). Section 9.3 covers methodologies for indicating meaning, and illustrates forensic linguistic analysis through discussion of a case involving the term *duppy*. Section 9.4 looks at word crimes such as threats and bribery, which relate directly to meaning. This chapter ends with an introduction to language and understanding, which feeds into the following chapter on language and legal processes.

Aims

This chapter introduces key theories of **meaning** and how it is conveyed. It explains **corpus linguistic methodologies** and illustrates how they can be applied in a case. It also considers **language crimes,** and the implications of failure to adequately convey **meaning in warning labels**.

DOI: 10.4324/9780367616595-9

9.2   Making meaning

We discussed in Chapter 8 how language is an inherently social phenomenon; if it was truly individual then no-one would be able to understand you, and communication would not be possible. But how exactly is meaning made? When talking about spoken language and meaning, we are talking about the relationship between two (or more) disparate things. For example, when we talk about the written words *coffee cup*, we usually relate these marks (c o f f e e c u p) on the page both to a series of sounds [kɔfi kʌp] that represents the word, as well as to the physical entity ▇. A user of a signed language might also relate this to a series of movements.

Language is a social construct, and meaning is largely determined by co-locuters and the context in which an interaction takes place. A good example of meaning being negotiated by the co-locuters is the 'Gazebo' sketch by the British comedian Michael McIntyre, in which he demonstrates the vast array of words a 'posh English person' can substitute to say they were drunk. *Trollied, wellied, hammered, plastered* are all common examples of terms used to mean *drunk* in colloquial British English, despite their roots having nothing to do with imbibing alcohol. McIntyre extends this to include other terms with different roots: *carparked, pajamaed*, and *gazeboed*. 'Did you have a drink last night? Are you joking, I got utterly gazeboed'. The point here is that the interlocutors (in this case McIntyre and the audience) are temporarily agreeing that the meaning of the words *carparked, pajamaed*, and *gazeboed* is the same meaning as the word *drunk* in this context. The clues to the meaning are provided by the beginning of the response – 'are you joking?' – which is understood as an affirmative in this case, and the confirmation with an adverb modifier, 'I got utterly ___'.

Context is another key factor that impacts meaning. For example, the word *mouse* has a variety of distinct meanings, among which are the electronic device we use to plug in to our laptop and move the cursor, or a small fluffy creature that might be a pet or an undesired living companion. If someone therefore asks you 'Have you seen my mouse?' both you and the speaker would be relying on the context to indicate which meaning was intended. If the speaker is at home, next to an empty pet cage, they are likely referring to the living creature, but if they are in the office standing next to a desk (which is apparently devoid of the

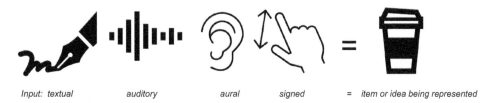

Input: textual   auditory   aural   signed   = item or idea being represented

Figure 9.1 Visualisation of input to representation.

electronic type of mouse) and looking angry, they are probably referring to the electronic kind. Furthermore, the tone of the utterance might indicate whether or not the speaker is accusing you of having stolen the mouse, or just asking a general question. Here the setting around the language is used as an indicator to which meaning is intended.

Now is a good point to undertake Activity 9A, which can be found on page 212, as it gives a hands-on understanding to the theories we are going to discuss below, and the discussion ties in a lot of relevant theories.

9.2.1 Types of meaning

It is important to remember that there are different types of meaning. When we are talking of meaning in abstract terms we tend to focus on literal meanings, e.g., for *coffee* this would mean we are talking about a bitter dark liquid. However, in daily life we regularly rely on different types of meaning. For example, when asking someone if they want to *go for a coffee*, depending on the context, it could mean that you are less focused on the specific warm beverage they drink, and instead asking to spend time together in a social environment. If a similar question is posed after a romantic dinner, the meaning might change again.

There are lots of different ways to understand the types of meanings that exist, however, there are two main overarching classifications: conceptual meaning and connotative meaning. **Conceptual meaning** (also sometimes called referential, denotative, literal, or cognitive meaning) relates to the literal meaning of an item, so a *hedgehog* is a small mammal that has spikes. **Connotative meaning** is sometimes considered a secondary meaning, in that it relates to the connotations around a word, term, or phrase. This includes the emotions associated with it. For example, for a budding chef, *knife* might have the connotative (associated) meaning of *cooking tool*, but for a police officer walking down a dark alley, it is more likely to have the associated meaning of *danger*. Now is a good time to undertake Activity 9B (page 213).

9.2.2 Language, meaning, and 'common sense'

Related to language and meaning is the concept of understanding and how individuals interpret the input they receive. In legal cases, a judge or court will often seek to determine what an average person would understand from something. Consider warning labels on medicines, household cleaners, and more. What they say is of course important, but what is even more important is that the right readers understand it, the right readers being those that might come to harm if the meaning is not accurately conveyed. It is not acceptable if the majority of people understand the warning label and understand they should not drink the toxic cleaning fluid, but a small minority of people (for example, children) do not understand the warnings and come to harm.

It is not a stretch to say that the times when people are read their rights are often very stressful. This might be shortly after someone has a car crash, or when they have been involved in a fight on a night out. There might be secondary issues such as drink or drugs that can affect attention and understanding. Furthermore, people are often so apparently familiar with the words that they do not focus on the implications of their meaning. Now is a good time to undertake Activity 9C (page 213).

The UK government website gives more official information that explains the meaning of the rights. This preamble states: 'The police may question you about the crime you're suspected of – this will be recorded. You don't have to answer the questions but there could be consequences if you don't. The police must explain this to you by reading you the police caution'. Look now at your answer to Activity 9C. Does this information match the bullet points of rights you wrote? People often don't realise that the 'right to silence' is not absolute but mitigated, in that it can have severe implications if you employ it 'wrongly'. In other words, you can stay silent, but there will be legal consequences if you don't explain, at this early stage, information such as an alibi.

Further, the language and grammar used in the rights are very complex, containing multiple sub-clauses ('But, it may harm your defence if you do not mention when questioned something which you later rely on in court'), lexical complexity (what does it mean to 'rely on' in the context of court?), and technical or jargonistic legal language ('given in evidence').

On the topic of language experts and common-sense meaning, consider this case of the former US President Bill Clinton and his relationship with the White House intern, Monica Lewinsky. In 1995, Clinton and Lewinsky began a sexual relationship that lasted 18 months. When the details of their relationship came to light, impeachment charges were brought against President Clinton.

According to the trial material (Starr 1998), Clinton told his top aides that 'there's nothing going on between us' in reference to his relationship with Lewinsky. However, a number of documents and statements were then provided to illustrate that there had been a sexual relationship with Lewinsky. When Clinton was confronted with this statement during a grand jury testimony, he responded with this statement:

*It depends upon what the meaning of the word 'is' is. If the—if he—if **'is'** **means is and never has been, that is not—that is one thing.** If it means there is none, that was a completely true statement.*

The meaning of *is* in the key sentence, and Clinton's response to the question about it, are unclear. The issue at stake, however, is whether *is* was intended to be restricted in scope to the present time, or whether it implied a possible event in the past. Based on these pieces of evidence, the attorney leading the trial, Ken Starr, concluded that Clinton had committed perjury since he had previously stated to his aides 'there's nothing going on'. Starr obtained further evidence of inappropriate behaviour by seizing Lewinsky's computer hard drive and email records. It is also worth noting that Clinton was himself a former lawyer, so perhaps he was aware of the manipulation of the common sense definition of 'is' (meaning there *is* nothing going on in the present time, and there has never been anything going on) and deliberately obfuscated his remarks to his aides by saying *there is nothing going on currently between us.*

9.3   Determining meaning through corpora

When we learn language as children, we predominantly learn it through observation and experience. We are not systematically taught the meanings of the words via explicit instruction (unlike when we learn a foreign language in school). However, as linguists, when we seek to determine the meaning(s) of a term or phrase, we have other tools and methodologies at our disposal that result in a wider understanding and more quantifiable insights. Chief of which is corpus linguistics: a linguistic methodology that uses a collection of texts. Corpus (plural: corpora) comes from Latin, meaning 'body'; linguists examine a body of texts that are collected. In forensic linguistics, corpora usually consist of written texts; however, corpora can also comprise speech recordings or transcriptions of spoken material. Spoken corpora are widely used in forensic phonetics, for example to establish population statistics for the calculation of likelihood ratios (see Chapter 4). Corpora are regularly used in a variety of ways by forensic linguists, and due to the variety of intended purposes can therefore look quite different. There are some key common traits, though. A corpus is usually a large collection of texts consisting of millions of words (though they can also be small, in the low hundreds). Corpora usually contain authentic language (that is, language that has occurred naturally and was not produced specifically for the purpose of being included in a corpus). They also usually contain known information about the author and document (such as the author's gender/sex, age, geographical origin, when the text was written, and what type of text it was). They can also include a variety of registers (e.g., books, online materials such as blogs, WhatsApp conversations, advertisements, court transcripts, pub conversations, etc.). There is a great range of pre-collected corpora, as well as tools to assist corpus building (this will be discussed further in section 9.3).

Previously when people (such as dictionary writers) wanted to determine the meaning of a word, they would think about how they use it, and write down a corresponding definition. This, however, severely limited the definition to that person's individual understanding of the word. Further, people are not always very good at observing their own language use. Tools such as corpora can help us gain more comprehensive insights into language and how it is used. These include the definitional meanings that make it into most modern dictionaries – how the word is used, rather than how someone thinks it should be used. Over the last 20–30 years, corpora and corpus linguistics have undoubtedly revolutionised linguistics and applications of linguistics.

A good example of the value of corpus methods is provided by the story of *Alice in Wonderland*. Most people, when asked, say that the story is about Alice having an adventure on her own through Wonderland, and meeting a variety of fantastical creatures including the White Rabbit and the Cheshire Cat. They therefore assume that the most frequent words in the text relate to such things. However, if we adopt a corpus linguistic methodology and create a word frequency list (removing so-called function or grammatical words, such as articles, pronouns, and other words that do not convey specific content), then we can see the following.

Rather than purely being about a girl going on an adventure alone, we can see from the most frequently occurring words that the text is actually very dialogical, with *said* being the most frequent word. If we include the function words in the analysis, we also see *she, I*, and *you* all in the top ten, further indicating the dialogic nature. This can also be shown through looking at the n-gram analysis, or how the words cluster. Looking at the bi-grams (two-word clusters) we see *said the*, and *said Alice* appearing regularly (Krishnamurthy 2018).

Surprisingly, a group of the frequently-occurring content words actually relate to size: the word *little* is the third most frequent term, *long* and *large* also feature in the top 50 words (when filtered to remove 'stop words' or terms that do not link directly to the content). Thinking about size terms specifically, we might remember that Alice gets bigger and smaller, the door is too small, the key is too big, etc. In fact, the author, Charles Lutwidge Dodgson, whose pen name was Lewis Carroll, was actually a lecturer in mathematics at Oxford University and specialised in geometry. It is therefore perhaps unsurprising that dimensions and size feature prominently within the most frequent words. But this emphasis often goes unnoticed by lay readers. A corpus linguistic analysis of the text, and consideration of the word frequencies, can therefore enable us to see core aspects of the text that we could easily have missed.

Table 9.1 Top 20 frequent terms in Alice in Wonderland

Frequency rank	Term	Count	Frequency rank	Term	Count
1	said	462	11	don't	61
2	Alice	386	12	I'm	59
3	little	129	13	began	58
4	know	87	14	turtle	57
5	like	85	15	mock	57
6	went	83	16	it's	57
7	thought	74	17	way	56
8	time	71	18	quite	55
9	queen	68	19	hatter	55
10	king	61	20	gryphon	55

For more exercises that can show how corpus tools can be used to teach English, or give insight into different texts, we recommend working through the exercises in the blog post from Birmingham University.

Forensic linguistics takes a **descriptivist approach** to language (describing how language is used) rather than a **prescriptivist approach** (saying how language *should be* used). In order to gain accurate information about how language is *actually* used (rather than how we think it is used), we need to rely quite heavily on the use of some form of corpora. Corpora are used across the whole field of forensic linguistics, but we will explore them a little further here with relation to questions of language and meaning.

9.4 Application and tools

There is a very broad range of tools available to undertake corpus analysis. This section will introduce a few of those and signpost where you can learn more. We then demonstrate how the approaches were used in a casework situation (section 9.4.3). However, corpus tools are not just used in language and meaning cases, but to some extent in virtually all cases. For example, in a socio-linguistic profiling case (Chapter 11) we might use a corpus to determine what dialect a particular feature is linked to, and in a comparative authorship analysis case (Chapter 12) a corpus might tell us how widely distributed that feature is. In fact, known (K) and questioned (Q) texts could themselves be considered mini-corpora.

9.4.1 Tools

There is a range of corpus tools available to assist an analysis. Most academic institutions and universities subscribe to a range of corpora, but there are also freely available corpora. For example, SketchEngine and the BNClab at Lancaster University have corpora that are openly available.

There is also a variety of tools available for analysing corpora. There are specific language analysis programs such as WordSmith and AntConc that enable users to analyse collections of texts (building word frequency lists, or collocations, through to more complex analyses). There are also online tools such as Birmingham University's CLiC project or Voyant, or for those with the technical coding skills, analysis can also be done using software such as R or Python. Again, most academic institutions will have access to some of these programs, and will be able to support the technical side of installation and access.

It is beyond the scope of this book to give a detailed discussion of the potential tools and techniques that are available, but Activity 9C (page 213) is an exercise that will help you develop some skills with corpus tools. It is highly recommended that you spend time familiarising yourself with corpus linguistic methodologies, tools, and resources. In particular, find out what tools you have access to through any institutions you are linked to, and research the benefits of what they can – and cannot – do.

9.4.2 Data selection

One question that needs to be considered is what makes a representative corpus for the purposes of what we are looking at? How relevant the data is to the context will impact the reliability of the findings and the strength of the conclusion drawn. As already stated, corpora are of high importance when determining meaning, but not all corpora are created equal. The analyst will need to decide which corpus is the best to use in any given situation. A corpus is a collection of language that is representative of certain conditions. It is impossible to capture all of a language within a corpus; by its very nature it is a representative sample of language use at a particular time and collected under certain conditions and with a set of assumptions. If, for example, we are focusing on how people use language on a new and emerging short-form video messaging platform, we might create a corpus of videos from existing similar platforms that have more data or are more accessible (such as TikTok). Note, however, that we would be making various assumptions: that the audiences are comparable, that the demographics of the users are comparable, and that the communicative purposes and fields of discussion are familiar – not just in the wider data but in the specific collected data. It is impossible to remove all assumptions, but the key is to be aware of them. The task for a forensic linguist working on a specific case is to get as close to the questioned context as possible. This might entail choosing the pre-existing corpora that are relevant enough for the particular situation. In other circumstances the analyst can create or collect their own corpus to match the characteristics of the questioned texts being analysed. Grant (2017) details a case, which we discuss in section 9.4.3, in which he needed to collect a very specific corpus in order to analyse meaning.

There is a considerable amount of material that covers the practicalities and matters that need to be considered when collecting a corpus. In particular, we would recommend O'Keeffe & McCarthy (2010).

9.4.3 *Duppy* case – Determining lexical meaning

Now that we have looked at how language input is received and how we can determine meaning, the question remains why this matters in forensic contexts. We have now shown that meaning is not as straightforward as people sometimes assume, and that a scientific analysis of the language brings many advantages in understanding terms. Nonetheless, early linguists have often had to justify how their skills could assist in a criminal case.

Tim Grant's *duppy* case (Grant 2017) highlights how forensic linguists can be of great use through applying linguistic methodology to terms with questioned meaning. This is a case from 2008, in which a pregnant 15-year-old girl was hit over the head with a crow-bar next to a canal in North London. She was rescued by a passer-by, and later told police that she had been there to meet the father of her unborn child, a grime musician called Brandon Jolie. As part of the investigation his phone and computer were seized. His phone showed him to be elsewhere at the time of the attack, but the computer contained incriminating Internet Relay Chats (IRC) between him and another grime musician, Kingsley Ogundele. The IRC platform used was MSN messenger, a text-based instant messaging system for group or private communication (that no longer exists). The language used in the chat between Jolie and Ogundele was predominantly in a variant of English popularly known as Multicultural London English (MLE) that is influenced by a range of languages and cultures (Cheshire et al. 2011). The chat also contained language features that are common in computer-mediated communication (CMC), including emojis, abbreviations, colloquial terminology, etc.

The forensic linguistic aspect of this case predominantly revolved around the following phrase:

I'll get the fiend to duppy her den.

MLE is not generally widely understood outside its own community of speakers, as it is a variety of English that contains a high number of non-mainstream British English features. The concern of the prosecution team was that the language used would be unclear to the court. They therefore hired Grant to give a 'translation of the language for provision to the court of any of the meanings which might be unclear' (Grant 2017: 2). A *fiend* is a drug user, and *den* represents a substitution of [d] for /ð/ that appeared throughout the texts (in this case *den* means 'then'). *Duppy* is a term commonly used in Caribbean Englishes, such as Jamaican patois, that alludes to a ghost or dead person that haunts people, or is an evil omen. Therefore, linguistic extrapolation of the term would suggest *duppy* as a verb in *I'll get the fiend to duppy her den* might refer to killing or harming the girl.

A logical next step for Grant to determine the meaning was to see how the term is actually used. At the time *duppy* did not (and still does not) appear in the majority of standard corpora, which might be based, for example, on texts from newspapers or literature. It does, however, currently appear in the Corpus of Contemporary American English (COCA). In order to understand how a term is used, linguists look at the **co-text** or the language that surrounds it. This can be done most easily through **concordance lines** which show the term in question, along with a number of words from before and after. Table 9.2 shows the outputs from a COCA search using SketchEngine.

Look carefully at Table 9.2 and consider the following questions. What do you see as the difference between how the term appears in COCA and how it appears in the case? How would you deal with this?

Table 9.2 Duppy COCA concordance lines – adapted from COCA export (www.engl ish-corpora.org/coca/)

Number	Year	Genre	Publication	Abridged context
1	2017	TV	Criminal Minds	And our second victim was burned. This is Obeah. It's **Duppy** rituals.
2	2017	TV	Criminal Minds	**Duppy?** Clara: Well, the Jamaican belief system Obeah is very similar to voodoo
3	2017	TV	Criminal Minds	And that earthly spirit can escape the body and become and malevolent spirit called a **Duppy**. And it's believed that **Duppies** roam the earth for all of eternity haunting
4	2017	TV	Criminal Minds	Yes, Jamaicans grow up hearing **Duppy** stories. They are used to impart a moral lesson, much like fairy tales
5	2014	FIC	HudsonRev	It's just you, just your white nightgown, but you've heard of **duppy** brides dressed all in white, riding the breezes to snatch lovelorn girls
6	2012	WEB	reggae141.com	music the band ever made. Such tracks as 'Soul Rebel', '**Duppy** Conqueror', '400 Years', and 'Small Axe' were not only
7	2012	WEB	reggae141.com	LP that included new versions of some of the band's older songs: '**Duppy** Conqueror', for instance
8	2011	FIC	Antipodes	? # You tink I is frighten fe you? # Because you Mudda see **duppy** # So put whitey wash in you' kin
9	2002	FIC	FantasySciFi	Dis de night dey be playin 'de **duppy** movies'. 'I beg your pardon?'
10	2002	FIC	FantasySciFi	On de television. Dey plays de **duppy** movies at midnight of a Saturday.
11	1998	FIC	Ploughshares	A **duppy** by default, he was drowned, but he came out of the sea.
12	1998	FIC	Ploughshares	'I tellin' her' bout da **duppy**'. The driver gestured with his thumb to Charlotte.
13	1998	FIC	Ploughshares	The driver gestured with his thumb to Charlotte. 'What **duppy**?' # 'Ah, you doan know, mahn?'
14	1998	FIC	Ploughshares	the bar which claimed the **duppy** each night. It was only a few blocks away.
15	1998	FIC	Ploughshares	Charlotte didn't need to believe the **duppy** story to check it out. No one else seemed to.

(Continued)

Table 9.2 (Continued)

Number	Year	Genre	Publication	Abridged context
16	1998	FIC	Ploughshares	A **duppy**, he explained, wouldn't enter a building without first counting all the grains
17	1998	FIC	Ploughshares	no, your average **duppy** couldn't do that before daybreak, the hour when all **duppies** are due back
18	1998	FIC	Ploughshares	'It's the **duppy**', the bartender said as soon as she took a stool at the bar
19	1998	FIC	Ploughshares	leaned back on his stool to call over to Charlotte, 'He's no **duppy**'.
20	1998	FIC	Ploughshares	It seemed clear that all the stories about the **duppy** were a joke. Anyone could see he was no sage.
21	1998	FIC	Ploughshares	'Yes, I heard you were a **duppy**', Charlotte offered tentatively. She still wasn't sure she wanted to get
22	1998	FIC	Ploughshares	That's why everyone's saying I'm a **duppy**.
23	1998	FIC	Ploughshares	Greg had drawn up to the bucket. 'Cause she friends with the **duppy**'
24	1998	FIC	Ploughshares	'He isn't a fuckin' **duppy**', Greg said.
25	1998	FIC	MassachRev	The notion of the shadow, our own ghostly self, what Jamaicans call the **duppy**, seems richer than Freud's unconscious, that demon within us.
26	1998	FIC	MassachRev	, has a breakdown and must return home, I wonder who has taken her **duppy**.
27	1998	FIC	MassachRev	'I believed you had my **duppy**', I say, provoking gales of laughter.
28	1998	FIC	MassachRev	Mon, the only time I got your **duppy** is when we play dominoes. I am dumbfounded.
29	1998	FIC	MassachRev	Ya mon, I got your **duppy** den. 'So I've been a dumb cluck'.
30	1997	FIC	AntiochRev	His upper body twitched a lot too. 'Maybe he a **duppy**', Azinta had suggested one September day
31	1997	FIC	AntiochRev	**Duppy** or not, tonight Sam was suffering from all his tics.
32	1992	ACAD	LatAmPopScult	This genre of Jamaican serials is directly related to the Jamaican '**duppy**' story. '**Duppy**' stories hold a special place in Jamaican folk culture
33	1992	ACAD	LatAmPopScult	'**Duppy**' stories hold a special place in Jamaican folk culture.

COCA shows only instances where *duppy* is used as a noun. It does not appear at all as a verb (as it was used in the case). On the basis of COCA alone, then, it is not possible to confirm the interpretation that *duppy* is being used as a verb to indicate intent to harm. However, a limitation of COCA is that it is not particularly representative of the data that of the case (an MSN conversation between two UK grime musicians). Furthermore, there were at the time no definitions in reputable slang dictionaries that related to it being used as a verb. Grant therefore collected language data for his own corpus for the case. His corpus was considerably smaller than the COCA corpus, but it was more representative of the data in the case. It was drawn from an online grime music forum where the people who were posting virtually all claimed to be from East London (i.e., were very much in the same community, and using the same variety of English). Using this he ultimately determined that the phrase can be seen as a conspiracy to murder (Grant 2017: 8).

Grant advocates three main strategies for determining meaning of slang in forensic linguistic cases:

1. Use a formal dictionary of slang.
2. Consult sources (such as less formal internet sources).
3. Collect a corpus.

This case also demonstrates how we can determine meaning when turning to a dictionary is not a solid option. As discussed in the previous sections, lexicographers now often rely on corpus linguistic approaches to determine meaning. In lexicography and forensic linguistics, when it comes to determining meaning, 'the reliability of the sources is key' (Grant 2017: 8). This is particularly true with relation to terms that could be considered slang, as there are a lot of online resources which would not be considered reliable in linguistic terms, despite framing themselves as dictionaries. This is because the 'definitions' are often written by individuals for purposes other than seeking to define the term; they are certainly not developed using solid corpus methodology. For example, if we put one of our names (Ria) into a leading online slang dictionary, it comes back with various definitions about being a good friend, smart and beautiful, and even as someone who is having love professed to them through the definition. The communicative purpose of these definitions is clearly not that of defining the word or term. While more common slang terms do receive true and meaningful entries, there is a community aspect to online sources where preferred definitions are 'upvoted' to receive public recognition, as well as the possibility that some people simply enjoy creative writing and contributing nonsense. It remains the fact that we are often unaware of how exactly language is used (think how hard the *table* task Activity 9A was) if we are not supported by corpus techniques.

The full analysis and the nuances around the *duppy* case can be read in Grant (2017), but the key observation for us is that 'translation' or interpretation between varieties of a language can be of much benefit in criminal proceedings. Groups of people will often develop new ways of using certain terms that may not be universal across all members of the wider community. Further, these speakers may not be aware of the lack of universality, or not be fluent enough in a different variety (or code) of the language to explain it in another way. Similarly, the wider population might not be aware that the term is established within that group. As Grant explains: 'It is this universality of non-standard language and the discriminatory patterns of comprehension that creates a need for explanation of slang terms to the Court' (Grant 2017: 3).

9.5   Language crimes

There is an entire class of crimes that linguists often term **language crimes**. These are crimes that are committed solely through communication, and include bribery, solicitation, threatening, and extortion.

A further complication to these crimes, and the reason they are of particular interest to linguists, is that people tend not to undertake them explicitly. In other words, if we are seeking to bribe someone, we tend not to state explicitly 'We will give you £1000 if you grant us the planning permission we want'. Instead, people will commonly allude to the transaction, or rely on shared indirect meaning, for example saying 'perhaps this will help matters', as they slide the money across the table. This lack of directness can make it hard to prove definitively that a particular communication was intended to have a certain meaning. It is also open to misunderstanding, or the claim that something else was meant. The following sections look at the determination of meaning with relation to potential threat and bribery word crimes.

9.5.1   Threats

It should be noted that not all threats are crimes, or would be considered criminal. Further, it is not always clear whether something is a threat or not. For example, if someone says 'break a leg', are they threatening the person they are talking to? Or is it a case of wishing them luck before a stage performance? (In both the UK and the US, it is commonly considered an alternative way of wishing an actor good luck.) Context plays a huge part in this. If you wish someone you've recently had a disagreement with to 'break a leg' at the top of a staircase, it is probably considerably more threatening than if they are a friend who is about to go on stage and they are aware of the superstition around breaking a leg and wishing luck.

The *Oxford English Dictionary* defines a threat as 'a statement of an intention to inflict pain, injury, damage, or other hostile action on someone in retribution for something done or not done'. The forensic linguist Bruce Fraser (1998) considered threatening from a linguistic perspective, and narrowed it down to three key points. In order to make a threat, a speaker must:

- express an intention to personally commit an act, or to be responsible for having an act occur;
- believe that the act will lead to an unfavourable state of affairs to the addressee; and
- intend to intimidate the addressee through the addressee's awareness of the speaker's intention.

It should further be noted that not all threats are criminal. For example, you might threaten a child with the consequence of not being allowed pudding if they don't eat their main course.

The Twitter Joke Trial in 2010 was a case that raised the issue of language and meaning within the UK media. After a bout of cold weather, significant travel disruption occurred, including the closure of airports. Twitter user Paul Chambers, who intended to fly to Northern Ireland, tweeted: 'Crap! Robin Hood airport is closed. You've got a week and a bit to get your shit together, otherwise I'm blowing the airport sky-high!!'

A week later, staff from Robin Hood Airport (situated between Sheffield and Doncaster in the north of England) discovered the tweet but did not consider it a credible threat. Nonetheless, they notified the police, who arrested and charged Chambers for sending a menacing communication. In May 2010, he was found guilty and ordered to pay a fine. However, the trial attracted considerable media interest as well as celebrity commentary, much of which focused on the language used and the difference between a joking threat and a real threat. Eventually Chambers appealed, and the appeal was upheld. The conviction was quashed 'on the basis that this "tweet" did not constitute or include a message of a menacing character' (Paul Chambers v. Director of Public Prosecutions 2012: 13). While the analysis undertaken was predominantly legal, not linguistic, this case can serve as an example between serious and joking threats, and how different interpretations by different audiences can have significant implications.

9.5.2   Discourse markers and bribery

Discourse markers – items such as *okay, um, oh, well, right, yeah, you know* – are linguistic items that act as cognitive, expressive, social, and textual indicators in an utterance (Schiffrin 1994). For instance, the discourse marker *oh!* indicates a change in cognition, a mental shift of sorts, as illustrated by examples such as *'Oh! That reminds me...'* The functions of discourse markers are so wide ranging, it is helpful to understand the characteristics of discourse markers as they relate to meaning. According to Holker (1991), discourse markers share the following criteria:

- They do not affect the truth conditions of an utterance.
- They do not add anything to the propositional content of an utterance.
- They are related to the speech situation and not to the situation talked about.

- They have an emotive, expressive function.

Put simply, you can remove discourse markers from a text without changing its conceptual or referential meaning. Compare, for example, *Oh, well, I was like ... uh... going to the shops, yeah?* with *I was going to the shops*. The discourse markers convey information about the speaker's certainty and attitude, but the core meaning of the narrated event remains if the discourse markers are removed.

What is important here is that the meanings of discourse markers are very much dependent on the context. Consider the use of *okay* in the following scenario:

Person A says: 'I've had a great idea!'
Person B replies: 'Okay'

When given in written form, there is a lack of context, which in turn obfuscates what *okay* is likely to mean. In general, the word can have a variety of different meanings. It could be used, for example, to mean the following:

- assent, an agreement to do whatever A is suggesting;
- extreme caution 'Okaaay';
- a desire to learn more;
- that the person is not actually paying attention at all to Person A and is instead engrossed in their phone;
- 'No. That is ridiculous';
- 'Here we go again' (often accompanied with an eye-roll or sigh);
- 'Let's move to the next topic';
- 'I won't commit and want to think about this'.

When spoken, the intended meaning (out of the long list of the potential options) can be indicated through phonetic elements such as intonation, rhythm, duration, and pausing. When the participants are face-to-face or able to see each other, there might be movement or gestures that indicate the meaning (e.g., a head nod, an encouraging hand wave, or a lack of eye contact). When written (for example in a WhatsApp message), there might be other markers such as emojis, punctuation, or amendments to spelling (e.g., *okaaay...*) that signal the intended meaning of the term.

Now consider that there was a recording in which, instead of a great idea, the proposition was an allusion to giving the person a bribe.

Person A says: 'What if I donate five million dollars to your wife's charity?
                          Can I be President of the University then?'
Person B says: 'Yeah'

What information would you require to determine whether this 'yeah' was an agreement to what A was asking, or something else? Perhaps there might be paralinguistic clues like the voice trailing off, as in 'yeah....I'm not so sure about that', or laughter as in 'haha yeah, there's no way', or sarcastic tone as in 'yeah right, that'll be the day!' Clearly we need to consider the wider context in which the utterance occurs, including its phonetic features. It is for this reason that linguists will regularly include much more information than just words when writing transcripts, information such as pauses, elongation, changes in tone, overlapping speech, etc.

In conclusion, we have already established how context can affect meaning, and is in fact deeply integral to understanding. So far we have been assuming that the speaker and the listener are sharing a common context. However, this is not always the case. Consider a listener (such as a police officer) who is monitoring a conversation via a covert recording. The context of a legally allowed covert recording instantly foregrounds the question of whether the speakers are doing or discussing things that are illegal. Consider then how this might affect the listener's interpretation of the discourse marker *okay*. Given the context, they might be more likely to interpret it as indicating (nefarious) agreement, rather than any of the other options. Under these conditions, we might talk about the priming effect that the context and wider situation might have on the listener.

This is not just a hypothetical situation, but instead reflects several real cases. One of the earliest was *Texas v. Davis* in 1979 (discussed along with similar cases in Shuy 2001) in which an oil tycoon was accused of soliciting the murder of his wife. Tape recorded conversations between Davis and an undercover employee allegedly showed him soliciting the murder. However, Davis never brought up the topic or killing himself, and mainly responded by changing the topic, saying nothing, or with the discourse marker 'uh-huh'. The prosecution argued that these discourse markers were Davis agreeing with the undercover employee's offers; by contrast, the defence argued that they were markers of listening not agreement. There was also an audio recording and accompanying transcript in which Davis seemingly replied 'good' to incriminating language from the employee. However, along with the context from a covert video recording of the encounter, Shuy was able to show that there were two conversations going on, and that Davis was unlikely to be able to hear the words of the employee. The comment 'good' was therefore more likely in relation to a different track of conversation. Looking at the transcript alone would have given a very different interpretation of events. This serves to demonstrate the sometimes uncontrollable and unintended effects of context, and how context can lead to misunderstanding or bias in interpretation.

9.6 Discourse analysis and meaning - ISIS case

So far we have largely been considering meaning at a lexical to sentence level. The following case shows how meaning is influenced by discourse level aspects. Karoli Christensen's (2022) case details a pragmatic discourse analysis of 195

Skype chat messages between a young man (pseudonym Kamil) and another (pseudonym Faisal), in which Faisal was seemingly encouraging Kamil to 'come' somewhere. The chat was in Danish with some Arabic phrases. The underlying question was whether this chat was evidence that Kamil was planning on travelling to Syria (though this question was not revealed to the linguist beforehand). Police approached Christensen to provide linguistic analysis. They had made their own attempts at explaining the implicit meaning of the chat messages, but recognised that there was much potential room for error or misinterpretation. They therefore approach Christensen to undertake a separate linguistic analysis. Giving the example of the phrase 'Akhi it went out' (written by Kamil, originally in Danish and Arabic) Christensen shows how the context is vital to understanding and interpreting the implicit meaning. *Akhi* is an Arabic term of endearment meaning *brother* or *my brother* (sometimes transliterated as *akii* in the data). However, the two authors did not seem to possess the level of knowledge about each other that would indicate a normal sibling relationship. This in turn indicates that the term is more likely being used to indicate non-literal kinship, such as people that consider themselves part of the same group might feel. Similarly, *it went out* is also unclear without consideration of the context. *Went out* (like much natural language) is polysemous, i.e., it could have more than one potential meaning. *I went out last night* might mean I left the house and went to a restaurant, or in the phrase *the fire/light went out*, it takes on the meaning of something stopping working. In addition, there was indication that the two men had switched modes of communication from Skype chat to a spoken conversation, and there was a significant time gap between Faisal's message and Kamil's response. The pronoun *it* does not clearly indicate something in particular, until you look at the message before from Faisal, where he writes *akii the connection it is bad*. This indicates that *it* is pointing back to Faisal's message, and more specifically means *the connection* or their mode for having a spoken conversation.

This sentence alone is arguably not vital to the wider case, but it is easy to see how it could be misinterpreted. Knowing that Kamil is in a place where the power often goes out can feed into the wider evidentiary picture. And a series of misinterpretations across the wider data could have a devastating effect. The police recognised the risk of this, and wisely consulted a linguist to provide input. This case demonstrates not only the importance of context in determining meaning, but how broad that context can be. It also shows how a linguist can aid in providing clarity and understanding, even when the judicial system operates in the main language used in the data.

9.7   Warning labels

An interesting area of legal discourse that people often overlook, but is prevalent in day-to-day life, is that of warning labels. The stereotypical 'bad' warning label is the warning label on a pack of peanuts that states 'Warning: May contain nuts'. There are so many warning labels that could be considered absurd that there are even contests to celebrate the most wacky. The 2007 winner was a warning on a small tractor that helpfully read 'Avoid death'. This might well raise the question of what is the communicative purpose of this label – is it to *warn* and help the reader (or user of the equipment), or is it to protect the author or manufacturer from legal implications ('well, we told the user not to die')? While we often focus on intent when looking at meaning – *what did the person mean to say* – there are also many situations when what is most important is what was understood – or not. This is exemplified in particular by warning labels.

A study by Hagemeyer & Coulthard (2015) looked at patient information leaflets (PILs) in Brazil and the UK. It demonstrates that there is a clear difference between simply understanding the words on the leaflet, and fully understanding the significance of the warning. So how is the meaning conveyed, and what constitutes an adequate warning? Tiersma (2002) distinguishes two types of warning – **imperative** and **informational**. He illustrates the difference with the following example.

> An imperative warning (stay on the trail) not only orders or advises the hiker, but indirectly communicates that there is some danger lurking off the trail. An informational warning (dangerous cliffs ahead) informs the hiker of the danger, but also indirectly suggests or directs the hiker to avoid the danger by staying on the trail.
>
> Tiersma (2002: 63)

Consider the following mandated Surgeon General's Warnings. These were required to be included on all cigarette packets or advertising as part of the US Congress's Comprehensive Smoking Education Act of 1984 (Public Law 98–474):

- SURGEON GENERAL'S WARNING: Smoking Causes Lung Cancer, Heart Disease, Emphysema, and May Complicate Pregnancy.
- SURGEON GENERAL'S WARNING: Quitting Smoking Now Greatly Reduces Serious Risks to Your Health.
- SURGEON GENERAL'S WARNING: Smoking by Pregnant Women May Result in Fetal Injury, Premature Birth, and Low Birth Weight.
- SURGEON GENERAL'S WARNING: Cigarette Smoke Contains Carbon Monoxide.

Let's focus on the final one: *Cigarette Smoke Contains Carbon Monoxide*. At first glance, you might consider that this is an adequate warning: there is carbon monoxide in cigarette smoke, which is therefore bad. However, what part of the language has actually warned you of this 'badness'? Understanding the risk requires the reader to draw on existing knowledge about carbon monoxide, and to infer that the danger of carbon monoxide carries over to the act of ingesting cigarette smoke. Can we be sure that such logical inferences and existing know-ledge would be available to all the readers it is intended to warn?

To look at the steps that are required to understand this warning, Dumas (1992) broke it down into the following series of conclusions that the reader needs to reach:

1. Carbon monoxide is bad for you.
2. You therefore shouldn't breathe it in.
3. Cigarette smoke contains carbon monoxide.
4. Therefore, smoking cigarettes is bad for you.

You likely jumped through all these conclusions nearly instantaneously, but consider your own educational and literacy background. It is worth recognising that you are likely somewhat privileged in these areas, a privilege that might not be shared by many other intended readers of cigarette warning labels (such as, for example, children who might be trying a cigarette for the first time, or people for whom English is not their first language). Further, the warning is potentially even more important for those without the privilege of higher education levels, as this might also result in less awareness of the dangers of smoking. As Roger Shuy (1990: 296) writes, 'The good writer does not provide information about X, then information about Y, and then expect the reader to infer the connection between X and Y'. The language that is used often complicates matters further:

> Federally mandated cigarette package warnings display characteristics of weak warnings: (a) qualifying language (e.g., the modal auxiliaries may and can), (b) unusual syntax (e.g., the double -ing construction as in Quitting smoking now), and (c) technical and semi-technical vocabulary (e.g., fetal injury, carbon monoxide). The warnings lack significant information (What are the precise dangers? Who will be affected? To what extent?)
>
> Dumas (2010: 371)

Dumas' (1992) recommendations, borne out of her work on the adequacy of cigarette warning labels, are as follows:

1. Either formulate the warnings as hypothetical or use strong conventional warning labels like POISON.
2. Avoid unnecessary qualifying language, e.g., the modal auxiliaries *may* and *can*.
3. List specific undesirable consequences of unsafe behaviour.
4. Make the warnings conspicuous in all ways, e.g., colour contrast, type size, and position on product.
5. Write the warnings in simple syntax and in ordinary vocabulary.
6. Include specific information about negative consequences on each label in a rotational series.

7. Do not narrow the target population by addressing specific labels to different portions of that population (e.g., pregnant women).
8. When considering the use of rotating warnings, consider that differences in the strength of individual warnings may have the effect of weakening stronger warnings.
9. Field-test all proposed warnings. (This step would appear to go without saying, but, given the history of proposed federally mandated warnings, it is clear that it does not.)

Dumas (1992: 300–301)

For those interested in further analysing cigarette warning labels in the USA, the accepted proposals are available online. They detail how they will comply with the Surgeon General health warning display requirements that manufacturers, packagers, and importers must submit to the Federal Trade Commission before selling in the USA.

With respect to the cognitive load required by readers, Pryczak & Roth (1976: 243) conclude, 'comprehension is a significant problem with safety warnings... many warnings on labels of over-the-counter drugs require 11ᵗʰ or 12ᵗʰ-grade reading skills, and in some cases a college education'. This assumes a level of reading and education that much of the world will not possess, thus further alienating these groups and potentially putting them in harm's way. Other experts have observed that words such as *accidental, contact, consult,* and *persist*, all common in warnings, caused comprehension difficulties overall (Lehto & Miller 1988: 236). Studies on literacy confirm that a large number of people do not have the reading skills needed to understand warnings and directions on the products they use every day (Marsa 2000). This has very real implications for people's safety.

9.8 Conclusions

Meaning, and the conveying of meaning (so that it is understood), are integral to language and communication. There is a considerable body of linguistic work that looks at how meaning is made and how it evolves. However, the main areas of importance for forensic linguistics are determining (or indicating) meaning (or what was meant) in a text, and conveying meaning. Corpora, and corpus linguistic methodologies, are central to this work.

This chapter has introduced some of the common types of cases encountered in forensic linguistic work in this area, as well as the theories and methodologies that can be applied to assist in them. The following chapters build on these theories and methodologies, while looking at other areas of forensic linguistics.

Further reading and resources

For more on meaning making through language in a forensic context:

Shuy, R. W. (2005). *Creating Language Crimes: How Law Enforcement Uses (and Misuses) Language*. Oxford University Press.

For more on corpus linguistics as a supplement to forensic linguistic research:

Hardaker, C. (forthcoming). *Corpus Linguistics for Forensic Linguistics: Research and Practice*. Routledge

O'Keeffe, A., & McCarthy, M. (eds.). (2010). *The Routledge Handbook of Corpus Linguistics*. Routledge.

For more resources on forensic linguistics, please visit this excellent repository of data collected by Tammy Gales of Hofstra University: https://forensicling.com/data-collections/. The repository includes everything from publicly-available threatening language (Threatening English Language [TEL] corpus and school shooter databases) to private collections (e.g., the Ted Kaczynski archives).

For more information on the cases discussed:

Grant, T. (2017). Duppying yoots in a dog eat dog world, kmt: Determining the senses of slang terms for the Courts. *Semiotica*, 216: 479–495.

Christensen, T. K. (2022). Joining ISIS? A pragmatic discourse analysis of chat messages in a counterterrorism case. In R. Perkins, M. Coulthard, & I. Picornell (eds.), *Methodologies and Challenges in Forensic Linguistic Casework*. Wiley, pp. 129–144.

Activity section

Activity 9A - Meaning

The following word is one that should be familiar to you. Without looking it up, or peeking forwards in the book, write a dictionary style definition for it:

Table

The understanding in the task comes from the process, rather than having the right answer. Give yourself three minutes exactly, then move forward to the following questions.

- It is an easy word to understand, but is it an easy task?
- If not, why not?

• How do you personally know what it means? How did you go about trying to determine the meaning of this word you know?

Activity 9B - Defining terms

Doing the same task as Activity 9A, we have found the following definitions of the word table on a website that labels itself as a 'Dictionary':

• A table is something to have sex on.
• A table is an insult – worse than calling someone a plank (which is a relatively standard British insult related to the idea that an individual is *as thick as a plank* or stupid).

Do these definitions help? Does it matter that we found them on Urban Dictionary? How is that different from a standard dictionary? Coming back to your definition, consider these questions:

• What method did you apply? How do you know what the word means?
• How have you determined how other people use it?

These might seem easy questions when they are first posed, but when you try and define a word yourself it becomes apparent that language is actually much more complex.

Activity 9C - Police caution

The current UK police caution is as follows:

> *You do not have to say anything. But, it may harm your defence if you do not mention when questioned something which you later rely on in court. Anything you do say may be given in evidence.*

Write down in your own words exactly what you think this does, and doesn't, mean.

Activity 9D - Corpus searches

Now go to Sketchengine.eu. There are a range of open corpora available including the Brown Corpus (1 million words) and the COVID-19 corpus (224 million words). Search for the word *table* in each of these corpora. How are the results different, and why?

Answer 9D

A few notes on defining the word *table*. Did you consider verb formats as well as nouns? e.g., 'let's table that till the next meeting'? What about specific or technical forms, e.g., it's in the Excel table?

Will you ever be able to cover all these potential specific definitions? Do they belong in your definition? Are there situations where a definition might need to include the Urban Dictionary definitions above? (e.g., specific dictionaries, perhaps a young person going to university might want to know that in certain areas/dialects they are being insulted and not being called strong and stable if they are being called a *table*). When people first started constructing dictionaries they adopted a very similar method to the one you used above, i.e., they thought about how they used the word and then defined it in line with that.

Words are used differently by different people. A commonly used example is the word *wicked,* which can be used to mean something along the lines of *bad or evil*, or it can be a positive term meaning *good or cool*. This is an example of a Janus word or contronym. Janus words are named after a Roman god traditionally depicted with two heads looking in opposite directions (and after whom the month January is named). These words have directly opposing meanings, and the meaning largely changes due to the context in which the word is used.

Similarly, who is using the word will also impact the likely intended meaning. For instance, consider how you might interpret the term *wicked* differently if it was said by a judge or a young British student. If you think about a stereotypical historical dictionary writer (in early days this would likely mean upper-class male scholars) they are unlikely to know the secondary meaning of the word *wicked* and therefore leave it out entirely. More recently, lexicographers have moved towards a corpus approach, based on observing language as it is naturally used, and then classifying the meanings from there. This means that the definition is less likely to be biased by the writers' own preconceptions of how a word is (or should be) used, and instead prioritises how it is genuinely used in the data that has been looked at. It is how a word is actually used, rather than how it 'should' be used, that is of interest to forensic linguists.

Activity 9E - Corpus task

STEP 1: Go to a corpus of your choosing, and search for the word *table*. Using collocation lists, re-visit your definition.

STEP 2: Compare your definition to a standard dictionary definition. How did it match up? What decisions did you make that differed from the dictionary writers?

Activity 9F - Warning labels

Notice how many warning labels you see or hear in a day. What linguistic, semiotic, and stylistic features are employed to accurately convey the warning? How does this interact with other communicative purposes, such as advertising, or selling something?

Take a moment and write down the key communicative purposes of a warning label. For each purpose, write down who is the key audience, then write down how this might affect the language.

References

Cheshire, J., Kerswill, P., Fox, S., & Torgersen, E. (2011). Contact, the feature pool and the speech community: The emergence of Multicultural London English. *Journal of Sociolinguistics*, 15(2): 151–196.

Dumas, B. (1992). Adequacy of cigarette package warnings: An analysis of the adequacy of federally mandated cigarette package warnings. *Tennessee Law Review*, 59: 261–304.

Dumas, B. (2010). Consumer product warnings Composition, identification, and assessment of adequacy. In M. Coulthard, & A. Johnson (eds.), *The Routledge Handbook of Forensic Linguistics*. Routledge, pp. 365–377.

Hagemeyer, C., & Coulthard, M. (2015). On product warnings. *Language and Law / Linguagem e Direito*, 2(1): 53–75.

Hölker, K. (1991). Französisch: Partikelforschung [Research on French particles]. *Lexikon der Romanistischen Linguistik*, 6: 77–88.

Krishnamurthy, R. (2018). Modes of analysis. In A. Čermáková & M. Mahlberg (eds.), *The Corpus Linguistics Discourse: In Honour of Wolfgang Teubert*. John Benjamins, pp. 35–75.

Lehto, M. R. & Miller, J. M. (1988). The effectiveness of warning labels. *Journal of Product Liability*, 11: 225–270.

Marsa, L. (2000) Illiteracy can be hazardous to your health, *Los Angeles Times*, 31 July, section S1.

Pryczak, F. & Roth D. (1976). The readability of directions on non-prescription drugs. *Journal of the American Pharmaceutical Association*, 16: 242–251.

Schiffrin, D. (1994). *Approaches to Discourse*. Blackwell.

Shuy, R. W. (2001). Discourse analysis in the legal context. In D. Schiffrin, D. Tannen, & H. E. Hamilton (eds.), *The Handbook of Discourse Analysis*. Blackwell, pp. 437–452.

Starr, K. (1998). Report to the house on President Clinton. *Washington Post*.

Tiersma, P. M. (2002). The language and law of product warnings. In J. Cotterill (ed.), *Language in the Legal Process*. Palgrave Macmillan, pp. 54–71.

Case

Paul Chambers v. Director of Public Prosecutions (2012). High Court of Justice, Approved Judgement [2012] EWHC 2157.

10 Language of the judicial process

This chapter is different from other chapters in that it does not focus on language use as evidence or investigative work, but rather how linguists can aid in understanding criminal justice systems and thereby feed into the larger process of justice. Integral to this is recognising and highlighting power dimensions and asymmetry of power within the legal institution(s).

When forensic linguists discuss language of the criminal justice system, it is important that we understand who the main players are. We are talking about an institution, or a place of work, with a shared set of norms and values, in which there are institutional representatives (e.g., police officers, lawyers, judges, bailiffs, court reporters) and lay people (e.g., witnesses, victims, suspects, jurors) who seek or participate in services from these representatives.

This chapter presents a discussion of the various techniques used by forensic linguists to analyse legal interactions, be it police interviews, testimonies in the courtroom, traffic violations, or any number of interactions in the criminal justice setting. Typically, as linguists, we try to find the linguistic feature or marker that signals a certain thing that is remarkable or worth analysing. However, in this chapter, we will focus more on qualitative and discursive features which, while sometimes not quantifiable, can allow us an insight into a vitally important aspect of the legal world which is experienced by many people, and often those with less of a voice.

In many court systems (particularly in the United States and United Kingdom) you can observe court cases either in a public gallery or by viewing court proceedings online, which we strongly encourage you to do. So much can be gained from simply observing the goings on of this critical interaction that quietly dictates so much of our lives. We encourage you to investigate the criminal justice systems in your own communities and apply what you learn here.

DOI: 10.4324/9780367616595-10

Aims

This chapter discusses **how forensic linguists can support the criminal justice system** through **analysing the language of the legal system**. It also explores how **power dimensions** play a role through language, and contribute to the asymmetries between lay people and institutional representatives. Finally, the chapter introduces **cases which illustrate these topics**, and how forensic linguists can help expose areas of potential improvement.

10.1.1 Multilingual legal jurisdictions

It is easy for monolingual scholars and students to fall prey to their own biases and forget the fact that the majority of the world is multilingual, which has clear implications for the criminal justice system. Not only does it have implications for what the *language* of the courtroom or police interaction is, but it also has implications on the individual level. Is someone able to understand the rights read to them (see McMenamin 2022)? Are they able to accurately answer the questions asked in an interview? Are there pragmatic differences in their dialect that differ significantly from the dominant variety in the courtroom, and which could affect how a person's speech is interpreted? An example to illustrate the import of this last question is presented by Eades (2012), in the context of Aboriginal English in Australia. In many varieties of Anglo English (i.e., dialects widely spoken by people of Anglo Saxon origin), a prolonged pause after hearing a question indicates the respondent is having difficulty formulating an answer. It also possibly has negative connotations, such as indicating the speaker might be constructing a lie. This is not the case in Aboriginal Englishes, however. In these varieties, lengthy pauses are a normal part of formal and informal conversation. These silences do not have a negative connotation but might instead indicate a desire of the respondent to think. This difference in interpretation can have severe consequences when talking about legal questions.

The United States and United Kingdom operate in an English-dominant criminal justice system. These are the jurisdictions in which the authors have most experience, hence our discussions in this book reflect that bias. However, there is extensive literature on multilingual forensic contexts. For example, McAuliffe & Trklja (2018) look at multilingual law in the European Union Court of Justice, showing that multilingualism has an impact on the very nature of the law. Eades (2012), referred to above, considers differences between standard Australian English and Aboriginal Englishes. Gumperz (1982) discusses non-native English speakers in the US courtroom, while African American Englishes and discrimination in the courtroom have been addressed by Lippi-Green (1994), McWhorter (2013) and Sullivan (2016), among others. See also the list of references at the end of this chapter for more details on international courts.

10.1.2 Power and asymmetries

Power is a central concept when considering justice, the legal system, or institutions. Power has been considered extensively in other fields such as sociology and philosophy, with different models being proposed for how power can be viewed in society. For example, a class-based approach in which society can be divided into the 'haves' and the 'have-nots' with the former having more power and economic resources than the latter; other models look at elite groups within societies, the elite group being a small number of people with a disproportionate amount of economic and/or political power. Readers interested in power at a societal level should further explore sociological and philosophical approaches to power. The link between language and power has been long established, with language both representing the power structures between individuals, and serving to enforce and propagate the power differences. Interest in the link between power and language can be traced back at least to Aristotle's work on rhetoric in the 4th century BCE, and it has remained of interest to intellectuals (including Foucault 1970, Habermas 1984, and Bourdieu 1992). It is virtually impossible to consider power without considering language. However, there has been a move from linguists and discourse analysts to understand better the links between language and power. There is therefore now a body of research that has analysed how power is realised and enacted through language (for an early example see Fairclough 1989), as well as how an individual's language will vary with relation to their role within a hierarchy. These studies have predominantly focused on very specific areas such as boardroom meetings (Baxter 2012) or courtrooms (Conley et al. 1979; Cotterill 2003). One thing that has been ascertained through the existing research is that the relationship between power and language is both strong and complex. Wodak & Meyer (2001) summarise that relationship in the following terms:

> Power is about relations of difference, and particularly about the effects of differences in social structures. The constant unity of language and other social matters ensures that language is entwined in social power in a number of ways: language indexes power, expresses power, is involved where there is contention over power and a challenge to power.
>
> Wodak & Meyer (2001: 11)

Power is a complex and nebulous entity. Concepts of power also link to concepts of identity. In the same way that we do not have one fixed identity, power is also not one absolute or homogeneous entity. Further, in the same way that identity is co-constructed, power is 'jointly produced' (Simpson et al. 2019: 2).

A person cannot be powerful in isolation – power needs to be exerted over someone or something else. Power is therefore inherently a social construct.

When talking about power, it is important to recognise that there are different types. You may be envisioning someone with physical power, be it having a size or strength advantage over another, but there are other types still. Imagine, for example, the stereotypical mob boss who has sent an underling from their criminal organisation to go and beat someone up in order to get money out of them. The mob boss then holds a meeting with the underling for a debrief. In this situation, the mob boss has what we term **institutional** or **hierarchical** power (it doesn't matter that the organisation is illegal or informal, it is still a form of institution with a hierarchy). The underling who went to visit the victim, however, holds the **situational** or **informational** power. They know what happened in the interaction (what the victim said, whether the victim handed money over, what extent of harm was done to the victim, and where the potential money now is). The underling has the power to decide whether or not they divulge that information to the mob boss (in whole, in part, honestly, or deceptively). The boss might use other motivating factors (such as the threat to harm, or opportunity for career advancement), but through possession of the information, the underling also holds a form of power. There are other forms of power, too. Some people are naturally charismatic and hold a form of **personal** power that is separate from both hierarchical power and situational power. The main point is that power is not a single, clear concept, or a measurable thing that one has, or does not have. The following sections illustrate the importance of understanding power relations in different contexts.

10.2 Police-civilian interactions

All professions, including law enforcement, approach their work with their own **professional vision**, or an organised way of seeing and understanding the world based on their institution (Goodwin 1994). In other words, our profession and our experience from the institution we are working for teaches us a certain way to see the world. This might lead people who are inside the institution (such as police officers) to interpret events very differently from those outside it (such as members of the public). Language can play a crucial role in how a professional vision shapes interpretations of events, and in establishing power relations between participants in an event. We outline a detailed example of this in section 10.2.1. First, however, we illustrate how institutional frameworks can shape the way people interpret events more generally. This example also provides important context for understanding the example detailed in section 10.2.1.

Goodwin (1994) examines the Rodney King case, in which a man was brutally beaten by police (see also Chapter 5). The professional vision of the law enforcement caused the police to see signs of aggression in King's physical demeanour. For example, when King's hands moved to the places on his body where he was being beaten, some interpreted this as a sign that he was grabbing for a gun. It was therefore (in their minds) a justification for the beating. Shuy (2005: xi), reflecting on Goodwin's concept of professional vision writes, 'Everyone makes use of their own professional vision in everyday life, but we should be alert to the fact that it can also interfere with finding truth'.

This may sound familiar with recent cases, such as the case of George Floyd. In 2020 Floyd was murdered by a White police officer, who pressed his knee to Floyd's neck for over nine minutes while Floyd was restrained on the ground, because he saw Floyd's behaviour as a threat. The officer was found guilty of murder, a rare (while still tragic) victory in holding police accountable in America.

10.2.1   Acknowledging socio-political contexts

It would be imprudent to consider the language of police-civilian interactions without first considering wider social sentiments around them. Your background and past experiences will likely shape your perceptions of the police. Furthermore, it is impossible to ignore the role that race and social identity may play in today's police-citizen interactions, especially in light of the history of race and policing around the world. Based on the reality of living as a person of colour (and the wealth of literature that supports this), it should not be a surprise that large swathes of the population are apprehensive and fearful of interactions with police, as seen most saliently with the Black Lives Matter movement.

For forensic linguists to analyse police-civilian interactions, one must attempt to understand the sociopolitical context that these interactions take place within. Since 2013, the Black Lives Matter movement has been a critical cornerstone of police-civilian between police and civilians of colour. The hashtag #BlackLivesMatter was used first in July 2013 by Facebook users Alicia Garza, Patrisse Cullors, and Opal Tometi in reaction to the acquittal of George Zimmerman who shot and killed a Black teenager, Trayvon Martin (see further 2015; this case is considered further in section 10.3.2, and also in Chapter 13).

Garza, saddened by the news of the acquittal, shared her love for the Black community on Facebook. Her post was then shared by Cullors, who added the hashtag #blacklivesmatter. After seeing their posts, Tometi contacted the two women to offer assistance in creating a platform for their voices. These three became the co-founders of an internationally-recognised civil rights movement of 21st century America. On July 13, 2013, Garza posted to Facebook: 'black people. I love you. I love us. Our lives matter'. On that same day, Cullors posted: 'declaration: black bodies will no longer be sacrificed for the rest of the world's enlightenment. i am done. i am so done. trayvon, you are loved infinitely. #blacklivesmatter' (Brown 2015).

The use of the #BlackLivesMatter hashtag evolved to be used widely on Twitter and other social media platforms. In 2014, the deaths at the hands of police of two more Black men, Michael Brown and Eric Garner, continued the #BlackLivesMatter movement throughout the protests around the United States and discussions on social media. The originators of the hashtag expanded the project in 2014 to become a national network of 30 chapters, aiding social justice activists around the US. The movement returned to national and international headlines during the global George Floyd protests in 2020 following his murder by the Minneapolis police officer, Derek Chauvin.

It is worth taking a moment to consider your own background, and the narratives around police that you were raised with. Were you raised that you could trust police, or that they might be corrupt, or that they were a danger to you or your community? How might your background frame your interpretation of situations, and thus inform how you perceive threats (or not)? What impact might this have on how you communicate about events involving the police?

10.2.2 Traffic stops

Consider now a traffic stop, or when a person driving is 'pulled over' by the police. In this interaction, police typically indicate – often through lights and sirens – that they want you to stop on the side of the road so they can talk to you. You may have been speeding, or you might not know why you're being stopped. You pull over, turn off the engine, and the police officer approaches your car. They may ask for your licence and registration documents, but what happens next is not commonly scripted in our schemas of how an interaction will go. This scenario offers a good example of how professional vision shapes interpretation of an event. It illustrates how different that interpretation can be for someone inside the institution compared to someone who is outside it, and furthermore exemplifies the role that language plays in the relevant institutional framework. Crucially, it also shows the importance of understanding the wider socio-political context in which an interaction takes place.

Research on traffic stops suggests that the interaction between an officer and a citizen is a question of authority and power, and perhaps legitimacy, or the determination of whether a 'power-holder is justified in claiming the right to hold power over other citizens' (Bottoms & Tankebe 2012: 124). By stopping another citizen, the police officer is claiming a certain right to behave in a manner of authority. The citizen is thus expected to act in a way that addresses that person's legitimacy over them.

The following case offers an option to analyse police-civilian interactions and the power asymmetries as signalled through language. In 2015, a State Trooper Officer in Texas, Brian Encinia, pulled over an African American woman, Sandra Bland, for failing to use her turn signal when changing lanes. The events that followed devolved into shouting, physical violence, and Bland's arrest for assaulting a police officer. This routine traffic stop resulted in Bland being jailed and then eventually losing her life to suicide in the county jail. The traffic stop is replete with power dynamics and Encinia's quest for legitimacy (for more see Lowrey-Kinberg & Buker 2017). One power feature that can be analysed in their interaction is the use of the term 'lawful order'. In US law enforcement, a *lawful order* is a direction from a police officer that a citizen is legally required to obey, and in its obeying does not require the citizen to break the law. The officer cannot lawfully order someone to go rob a bank, for example, but they can lawfully order someone to step out of their car, which is what Encinia did in this instance. Excerpt 10.1 provides a transcription of part of the interaction, which was recorded on Encinia's dashboard camera.

Bland:	I am getting removed for a failure to signal?
Encinia:	(Overlapping) Step out or I will remove you. I'm giving you a lawful order.
(Pause)	Get out of the car now or I'm going to remove you.
Encinia:	(Overlapping) I said get out of the car
Bland:	Why am I being apprehended? You just opened my-
Encinia:	I'm giving you a lawful order.
Bland:	Why am I being arrested?
Encinia:	Turn around.
Bland:	Why can't you tell me...
Encinia:	(Overlapping) I'm giving you a lawful order. I will tell you.
Bland:	(Overlapping) Why am I being arrested?
Encinia:	Turn around!
Bland:	Why won't you tell me that part?
Encinia:	I'm giving you a lawful order. Turn around...

Excerpt 10.1 Interaction between Encinia and Bland. (Adapted from Lowrey-Kinberg & Sullivan Buker 2017: 401)

Encinia uses the phrase *lawful order* as a way to signal to Bland that he is in complete control and can exercise this control over her. However, the problem is that Bland tries to ask clarifying questions. Combined with her lack of acknowledgement of the *lawful order*, this could indicate that she does not understand the term (as in fact many people might not). When Lowrey-Kinberg & Sullivan Buker (2017) were investigating this case, they turned to the Corpus of Contemporary American English (COCA) (see Chapter 9, Davies 2008) to research the frequency of the term as it was clear from the data that Bland did not understand the term. There were 21 instances of the term *lawful order* in the corpus, and all of these instances were direct quotes from law enforcement or a paraphrasing of a law enforcement official. This suggests that the term is highly concentrated in the law enforcement profession, and therefore there is a good chance that it is not familiar to ordinary citizens.

Why does this matter? A police officer issuing commands is trying to use their (legal) power over someone to get them to do something. This in itself is not an issue. They usually receive extensive training on working with the public, and might also have a range of experiences impacting their approaches. There is the question of whether the police officer is exerting a reasonable amount of power, and is able to adapt their communication to fit the purpose. In this instance, we see Encinia seemingly attempting to exert his authority over Bland, but the manner of his communication also serves as a tool to further alienate her from the interaction. Consider if someone you were speaking to used a foreign term you did not know, and despite your requests for clarification, they just kept using the unfamiliar term. You would likely view this as uncooperative and might feel left out and alienated. This is further evidenced by the interaction shown in Excerpt 10.1 when Bland asks *Why won't you tell me that part* and he responds *I'm giving you a lawful order. Turn around.* He does not explain to the citizen, Bland, what he is actually asking of her. Seemingly frustrated by this, she is thus more insistent in her quest for clarification and just treatment. Unfortunately, Bland was eventually pulled from her car and forced to the ground by Encinia. The interaction on the ground was off camera and the details of what occurred with her subsequent arrest are unknown.

10.2.3 Police-civilian interviews

Another power imbalance in the judicial system can be seen with the police interview, where the civilian enters the realm of the institutional representatives in a new physical space. A brief note on terminology: interviews are used in an investigation to gather information – objective facts – by asking open-ended questions and allowing the witness to supply the evidence. Interrogations, on the other hand, are designed to extract confessions where police already have other concrete evidence connecting the suspect to the crime. The aim of investigative interviewing is *not* to secure a confession from a suspect; instead, it is for investigators to acquire clear, accurate, trustworthy information that can further the investigation and the delivery of justice. To do this, witnesses, including victims and suspects, often need to be questioned, enabled, and encouraged through the interviewing processes to give their understanding of events in a truthful, accurate, and understandable manner. How these aims can best be facilitated are of interest to police and other law enforcement agencies. There has been a significant amount of interdisciplinary work in the area, namely from psychology, social, legal, and practitioner perspectives. Given that interviewing is a communicative process, there has also been a considerable number of linguistic contributions, which is what we focus on in this section.

We can again use our imaginations to consider ourselves in this situation. You've been asked to arrive at a police station, perhaps you know why, perhaps you don't. You probably have some preconceptions of what might happen based on TV shows and books (which might not be from the same jurisdiction you are in, and will likely be sensationalised). You arrive, you tell someone at the front desk why you're there, and then... most ordinary people who are new to the situation would not know what to expect next. The police officers do know, however, and that's just the beginning of the power asymmetries that you will experience. In police interviews in the US, it is legal for a police officer to lie to a suspect and say they have incriminating evidence against them (note this is not the case in many other jurisdictions including the UK). This deception in the criminal justice system is a tool that is readily used in police-civilian interactions (for more on this, see Shuy 2005).

Overall, there has been much interest from scholars of investigative interviewing around question types and how these might elicit information differently. For example, open questions (e.g., *What happened yesterday?*) are often encouraged as ways to elicit more detailed responses from an interviewee. (We also noted the value of using open questions in asylum interviews in Chapter 7.) By contrast, closed questions (e.g., *did you steal it?*) are discouraged as they do not invite elaboration from the interviewee. However, closed questions can have a benefit in certain stages of the interview, such as initial fact checking. Linguists have demonstrated that it is not always easy to categorise questions as *open* or *closed* (for further information, see Oxburgh, Myklebust, & Grant 2010).

In general, there are two main approaches to investigative interviewing that are used around the world: the Reid technique, and the PEACE model. The Reid technique was developed in the United States, where it is still widely used. It is a method of interrogation that has nine steps in order to increase the pressure on a suspect and to encourage a confession. The PEACE model was developed in the UK as a deliberate move away from more psychologically coercive techniques, which could often lead to false confessions (and has indeed been found to do so). It has been adopted by police forces in other countries including Australia, Canada, and Norway. The emphasis is on creating and encouraging dialogue between the interviewee and the interviewer.

The Reid technique has become infamous because deception and manipulation are a main component of the method. Developed in the 1950s by John E. Reid, a psychologist and former Chicago police officer, the technique creates a high-pressure environment for the civilian interspersed with sympathy and understanding (and outlets for help) but only, critically, if they will give a confession. It has been greatly popular in the United States legal system and is taught to law enforcement to this day, both on the local and federal levels.

The Reid technique's nine steps of interrogation are:

1. Positive confrontation.
    - Advise the suspect that the evidence has led the police to the individual as a suspect.
    - Offer the person an early opportunity to explain why the offense took place.
2. Try to shift the blame away from the suspect to some other person or set of circumstances that prompted the suspect to commit the crime.
    - Develop themes containing reasons that will psychologically justify or excuse the crime.

- Themes may be developed or changed to find one to which the accused is most responsive.
3. Try to minimise the frequency of suspect denials.
4. At this point, the accused will often give a reason why he or she did not or could not commit the crime.
   - Try to use this to move towards the acknowledgement of what they did.
5. Reinforce sincerity to ensure that the suspect is receptive.
6. The suspect will become quieter and listen.
   - Move the theme of the discussion toward offering alternatives. If the suspect cries at this point, infer guilt.
7. Pose the 'alternative question', giving two choices for what happened; one more socially acceptable than the other.
   - The suspect is expected to choose the easier option but whichever alternative the suspect chooses, guilt is admitted.
   - There is always a third option, which is to maintain that they did not commit the crime.
8. Lead the suspect to repeat the admission of guilt in front of witnesses and develop corroborating information to establish the validity of the confession.
9. Document the suspect's admission or confession and have him or her prepare a recorded statement (audio, video, or written).

In contrast, in the United Kingdom in the 1970s and 1980s, the Court of Appeals found a number of confessions were made involuntarily. They therefore decided to implement a change. In the early 1990s, in a collaboration with law enforcement and psychologists, a new interviewing framework was developed to combat the number of false confessions that were identified and to make the interviewing process less manipulative. John Baldwin was a lead researcher involved in this process. Baldwin published a report which identified a number of weaknesses in police interviewing: 'in many cases officers are unacquainted with even basic details of the investigation; they frequently make assumptions of guilt and exert undue pressure upon suspects; and they are unduly repetitive or laboured in pursuing particular lines of questioning' (Baldwin 1993: 336).

Baldwin's research motivated the creation of the PEACE model to address these issues. This framework has since been widely praised and adopted by law enforcement around the world. The acronym PEACE provides a mnemonic for law enforcement throughout the interviewing process:

P: Preparation and Planning – identifying key issues and objectives, making practical arrangements, and developing an interview plan.

E: Engage and Explain – building rapport, identifying topics and evidential information during the interview, and showing interest in the interviewee and their account of events.

A: Account – obtaining an accurate account through both initiating and supporting through tools such as open-ended prompts.

C: Clarification, Challenge, Closure – clarification and challenge are sometimes included with account, where the account can be further probed with different question types. Closure relates to making sure the interview does not end abruptly and that everyone has asked any questions, and readying a witness statement if needed, and explaining next steps to the interviewee.

E: Evaluation – the interviewer evaluates what has been said with relation to the rest of the investigation, and to determine any future actions, and to reflect on the interviewer(s)'s performance.

This model recognises that the responsibility lies on the interviewer themselves and they hold the power, but it must not be manipulated. The PEACE model also acknowledges that interviewers walk into every interview with bias and preconceptions, and the PEACE framework provides a basis to constantly evaluate such subjectivity.

 More information and guidance on the PEACE model and how it is taught to UK police can be consulted via the UK College of Policing website.

10.3 Power and participation in the courtroom

Much of the literature on the courtroom institution has focused on the asymmetries of participation. Consider Table 10.1, which summarises the hierarchical nature of the courtroom participants as described by Janet Cotterill's (2014) work on court proceedings in the United Kingdom. Pay attention to the participants in relationship to themselves with respect to legal training and interactional rights. For instance, the judge has the most power in terms of legal training but also interactional rights. Terminology from the US legal system is provided in italics.

This hierarchy illustrates an interesting aspect to the courtroom institution and how language follows suit. Firstly, consider that the judge and the attorneys are listed in the same hierarchy in both columns. As Cotterill (2014: 46) writes, 'their interactional potential is commensurate with their legal training

Table 10.1 Courtroom participants (based on Cotterill 2014: 46)

Level of legal training/seniority	Level of interactional rights
Judge	Judge
Barristers (*attorneys*)	Barristers (*attorneys*)
Solicitors	Solicitors (*attorneys/advocates*)
Interpreters	Expert Witnesses
Jurors	Witnesses/Defendants during examination in chief (*direct examination*)
	Witnesses/Defendants during cross examination
	Jurors

and seniority'. This means that the relative expertise these two main institutional representatives have directly correlates with their level of interactional rights. The lay people involved in the courtroom (witnesses and jurors) both have the lowest amount of training and lowest institutional knowledge, and lowest amount of interactional rights. Witnesses are not only poorly placed in the hierarchy of seniority or experience in the courtroom, particularly during cross-examination testimony, but also poorly placed in the hierarchy of linguistic rights, i.e., what they can say and when, within the interaction. Throughout most of the literature on language in the judicial process, researchers explain the disadvantages that witnesses are faced with in terms of constraints on what they can say and when they can say it.

The courtroom is a good area to look at the linguistic effects of power hierarchies, as the roles are firmly set. Witnesses are typically required to conform to a yes or no answer during a cross-examination (Agar 1985) and are interrupted by the judge if their response becomes too 'narrative-like' (Conley, O'Barr, & Lind 1978). However, this is not found with all witness questioning. Conley, O'Barr, and Lind's (1978) work on style in the courtroom finds that 'legal tacticians have advised that the credibility of a witness can be enhanced on direct examination if the lawyer allows and encourages the witness to testify in the narrative style' (p. 1387). The narrative style in their framework is similar to the canonical examples of narrative introduced to the field of linguistics by Labov & Waletsky (1967). That is, a narrative follows a temporal order of events and includes a description of where, when, and to/by whom some sequential order of events occurred. Conley, O'Barr, & Lind's (1979) conclusions suggest that if those hearing the testimony (i.e., members of the jury) hear a narrative style from the witness, then it indicates that the lawyer has faith in the witness's competence. Also, by nature of the structure of examination, witnesses are restricted from asking questions. However, if they do, their questions are typically limited to requests for clarification (Agar 1985; Cotterill 2014).

Understandably, much of the interest in power focuses on disparities or differences in power and the inequalities this presents. A clear example of power on the interactional side of legal discourse can be seen with the asymmetrical power in the courtroom. There are four types of asymmetries, or imbalances, in institutional conversations (adapted from Heritage 1997):

1. Asymmetries of participation.
2. Asymmetries of interactional and institutional 'know-how'.
3. Asymmetries of knowledge and levels of epistemological caution.
4. Rights of access to knowledge.

Consider a typical cross-examination in adversarial legal systems (which is the legal system in the UK and the US, as opposed to the inquisitorial legal system of France, Italy, Saudi Arabia, etc.; for more discussion of this see Chapter 13). The cross-examination is a fascinating interaction because it is restricted by a set of institutional rules of the courtroom that all participants must adhere to. Not adhering to these rules can have severe consequences in the form of official legal punishment. As such, the adversarial cross-examination has been the focus of much analysis (see Atkinson & Drew 1979, Drew & Heritage 1992). Overall, cross-examinations are restricted to a question-answer sequence where the attorney provides the question, and the witness provides the answer. As has been attested by many researchers and scholars, witnesses are by design not *allowed* to give unrequested information.

Consider, for example, a cross-examination of a rape victim. The victim (acting as a witness on the stand) answers an attorney's question but provides additional explanation to contextualise their answer. This extra information is not allowed under the court rules, so the opposing attorney would likely object. The judge would then consider the situation, and likely say that the extra information should be struck from the record (with any jurors instructed to ignore it). This power asymmetry means that the victim is disempowered from being allowed to include what they consider relevant (for discussion on interviewing of rape victims in police interviews see MacLeod 2020). Let's consider the scenario with respect to Heritage's (1997) asymmetries mentioned above:

1. Asymmetries of participation: the attorney is allowed to ask questions, but the witness is only allowed to answer the question asked. The witness is *not* allowed to ask questions, unless a request for clarification. The attorney has fewer participatory constraints but is required to adhere to certain institutional restrictions on what questions to ask, and the judge is the final decision-maker (gatekeeper) for whether the participation is allowed in the courtroom.
2. Asymmetries of interactional and institutional 'know-how': the attorney knows what is expected on the interactional level (thanks to their years of training and experience), but the witness does not have knowledge of what is expected. Therefore, the witness has likely worked with someone with this knowledge to prepare for testimony.
3. Asymmetries of knowledge and epistemological caution: this component of asymmetry is trickier to understand. A fair amount of caution is brought to the courtroom. For example, the witness is generally more apprehensive about what they are allowed to say and what they *should* say. The institutional representatives (e.g., lawyers and judges) are more savvy about what is allowed, but are generally cautious about what information to share and when. The knowledge they both have access to and their motivations for caution are subtly different.
4. Rights of access to knowledge: this is critical to the discussion of participation and power. Who is allowed to know what information is kept under tight control by the institutional gatekeepers, such as the attorneys and notably the judges. This is most obvious when judges decide whether or not a lawyer is allowed to talk about a particular piece of potential evidence in front of the jury.

10.3.1   Power and language in the courtroom

One of the areas where power differences are most visible is the courtroom. It is unsurprising therefore that this has attracted a lot of research into language and power. This started in the US with the work of Conley & O'Barr (1990). They examine how language is treated in the courtroom on the institutional level, and explore how variations in language have, historically, been perceived on a systemic level. The researchers argued that the speakers who spoke in what they deemed a more 'powerless' speech style (i.e., they used a high frequency of intensifiers, hedges, hesitations, question intonation, and politeness) are less likely to be considered credible than speakers who patterned with a more 'powerful' speech style (i.e., an absence of the aforementioned features). However, categorising linguistic features into a binary powerful versus powerless dichotomy cannot define an individual as such. Forensic linguists who utilise discourse analytic approaches therefore consider the socio-political environment in which an interaction takes place to understand why someone may be *considered* powerless (i.e., a marginalised class or speaker of a non-standard variety of English).

However, the concept of power cannot be considered in isolation or separated from other social aspects. A further consideration is the codes, or varieties of language, that people have access to. Translators and interpreters are provided in most jurisdictions if you are not a native speaker of the official language(s) of the court. However, there is not a clear definition of what it means to be a speaker of a certain language. In a British context, we could say that both the King and a person who speaks with a very strong Cornish accent filled with dialect terms speak English. However, that does not mean they necessarily fully understand each other. In everyday life, this might cause frustration, but in a courtroom setting the stakes (e.g., personal liberty) are arguably much higher if someone has restricted access to the institutional language code. Put more simply, a defendant or witness may be at a disadvantage if they lack understanding of the linguistic conventions or terminology used in the court or legal system.

Work in this area started with O'Barr (1982), who lays out the four varieties of language that may appear in the courtroom from data collected in American courts. The four are: formal legal language, standard English, colloquial (or informal) English, and 'subcultural' varieties. It is obviously problematic to call something 'subcultural', so let's refer to these terms as what linguists categorise as **non-standard** (though we fully recognise that this is also potentially a loaded term, and falsely implies that there is necessarily a **standard** that is accepted or used by the majority). O'Barr found that no one speaker ever used all four varieties of language, but most speakers tended to shift between the four possibilities when context required it. O'Barr (1982: 25) provides examples: lawyers are more likely to address prospective jurors during *voir dire* (when jurors are selected) using the colloquial variety 'as though seeking solidarity with them' or 'emulating the speech styles of "ordinary folks"'. By contrast, when questioning

witnesses in court, lawyers are 'likely to remove themselves from hostile witnesses
… by attempting to make the colloquial or subcultural varieties of language
appear "stupid" and unlike their own speech' (p. 26).

The difficulty of the lack of mutual intelligibility can be seen in a 2003 copyright case concerning rap lyrics. The judge had to try and determine the meaning
of a variety of rap terms including *shizzle my nizzle* and *mish mish man*. Although
the judge conducted his own research, by consulting Urban Dictionary, it is clear
that a linguist could have been of use.

The following case study demonstrates in detail how valuable expert opinion
can be.

10.3.2 Case study on language and power in the courtroom

On a rainy night in February 2012, a seventeen-year-old African American male,
Trayvon Martin, walked to his father's house in a gated community in Sanford,
Florida. George Zimmerman, a twenty-eight-year-old Peruvian American
male, was on duty as neighbourhood watch for the community. He started
following Martin under the suspicion that he was 'up to no good', according to
Zimmerman's call to 911 (Baldwin 2012). Meanwhile, Martin was on the phone
with his childhood friend, eighteen-year-old Rachel Jeantel, and he allegedly told
her that a man was watching and following him. According to Jeantel, dialogue
was exchanged between the man and Martin before she heard muffled sounds,
after which the phone went silent. Martin was shot and killed by Zimmerman,
who argued that he shot Martin in self-defence. The State of Florida filed an affi-
davit stating probable cause, alleging that Zimmerman racially profiled Martin
and shot him, as Martin was committing no crimes. Zimmerman was charged
with second-degree murder and manslaughter. However, after about a month
of highly publicised trial (see also Chapter 13), the six-member jury acquitted
Zimmerman of all charges. It came to light later that although the jury deliberated
for over 16 hours, they did not consider Jeantel's testimony even though she was
an earwitness to the altercation between Zimmerman and Martin.

During the trial itself, the race of both the defendant and the deceased was a
key component of both sides' arguments. It appeared obvious that the State of
Florida pursued a line of evidence that Zimmerman racially profiled Martin, as
Martin was an unarmed Black teenager walking back from a convenience store.
However, in a surprising turn, the Defense used a portion of Rachel Jeantel's testimony to position Martin as being the one who racially profiled and attacked
Zimmerman, whose only recourse was to stand his ground. The Defense used
Florida's Stand Your Ground Law (2005) as support for this claim, which states
that a person is justified in the use of deadly force and has no obligation to
retreat if the person believes that force is necessary to prevent their own or
another's bodily harm or imminent death.

Consider the exchange in Excerpt 10.2, which occurred during the cross-examination of Rachel Jeantel. Here the defence attorney, Don West, challenges what Jeantel said during an interview with the Martin family attorney, Benjamin Crump, about the dialogue exchanged between Martin and Zimmerman. The notation in Excerpt 10.2 indicates the initials of the person being voiced and the scope of their utterance (marked with brackets).

1 So what you are saying is that, *indeed,*
2 what you told Mr Crump in this recorded interview,
3 [$_{RJ}$ that what George Zimmerman said in response to *him* saying
4 [$_{TM}$ 'what you followin' me,'
5 or 'why you following me?']
6 [$_{RJ}$ George Zimmerman said,
7 [$_{GZ}$ 'what are you talking about?']]]

Excerpt 10.2: extract of cross-examination by Defense Counsel in the Zimmerman trial (adapted from Sullivan 2016)

This line of questioning is not only temporally complex, but it is complex in the voices being portrayed. Figure 10.1 serves to clarify the embedded nature of the voices at play during this exchange by illustrating speakers and their utterances.

What is crucial to recognise here is the contrast in voice between Lines 4 and 5 and Line 7. In Lines 4 and 5, the Defense is repeating what Jeantel

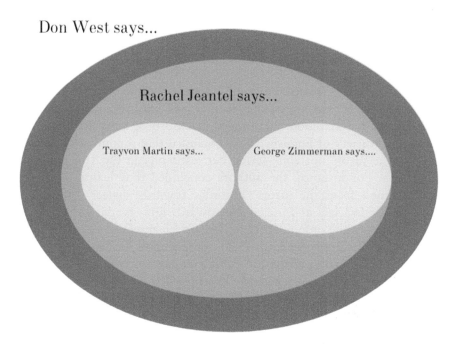

Don West says...

Rachel Jeantel says...

Trayvon Martin says...   George Zimmerman says....

Figure 10.1 Structure of voices in the cross-examination of Rachel Jeantel.

had previously testified to, concerning what was said between Martin and Zimmerman. In these lines, it appears that he is re-voicing Jeantel's production of Trayvon Martin's words. In Line 4, the non-standard spelling of *followin'* draws attention to non-standard pronunciation (i.e., [-n] rather than [-ŋ]) – a variant that is in fact common in most accents of English. Line 5, *why you following me?*, contains a vernacular variant found in many varieties of African American English (AAE): deletion of the copula (the verb *to be*). Compare this to Line 7, George Zimmerman's response. Although this line is theoretically within the same scope of Jeantel's voice (as indicated by Line 2, *What you told Mr. Crump...*) it does not contain any vernacular variants associated with AAE. Instead, Zimmerman's voice is portrayed in the standard variety, with a copular *be* present and the velar variant of –ING. It could also be argued that the Defense is voicing Trayvon Martin with the vernacular variant in Line 5: *why you following me*.

It is fascinating that there is this subtle vernacular-standard distinction between the two parties. The question remains, why does the Defense, an individual who is not a speaker of AAE, choose to voice Trayvon Martin or his proxy, Rachel Jeantel, as having vernacular features associated with AAE? The example is reminiscent of the findings of William O'Barr (1982), quoted earlier: lawyers distance themselves from hostile witnesses by highlighting colloquial or non-standard language varieties, and emphasising the differences relative to the lawyer's own speech (and by extension, that of the court). Perhaps this strategy is utilised consciously by West to distance himself from the quoted speech, and to undermine the witness's credibility in the eyes of the jury by drawing attention to her non-standard language use. Whether or not that was his intent, Jeantel's testimony was subject to extremely harsh criticism in the media and in online commentary. Her dialect and her voice were explicitly targeted to call her intelligence and reliability into question.

Rickford & King (2016) analyse many other features of Jeantel's voice and dialect, and the negative effects they had on the evaluation of her testimony. They cite one of the jurors (referred to as B37) from a TV interview with CNN's Anderson Cooper, where the juror states Jeantel was 'hard to understand' and 'not credible' (as cited in Bloom 2014: 148). Rickford & King attribute this to her vernacular variety of English. They concluded that a number of factors contributed to the jurors not considering her testimony in the 16+ hours of jury deliberation. For instance, the authors concluded that Jeantel's lack of credibility stemmed from the jurors' attitudes towards dialect differences, and institutionalised racism and judgement towards non-standard varieties of English, in addition to the unfamiliarity of AAE and Jeantel's voice quality.

Sullivan (2017) takes this a step further and examines how the institution of the courtroom, not just the media and the adversarial participants, treats Jeantel on the stand. She finds that Jeantel was repeatedly interrupted and 'corrected' in a sense by the non-adversarial and institutionally 'neutral' participant, the court reporter. In this trial, the court reporter was the individual tasked with transcribing the verbatim record of the court. According to the research, it is rare for court reporters to participate in the trial, but in this testimony, the court reporter participated no fewer than 108 times (cf. the around 250 times the judge participated). Within the 108 instances of participation, the court reporter would ask clarifying questions: *can you repeat that?* They even repeat Jeantel's utterances in a more standard form (e.g., *the mailing area* vs. *the mailin' area)*. Sullivan concludes that if the jury and public opinion 'blamed' Jeantel's intelligibility and credibility on her linguistic performance, as Rickford & King (2016) claim, Jeantel's lack of credibility may have been exacerbated by the court reporter's consistent clarification and repetition of Jeantel's utterances in a more 'standardised' way.

Sullivan's examination of language in the courtroom illustrates that forensic linguists can benefit from acknowledging the socio-political context of the legal interactions, such as institutional racism and ideologies towards non-'standard' varieties of language in the courtroom and police encounters.

10.4   Conclusions

As we have seen in this chapter, the field of forensic linguistics involves more than analysing death threats and ransom notes to aid legal investigators. This chapter illustrates how forensic linguistics applies to language and the judicial process. Forensic linguistic approaches can be used to analyse how power asymmetries play out in the criminal justice system and, as such, provide methods for improvement and reform. Forensic linguists can be instrumental in helping access the truth and ensuring that justice is served for all parties involved.

As linguists first and foremost, forensic linguists provide valuable insight on the stand as well and can be relied upon to provide expert perspectives on the issues at hand.

Further reading

A key resource for investigative interviewing:

International Investigative Interviewing Research Group (iIIRG).
    https://iiirg.org/

For more on police interviewing:

Mason, M., & Rock, F. (eds.) (2020). *The Discourse of Police Interviews*.
    University of Chicago Press.

For more on the history of race and policing around the world:

Berry, M. F. (1994). *Black Resistance, White Law: A History of Constitutional Racism in America*. Penguin.

For more on this history of race and policing around the world:

Hawkins, H., & Thomas, R. (1991). White policing of Black Populations: A history of race and social control in America. In E. Cashmore & E. McLaughlin (eds.), *Out of Order? Policing Black People*. Routledge, pp. 65–86.

For more on police shootings of African-American men and women, and protests against the police use of force:

Davey, M., & Bosman, J. (2014). Protests flare after Ferguson police officer is not indicted, *New York Times*, 24 November.

Lee, T., & Landy, B. (2015). Protesters demand answers after death of Sandra Bland in police custody. *MSNBC*, 20 July.

Mueller, B., & Southall, A. (2014). 25,000 march in New York to Protest police violence, *The New York Times*, 14 December.

Yan, H., & Ford, D. (2015). Baltimore riots: Looting, fires engulf city after Freddie Gray's funeral, *CNN*, 28 April.

For more research on police-civilian sentiments and race:

Hagan, J., & Albonetti, C. (1982). Race, class, and the perception of criminal injustice in America. *American Journal of Sociology*, 88: 329–355.

Hagan, J., Shedd, C., & Payne, M. R. (2006). Race, ethnicity and youth perceptions of criminal injustice. *American Sociological Review*, 70: 381–407.

Weitzer, R., & Tuch, S. A. (2004). Race and perceptions of police misconduct. *Social Problems*, 51: 305–325.

Wortley, S., Hagan, J., & Macmillan, R. (1997). Just des(s)erts? The racial polarization of perceptions of criminal injustice, *Law & Society Review*, 31: 637–676.

Activity section

Activity 10A – Legal institution

Consider the following fictional example: where does the legal institution play a role for both me and Ben?

I covet my co-author's dog and decide that I am going to steal it. I know this is illegal, so I keep my plans secret, but come up with an elaborate plan to lure the puppy into a rented van with treats, so that I can drive it back to my house. Once the dog has gone missing suspicion falls on me and our other colleague Ben. The police decide to interview Ben first. He had known the dog was missing, but is completely innocent and was not expecting to be interviewed. They then decide to interview me after Ben mentioned seeing me covered in dog hair. They apply to the court for a warrant to search my house, and upon finding the dog in my house arrest and charge me. This case then proceeds to trial.

Answer 10A

This is not an absolute answer, but you should consider the following.

You could say that for Ben the legal institution comes into play when the police come and question him. For me it is already playing a role when I am plotting my crime. I am clearly aware of the laws, and actively choosing to try and circumvent them.

Activity 10B – Police-civilian interactions

Much forensic linguistics research relies on open-source data, such as televised testimony or depositions that are later uploaded to sites like YouTube. You can also find recordings of many police-civilian interactions publicly available from dashboard cameras and bystander recordings.

For this exercise, browse through some of the open-source sites, such as YouTube, to find police-civilian interactions. You can search for specific interactions you have heard of from the news, e.g., the George Floyd arrest, or you can search using keywords such as 'recordings of police arrests/interrogations/interviews'. Take care that the videos aren't abridged or edited in any way so that you can get the full context. Then answer the questions here and in the following activities:

What type of interaction is it? Who are the participants? What sociocultural details may be important to the interaction?

Answer 10B

This is not an absolute answer as your answer will depend on your data, but an example of points you might want to consider in an answer.

E.g., *This is a police interview with a minor suspected of assaulting a class-mate. The minor is a 16-year-old White male with a learning disability and his lawyer (Black female around 40–50 years old) is present. There are two police officers, one is a Hispanic male, around 30–40 years old and the other is a White male around 50–60 years old. The interaction takes place in Tennessee, United States.*

Activity 10C – Mood

For the interactions you looked at in Activity 10B, how would you categorise the mood of the interaction (e.g., amicable, cooperative, aggressive, etc.)? What are the linguistic cues that support your findings?

Answer 10C

This is not an absolute answer as your answer will depend on your data, but an example of points you might want to consider in an answer.

E.g., In this interaction, the minor is clearly trying to be cooperative as can be seen by the use of the phrase 'I'm trying to explain', but the officers are unwilling to accept this as cooperation 'I don't believe you!'

Activity 10D – Power asymmetries

Consider the interactions in the prior activities. What theories of power asymmetries do they illustrate? Can you pinpoint who in the interaction has the power and how are they showing it?

Answer 10D

This is not an absolute answer as your answer will depend on your data, but an example of points you might want to consider in an answer.

E.g., Participatory asymmetry: The police officers are the only ones that are 'allowed' in the interaction to ask questions. The minor's lawyer, albeit an institutional representative herself, would ask questions such as 'Are we done here?' and the officers would dismiss her and not answer. The minor would also ask questions, such as 'How long will I be here?' and similarly the officers would ignore that question. However, the officers expected their questions to be answered. When the lawyer would state, 'you don't have to answer that', the officers would scoff and get frustrated and try to rephrase the question in a different way to elicit an answer.

Activity 10E – Power dynamics

Are there any other cues in the interaction that illustrate power dynamics at play that could be transferred to your daily life?

Answer 10E

This is not an absolute answer as your answer will depend on your data, but an example of points you might want to consider in an answer.

E.g., The combative style of communication as seen with interruptions and dismissive behaviour is reminiscent of some interactions I've experienced with classmates. These interactions make me feel powerless and like I can't get a word in during class. Many times, classmates will interrupt the flow of conversation to derail it to a topic of their choosing, and it's very frustrating. I will take my cue from the minor's lawyer from the video and remain calm and collected, and defend my fellow classmates when they're interrupted by saying something like, 'I'm sorry, you were interrupted, I'd love to hear what you had to say'.

References

Agar, M. (1985). Institutional discourse. *Text – Interdisciplinary Journal for the Study of Discourse*, 5(3): 147–168.

Atkinson, J. M., & Drew, P. (1979). *Order in Court: The Organisation of Verbal Interaction in Judicial Settings*. Macmillan.

Baldwin, J. (1993). Police interview techniques. Establishing truth or proof? *British Journal of Criminology*, 33(3): 325–352.

 Baldwin, S. (2012). *Transcript of George Zimmerman's Call to Police*.

Baxter, J. (2012). Women of the corporation: A sociolinguistic perspective of senior women's leadership language in the UK. *Journal of Sociolinguistics*, 16(1): 81–107.

Bloom, L. (2014). *Suspicion Nation: The Inside Story of the Trayvon Martin Injustice and Why We Continue to Repeat It*. Counterpoint.

Bottoms, A., & Tankebe, J. (2012). Beyond procedural justice: A dialogic approach to legitimacy in criminal justice. *Journal of Criminal Law and Criminology*, 102(1): 119–170.

Brown, J. (2015). One year after Michael Brown: How a hashtag changed social protest. *Vocativ*, 7 August.

Conley, J. M., & O'Barr, W. M. (1990). *Rules Versus Relationships: The Ethnography of Legal Discourse*. University of Chicago Press.

Conley, J. M., O'Barr, W. M., & Lind, E. A. (1979). The power of language: Presentational style in the courtroom. *Duke Law Journal*, 6: 1375–1399.

Cotterill, J. (2003). Just one more time…: Aspects of intertextuality in the trials of O. J. Simpson. In J. Cotterill (ed.), *Language in the Legal Process*. Palgrave Macmillan, pp. 147–162.

Cotterill, J. (2014). Discourse and discord in court: The role of context in the construction of witness examination in British criminal trial talk. In J. Flowerdew (ed.), *Discourse in Context*. Bloomsbury, pp. 71–90.

Davies, M. (2008). *The Corpus of Contemporary American English: 450 Million Words, 1990–Present*. Available at: http://corpus.byu.edu/coca/

Drew, P., & Heritage, J. (1992). Contested evidence in courtroom cross-examination: The case of a trial for rape. In P. Drew & J. Heritage (eds.), *Talk at Work: Interaction in Institutional Settings*. Cambridge University Press, pp. 470–520.

Eades, D. (2012). Communication with Aboriginal speakers of English in the legal process. *Australian Journal of Linguistics*, 32(4): 473–489.

Fairclough, N. (1989). *Language and Power*. Longman.

Goodwin, C. (1994). Professional vision. *American Anthropologist*, 96(3): 606–633.

Gumperz, J. (1982). Fact and inference in courtroom testimony. In J. Gumperz (ed.), *Language and Social Identity*. Cambridge University Press, pp. 163–180.

Heritage, J. (1997). Conversation analysis and institutional talk: Analyzing data. In D. Silverman (ed.), *Qualitative Research: Theory, Method and Practice*. Sage, pp. 161–182.

Labov, W., & Waletzky, J. (1967). Narrative analysis: Oral versions of personal experiences. In J. Helm (ed.), *Essays on the Verbal and Visual Arts*. University of Washington Press, pp. 74–104.

Lowrey-Kinberg, B. V., & Buker, G. S. (2017). I'm giving you a lawful order: Dialogic legitimacy in Sandra Bland's traffic stop. *Law & Society Review*, 51(2): 379–412.

McAuliffe, K., & Trklja, A. (2018). Superdiversity and the relationship between law, language and translation in a supranational legal order. In A. Creese & A. Blackledge (eds.), *The Routledge Handbook of Language and Superdiversity*. Routledge, pp. 426–441.

McWhorter, J. (2013). Rachel Jeantel explained, linguistically. *Time*, 28 June.

MacLeod, N. (2020). The discourse of (re)exploitation: Female victims in the legal system. In C. R. Caldas-Coulthard (ed.), *Innovations and Challenges: Women, Language and Sexism*. Taylor & Francis, pp. 131–143.

McMenamin, G. R. (2022). Mourning the slow death of Miranda: California v. Ceja. In I. Picornell, R. Perkins, & M. Coulthard (eds.), *Methodologies and Challenges in Forensic Linguistic Casework*. Wiley, pp. 95–113.

O'Barr, W. (1982). *Linguistic Evidence: Language, Power and Strategy in the Courtroom*. Academic Press.

Oxburgh, G. E., Myklebust, T., & Grant, T. (2010). The question of question types in police interviews: A review of the literature from a psychological and linguistic perspective. *International Journal of Speech, Language & the Law*, 17(1): 45–66.

Rickford, J. R., & King, S. (2016). Language and linguistics on trial: Hearing Rachel Jeantel (and other vernacular speakers) in the courtroom and beyond. *Language*, 92(4): 948–988.

Shuy, R. W. (2005). *Creating Language Crimes*. Oxford University Press.

Simpson, J. A., Farrell, A. K., & Rothman, A. J. (2019). The dyadic power-social influence model: Extensions and future directions. In C. Agnew & J. Harman (eds.), *Power in Close Relationships*. Cambridge University Press, pp. 86–101.

Sullivan, G. (2016). In your own words: Intertextuality and witness credibility in the George Zimmerman trial. *Proceedings of the Linguistic Society of America*, 1(13): 1–15.

Sullivan, G. (2017). *Problematizing Minority Voices: Intertextuality and Ideology in the Court Reporter's Representation of Rachel Jeantel's Voice in the State of Florida v. George Zimmerman Murder Trial*. PhD thesis, Georgetown University.

Wodak, R., & Meyer, M. (eds.) (2001). *Methods of Critical Discourse Analysis*. Sage.

11 Authorship profiling

Authorship profiling is in many ways similar to speaker profiling, as discussed in Chapter 3. Sociolinguistic theory and knowledge are used to develop a profile, i.e., an indication or outline of the author's potential social characteristics based on features in the language they use. This has been used in a variety of cases, including where there is limited other evidence to narrow the suspect pool to aid in investigations. This is exemplified by cases involving text from anonymous threat notes, or online 'dark web' paedophile forums.

This chapter introduces the underpinning theories of authorship profiling, the methodologies that are employed, and some key cases, before taking a closer look at a sub-field of authorship profiling, other language influence detection (OLID).

Aims

This chapter **introduces and defines authorship profiling** as it relates to analysis in forensic linguistics. It discusses **relevant linguistic theories and methodologies** for approaching authorship analysis, and outlines a number of **cases** in which authorship profiling supported the provision of justice.

11.1 Introduction to linguistic authorship profiling – Theory

In this section, we develop ideas introduced in the previous chapters to demonstrate how understanding the social aspects of language can aid in forensic situations and enable sociolinguistic profiling. Importantly it also demonstrates the need for a linguistically grounded approach.

With respect to terminology, when discussing forensic linguistic or sociolinguistic profiling we are talking about developing a linguistic profile based on scientific research and analysis. We acknowledge that the term 'linguistic profiling' may also be used to describe the discrimination and racist stereotyping

DOI: 10.4324/9780367616595-11

that people face on the basis of their language, akin to racial profiling. This is discussed in length in John Baugh's (2003) examination of linguistic profiling found in housing discrimination. Therefore, we will be using the term **socio-linguistic profiling** to reflect the creation of a profile of an individual based on sociolinguistic features that suggest demographic information such as race, age, gender, socioeconomic status, and more. The term **forensic linguistic profiling** relates to sociolinguistic profiling used in forensic contexts, so for the purposes of this chapter will be largely interchangeable.

Sociolinguistic profiling is a type of authorship analysis that looks at 'open set' issues, meaning there is often little contextual information that narrows down who might be the likely author; in other words, there is an open set of potential authors. When making a sociolinguistic profile, if there are a few key suspects, then we can seek data for comparison with the questioned texts (Q texts) and compare them to the known texts (K texts). This comparison would allow us to see which texts are most linguistically similar; this would then become a **comparative authorship analysis** (see Chapter 12). In many ways, this is similar to the relationship between speaker profiling and speaker comparison, discussed in Chapters 3 and 4.

With an open set or profiling question there is no such comparative option. The range of data types that might be analysed is exceedingly broad, but typically this might be someone sending anonymous hate or threat letters, or it might be someone on the dark web discussing paedophilic activity. In such situations, investigators will often be looking for information that can help to narrow down where they should be placing their efforts. This is where sociolinguistic profiling can be of investigative use.

As noted in Chapter 8, sociolinguists have consistently demonstrated that an individual's language is influenced by their social background. This might include their age, gender, class, or other languages spoken based on the linguistic data the forensic linguists receive. Assuming that our language is influenced by our social background, it follows that we can look at the language produced by anonymous individuals in order to infer what social categories they might belong to. It should be highlighted here that we are looking at explanations, and not purely computational or 'black box' approaches (in which the data is input, and a result is output, but the manner by which the result was reached is not transparent). These are often not grounded in sociolinguistics and do not account for context and how language works. There is a growing push for such automatic approaches to provide explanations as to how the final conclusions were drawn (i.e., being less of a closed black box) but currently this explanation is often added in post-fact as it is not always clear or grounded in linguistic theory.

Consider this hypothetical scenario: A police officer in a small town near Boston, Massachusetts, USA begins receiving harassing comments on her Facebook page. The poster is anonymous and does not reveal any personal information about themselves. The harassing comments look something like this:

I know all about you and your trash squad. How DARE you think you can get away with your corruption, your complicity, your collusion! Why don't you go down to the Dunkies next to Dag's Deli and get another donut, pig.

First, a forensic linguist would look at all the comments posted by the same username to ascertain whether there was one individual responsible for writing this Q text. If there is reasonably strong evidence that there is one author, based on the linguistic and stylistic choices used by the author, then the forensic linguist would move on to develop a sociolinguistic profile of the person.

Let's say all these comments were syntactically and semantically clear with no non-standard spelling or grammar. Perhaps all the comments also included a rich level of vocabulary, complex sentence structure, and other literary devices, such as alliteration (see: *corruption, complicity, collusion; Dunkies, Dag's Deli, donut*). These could all indicate a native-level proficiency of English. Another feature that would be interesting to explore in more detail are the indicators of regional influence. If this law enforcement officer was a part of a small town police department and had little fame outside this small network, it would be important for the forensic linguist to note the direct mention of a 'Dunkies', which is what Dunkin Donuts is known as colloquially to those in New England.

The importance of considering context when profiling can be seen in the example above, where *Dunkies* is a colloquial term in the area the case occurred in but could be highly unusual in other areas (this develops an idea raised in Chapter 9, showing how vital context is to meaning and understanding). Language is not produced in isolation, and it is this surrounding information that can be considered the context of a document. The reference to the location which is next to a specific deli could indicate that the author is either familiar with the police officer attending that particular coffee shop, or that the author is also from that area. However, this would be a content-based conclusion, not a linguistic one. It is therefore outside the scope of a linguistic analysis, but would be something investigators would consider.

With more comments and more language, the forensic linguist could use this similar methodology to identify both patterns and inconsistencies that align with certain demographic information.

This brings us to a discussion of the different methodological approaches used by forensic linguists seeking to create a demographic profile. Like speaker profiling, sociolinguistic profiling involves considerable qualitative judgement on the part of the analyst. There are some who consider profiling from a purely computational perspective; rather than being based on how language is used, they train algorithms to identify language-based features, and to infer from those features conclusions about the author. For example, in recent years a variety of applications have claimed to be able to determine if you are male or female based on the language of your Tweets. Their accuracy was variable, but one of the common issues with such approaches is their lack of transparency, meaning it was unclear what features were being used to assign gender. When we are considering linguistic profiling in a forensic context, it is exceedingly important that there is a high emphasis on explainability and replicability. A parallel can be seen in automatic speaker recognition (see Chapter 4). These systems are often not able to account for the context (for example, the register of the data). One of the authors discovered when experimenting with one system many years ago that any of her academic texts input to the system were falsely classified as being written by male authors. The algorithm had likely been biased by being trained on data where the academic texts were predominantly authored by men.

A lot of computational profiling research, which underlies the 'black box' applications, requires large volumes of text to train the algorithms. Collections (or corpora) of student data are often used for this, as information about the author can be more easily ascertained. There is no such thing as standard forensic data – it can be exceedingly varied. However, with the exception of specific plagiarism research or cases, student data rarely appears in forensic contexts. This is important because the communicative purpose – and therefore linguistic devices – used in a student essay and a forensically relevant text such as a threat letter, are very different. Corpora of formal texts such as books and newspapers are also sometimes used, but again the communicative purpose and the language style differ significantly from many texts that appear in forensic cases. They also introduce the issue of editors and multiple authors.

For these reasons we caution against a purely computational approach to forensic linguistic profiling. Instead, we recommend a combination of computational and sociolinguistic approaches. Significant strides have been made in this respect with work by linguists such as Andrea Nini and Jack Grieve (see Grieve et al. 2019 and Nini 2018).

11.2   Kidnapping case

This seminal case, revolving around a kidnapping ransom note, demonstrates how useful sociolinguistic profiling can be to a polce investigation. The note below was found as part of a kidnapping case in Illinois, USA. Roger Shuy was asked by the FBI to analyse the note and develop a linguistic profile, which might help to guide the investigation. This is a typed version of the handwritten note that was found on the doorstep of the parents of a missing juvenile. The formatting, spelling, and grammar has been kept as consistent as possible.

Take a moment to read the note, and look for any unusual language features. Ultimately, we are looking for any features that might indicate geographical origin, first language, age, gender, education level, etc. However, the first stage is highlighting any unusual or marked features even if you are not sure yet what they might mean.

Do you ever want to see your precious little girl
again? Put $10,000 cash in a diaper bag. Put it
in the green trash kan on

243

> the devil strip at corner 18th and Carlson.
> Don't bring anybody along.
> No kops!! Come alone! I'll be watching you
> all the time. Anyone with you,
> deal is off and dautter is dead!!!

There is a brief discussion of the key points and analysis of this case below. The case is also discussed in more depth in Shuy (2001).

You will notice that it is a very short note, as is often the case in forensic casework. However, despite its brevity it has a remarkable number of identifying features.

The first things that people commonly notice are the Americanisms (dollar signs, *diaper, kops, trash*) and misspellings (*dautter, kan, kops*). The use of Americanisms is perhaps not surprising (or particularly useful) given that the case took place in America – this serves to highlight the variability of a feature's significance based on the context of a case. If this case happened elsewhere, then the Americanisms might have had more significance to the wider case. The misspellings are interesting: *cops* and *trash can* are quite simple commonly used terms, while *daughter* is understood to be a bit harder to spell. Misspelling such simple words sometimes leads people to hypothesise that the author has a low level of education, or writing ability, but it is important to test any such hypothesis more thoroughly, and look for evidence that might indicate a different explanation. In this situation, we can see that *precious* is spelt correctly, and this is a considerably harder word to spell than *cops* or *can*. It is worth noticing that there are some languages in which the letter <K> is often used when we would use a <C> in English – most notably German (for example, *der Kaffee, die Kamera*, and *der Konjunktiv*). Again, this sometimes leads people to question if the author might be a native German speaker. It is equally important, however, to look for what is *not* there that we would expect in either of these situations. Despite the <K/C> replacement, there are no other features (such as unusual or marked word order, awkward preposition use, or tense errors) that might indicate non-native authorship. In fact, there are numerous markers of advanced, native-like proficiency. The text is very well structured, with broadly standard punctuation use, and some difficult words are spelt correctly. Further, the communicative purpose is clear and in no way hindered by any slips. This leaves another option: that of attempted disguise. An author might well choose to pepper a ransom note with features in order to give the impression that it is written by a person of a different profile from them (e.g., less educated). However, it is well documented that people are generally not very good at disguising their language, as they tend to focus on the more conscious surface level features, such as spelling, rather than grammatical and construction features (Shuy 2001). For more on vocal disguise, see Chapter 4.

The other striking feature not yet discussed is the term *devil strip*. The context indicates that this is a location term of some sort, but it is not a commonly used one. The rarity can be evidenced by corpora such as the Corpus of Contemporary American English (COCA), which on our last search showed zero instances of the term in over a billion words. It refers to the strip of grass that sometimes separates the road from the pavement (or sidewalk). However, it is a dialect term that is seemingly restricted to a dialect from Akron, Ohio. As a reminder, this case happened in Illinois (at least 400 miles away from Akron). The use of this term was therefore unusual in the context. It is reported that the profile Shuy gave the investigators concluded that the author's language showed features indicative of an educated person from Akron, Ohio. One of the suspects fit that description and later confessed to the kidnapping. It is exceedingly rare for a case to have such a distinctive and useful feature, but it serves as a fine example of how a seemingly innocuous use of language can be exceedingly useful in helping to solve an investigation. Of course, had the kidnapping occurred in Akron, Ohio, this feature might have been much less useful. The case also serves to demonstrate the importance of the case context when considering how distinguishing a feature might be. Despite being a very short note, it can be considered **feature rich** as it contains a lot of features. Not all forensic data is like this, of course.

11.3   Identity performance

The key concept when looking at authorship profiling is identity, and how that manifests in language. There are a number of facets of yourself that make up your identity. A number of those will be shared with other people, but there will be others that are different. Throughout your daily life you present different components of your identity through language (for example, where you're from, your age, gender, profession, etc.). It is not always as overt as saying 'As a Manchester City fan…' but it leaks into your language in more subtle ways, like the phrases you use with certain people as opposed to others. For instance, when discussing social media events with friends, you rely on a shared terminology from social media and trending themes (e.g., *DM me*), but this terminology might be alienating if you were talking to the average grandparent.

There are many different elements that make up an individual's identity. Consider for a moment your own identity. Do you consider yourself to be tall, smart, southern? How many of these aspects of your identity are in relation to other people? It is difficult to develop a strong sense of identity if you do not have other people to compare yourself to. Similarly, the concept of region is largely dependent on physical space: who we are geographically close to and who we are geographically further away from. However, it might also involve political boundaries or psychological factors, which yet again involve influence from other people. It is worth noting that there are different forms of space, for example geographical (or Euclidean) space is different from social space, or psychological space. We might also discuss how Calais is geographically closer to London than Cornwall is, but as it is a different country is socially further away, and the impact of the channel sea will make it seem psychologically further away to many (for more discussion see Britain 2013).

This leads to us construct a sense of identity that comprises aspects that are shared with others, and aspects that are different from others. These will vary from person to person that we encounter.

The concept of identity gets even more complex. We commonly think of identity as a homogeneous construct, though this is not truly representative of the situation. Let's say your height is 5 feet 10 inches (178 cm). You might consider yourself tall in a group of people under 5'10", but in another group of people above 5'10" you might consider yourself short. So not only does our identity vary with relation to those around us, but also we have different identity elements that we might emphasise. For example, you would portray a different identity when talking about linguistics in a lecture hall from when you are *chilling with your mates*. In a lecture hall, you would likely emphasise aspects of your identity that draw on any credentials and experience in the field of linguistics. Whereas *chilling with friends*, you'd bring different aspects of identity to the fore, focusing on social ties and shared histories. Along with this shift in focus, there can also be a marked shift in language. Consider a chemistry student talking about salt. In a social setting it would likely be referred to as *salt*, but in an academic setting, *sodium chloride*. This is because the language we use is a key part of how we portray identity.

Stop and think about the different aspects of your own identity. How many identities do you have and portray? How does your language change in relation to these different aspects of yourself?

While it might make more sense to talk about identities in the plural, it is worth noting that there is still a limit on the number of identities that you can choose to portray. A monolingual English speaker would struggle to convincingly perform the identity of a native Arabic speaker in most contexts, as their level of Arabic language would likely not be sufficient. While we might be able to draw on different aspects of ourselves in order to perform different identities, we are still constrained by what we have within our repertoire. Grant & MacLeod (2020) discuss this understanding of identity with relation to the identities people perform online, looking specifically at undercover policemen and how they can and do perform different identities through their language use. For example, officers might need to perform the identity of someone who belongs in a particular forum (e.g., a paedophile forum); it isn't a case of just using the correct terms, but the entire linguistic portrayal needs to be appropriate for the context and persona (e.g., what topics are introduced, and how). This is a strong example of how understanding of linguistic theory can be applied in forensic situations to support the delivery of justice.

The concept of identity performance is integral to forensic linguistics. When sending a threat letter, a person is normally trying to minimise their real identity, yet also trying to enhance any threatening aspects of their identity. Comparing someone's work emails to a questioned threat or love letter means that, even if it is the same author, you are looking at performances of different identities. Similarly, people often only see a very small number of the different identities that people portray. For example, you are unlikely to have seen how your partner uses language in their professional work persona, unless you also work together. That would make it harder for you to mimic their work style. In sum, this means that we need to pay attention to the context within which a text was created. We need to look at register elements, including field, tenor, and mode, and consider the wider role these might have on the context of the language being produced. This will be discussed further in the next chapter where we are looking at consistency in linguistic style across authors, and by extension, within authors.

11.4 Social variables

One common misconception around sociolinguistic profiling is that it is similar to psychological profiling. Psychological profiling has been made popular by a range of books and media (for example, the TV show *Criminal Minds*, which focuses on fictional stories around the FBI's Behavioral Analysis Unit). Like most forensic sciences that are represented in the media, there is an oversimplification of the analysis, and an increase in the apparent certainty, speed, and ease with which analysts will make their conclusions.

What a standard sociolinguistic profile cannot indicate:

- Whether someone is lying.
- Whether a threat is genuine.
- The psychological state or behavioural profile of the author.
- *Who dunnit...* or who did the crime in question.

In order to develop an accurate psychological profile, or comment on psychological state, an analyst would need to have extensive knowledge, skills, and training as a psychologist. There are areas of research that are looking to bring together these areas, but at present it would be beyond the sphere of knowledge of most linguists to comment on psychological elements, and it would be exceedingly dangerous if they tried. An important part of being an expert is recognising the bounds of your knowledge. There is growing work in linguistics and deception, and threat assessment, but these are separate areas and would not be a part of a standard authorship profile. Further, it is important to remember that forensic linguistics does not solve crimes or deliver justice (this often gets lost in the Hollywoodisation of many forensic sciences). Instead, forensic linguistics can help provide evidence that lets investigators and the judicial system do their jobs.

As a forensic linguist, you might be able to say that the apparent suicide note found next to deceased Person A, was actually more likely to have been written by Person B. But that does not mean that Person B murdered Person A; that is for the wider investigation to determine (and forensic linguistics might be a useful part in that). We consider these issues further in Chapter 13.

Similarly, the success of a case does not equate to the success of the analysis. Person B might be found not guilty of murder, due to an overall lack of evidence, but in reality, he still wrote the note. Or Person B might be found guilty, on the strength of the non-linguistic evidence, and it might remain legally undetermined whether they actually wrote the note.

Forensic linguistic profiling is particularly useful in providing evidence that can guide investigations. In Perkins (2022), a case is detailed in which linguistic analysis helped indicate which jurisdiction an investigation might belong to. In this case, there was a suspicion that an anonymous author was detailing horrific paedophilic attacks that they were carrying out. The question the UK police unit were initially focused on was whether the author of these posts was likely in the UK, i.e., under their jurisdiction, or located elsewhere, and thus better passed to the authorities which cover the relevant jurisdiction. They had a suspicion from the content (both of the language, and things such as photos) that the author was based in Germany or the Netherlands. The question was whether sociolinguistic profiling would indicate social variables that might support this hypothesis. In particular, they were interested in the linguistic profile focusing on the potential first language of the anonymous author. They had noticed a few interesting linguistic features (such as potential other language influence in the username, and grammatical errors) that indicated the author was possibly a native speaker of a language such as German or Dutch. The Other Language Influence Detection (OLID) aspects of profiling are discussed later in this chapter (in section 11.7 Native or other language influence), but the relevance for now is that the profile indicated that the author was likely a native German speaker (with influence from a specific regional German dialect). The case was sent to the relevant authority, and the perpetrator was found and prosecuted. The analysis did not solve the case, far from it, but the police being informed as to the most likely potential linguistic influences on the anonymous author's language played into the successful resolution.

For more examples see section 11.7.

11.5 Linguistic features and content

There is a key difference between language and content. As forensic linguists we are focusing on drawing our conclusions based on the linguistic features used rather than the language content. Much of the data that we are looking at has been constructed in situations where the author is aware that there might be negative consequences for them if they were identified as the author. Consider, for example, the authors of death threats, ransom notes, or paedophiles on the dark web. These authors commonly do not identify themselves, or they might use false names or insert false information. The reasons for this are clear when you consider the legal implications of being found to have written such documents. The context behind the letter construction might also be more complex, and the analyst needs to be prepared for the potential existence of such complexity, even if it is not initially apparent to investigators. We can use the content of a document that we are analysing to form a hypothesis that can then be tested through further analysis. For example, if there is a series of hate letters that claim to be from multiple authors, we might choose to see if there is variation in the linguistic style across the texts, such as one might find from different authors. Or if an author is claiming to be from a particular geographical region we might see if there are linguistic features in their language that support their being from this region. But any findings should be derived from the linguistic features.

A linguistic feature is something that corresponds to a particular element(s) of the language. This might be standard or marked (i.e., non-standard or otherwise unusual) language use, and is something that can be described and measured. Examples can be found from the full range of language levels (as discussed in Chapter 8), including dialect features (e.g., as discussed earlier, *devil strip*), and stylistic features. The latter include things like use of Oxford commas. (That's the comma used in a list prior to the final *and*: *apples, oranges, and bananas* rather than *apples, oranges and bananas*.)

Forensic linguists, like sociolinguists, are less concerned with how language *should* be used or prescriptive approaches to grammar, and more interested in descriptive approaches to grammar, or how it actually *is* used by people. For example, a prescriptive grammar approach says that *they're, their,* and *there* are all different and non-interchangeable words. However, it is not unusual to see authors using them somewhat interchangeably in certain settings such as in informal online forums. Therefore, in a profiling case focusing on forum posts, it is unlikely that an author using *their* instead of *they're* would be a particularly distinguishing feature.

In forensic linguistic profiling, we are predominantly looking for features that might be indicative of membership of a certain social group, as these tend to be distinctive or marked in some way. These features, as seen in the *devil strip* example, can provide additional information to law enforcement or investigators to help narrow down a suspect pool or to create a list of indicators that could help create a suspect's profile. In order to determine whether a feature is in fact marked in some way, we can use corpora of collected language. Corpora were introduced more thoroughly in Chapter 9 when discussing language and meaning. In the case of *they're, there, their,* a corpus could be used to tell us that using *there, their,* and *they're* interchangeably is not particularly unusual among the standard L1 English speaking population, especially if we're looking at online or computer-mediated communication. Contrast this to a grammar book, which would tell us that using these words interchangeably is wrong.

A corpus can tell us that while it might be grammatically wrong, it does in fact occur with quite a high frequency. It does so across the majority of social groups, though less frequently in more formal registers of language such as academic texts or news media.

A further distinction when looking at linguistic features is consistency within the author's language. In the *devil strip* case, we saw that the author used a letter <K> twice to represent the /k/ sound, when we would expect a <C> in standard English orthography. This indicates that there is an element of consistency to this feature within the author's writing, though it should be noted that there was not absolute consistency, as both *Carlson* and *cash* were spelt with a <C> not a <K>.

We also need to consider whether there are other situations in which the feature might have occurred. Greetings, such as salutations of a letter, are an example of a feature that usually only occur once in a text. When looking at the frequency of a feature, then, a simple raw frequency alone might not tell us much. It is also important to distinguish between a genuine, consistent feature of an author's language and a possible slip. It would quite clearly be a waste of time to spend a lot of time searching for which languages or groups use two full stops in a row (like this ..) if this feature only occurred once in questioned author's data, particularly if the context indicated that what was intended was an ellipsis (i.e., ...). It is more likely that the author merely did not press the full stop key fully the third time, rather than it being an influence from a particular social variable.

Similarly, there are some very useful indicative features which an author will not use 100% of the time. There are likely examples of this in your own language. You might have a heavy tendency to use EM dashes (—), or a particular smiley, or unusual greeting, but that does not mean you use them in every situation where you could use them.

We can talk about a text being feature rich, or feature poor. This essentially relates to how many features of note appear within the document being analysed. As already mentioned, the letter in the *devil strip* case is unusual in that it has a large number of features in a very low number of words – it was very feature rich. Furthermore, the features proved particularly useful to the case. If the letter had related to a kidnapping in Akron, Ohio (rather than one in Illinois) the use of the term *devil strip* would not have been so useful.

11.6 The link between social and linguistic variables – The research

It is far beyond the scope of any textbook to document the full extent of how social variables manifest in language. There is extensive literature and an entire field of sociolinguistic variation for your further reading. Furthermore, due to the constantly changing nature of language, we cannot fully know all potential manifestations of social differences in language. However, this section pulls together a few key findings that are widely recognised as being indicative of certain social or demographic features. It should be noted that these are generally context dependent. Nini (2018) demonstrates how important context is to profiling and that fully automated approaches that has been trained on data from a different context from forensic texts can be unsuitable for forensic work. He conducted an experiment looking at the writing of 96 participants from a variety of backgrounds, producing texts that replicate forensic materials. He argues that profiling should begin with a register analysis of the text, because the influence of register is generally stronger than the effect of social factors. When considering the register, we should include the *field*, *tenor*, and *mode* (see Chapter 8 for more). As a reminder, **field** is the topic or subject of the text or discourse; **tenor** is the relationship between the people involved; and **mode** refers to the channel or method of communication. Consider how you write versus how you speak, and the differences between WhatsApp and email. If we develop an understanding of how different groups of people use language based purely on student essay data, then we cannot be sure if those features also transfer to WhatsApp or not.

The reason this is important for us as forensic linguists is because these all matter when understanding the context of the text we are analysing. Finegan & Biber (2001: 265) lay out this phenomenon as follows:

> If a linguistic feature is distributed across social groups and communicative situations or registers, then the social group with greater access to the situations and registers in which the features occur more frequently will exhibit more frequent use of those features in their social dialects.

Therefore, it is important for the forensic linguist to be attuned to these linguistic features to then build components of an author profile.

11.6.1 Gender

It is now widely understood that gender is not a binary concept, and that gender does not always equate to physical sex. However, many studies do treat it as a binary concept. For more contemporary research accurately reflecting the spectrum of gender, we recommend current sociolinguistic texts in this area, and fields such as lavender linguistics. Wardhaugh & Fuller (2021) give a nice overview of some of the current literature in this field. We hope that future research in this area can more fully represent and understand the complex nuances of gender, and how that relates to language.

It is also worth remembering that academic literature is also not always free from bias and can reflect the views of its time; as such it is not uncommon to find literature that propagates stereotypical, or even misogynistic views of the difference between men and women's language. This will usually be older literature, and not adequately grounded in rigorous research. It is usually easy to determine whether work falls into this category with a few questions. Such questions might include: What is this conclusion based on? What is the data? What exactly in the data supports the finding, and to what extent? Does the data support the depth and breadth of the conclusion? Is there appropriate mitigation, caution, and hedging around the conclusions? When looking at research representing stereo-typical or misogynistic views, it often becomes clear quickly there is no empirical data, or specific findings on which the conclusions are based. And if there are, the findings are extended beyond the bounds of what the data objectively indicate. For example:

> The vocabulary of a woman as a rule is much less extensive than that of a man. Women move preferably in the central field of language, avoiding every-thing that is out of the way or bizarre, while men will often either coin new words or expressions or take up old-fashioned ones, if by that means they are enabled, or think they are enabled, to find a more adequate or precise expres-sion for their thoughts.
>
> Jespersen (1922), from the chapter entitled 'The Woman'

Previous stylistic research has, however, indicated certain correlations between language use and the socio-cultural gender of the author. For English, at least, the main difference lies on the spectrum between the nominal and clausal styles of language (Nini 2018). A nominal style of language, comprising features such as nouns, adjective, prepositions, and complex noun phrases, is typical of men, while the clausal style, comprising simple noun phrases, verbs, and adverbs, is typical of women. Please note, though, that these are based on statistical differences (derived from corpus analysis) and not absolute ones; an author is not restricted to one style of language because of their gender. This pattern has been found by multiple different studies, across different times, and focusing on different registers (see Biber et al. 1998, or Schler et al. 2006).

An individual might also change in their language use. You might identify as female, but choose to use more stereotypically masculinised language (e.g., more direct with less hedging, mitigation) in certain contexts. For instance, Holmes (2006) showed that women in leadership roles draw on masculinised language in 'masculinist' workplaces, whilst Baxter (2008) showed how men and women both use different communicative strategies to perform as leaders, drawing on different discursive resources that they have at their disposal (Baxter 2012).

Therefore, linguistic gender performance is perhaps better considered not in binary terms but as a continuum. In a study examining stereotypically 'gendered' features of English language, Argamon et al. (2003) concluded that more fem-inine language usually contains more intensifiers, hedges, and pronouns. Earlier studies in American English (such as Lakoff 1973) claimed that women use more intensifiers, hedges, tag questions, and politeness, all of which have also been argued to constitute less powerful language (also discussed in O'Barr 1982; see Chapter 10 for more on this in the legal context). However, re-examining these features with a modern lens raises the question of what social characteristics are actually being represented with these linguistic features and whether these conclusions can be generalised to a larger audience. More recent research, such as Bamman et al. (2014), found that on Twitter the gender composition of an individual's social group was a significant factor influencing the gendered features in their language. However, much more research is necessary to facilitate the analysis of a forensic linguist in creating a profile of a person.

A good demonstration of the importance of context in practice is the use of automated computational tools for predicting the gender of an author of a text. Now is a good point to do Activity 11A (page 260) and read the accompanying discussion.

11.6.2   Age

Age is another factor which on the surface might seem unproblematic, as we all have a biological age that increases with time. However, language does not usually correlate with biological markers. Instead, it correlates with a person's social age rather than their biological age. Social age categories depend on the societal context of the individual. Social interactions change quite dramatically from childhood into adolescence, and then again into adulthood. At this age, social circles widen rapidly as we enter high school, and many adolescents spend much less time in the family context than they did as children. Such changes can have a marked effect on language, such as the sharing of new slang terms within the adolescent group. Social and biological age do often correspond to each other within an individual, but there are many times when they do not. (For discussion around speaker profiling of age, and related issues, see Chapter 3.)

Many studies have confirmed a link between social age and differences in language use. Kemper et al. (1989), looking at oral interviews and written essays, found that complexity – the average number of clauses per utterance – decreases with age in adults. This is similar to Byrd's (1993) findings that older adults produce less cohesive text, which means, for example, that they use fewer cohesive ties such as *thus, finally, however*. Differences in swear word usage has also been documented over different age groups. McEnery & Xiao (2004) showed that use of the word *fuck* varied across different age groups within the British National Corpus, with younger people using more swear words. Barbieri (2008), looking at conversational corpora, found that younger speakers use more slang, more swear words, and index their stance and emotional involvement more, whereas older speakers use more modal verbs.

11.6.3   Geographical background

As discussed above, a person's geographical background might also be indicated in the language they use. For example, if there is a heavy use of dialect features, it could be indicative that they are from a particular region where that dialect is spoken. However, it is not always that simple. It should be remembered that many people have complex backgrounds and histories, and therefore contact with lots of different languages and language varieties. Significant movement of people both within countries and around the world can result in complex layering of language features. We considered examples of this in Chapter 7 on language analysis of asylum seekers. For example, we discussed a man who claimed to come from Syria but whose speech showed the influence of an Egyptian dialect, which was attributed to him having shared accommodation with Egyptians. This potential complexity serves to highlight why we cannot approach sociolinguistic profiling purely as a classification task, and why we are focusing on a range of features as opposed to individual features. It is the role of the forensic linguist to understand the potential influences on an author's language, i.e., which social and background profiles might potentially account for those features.

There is a range of tools that a linguist can use when determining which features are indicative of which dialects or regional language usage. The majority of these are corpus based. However, for English and a limited number of other languages there are also a great number of reference texts due to the long and prolonged interest in dialectal and regional language. However, good reference texts will indeed be informed by corpora themselves. Many reference texts focus on stereotypical dialectal items as opposed to more structural elements (e.g., for Brummie, the dialect of Birmingham in the West Midlands of England, the address term *alright Bab*). It is also worth remembering that geographical regions are not homogeneous: there is not usually a distinct boundary between where one dialect stops and another begins (we discussed the continuum of dialect areas in Chapter 7). The clearest example of geographical background being indicated through language use is the *devil strip* case discussed above, but elements of it occur in many cases.

Now is a good time to undertake Activity 11B.

11.6.4 Social class and group membership

Social class and group membership are often considered in stylistic variation studies, but rarely with relation to profiling. This is largely because they are very complex concepts and difficult to define, which in turn makes them difficult to analyse, or even to compare studies and disseminate findings.

People also belong to a number of different groups or communities of practice. Consider, for example, job role. It is well documented that certain jobs have specific jargons and perhaps even styles of speaking. It is therefore conceivable that such features might filter over into language being used for other areas. Consider, for example, 'police speak', legal language (or legalese, and the reason for the plain language movement), or military jargon (which features a lot of acronyms). People who regularly use job-specific language often find it becomes natural, and therefore are not always sufficiently aware of it that they think to disguise it in forensic contexts. An example of this was introduced in Chapter 8 with the Derek Bentley case. Elements of a statement that was supposedly a verbatim transcription of Bentley's confession contained features that were more typical of police officer statements (most notably the frequent use of *then* and specifically where if followed a pronoun rather than preceded it).

11.7   Native or other language influence

A further consideration in profiling is that of native language. Linguists often speak of an L1 rather than a native language or 'mother-tongue', but these concepts are not as straightforward as they might at first seem (as noted in Chapter 7). Consider the hypothetical example of Joe Bloggs: He grew up in the UK only speaking English, before learning French at school and later moving to work in France. He might have a relatively simple linguistic background. In this situation, his L1 is English, the language he learnt first. His L2 is French, the language he learnt second. It is highly likely that his French will always show some indication, even to a lay person, that English was his first language. This might be in the form of accent, or unusual word choice, or marked constructions.

However, if Mr Bloggs had a French parent who taught him French along with English when he was first learning to speak, or if Mr Bloggs settles fully in France, never returning to an English-speaking country, marrying a French man, working exclusively in French, never using English, and even dreaming in French – what is his first language now? Does 'first' mean the first language a person learns – even if they later lose it (consider the issue of language attrition, also discussed in Chapter 7)? Or does it mean the language that predominates in someone's life? Is someone's L2 the language they learnt second, or the one that they are second best at? What about the person raised as a balanced bilingual, or trilingual?

These questions highlight the complexity of a seemingly simple concept that underlies Other Language Influence Detection (OLID). There is no consensus in linguistics as to what the answers are, but some interesting discussions can be seen in Davies (2003). What matters when working with OLID is understanding that the underlying concept of an L1 or Native Language is itself highly variable.

11.7.1   Other language influence detection (OLID) analysis

In OLID analysis we are firstly seeking to identify any unusual or marked features. The second step is to determine if there is a potential L2 influence that might explain those unusual features. Again, we are not just focusing on errors, but instead we are looking for marked patterns of language use that might be indicative of specific influence. The features can have three different types of explanation: lexico-grammatical, typological, or sociolinguistic (further discussion on this division can be read in Kredens, Perkins, & Grant 2020). Lexico-grammatical explanations focus predominantly on formulaic sequences (e.g., fixed idioms), typological explanations are ones that relates to typological differences between languages (e.g., whether they use a definite article or not), and sociolinguistic explanations include conceptual or cultural phenomena. These categories of explanations do not have hard boundaries – features can belong to multiple categories. However, this framework is useful for ensuring that a range of explanations have been considered. It also serves to highlight that we are not just looking at errors, but instead we are looking at influence from other languages which can come across in different ways.

A good example of how lexico-grammatical features and explanations feed into an understanding and development of a potential OLID profile can be seen through the use of the term *tongue breaker*. If we were to see this appear in a text in a context where we might expect the phrase *tongue twister*, then we could hypothesise that this is likely to be a direct influence from another language, in particular, a language that uses a phrase that translates directly as *tongue breaker* rather than *tongue twister*. If there were further contextual information that indicated the author was most likely the native speaker of a Germanic language other than English, then an analyst might look to see what the equivalent term is across a range of Germanic languages. Table 11.1 shows the literal translations for this idiom across a range of Germanic languages.

We can see that in this hypothetical situation (which closely mirrors real cases we've dealt with), the appearance of the term *tongue breaker* could be indicative of a German influence on the author's English. It should, of course, be noted that this feature alone would not be particularly indicative of this profile. Instead, we would need to look for consistency across a range of features before we could determine whether or not this was the likely cause of influence, and hence, whether or not we could develop a sociolinguistic profile indicating that the author is potentially an L1 German speaker.

Typological features look at the different language structures that might be present. It is possible to determine the typological structures of different languages using reference texts and online corpora. One particularly useful online reference text is the World Atlas of Language Structures (WALS). For example, if a forensic text contained unusual article uses, we might want to know how articles

Table 11.1 Tongue twister variants

Language	Term	Literal English translation or potential calque
German	Zungenbrecher	Tongue breaker
Dutch	Tong twister	Tongue twister
Afrikaans	Tongdraaier	Tongue spinner
Swedish	Tungvrickare	Tongue sprainer
Norwegian	Tungetvinger	Tongue forcer

Table 11.2 Article use cross-linguistically

Feature	Number of languages	Examples of languages in the category
Definite word distinct from demonstrative	216	German, Dutch, Frisian, French, English, Cornish
Demonstrative word used as a marker of definiteness	60	Latvian, Indonesian, Xhosa
Definite affix on noun	92	Arabic, Danish, Swedish, Norwegian, Albanian
No definite article but indefinite article	45	Turkish, Persian
Neither definite nor indefinite article	198	Yoruba, Hindi
	620 (total)	

are used across different languages (see Table 11.2) in case it was indicative of interference from a specific language.

Sociolinguistic explanations are those that reflect cultural and conceptual aspects that might transfer into an L2. This can also include structural features. For instance, if you ask a colleague to do a piece of work you will likely start the email by asking how they are and how their family is, before proceeding to ask them about the piece of work. This is considered polite in British English. However, a native Chinese speaker might flip the order, starting with the questions about the piece of work, then progressing to the politeness and face work (methods for maintaining the dignity and respect of those in the conversation) in the form of questions about the colleague's family. This approach might be considered direct and abrupt in British English, but prefacing the work questions with social questions might be considered indirect and wasting someone's time to a native Chinese speaker.

Sociolinguistic features can also be influenced by the history and cultures related to the relevant language(s). An example of this can be seen in the variation in ways that you inquire after someone's daily health in different languages. In British English, upon meeting someone, we might ask them 'how are you today?' Previously in Korean or Malay it would have been normal instead to ask someone; 'Have you eaten today?' And in Indonesian, people might ask 'Have you showered today?' Both of these questions could be considered a proxy in the respective cultures for how someone is doing on that particular day. It is clear to see how society has fed into influencing what questions are considered as the proxy for how someone's day is going. Historically, food could be quite scarce in Korea, and the weather is consistently warm and humid in Indonesia. Therefore, if a Korean speaker has eaten, and the Indonesian speaker has showered, that might indicate that they are largely ok at that moment.

Another example of a sociolinguistic feature can be seen in a case by Hannes Kniffka (1996) which related to threat notes written in German, with a very high level of German fluency but with a variety of lexico-grammatical features and unusual linguistic constructions. This included non-standard spelling, errors with umlauts, awkward lexical collocations, and the non-idiomatic use of German proverbs. In particular, the writer used a German idiom which translated literally as 'A sparrow in your hand is worth more than a pigeon on the roof' (the English equivalent being 'A bird in the hand is worth two in the bush'). However, the version that appeared in the letter translated literally into English as 'A sparrow in your hand is worth more than two in the bush.' While this is grammatically correct and conveys the same sense, it is not native-like in either language, instead demonstrating elements of both the English and the German idioms (Kniffka 1996: 89). Kniffka concluded that the author was likely a native English speaker writing in German. This demonstrates how an analyst with an in-depth knowledge of the relevant potential languages and the cultural contexts around them might be able to ascertain which language the influence has come from.

11.8   Certainty levels

Grant (2008) acknowledges that forensic linguistic authorship profiling will not reach the certainty levels needed for it to be admissible in court, but has a considerable potential to be supportive at investigative stages. He highlights that this is similar to the case of psychological profiling. The reasons for this are complex and varied. Of particular importance is that language is constantly varying and changing, the impact of context is huge, and there are always new and varied contexts which impact language in new and varied ways. Furthermore, even if we create the world's most useful profile there are still many, many people in the world that might fit that profile. This can be seen in some of the discussion around the Lindbergh baby kidnapping in America from the 1930s. This case was discussed in Chapter 5, with respect to the earwitness testimony given by Lindbergh after hearing the kidnapper's voice.

However, the case also has relevance for forensic linguistics. It was noted (in the press and likely the investigation) that the first ransom note contained features indicative of a native German speaker (International Herald Tribune 2010). While this might on the surface be exceedingly useful information, it is only useful at an investigative stage – it would be problematic used in a court case or as evidence against a specific individual.

Although Bruno Hauptmann was born in Germany, there were a great many native German speakers living in that area of America at the time. Therefore, the appearance of German features in the texts did not indicate that the note was likely written by Hauptmann. Failing to consider this evidence within a likelihood ratio framework (see Chapter 4) would lead to what is referred to as the

Prosecutor's Fallacy. This is a logical flaw in reasoning. Given a piece of evidence with low probability (in this case, German features in writing), and a suspect who could have produced the evidence (because he is German), the conclusion is drawn that there is a high probability the suspect is guilty. The problem is that no alternative proposition has been considered: what is the probability of other people producing that evidence? The suspect is one of many Germans in US, all of whom could, in principle, have written the text. Without further evidence to place the suspect at the scene of the crime, it is in fact far more likely that the evidence was produced by another member of that relevant population. Such logical errors are common both in legal cases and in everyday life, and in part explain why the text was seen as so incriminating against Hauptmann. It should be noted that the main textual analysis was handwriting analysis (not forensic linguistics), and there was little discussion of the identification of the features that indicated the author was a native German speaker. Nonetheless the implications are clear for both forensic linguistics and forensic phonetics.

Despite the fact that forensic linguistic profiling is unlikely to reach the certainty levels required for inclusion as court evidence it has many benefits at an investigative level. There should be a rigorous scientific methodology to ensure good processes, and findings should be represented with the level of certainty clearly demonstrated (most likely via verbal likelihood ratios; for more see Chapter 4).

11.9   Conclusion

Authorship profiling can be of much use to forensic situations, especially where there is limited information about an author, for instance, the language you may encounter on the dark web. This chapter has introduced a variety of cases, showing how sociolinguistic theory can be used to support an investigation. The following chapter develops on this to look at authorship comparison, where there is a closed set of potential authors.

Further reading

For more on the relationship between computational analysis in forensic linguistics:

Nini, A. (2018). Developing forensic authorship profiling. *Language and Law/ Linguagem e Direito*, 5(2): 38–58.

For more on how authorship analysis is evolving:

Grant, T. (2022). *The Idea of Progress in Forensic Authorship Analysis*. Cambridge University Press.

For more on the assumption of identities online and undercover police work:

Grant, T., & MacLeod, N. (2020). *Language and Online Identities: The Undercover Policing of Internet Sexual Crime*. Cambridge University Press.

For more on OLID and its applications in a casework situation:

Kredens, K., Perkins, R., & Grant, T. (2020). Developing a framework for the explanation of interlingual features for native and other language influence detection. *Language and Law/Linguagem e Direito*, 6(2): 10–23.

Perkins, R. (2022). Other language influence detection: Profiling the native language of a dark web pedophile. In I. Picornell, R. Perkins, & M. Coulthard (eds.), *Methodologies and Challenges in Forensic Linguistic Casework*. Wiley, pp. 63–76.

For a discussion of a non-Anglocentric case:

Queralt, S. (2022). Linguistic profiling: A Spanish case study. In I. Picornell, R. Perkins, & M. Coulthard (eds.), *Methodologies and Challenges in Forensic Linguistic Casework*. Wiley, pp. 44–62.

Activity section

Activity 11A – Automatic gender analysers

Look for a gender text analyser online and try searching for sentences from your academic essays or less formal texts. See how consistent and accurate the answers are.

(Note that we would recommend not downloading any software, and being cautious about what text you put in.) To make it clear, we are not advocating the use of such automatic tools, but instead seeking to highlight the risks.

Answer 11A

At the time of writing there is a variety of free sites that claim to identify the gender of an author from the language used, for example, Gender Analyzer, Gender Guesser, and Gender Genie. The Gender Guesser page claims the following: 'The words you use can disclose identifying features. This tool attempts to determine an author's gender based on the words used.' When we inputted the following sentence: 'forensic linguistics is the scientific study of language and the law' the Gender Guesser came up with 'male' as the final verdict, although the author identifies as female. As you have likely found through playing with the gender text analyser it appears that the more formal the text is, the higher the likelihood that the Gender Guesser tool will yield a 'male' result. This is because they are not adequately considering the role of register (which a human analyst should do), and whether there is an adequate representation of all groups of authors (in this case different genders) in the training data for each register.

Activity 11B - Personal geographical background

From August to October 2013, over 350,000 respondents were surveyed by Josh Katz, a graphics editor for the *New York Times*. The survey questions were based on a linguistics project by Bert Vaux and Scott Golder. Katz has since created an interactive map of the United States.

Answer the questions on the quiz and see if the dialect map aligns with your geographical origin. If it doesn't align with your origin, does it match the location that most closely represents your regional identity? For instance, if you were an 'army brat' (i.e., moved all over the country/world) but you spent your high school years in Providence, Rhode Island and identify as a New Englander, did the dialect map peg you as a New Englander?

Activity 11C - Celebrity social media identity task

Chose a social media feed for a celebrity and look at how they portray aspects of their identity through their language. One research questions to pursue is: how do Pitbull, Enrique Iglesias, or Shakira code-switch between English and other languages on Instagram? What are the differences in their 'rules' around code-switching? And what does this mean for the identities they're representing?

Answer 11C

We don't offer any specific answers here, as the activities can take many different forms depending on the participant's findings on social media. However, the following table outlines some of the things that could be considered at different levels of language (see Chapter 8 for a discussion on the language levels)

	Level description	Questions that could be considered
Discourse	Larger units of language, interaction, text or document level and above	• What media is included? Is the data just text based or are they multi-modal? • Are the posts for news dissemination and the other for more personal context? (for example some artists post about upcoming tour dates on Twitter, but Instagram is more personal)
Pragmatic	Paragraph and text level	• Are all the posts in the same language? • Are the posts long or short? Do they contain embedded media such as photos of a notes document?

(Continued)

	Level description	Questions that could be considered
Syntactic	Clause level, structure of sentences, phrases, and clauses	• Is there code-switching? Do the sentences contain the same number of clauses? How complex are the sentences?
Semantic/ lexical	Clause level, vocabulary or words used, alone and in combination	• Is there colloquial language? Is there dropping of certain words, e.g., articles or pronouns? Is this is in keeping with other's norms on the platform?
Morphological	Internal structure of words and morpheme elements	• Are words represented as they might be said? (e.g., *gonna*, *walkin*) • Are emojis used to replace or duplicate certain words?
Semiotics	Relationship between textual and visual	• Have fonts been changed? Are there bold, italics etc.? • Are pictures included? Are there videos? What is the music accompanying the video (is this used to change the meaning?)
Phonological	Relating to the sound patterns and phonetic properties	• Is the speech standard or sung? Are there certain phonological elements that might change the meaning (such as rising intonation)?

Activity 11D - Case task

For ethical and legal reasons it is often very difficult to get realistic case data that we can use for tasks (the reason for this is apparent when you consider the sensitive nature of many of the cases that involve forensic linguistic profiling). Below is a simulated threat letter that was created for teaching purposes. For this reason, it is a poor example of a threat note because it is not genuine, and the communicative purpose was not actually to threaten. However, the ethical and methodological issues of including a real threat note in this book make this useful data for authorship analysis. There are a great number of real known threat texts, but they tend to be older, or lacking certainty around the author's profile information. It is true of many forensic cases, both in linguistics and in phonetics, that the truth behind the evidence is never established for certain.

Below you'll find the fictional case context as well as the note itself. Your task is to analyse the note. Notice any particularly interesting linguistic features. You can then search for potential explanations for these features using corpora, online web searches, and other reference works. Because this is a simulated note you can also search for extracts of the note in corpora or online, without news reports biasing the results.

Remember, your task is not to get the right profile answer, but to get used to the methodology of identifying potentially interesting linguistic features and then seeking out potential explanations for those features.

Case context

Ms Susan Taylor was found murdered in her home. As part of the investigation the police are looking at the hate mail she has received at her place of work, a research facility that tests products on animals. She is a research scientist there. Below is a letter that was received at the facility, by post, three months before her death.

Data

Dear Ms Taylor,

I am writing to you as an avid and concerned member of [redacted – animal rights organisation]; I found your name on your company website and am writing to you and your colleagues individually to appeal to you all as scientists. As you may have guessed, this letter is about the unnecessary animal testing done in your laboratory. I imagine that you receive hate mail frequently and are unmoved by any sense of compassion or ethics regarding this truly cruel practice. As basic decency has not been able to entice you to modify your work, perhaps cold hard facts will (as, ultimately, that's all you and your lot really care about).

Animal testing is unreliable. You know this and I know this. People have known this for years. Few dangerous side effects or reactions to these products are actually predicted by animal testing. Beyond side effects, the overt uses of these products are not accurately tracked in animal bodies because, unsurprisingly, animals react to human medications and products differently than humans would react. They do not contract most of the same diseases that humans contract, nor does their skin or hair react in predictably human ways.

Animal testing is also wasteful and expensive. It has led to hundreds of false results in recent years, opening up your company and the manufacturers to serious lawsuits. This is, at a fundamental level, plain bad research.

I very much doubt that this letter will change your mind, either, but with any luck karma will succeed where I have failed.

Sincerely,
Julie Johnson

Answer 11D

On initial reading, many students comment that the letter does not seem to have many significant features. However, the lack of obvious anomalies is in itself an important observation. We can say that there is a high level of standard language use, based on the following three main features:

- The structure of the letter is very formal, clear, and articulate.
- There are some complex sentence structures, including subclauses.
- Punctuation is used following standard conventions, including the use of semi-colons.

This does, however, leave us with some questions to consider. The first of which is that quite often with letters written for formal or pseudo-formal purposes, on the behalf of a specific cause, there might well be based on a proforma template which authors are encouraged to use. It would be important to distinguish sections of the letter which are directly borrowed from a proforma template, as features based on a model would not be indicative of the language of the letter's author, but of the author of the proforma template. We would therefore also want to look for consistency within the language use which might indicate multiple authors or influences on the language. In this instance, the author did not use a specific template, but it is a question that would need to be considered if this were a genuine case.

This leaves us with the following potential comments and observations that could be included in a profile:

- The letter demonstrates a high level of academic English, indicating that the author might well have a high level of academic qualifications.
- It is unlikely that the author is particularly young given the high level and ability with formal English.
- There are no strong indicators that the author is a non-native English speaker.
- There are no strong regional features. This could in part be due to the register of the text. There are no strong gender markers (the name is typically feminine, but this is a content feature and not a linguistic feature).
- Overall, there are not many potentially useful features within the data. In a real casework situation we would likely feed this back to the investigators at an early stage, indicating that more data would be useful.

We would of course need to address certainty levels, and there are many considerations for report writing, which are discussed more thoroughly in Chapter 13. More details on biographical information about the actual author of this document are included at the end of Chapter 12. It is not included here as the following chapter will expand on this case.

It is important to note that we will not always be able to identify every feature of an author's profile from their language. This is why more data is always important.

The information and the findings are given for reference. It is not expected that anyone could have developed such an accurate profile from the language contained in the letter. This could be considered quite feature poor data. Nonetheless, such analysis is still worth doing as it can often indicate useful directions for the police. Also, as we will see in the next chapter, there are many cases in which the investigation uncovers more language data, which can then be compared to the original sample.

References

Argamon, S., Koppel, M., Fine, J., & Shimoni, A. R. (2003). Gender, genre, and writing style in formal written texts. *Text & Talk*, 23(3): 321–346.

Bamman, D., Eisenstein, J., & Schnoebelen, T. (2014). Gender identity and lexical variation in social media. *Journal of Sociolinguistics*, 18(2): 135–160.

Barbieri, F. (2008). Patterns of age-based linguistic variation in American English. *Journal of Sociolinguistics*, 12(1): 58–88.

Baxter, J. (2008). Is it all tough talking at the top. A post-structuralist analysis of the construction of gendered speaker identities of British business leaders within interview narratives. *Gender and Language*, 2(2): 197–222.

Baxter, J. (2012). Women of the corporation: A sociolinguistic perspective of senior women's leadership language in the UK. *Journal of Sociolinguistics*, 16(1): 81–107.

Biber, D., Conrad, S., & Reppen, R. (1998). *Corpus Linguistics: Investigating Language Structure and Use*. Cambridge University Press.

Britain, D. (2013). Space, diffusion and mobility. In J. K. Chambers, & N. Schilling (eds.), *The Handbook of Language Variation and Change*, 2nd edition. Blackwell, pp. 469–500.

Byrd, M. (1993). Adult age differences in the ability to write prose passages. *Educational Gerontology*, 19(5): 375–396.

Davies, A. (2003). *The Native Speaker: Myth and Reality*. Multilingual Matters.

Finegan, E., & Biber, D. (2001). *Register variation and social dialect variation: The register axiom*. In P. Eckert & J. Rickford (eds.), *Style and Sociolinguistic Variation*. Cambridge University Press, pp. 235–267.

Grant, T. (2008). Approaching questions in forensic authorship analysis. In J. Gibbons & M. T. Turrell (eds.), *Dimensions of Forensic Linguistics*. John Benjamins, pp. 215–229.

Grieve, J., Montgomery, C., Nini, A., Murakami, A., & Guo, D. (2019). Mapping lexical dialect variation in British English using Twitter. *Frontiers in Artificial Intelligence*, 2: 11–18.

Holmes, J. (2006). *Gendered Talk at Work*. Blackwell.

International Herald Tribune (2010). Opinion From the *International Herald Tribune*— 100, 75, 50 Years Ago. 24 January.

Jespersen, O. (1922). *Language: Its Nature, Development and Origin*. Allen and Unwin.

Kemper, S., & Anagnopoulos, C. (1989). Language and aging. *Annual Review of Applied Linguistics*, 10: 37–50.

Kniffka, H. (1996). On forensic linguistic "differential diagnosis." In H. Kniffka, S. Blackwell, & M. Coulthard (eds.), *Recent Developments in Forensic Linguistics*. Peter Lang, pp. 75–122.

Kredens, K., Perkins, R., & Grant, T. (2020). Developing a framework for the explanation of interlingual features for native and other language influence detection. *Language and Law/Linguagem e Direito*, 6(2): 10–23.

Lakoff, R. (1973). Language and woman's place. *Language in Society*, 2(1): 45–79.

McEnery, A., & Xiao, Z. (2004). Swearing in modern British English: The case of fuck in the BNC. *Language and Literature*, 13(3): 235–268.

O'Barr, W. (1982). *Linguistic Evidence: Language, Power and Strategy in the Courtroom*. Academic Press.

Schler, J., Koppel, M., Argamon, S., & Pennebaker, J. (2006). Effects of age and gender on blogging. *2006 AAAI Spring Symposium on Computational Approaches for Analyzing Weblogs*. Stanford, CA, pp. 199–205.

Shuy, R. (2001). Forensic linguistics. In M. Aronoff & J. Rees-Miller (eds.), *The Handbook of Linguistics*. Blackwell, pp. 683–691.

Wardhaugh, R., & Fuller, J. M. (2021). *An Introduction to Sociolinguistics*, 8th edition. Wiley.

12 Comparative authorship analysis

12.1 Introduction to comparative authorship analysis

Chapters 8 and 9 looked at how language evolves and how meaning is made, and determined that it is very much a social creation. A language that is truly unique to an individual would fail as a tool for effective communication. Chapter 11 looked at the implications of this for sociolinguistic profiling, and how certain linguistic variables might indicate an author's social background. This chapter expands on the theory and methodology that we have looked at so far and applies that to closed set authorship questions. This chapter introduces theories and core concepts of comparative authorship analysis and discusses methodological approaches as they relate to real-world casework.

To understand the basic context for comparative authorship analysis, consider the following scenario:

Imagine that you are meant to meet your tutor in their office in order to pick up a copy of a class handout. There was a problem with your bus and you are going to be half an hour late. Send the tutor an email to explain this.

This is based on an exercise one of the authors has done numerous times in classroom or training settings. We would then collect these emails and compare them. A key point of this exercise is that there is little room for variation in the interpretation of the situation. However, no matter how many students are in the room, the scenario has never occurred in which any of the emails used identical language. Some emails might use the same words or short phrases, but it would never be more than a few words that are the same. Why does this matter? It illustrates the fact that even though language is a shared phenomenon, it is also highly individual, meaning that features can be indicative of who wrote a text. You could easily repeat this yourself with your friends or classmates, to see just how different the language really is.

DOI: 10.4324/9780367616595-12

Aims

This chapter expands upon Chapter 11's exploration of authorship profiling and discusses the comparison of two or more texts to determine authorship. We outline aspects of linguistic theory that provide a **framework for forensic linguists when undertaking comparative authorship analysis**. We continue the dialogue about the **utility of computational methods** in supporting analysts in their research, and finally we discuss **cases** in which comparative authorship analysis was vital to provide evidence to a legal team.

12.1.1 Terminology and theory

First, a note on terminology. When we conduct comparative authorship analysis, we compare texts by an unknown writer to samples from known individuals. Q texts are the questioned texts of unknown or disputed authorship, and K texts, or known texts are the texts where we can be as certain as possible who wrote them. Imagine, for example, that we hosted a small dinner party and the next morning we received an anonymous threatening hate email with content that indicates it must be written by one of the attendees of the dinner party. We might choose to compare the threatening hate email (Q text) with known emails (K texts) previously sent by the guests, in order to determine whose linguistic style is most similar to the language of the anonymous threatening hate email.

This dinner party scenario would be considered a closed set analysis, where (due to wider information we can be quite sure of) we know there is a small, closed list of potential authors. However, this is not always an accurate representation of how language works. Rather than seeking to attribute the text to a specific author, it is instead more realistic to speak of whose linguistic style is most similar to the questioned text. Approaching the task comparatively, assessing how similar each known author's linguistic style is to the Q text, is also more realistic as it allows for the potential that there is someone from outside the closed set whose linguistic style is in fact more similar to the question text. For instance, this might occur if the primary investigation had (at the time of analysis) failed to identify a potential suspect. In the example of the dinner party, there could have been an eavesdropper who had gathered enough information that the content of their hate letter looked as if they were one of the people present. The investigation might not have determined that they were eavesdropping on the dinner party until later in the process. This could result in them not being included in the initial list of suspects, and hence K texts from them not being collected until later. To attribute the Q text to one of the earlier K text authors would therefore be misleading, as well as incorrect. Sometimes (as seen with the case example in the activities at the end of this chapter) none of the texts are of 'known' authorship. In this situation we might talk about author Q1 and author Q2.

The concept of **idiolect** is a key one for authorship analysis. Idiolect refers to the idea that an individual's language style is, to some extent, unique to them. There are no features that are truly unique, but in authorship analysis we are considering a combination of features and linguistic style. There have been studies (e.g., Johnstone 2009 & Kredens 2002) that indicate aspects of an individual's language, such as linguistic stance (e.g., their attitude or opinion towards something), show consistency across long periods of an author's life (as well across texts and contexts). This is not to say that once an individual develops a way of speaking, they're entirely constrained by their idiolect; they can still adopt new words, and they might still adopt different constructions in different situations. However, the underlying features of a person's idiolect that make up their personal sociolinguistic profile (e.g., regional identity, academic or literacy level, potentially gender expression, speech communities, etc.) will, to some extent, remain consistent.

You may have heard the term 'linguistic fingerprinting'. This term is largely avoided by linguists as it misrepresents the situation (recall also the discussion of voiceprinting in Chapter 4, which is misleading for similar reasons in the context of voice comparison). The term *fingerprint* indicates that language is truly unique to the individual. However, as we have discussed in prior chapters, if language were completely unique to the individual it would not be fit for purpose as it would not allow communication between people. Therefore, there is no such thing as a linguistic fingerprint. The nearest concept is an idiolect, which allows for the dichotomy that language is both unique and socially constructed, and will vary given the context of the production of a particular piece of language.

A further key concept to explain at this point is that of **linguistic style**, which is very similar to idiolect as it reflects the stylistic choices that an individual might habitually make. These choices might reflect things such as who the recipient of the message is, or what is being discussed, among other contextual factors. Related to this is **linguistic repertoire**, which relates to the resources an author has to draw on. For example, someone could have conversational German, but exceedingly limited Arabic, meaning they can draw on their German to portray the identity of a German speaker, but cannot do the same with Arabic. Similarly, a writer might have some knowledge of a regional dialect or specialist terminology used in a particular field or job.

Comparative authorship analysis is not just about determining which known author's linguistic style is most similar to the questioned texts. It can also be about determining whose style is least similar to the questioned texts, or whose style is consistently different. This is commonly called **exclusionary analysis**. A variant of this can be seen with the Ayia Napa case discussed below.

When we are considering an author's linguistic style, we cannot ignore the role of **context**, as discussed in Chapter 8. Think about the way that you email your boss or tutor: the language and linguistic features that you use will in some ways be different from the way you message your partner or your grandparents. Therefore when we are developing a picture of somebody's linguistic style, we need to consider who their audience was. We also need to consider the mode through which the communication took place. For example, was it an SMS text message, an email, or video call? In addition we need to consider what the topic of the conversation was. Your linguistic style will vary if you are discussing the recent sad passing of a person's pet, instead of a mutual hobby that you share with your addressee, and are passionately enthusing about. These areas cover the three main elements that we often think of making up register: field, tenor, and mode (see Chapters 8 and 11).

Forensic linguistics systematises and brings a scientific approach to comparative authorship analysis, but it is worth noting that comparative authorship analysis is a common aspect of humans using language. Think, for example, of the times that you have noticed that a person's messaging style has changed, indicating that your sibling is messaging you from your parent's phone (or similar), or even the many times that you subconsciously note that the language is consistent with the named author. The following example demonstrates a lay variety of comparative authorship analysis. It comes from the brother of Ted Kaczynski, a.k.a. the Unabomber, who set a series of bombs in the US between 1978 and 1995. Kaczynski's sister-in-law, Linda Patrik, saw elements of the Unabomber's manifesto in the media and noticed that the linguistic style was similar to that of her brother-in-law. She eventually persuaded her husband to read the manifesto, to see if he agreed with her observations. The following is his commentary:

> *The tone of the opening lines was hauntingly similar to that of Ted's letters condemning our parents, only here the indictment was vastly expanded. On the surface, the phraseology was calm and intellectual, but it barely concealed the author's rage. As much as I wanted to, I couldn't absolutely deny that it might be my brother's writing.*
>
> Kaczynski (2016)

This is a form of exclusionary analysis, as he was seeking to either include or exclude his brother from being a potential author based on how similar his language style was. The case furthermore demonstrates that authorship analysis is a common part of daily life. This case is also famous for demonstrating to the FBI the potential for linguistic analysis to support some investigations. As forensic linguists we bring rigorous, reliable, and replicable linguistic methodology.

12.2 Starbuck case

Comparative authorship analysis has been used to help further numerous investigations. One example is the Starbuck case (Grant & Grieve 2022). In 2012, Tim Grant and Jack Grieve were contacted by Nottinghamshire Constabulary to aid in a missing person inquiry. Two years previously, Debbie and Jamie Starbuck got married, and embarked on an around the world trip, seemingly sending emails to loved ones to keep them updated on their progress over the following 31 months. However, the friends and family of Debbie started to get concerned as they noticed inconsistencies in the emails and the language style of the emails coming from Debbie's account compared to emails she had sent when on previous trips. They contacted the police, who in turn emailed Jamie and Debbie separately. They received responses that indicated that the couple had been separated for a while, but had now reunited, and that both were safe and well. However, the police became suspicious that Jamie was not only sending the emails from his account, but also the ones from Debbie's. They therefore approached Grant and Grieve, who undertook a comparative authorship analysis. Adopting a methodology to minimise confirmation bias, they focused on a range of features across all levels of language (including features such as common sentence-initial words, and non-standard colon use). Their analysis concluded that the later messages were consistent with the previous emails of Jamie Starbuck, but inconsistent in style with known examples from Debbie Starbuck. This linguistic report was used by police as part of the evidence to aid in getting an international arrest warrant. However, after repeated appeals from the police Jamie returned to the UK of his own volition. He later admitted to murdering Debbie shortly after their marriage and before leaving to travel the world. The timeline he indicated matched the findings of Grant and Grieve (though he has never disclosed the location of Debbie's remains). Jamie Starbuck was found guilty on the evidence of his confession.

Had Starbuck not confessed, the absence of remains would have made this a much harder case to prosecute. Murders in which no body is found are notoriously hard to prosecute due to the lack of evidence. However, there have been several cases similar to this one in which linguistic evidence has been exceedingly useful in assisting a prosecution. This includes the cases of Jenny Nicholl, who was murdered by her boyfriend David Hodgson (as discussed in detail in Chapter 8), Danielle Jones, who was killed by her uncle Stuart Campbell, and Amanda Birks, who was murdered by her husband Christopher. All the murderers sent messages from their victims' phones in an attempt to cover their tracks and mislead later investigations. From a technical point of view, it is significant that in the Jenny Nicholl case the forensic linguistic evidence was upheld at the highest level of the Court of Appeals in the UK. This sets a very strong precedent for comparative authorship analysis being accepted as methodologically valid evidence in UK law courts.

12.3   Approaches to comparative authorship

12.3.1   Comparative authorship conditions

In order to undertake comparative authorship analysis, there are a few key conditions that need to be met. Firstly, there needs to be a defined set of potential authors. Normally these are 'known' authors. This needs to be a manageable number of candidates so that we can reliably analyse the linguistic style for each author in the given time. In turn this also requires a level of certainty that there are no other potential suspects beyond the known group. This certainty and the narrowing of the group is most likely to come from wider investigative evidence. This might be based on the content of any known data (for example if a letter contained information that only a few people know), but it cannot be based on the language use, as that is a precursor for setting up the methodology for the linguistic analysis (and so would be circular).

The second main condition that needs to be met before comparative authorship analysis can be undertaken is that there is sufficient and comparable data for each of the candidate authors. There are no hard and fast rules as to what constitutes sufficient and comparable data for this sort of analysis. However, there are a few considerations that guide decision-making. First is the question of accessibility and volume. We need to be able to access data for each of the potential authors, and we need to be certain that these known texts were indeed authored by the questioned author, and the questioned author alone. In a casework situation, it is usually the investigators who collect and assure the certainty of this data, under the guidance of the linguist. Next is the question of comparability. When considering what makes a good comparison text, we ideally want the medium used (e.g., how the text was produced) as well as the type of text (e.g., comparing e-mails to e-mails, not e-mails to speeches) to be as similar to the questioned documents as possible. It would be far more appropriate to compare a questioned blog post with a known blog post than it would be to compare a questioned blog post with a journalistic essay. The linguistic style between the two is likely to vary greatly, even within the same author.

The three strands of register – field, tenor, and mode – provide a good framework for understanding the differences between texts in a comparative authorship situation. It is also worth considering the communicative purpose of any data being considered (for example, an email to a colleague where the purpose is to inform them about your work will likely contain different language structures than an email where the communicative purpose is to threaten the colleague to get them to do that work). While in an ideal world we would want the mode of the questioned texts and the known texts to be identical, in reality that is often neither possible nor practical. So, we need to find data that is as similar as possible, yet also allows for there to be sufficient volume of comparison data. Where this is not feasible, it will not be possible to do the analysis. It is worth noting that an initial stage of any analysis involves evaluating whether or not the conditions can be sufficiently met for the analysis to be undertaken. The reality of this is that in many casework situations we are not able to perform the analysis.

The following case outlines the importance of the methodological conditions.

12.3.2 *Belle de Jour* – Profiling versus comparative authorship analysis

A commonly cited example of when comparative authorship analysis was attempted without these conditions being met is the *Belle de Jour* case. This was a case that largely played out in the British media in the early 2000s. The case revolved around an anonymous online blog, in an era when weblogs were just beginning to gain popularity. The blog was titled *Belle de Jour: Diary of a London Call Girl*, written by an anonymous author under the pen name Belle de Jour. It seemingly detailed her real-life experiences as a 'high-class' London sex worker. The blog attracted a lot of attention, being voted blog of the year by *The Guardian* newspaper in 2003, with book deals (and later TV deals) following. Perhaps inevitably speculation arose as to who the anonymous author actually was. Armchair detectives combed the content of the blog, developing sociolinguistic profiles and hypotheses of who the author might be. Multiple names were linked to the anonymous author, with several people denying that they were the author. However, the real author, Brooke Magnanti, managed to stay anonymous until she revealed her identity in *The Sunday Times* in November 2009. This is despite *The Sunday Times* in 2004 claiming they had found the author using a variety of stylometric analysis undertaken by Donald Foster. Indicating that there was an exceedingly high level of certainty, the newspaper claimed that the anonymous author was in fact the journalist Sarah Champion. This led to a denial by Champion, and shortly after a denial by Foster that he had concluded that Champion was the author. Instead, he claimed that she had been identified as a 'person of interest'. An expert report has never been made public. However, based on what has been publicised, and what was discussed in the newspaper, it seems that the main problem with the analysis (or how it was understood and portrayed by the paper) was that it was treated as a classification problem, rather than the profiling case that it should have been. It is included here as an example of common pitfalls that could occur when attempting comparative authorship analysis. The sheer number of potential authors was too high for it to be considered a closed set case. The author that the blog was misattributed to could in fact have had a similar linguistic style to the real author, but many people have similar linguistic styles to each other. There were further potential issues relating to other aspects of the analysis, which are nicely and entertainingly discussed in the podcast *En Clair* by the forensic corpus linguist Claire Hardaker.

12.4 Levels of analysis, consistency, and variation

Both Chapter 11 and this chapter so far have mainly been looking at questions where there is a single author. However, in a real casework situation it cannot be assumed that there will be a single author. Consistency of linguistic features should be considered within a text and across texts by the same nominal author.

It is easy to think that the question of whether or not someone wrote something is a simple one. However, in reality the concept of *writing something* is not always straightforward. Consider the following example: your close friend has received a message from someone she fancies, and wants your assistance in responding. You make some suggestions that she likes, and she types your words down. You suggest including a joke, and find a flirty humorous joke online that fits the bill perfectly. Again, your friend copies this word for word. Who wrote the message? Your friend might have written the words down (or typed them), but some were your words. Perhaps she edited them, or there was co-construction, but to what extent: did she just switch a few words, or are there phrases and sections that were more her creation than yours? What about the joke that you borrowed from the internet? Who wrote that part of the message? Now compare the different linguistic involvement and input to whose name is technically on the text message. Your friend's romantic interest will receive a message, purportedly from one author alone, your friend. We see a similar phenomenon in business. A CEO might write a public announcement. It will be their name at the end of the message, and we all accept that it is nominally from them, but most likely crafted by a multi-person Public Relations team and further edited before being released. From a linguistic point of view, these different authors will leave their own linguistic styles on the text in different ways, depending on how they have contributed to its construction. Below are a few different types of authorship that are worth considering when undertaking authorship analysis.

- Nominal (or named) author
  (When dealing with Q texts, this is often the disputed author, or an anonymous author.)
- Actual author(s)
- Co-author
- Editor
- Plagiarist
- Quoted author (or plagiarised author)
- Proof-reader
- Dictating author – which might also include an amanuensis, transcriber, or scribe who writes down what is said, potentially contributing linguistic features (especially in the form of punctuation). They might also summarise, putting the dictation into their own words and hence becoming a co-author
- Computationally assisted authorship
- Translator

The first step should be looking for linguistic consistency within author and within text. Where this cannot be determined to a reasonable level, the separate texts should be treated as distinct and different authors. The reason this matters so much for authorship analysis is because this potential complexity must be recognised before undertaking any authorship analysis, and it must be considered during the analysis. Not considering that different forms of authorship could account for different manifestations of features could lead to false findings. The importance of this can be seen in the Bentley case (Chapter 8) where the question about the confession statement was not a simple 'who wrote this' but was this genuinely a dictation from Bentley written down verbatim by an officer. In that context the grammatical structures and word choices should reflect Bentley's linguistic style, but spelling and punctuation would be the officer's.

12.4.1 Selecting features

In order to form a picture of someone's individual linguistic style, we need to understand which features are indeed unusual. This brings us back to the paradoxical situation that we experienced in previous chapters: language is in a sense both unique and individual, but also social, and holds similarities across different users. When comparing two linguistic styles, we need to identify features that are somewhat rare. There is little to no point indicating that two authors share the similarity of using the definite article *the*. This would in fact be true for just about any author using the English language. That is not to say that it would be sufficient to rely only on exceedingly rare features, as there needs to be demonstrable consistency. If we focus purely on *hapax legomenon*, i.e., a term that only appears once in a document or text, then we will not be able to look for consistency of spelling, and the term is most unlikely to occur in another text of a shorter length.

In Chapter 11, you read the *devil strip* ransom note, which contained the terms *kops* and *kan* where we would typically expect *cops* and *can*. It is clear to see that these are not two unrelated misspelling features, but that instead they are similar. In both cases a <K> has been substituted for a <C>. Understanding this higher level of similarity (rather than seeking *kops* instead of *cops* and *kan* in the place of *can* as unrelated features) allows us to develop potential explanations in a forensic authorship profiling situation. For example, questioning whether there is an influence from a Germanic language in which <K> commonly occurs when a <C> would be used in English. In a comparative authorship analysis situation, it enables us to have a better understanding of what the author's style is. This is called **taxonomical similarity**. Woodhams et al. (2007) look at how taxonomical similarity is being used in marine ecology, and it can be extended to criminology and forensic linguistics. If a questioned document contained the terms *kops* and *kan* and a known document contains *kapture* and *kut* (instead of *capture* and *cut*) we need to see that these are not four unrelated spelling mistakes, but could all be manifestations of the same feature: <K> for <C> substitution. However, it should be noted that this was not completely consistent in the Q text, as *Carlson* and *cash* were spelt with both spelt with a <C>.

Traditionally we would turn to a corpus in order to determine how unusual a particular linguistic feature might be, as this will enable us to see the distribution of a particular word, phrase, or construction in the wider population. However, in comparative authorship analysis the main focus is on how unusual it is within the given set (though there will often remain a secondary interest of how unusual a feature is within the wider information).

When looking at linguistic style, this should cover the full range of levels, as introduced in Chapter 8. We do not want to just focus on the lexical – or word level features – such as spelling mistakes, or unusual words used. Instead we want to consider everything from phonological and morphological properties, up through lexical, syntactic, semantic, and pragmatic, to discourse level features. Table 8.2 in Chapter 8 outlines the levels that might be used in developing an understanding of an author's linguistic style, and for authorship analysis.

12.5 Ayia Napa case

The Ayia Napa rape case comprises comparative authorship analysis, though in a slightly different form from the cases discussed above. It also demonstrates how comparative authorship analysis and forensic authorship profiling use similar methodologies and are not completely distinct.

In 2019, a British woman attended a rape clinic in Ayia Napa in Cyprus, to report that she had been gang raped. The doctor at the clinic called the Cypriot authorities and the woman subsequently gave a statement about the attack. A few days later the woman was asked to return to the police station, seemingly to clarify inconsistencies within her statement. This visit resulted in the production of a document, signed by the woman, that retracted her original statement, and confessed that the accusation was a lie. This led to the woman being arrested and charged with 'public mischief'. It is around this charge that this case focuses, with the woman as the defendant.

The key question was around the production of the retraction statement. There was no dispute that it was indeed her signature at the end of the document, or that the statement was written in her own handwriting. However, the defendant claimed that she had been put under duress to write it after being detained for hours, denied a lawyer, and was afraid for her life. She also claimed that the original statement was her own true account of her experience, but that the retraction statement was in fact dictated to her by a police officer.

Methodologically this case sits between contextual analysis and authorship analysis. It is worth noting here that the methodologies utilised for a case will depend on the specific context and conditions, and that there is often a lot of overlap in the approaches, as seen when you compare the methodologies from Chapter 11 to those in this chapter. As discussed earlier in this chapter, there are different types of authorship. Here the woman is the undisputed nominal author, as her name is at the end of the document. The question is whether she is in fact the actual author, with all the language being hers, or if there was evidence of other authors.

One key difference between the potential authors was the native language. The defendant was a native English speaker, but the police officers were non-native

English speakers. The retraction statement read as follows (bold formatting added for ease of reference):

> The **report I did** on the 17th of July 2019 that I was raped at ayia napa **was not the truth.** The truth is that I wasnt raped and everything that happened in that **appartment** was with my consent. The reason I made the statement with the fake report is because I did not know they were recording & humiliating me that night I **discovered them recording** me **doing sexual intercourse** and I felt embarrassed so I want to appologise, say I made a mistake.
>
> quoted in Donlan and Nini (2022)

The linguists who worked on the case, Donlan & Nini (2022), identified five key constructions in the 85-word disputed retraction statement that would be of use for building a profile of the author. The lexemes are as follows, broken down into a bare syntactic or semantic form:

1. [DO [REPORT]]   (Line 1 above)
2. [BE *not the truth*]   (Lines 1–2)
3. [APARTMENT]   (Line 2)
4. [DISCOVER [NP V-*ing*]] (Lines 4–5)
5. [DO [*sexual intercourse*]] (Line 5)

Note: This follows standard linguistic lexeme conventions, where a capitalised word includes all the related forms of it, e.g., DO includes all the third person forms of the different tenses, i.e., present tense *does*, past tense *did*, continuous *doing*, and perfect tense *done* (see Donlan & Nini 2022 for more).

Donlan & Nini (2022) then analysed the occurrence of these features across a range of corpora, determining that for the majority of the features identified, they were much less likely to have been produced in the way they occurred in the disputed text by a native British English speaker than they were by a non-native English speaker. For example, their analysis (across a range of relevant corpora) showed that the term *report* co-occurred with *do* is marked and atypical (or unusual) in English writing. Instead *report* correlates more frequently with the verb *make*. Their report detailed these findings, and Donlan testified in court, but the court still decided to allow the disputed statement as evidence. The case later went through appeals on the grounds that the trial breached national and international laws (Justice Abroad 2019). The conviction has since been overturned, with the judge ruling that the woman did not receive a fair trial.

12.6 Plagiarism

Plagiarism is an area that is often covered under forensic linguistics. As the processes around prosecuting plagiarism are less directly criminal, people often think it might fall outside the bounds of forensic linguistics. However, there are direct civil legal implications of plagiarism cases. There are many ways in which forensic linguistic methodology can support civil or academic processes.

Plagiarism is the act of portraying someone's thoughts, words, or ideas as your own. In most universities, this is a punishable offence that can have severe implications on the plagiarist's qualifications and reputation. There are also various public figures, such as politicians, who have been accused of plagiarism, and in some cases publicly stripped of their degrees (for example Karl-Theodor zu Guttenberg, Germany's Defence Minister, in 2011).

Most universities use software in order to screen for plagiarism. It should be noted, however, that software alone cannot indicate plagiarism. Such software is often confused by correctly attributed quotes, and further, it might not notice plagiarism where there has been a rewording or restructuring of ideas. A further area in which it is known to struggle is that of translingual plagiarism, when a person has plagiarised from an author in another language. For these reasons, academic malpractice processes tend not to rely on plagiarism detection software alone. Instead, it might flag that there is a concern in a particular area of a text, which an academic will then evaluate, putting the evidence before a committee if they consider that the software has indeed correctly flagged plagiarism. There are also methods for academics to flag plagiarism when the software has not been triggered.

One of the key indicators for academics that plagiarism has taken place is a change in linguistic style. When there is inconsistency in the linguistic style within an essay, one large and potential explanation for this is that sections have been plagiarised from elsewhere. A further indicator that is sometimes seen is more akin to an exclusionary authorship analysis: the teacher, who knows the student and their writing style well, knows that the linguistic style of the essay is not within that student's standard repertoire of linguistic styles. For example, consider an essay purportedly from a student who is new to the field, still grappling with academic English, and who doesn't regularly use semicolons, is unlikely to include a paragraph in perfect technical academic English including semicolons. Furthermore, if this paragraph is different from the wider essay, it might indicate to the teacher marking it that someone else's linguistic style is present in that part, potentially through plagiarism.

Sousa-Silva (2022) identifies three key plagiarism strategies: literal or verbatim plagiarism (taking words from elsewhere and copying them word-for-word with no changes); paraphrasing or altering some of the words, phrasing, or grammar; or translation plagiarism (which is similar to paraphrasing, but there is a change from one language to another). Naturally the techniques that are needed to detect each type are different. Automated and semi-automated approaches of plagiarism detection can cope quite easily with the more basic word-for-word plagiarism. However, they struggle when the concepts and ideas are plagiarised, but the language altered to different degrees. This is compounded when looking at plagiarism by translation. In detecting and determining plagiarism by translation, Sousa-Silva (2022) shows that there are three steps, first determining if the questioned text is a translation, second identifying the most likely original or source language, and third reverse translating the text the same way as the plagiariser likely did (e.g., machine translation). Only then can the linguist start looking for the likely source text.

12.6.1 ChatGPT, technology, and plagiarism

In November 2022, the research firm OpenAI released a natural language processing tool and artificial intelligence chatbot, ChatGPT. The goal of ChatGPT is to mimic a human conversation, but it is also able to create a large section of writing if given a prompt such as 'write me one hundred words about comparative authorship in Forensic Linguistics'. When prompted by this input, ChatGPT returned the following:

Comparative authorship is a technique used in forensic linguistics to compare the writing styles of different authors in order to determine whether they were written by the same person or not. This technique involves analyzing various linguistic features such as word choice, sentence structure, syntax, and punctuation, among others. By comparing these features across different texts, linguists can identify patterns and similarities that can help them determine the authorship of a particular text. This technique can be particularly useful in legal cases where authorship is in question, such as in cases of plagiarism or anonymous threatening messages. However, it is important to note that comparative authorship analysis is not foolproof and should be used in conjunction with other forms of evidence.

Impressive, right?

In a separate field, *New York Times*' recipe writer and chef, Priya Krishna, used ChatGPT to create a Thanksgiving menu complete with recipes (Krishna & Metz 2022). To be fair to ChatGPT, some of the recipes it came up with were not entire failures, but others received the review of: 'oh man, they messed up dessert, too' from chef Melissa Clark. The point is that there is considerably more to creating textual data (such as a recipe) than correct grammar and lexis.

Although playing around with ChatGPT on the internet yields impressive or sometimes amusing results, many scholars and universities are concerned about the implications it has for plagiarism. Many school systems are attempting to block ChatGPT, while others are attempting to enlist the help of competing algorithms that would detect the use of ChatGPT. OpenAI has also suggested that they will be implementing a digital watermark of sorts on the responses from ChatGPT that would signal to readers that this was generated by an AI. However, with all of these fixes, there would be opportunities to work around these barriers. Others, on the other hand, advocate for utilising ChatGPT as a tool to *help* students and writers. They suggest that ChatGPT could be used as a mechanism for creating an outline or foundation for an argument, but the student would then have to go in and improve the writing and add sources.

The development of AI and machine learning mean we face another layer of authorship to consider when undertaking authorship analysis. This does *not* mean that AI will make authorship analysis impossible, rather that we need to consider it as another potential input (much like a plagiarised author, or a co-author). For further reading on large language models, and their risks and implications we highly recommend Bender et al. (2021). Bender was also a guest on the BBC *Word of Mouth* podcast.

12.7   Conclusions

In conclusion, this chapter demonstrates underpinning theory, and some of the key approaches for comparative authorship analysis, and how that can be of use in the wider legal and social spheres. It has direct implications for providing evidence to support or refute claims of authorship. As seen with the cases above, there is a wide array of applications of comparative authorship in casework. This also raises many questions regarding detecting authorship in other arenas, such as plagiarism. As our colleague ChatGPT says:

> *This technique requires a high level of linguistic expertise and careful analysis, which may not always be available. Nevertheless, comparative authorship remains an important tool in the forensic linguist's arsenal for investigating authorship and determining the origins of written texts.*

Further reading and resources

For more on the intersection between corpus linguistics and authorship analysis:

Kredens, K. J., & Coulthard, R. M. (2012). Corpus linguistics in authorship identification. In L. Solan & P. Tiersma (eds.), *Oxford Handbook of Language and Law*. Oxford University Press, pp. 504–516.

For more on forensic linguistics and its utility in casework as it relates to authorship analysis:

Ainsworth, J., & Juola, P. (2019). Who wrote this?: Modern forensic authorship analysis as a model for valid forensic science. *Washington University Law Review*, 96: 1161.

For more information on the Ayia Napa case:

Donlan, L., & Nini, A. (2022). A forensic authorship analysis of the Ayia Napa rape statement. In I. Picornell, R. Perkins, & M. Coulthard (eds.), *Methodologies and Challenges in Forensic Linguistics Casework*. Wiley, pp. 29–43.

For more on anonymity and authorship in online forums:

Marko, K., & Buker, G. S. (2022). "Hope you're in the mood for Cookies": An exploratory study of individual writing styles across social media platforms. *Journal of Indonesian Community for Forensic Linguistics*, 1(1): 14–25.

For more on translingual plagiarism:

Sousa-Silva, R. (2022). Forensic plagiarism detection and analysis. In I. Picornell, R. Perkins, & M. Coulthard (eds.), *Methodologies and Challenges in Forensic Linguistic Casework*. Wiley, pp. 77–92.

Activity section

Activity 12A - Social media language across platforms

Choose a celebrity's social media feed (you can use the same celebrity from Chapter 11) and compare their language use on another platform. How does the change in mode manifest in the language use across the platforms?

Answer 12A

We don't offer any specific answers here, as the activities can take many different forms depending on the participant's choices. However, the following table outlines some of the things that could be considered at different levels of language (see Chapter 8 for a discussion on the language levels).

	Level description	Questions that could be considered
Discourse	Larger units of language, interaction, text or document level and above	• Do the different platforms contain the same media? Are they just text based or are they multi-modal? • Is one for news dissemination and the other for more personal context? (for example some artists posts about upcoming tour dates on Twitter, but Instagram is more personal)

(Continued)

	Level description	Questions that could be considered
Pragmatic	Paragraph and text level	• Is one platform for raising questions and another for making statements? • Are the texts the same length? Are longer texts included as a screenshot from a notes app?
Syntactic	Clause level, structure of sentences, phrases, and clauses	• Does one platform have more complex sentence structures? • Do the sentences contain the same number of clauses? Is there code-switching?
Semantic/ lexical	Clause level, vocabulary or words used, alone and in combination	• Does one platform contain more colloquial language? • Some applications have character limits. Does this impact the word constructions or choices? Is there article or pronoun dropping?
Morphological	Internal structure of words and morpheme elements	• Are words represented as they might be said? (e.g., *gonna*, *walkin*) • Is the alveolar -ING variant used on both platforms for words that end in *-ing* (e.g., *dropping/droppin*)? Is this marked with an apostrophe (*droppin, droppin'*)? • Are emojis used to replace or duplicate certain words?
Semiotics	Relationship between textual and visual	• Have fonts been changed? Are there bold, italics etc.? • Are picture included? Are there videos? What is the music accompanying the video? Is this used to change the meaning?
Phonological	Relating to the sound patterns and phonetic properties	• Does your celebrity use a more regional or standard accent or dialect on one platform? • Is the speech standard or sung?

Activity 12B - Taylor case - Authorship analysis

This activity develops on Activity 11D in the previous chapter. This mirrors how cases can, and often will, unfold. A case might start as a profiling situation with a very limited number of suspects, but then as the investigation progresses there might be a narrowing of the suspects, either down to a small group, or to a specific individual. More data is often regularly uncovered in the progression of the case, as is the situation here.

Again, this is a simulated case. The case context is based on real situations, but the material was produced specifically for the purpose of a forensic linguistic exercise.

Case context

During the investigation in to Ms Susan Taylor's murder, an email is uncovered on her private email account. Investigators want to know if it is linked to the letter she received at work (see previous chapter). Unlike the letter – which Ms Taylor reported to her company – the email was not reported via the company procedure, though it had been read. It was received just over a month after the letter on her personal email.

Read the following email and consider.

- Can you help the police with this case?
- Is the data comparable to the letter in the previous chapter? How might this limit your findings?
- Are the linguistic styles similar?
- How might you express your findings?

Received by: J.Taylor@madeupemail.com
Sent from: Avengingangel@madeupemail.com

You are a disgusting human being and I swear you're going to pay for what you do every day. I hope that somebody will do to you exactly what you do to those poor animals every day. And all that 'for science'? Fuck off. I will fuck you up. It will be my pleasure to give you a dose of your own medicine and see how you like being locked away and tortured day after day. I know where you work and I know where you live. That's right Susan Taylor. You better watch your back.

Answer 12B

The difference in genres between an email and letter mean that this case is a difficult one, and one that we would be reluctant to take on without there being further data. Nonetheless, for the purposes of discussing analysis here, we can still look at the linguistic styles and how the work might be approached.

- The email is much shorter than the letter.
- It does not contain a greeting or signature.

- There is more explicit language, featuring taboo terms. This is different from the letter. The change in mode (letter to email) might have some impact on this.
- Similar to the letter, the language is well structured and broadly formal.
- There is idiomatic language use ('a dose of your own medicine') that is used correctly and fluently.
- The communicative purpose seems to be more directly threatening – but with no specific aim (though as with the letter in Chapter 11, this is a simulated email and therefore not much can be drawn from this observation; it is not a real threat note).
- Overall the main similarities between the email and the letter are the clear structure and the high level of standard English language use.
- Given the short volume of text, and the low level of features, it is hard to say definitively whether the email and the letter are written by the same person – but there are certain differences (such as more explicit and direct language, and taboo language use) that seem to be more significant than can be accounted for by the change of genre.

The letter in the last chapter (like this email) was written by a former colleague of one of the authors. As such, it is not a good example of a threat letter. However, it does mean that we have certain demographic information that we would not usually have access to. Further, as it is not a real case it is possible to search for sections of the data without instantly finding the answer.

Letter from Chapter 11
The author was a female academic, with a permanent job lecturing within a languages and social sciences department at a UK university. She has a PhD relating to literature, identifies as female, and at the time of writing was around 30 years old. She is American, with her family being based in a region of America close to Canada. At the time of writing the note she had been in the UK for about five years, initially based in Scotland and relocating to Birmingham about a year before the letter was written. The instructions given were deliberately vague and non-prescriptive. She was asked to write a threat note to someone who worked as a research scientist at a place that tested on animals. The rest was up to her.

Email
This email was written by a different former colleague. At the time of writing she was an academic close to completing her PhD in a social sciences field. She was 25 and identified as female. She has a native-like ability with English and fluency in other European languages.

This information and the findings are given for reference. It is not expected that anyone could have developed such an accurate profile from the language contained in the letter (though information such as where a person has lived *could* have left a linguistic trace). This could be considered quite feature-poor data.

A report could indeed note the differences in linguistic style between the email and the letter, as well as the similarities. This might tentatively indicate that the style difference could be due to there being different authors. However, it would also need to discuss the confounding impact of the different genres. The certainty level would be very low. It is unlikely that the report could include any of the social profile information about this second author (it is included here purely for completeness).

References

Bender, E. M., Gebru, T., McMillan-Major, A., & Shmitchell, S. (2021). On the dangers of stochastic parrots: Can language models be too big? In *Proceedings of the 2021 ACM conference on Fairness, Accountability, and Transparency* pp. 610–623.

Grant, T., & Grieve, J. (2022). The Starbuck case: Methods for addressing confirmation bias in forensic authorship analysis. In I. Picornell, R. Perkins, & M. Coulthard (eds.), *Methodologies and Challenges in Forensic Linguistic Casework*. Wiley, pp. 13–28.

Johnstone, B. (2009). Stance, style, and the linguistic individual. In A. Jaffe (ed.), *Sociolinguistic Perspectives on Stance*. Oxford University Press, pp. 29–52.

Kaczynski, D. (2016). My brother, the unabomber, *Psychology Today*, 5 January.

Kredens, K. (2002). Idiolect in authorship attribution. In P. Stalmaszczyk (ed.), *Folia Linguistica Anglica 4*. Lodz University Press, pp. 191–212.

Krishna, P., & Metz, C. (2022). Can A.I. write recipes better than humans? We put it to the ultimate test. *New York Times,* 21 November.

Woodhams, J., Grant, T. D., & Price, A. R. (2007). From marine ecology to crime analysis: Improving the detection of serial sexual offences using a taxonomic similarity measure. *Journal of Investigative Psychology and Offender Profiling*, 4(1): 17–27.

13 Expert witnesses and legal contexts

We have seen throughout this book that speech, language, and audio experts become engaged in many different types of legal case. Phoneticians are most often asked to address questions of speaker identity. They also become involved in determining what was said in a recording, or helping to test an earwitness via a voice parade. Audio engineers may help with technical matters such as enhancement of recordings. Linguists with training in corpus methods or discourse analysis may offer expert opinion on authorship or to advise courts on the meanings of dialect or slang terms. In all such examples, the expert is engaged to provide an opinion or specialist service to assist in a legal case. Their specialist knowledge and skills means they are classified as an expert witness.

This final chapter focuses on the **role of speech and language experts as expert witnesses**. We discuss how an expert witness is defined. We outline the **principles an expert witness must understand** and adhere to when conducting their work, and the ways in which **forensic sciences are regulated**. We consider **how the expert should report their opinion**. Finally, we discuss **what happens when a case reaches court**.

13.1 Introduction

Expert witnesses are used throughout the world in many types of cases and in all levels of courts. Indeed, there is even a very long history of language experts being consulted in legal cases. As long ago as 1494 a court in Ireland summoned 'masters of grammar' to explain the meaning of a Latin word.

The specific jurisdiction in which a case is tried might impose different rules on what sort of expert evidence can be called, and who is considered an expert. However, expert witnesses are generally defined with respect to their specialist knowledge, training, and skills. In the UK, for instance, expert evidence is defined as 'information which is likely to be outside the experience and the knowledge of a judge or jury'.

DOI: 10.4324/9780367616595-13

Most cases involving forensic experts are tried in criminal justice systems. They are usually heard in national or state courts, but some are heard in international courts. As we noted in Chapter 4, for instance, speaker comparison evidence was brought in war crimes trials heard by United Nations International Criminal Tribunals (against Radislav Krstic in 2001, and Slobodan Milošević in 2003–6). Experts are also sometimes called in non-criminal cases. Examples include professional tribunals (for example, to address a claim of wrongful dismissal from a job, as was the case when Sarah Forsyth successfully sued Eton College after accusing Prince Harry of cheating in his exams), or civil cases, where one party sues another to settle a dispute (e.g., in trademark disputes).

Many countries lack understanding about the value – and limitations – of forensic sciences. Judges might decide in the context of a specific case whether to admit expert evidence for the first time in the jurisdiction. In such cases the expert might be asked to explain the general aims, methods, and limitations of the science as well as to produce an expert opinion on materials integral to the case. This is what happened, for example, in the 2007 drugs case in Ghana mentioned in Chapters 4 and 6. The case was the first in Ghana in which forensic speech and audio analysis was used. The forensic team produced a short general report on the field for the judge prior to trial, and responded to the judge's questions in order to help him assess whether to admit the evidence.

An issue of major concern in the legal system is public confidence. For that reason, many legal systems now impose regulations on forensic sciences to ensure they meet acceptable standards. It is vital that courts should only engage reputable practitioners working within the limits of their area of expertise. Just as important is that expert evidence is only sought from reputable and valid disciplines. (We would not expect astrologers or readers of tea leaves to be called to assist in a legal case, though some people believe in these methods.) Science advances all the time, and new methods may become available that have not previously been used in legal cases. Automatic speaker recognition (ASR, see Chapter 4) is a good example of a relatively new and reputable discipline that has made very rapid advances. ASR is used in evidence in several countries. It has not yet been accepted as evidence in a UK case, but that is likely to change in the near future.

As we shall see below, speech and language cases have sometimes been the focus of debate on how expertise is defined in general within a legal system, with wide-ranging consequences for other forensic sciences.

13.2 Expert witness credentials

Around the world, expert evidence and expert witnesses are defined in various ways. As we have already noted, sometimes a court must decide in the context of a case whether to call for expert evidence, or whether to admit expert evidence brought by a legal team. Rules are therefore laid down to assist judges to make those decisions. Inevitably, rules differ around the world. Some sciences are well established, while others require more careful consideration in the context of the specific case. We'll take a detailed look here at practice in the United States and United Kingdom, and in particular how legal systems in these countries have addressed speech and language evidence. The US and UK situations are interesting in themselves, but other countries often refer to these jurisdictions when deciding on whether to admit evidence for the first time. The UK, for example, is influential on other Commonwealth countries (as it was in the Ghana case).

It is worth noting, however, that the legal systems in both countries are very complex. The UK consists of three separate legal systems (Northern Ireland; Scotland; England and Wales), while the fifty American States have their own legal systems sitting beneath a country-wide set of federal laws (Finegan 2021).

13.2.1 Experts in the United States

In the United States, the legal system requires a level of replicability and validity in the methodology presented by the expert, which allows for an expert's scientific method and findings to be verified. For decades, the standard by which expert testimony was allowed in the US court system was the *Frye* test, so named after the case in which the rules were first established (*Frye v. United States* 1923). The Frye test allowed scientific evidence if it had 'gained general acceptance in the particular field in which it belongs'. The basis of the Frye test was a case that involved a lie detector test that measured systolic blood pressure. This was a new method at the time. However, in the years that followed this case, lawyers began ambiguating the phrase 'particular field'. In the case of *Frye v. United States,* for instance, the 'particular field' could have been interpreted as the field of lie detector technicians, or haematologists, or medical experts more generally. Needless to say, the crucial matter of 'general acceptance' would differ depending on the way in which the 'field' was delimited. We comment further on this question below, in respect of so-called voiceprint evidence.

These and other problems with the Frye test came to a head in 1975 when the Federal Rules of Evidence (FRE) were first adopted. Under FRE Rule 702, the admittance of scientific expert evidence is allowed if it will 'assist the trier of fact to understand the evidence or to determine a fact in issue'. However, it was still unclear whether this language was intended to be added to the Frye test, or, rather, it was intended to replace the Frye test. In the 1990s, the US Supreme Court sought to clarify this situation with three cases that have now been dubbed the *Daubert* trilogy. The first case, from 1993, *Daubert v. Merrell Dow Pharmaceuticals, Inc.* examined whether the anti-nausea medicine taken during pregnancy, Bendectin, caused birth defects in the plaintiffs' children. Most of the medical field had concluded that Bendectin was perfectly safe to take during pregnancy, but the plaintiffs had an expert testify to challenge the literature and discuss studies that did show some birth defects in animals. The Supreme Court sent the case back to a lower court, which ruled that the scientific testimony of the plaintiffs' expert was not admissible because it lacked scientific validity (specifically, there had been a few studies that showed a link between Bendectin and animals with birth defects, but these findings were not substantiated by peer-reviewed research). This outcome then changed the standard by which expert testimony could be admitted. Henceforth, it had to be demonstrated that the evidence had a 'grounding in the methods and procedures of science'. To be admissible, the testimony had to meet four criteria:

1. whether the theory offered has been tested;
2. whether it has been subjected to peer review and publication;
3. the known rate of error;
4. whether the theory is generally accepted in the scientific community.

It is up to the discretion of trial judges to admit or reject expert evidence by evaluating it against these criteria.

The other two cases in the Daubert trilogy, *General Electric Company v. Joiner* (1997) and *Kumho Tire Company v. Carmichael* (1999), add more specificity for guidance on expert testimonies. The *Kumho Tire Company* addendum is critical to us as forensic language experts because in this case the Supreme Court ruled that the Daubert standard can also apply to experts who testify based on their experience, not just to 'scientific' testimony. This, of course, raises the very difficult question of how we can separate 'science' from 'experience' (or 'hard science' from 'soft science') but the ruling allows for more qualitative findings in scientific analysis (i.e., those without a 'known rate of error') to be admitted as evidence. The determining factor of the *Kumho Tire* case is whether the expert 'employs in the courtroom the same level of intellectual rigor that characterises the practice of an expert in the relevant field' (*Kumho Tire Company v. Carmichael* 1999: 152).

Following the Daubert trilogy the Federal Rules of Evidence were amended to allow an expert witness's testimony to be admitted if the testimony will 'assist the trier of fact to understand the evidence or to determine a fact in issue' and if:

• the testimony is based upon sufficient facts or data;
• the testimony is the product of reliable principles and methods; and
• the witness has applied the principles and methods reliably to the facts of the case. (Revised FRE Rule 702)

The US has therefore operated with four different sets of criteria to define expert evidence in the last 100 years (i.e., Daubert, Frye, FRE 702 and the Revised FRE 702). Although the Daubert standard is now law for federal courts and more than half of the fifty States, the Frye standard remains the metric for evaluating expert witness testimony in the state-level jurisdictions of California, Illinois, Maryland, Minnesota, New Jersey, New York, Pennsylvania, and

Washington (Matthiesen, Wickert, & Lehrer 2022). The Daubert criteria in particular have generated a huge amount of debate (a lot of information is collected on the Daubert on the Web website).

The fifty States have also made different decisions on which criteria should be applied and for which level of their courts. For instance, Florida's lower courts adopted Daubert in 2013, but their Supreme Courts only adopted it in 2019. In 2020, Maryland's Court of Appeals adopted the Daubert Standard. And to complicate matters more, several States (including Georgia, Idaho, Maine, Montana, Nevada, North Dakota, South Carolina, Utah, Virginia, and Wisconsin) have evaluation standards that do not strictly follow either Frye or Daubert. Instead they generally allow experts with different positions to testify, relying on cross examination to reveal which is more persuasive. Keierleber & Bohan (2005: 9), however, summarise that position in the following terms:

> This approach knowingly allows a jury to be exposed to opposing expert testimony on a topic, one delivered by an individual who speaks in accord with most or all of the accepted opinion within his field, and the other of whom is regarded as a crackpot by his own field. The cross examination of the crackpot is supposed to cancel out the impression that the two experts represent equally respected views—always a danger when there are only two of them and the jury is forbidden to do any of their own literature research.

Keierleber & Bohan's (2005) survey on the Frye v. Daubert standards across the fifty States also revealed that judges interpreted the criteria in different ways, and some sciences were therefore treated unevenly across the country. This is amply illustrated by the treatment of so-called voiceprint analysis – i.e., the visual inspection of spectrograms as if they were unique and similar to fingerprints (see the box on pages 60–61). In the 1960s–1970s the method was established among a relatively small group of practitioners, but widely regarded as invalid by the majority of people working in phonetics. A judge faced with voiceprint evidence under the Frye rules would therefore have to decide whether this method was 'generally accepted' in the narrowly-defined field, or the broader field of speech science. Different judges reached different decisions on this particular question, as well as whether it met the Frye standards in general. The result is that voiceprint evidence has been accepted under Frye in some States (Alaska and Maine), but rejected in others (California, Maryland, Pennsylvania; see further Tiersma & Solan 2002).

Tiersma & Solan (2002) provide a summary of how US courts have handled expert testimony involving forensic linguistics. Over 100 published judicial opinions (excluding voiceprint cases) include mention of 'language experts'. In the twenty years since this publication, there has been an increase of linguistic experts participating in the courtroom, but still areas of forensic linguistics which are yet to become established as fields of expertise. This is particularly the case for opinion on legal language, discourse analysis, and expert testimony on the meaning of a text in standard English. In contrast, judges routinely admit testimony on foreign languages or on non-standard registers, and linguistic or phonetic analysis in trademark disputes. Forensic stylistics and authorship analysis have not been admitted in some courts, or have been shown to be seriously flawed in specific cases such as the JonBenét Ramsay murder. Phonetic analysis has, however, been provided in numerous American cases, especially concerning speaker comparison. Hollien (2016) suggests that speaker comparison based on forensic phonetic methods has been used in over 150 cases and heard in 40 trials. Detailed reports of specific cases are provided by Ash (1988) and Labov (1988; the Prinzivalli case mentioned at the very start of this book). ASR has been employed as a component of speaker comparison analyses in recent terrorist cases involving Ali Yasin Ahmed in 2015 and El Shafee El-Sheikh and others in 2022 (although the ASR evidence was not presented at trial). Examples can also be found of the use of voice parades and audio tape authentication.

Worryingly, however, there are also examples of serious miscarriages of justice that might have been averted if lawyers had greater awareness of basic linguistics and the contributions expert witnesses might make. Rodman (2002) documents one such example. A Haitian-born American citizen was sentenced to jail for drug dealing, based on a covert recording of a drug deal. The court agreed that the dealer on the recording clearly spoke African American English. The defendant, by contrast, spoke English with a Haitian Creole accent. Anyone with training in forensic phonetics or English dialectology would therefore likely conclude that the recording was of a different person (assuming the recording was of sufficient length and quality). The jury were nevertheless persuaded that the defendant was the speaker on the incriminating tape. The prosecution case was built around what Rodman rightly describes as an 'absurd chain of nonsequiturs'. They claimed that the defendant disguised his voice by changing his accent. He had worked as an interpreter in the army, and was therefore a 'linguist'. The definition of 'linguist' in the Webster dictionary makes reference to 'sound change', referring to the types of historical change that affect languages and dialects over time. The prosecution, however, misinterpreted this as 'an ability to change sound' (i.e., one's voice), which therefore explained his ability to disguise his voice via a different accent. No expert witness was called for either side to challenge this claim.

13.2.2   Experts in the United Kingdom

In the United Kingdom, expert testimony has been assessed in a very different way. In general, the United Kingdom has focused on the credentials and expertise of the witness themselves rather than the methods they use. Expert scientific evidence was first addressed in the case *R. v. Silverlock* (1894; note that the *R.* in UK case titles refers to *Rex* or *Regina* – the King or Queen, representing the state). In the Silverlock case, a solicitor was permitted to offer evidence as an expert on handwriting. Clearly he lacked any formal qualifications in the subject (forensic science was not an established thing in the Victorian era), but he had studied handwriting as a hobby for some time. The judge accepted that he possessed knowledge about handwriting patterns that would be beyond the knowledge of members of the jury. This set the pattern for expert witnesses, whose credentials would be judged in respect of the individual practitioner's competence rather than with reference to the methodologies they used. The procedures for criminal cases, including the role and duties of expert witnesses, are reviewed regularly in the UK and summarised in the Criminal Procedure Rules.

This position held firm for almost a century before it was tested in the case *R. v. Robb* (1991). The subject of the expert testimony in this case was forensic phonetic analysis in a speaker comparison case. The prosecution expert analysed the recordings using auditory analysis alone. The defence expert, however, argued that acoustic analysis was necessary to reveal relevant information about the voice(s) in the recordings. (Note that acoustic analysis of speech was well established at that time, but much more cumbersome to conduct than it is now thanks to powerful software like Praat.) Thus the judge was forced to assess whether the expert evidence should be required to use a particular methodology. In this case, the judge ruled in favour of the prosecution and thus the *status quo* in terms of expert evidence rules. The judge's ruling acknowledged that the prosecution expert's methodology was used by a minority in the field, but his evidence was not proved to be wrong or misleading. A few years later, an appeal court in Northern Ireland did insist that certain methodologies were used, and thus for the first time in UK law changed the way in which experts were assessed. This case, *R. v. O'Doherty* (2002), also concerned forensic phonetic analysis. It was in fact rather similar to the Robb case, but crucially this time the acoustic evidence was shown to be critical to the conclusion drawn about the recording. The judge therefore ruled that most cases in Northern Ireland in which forensic phonetic evidence was brought should include acoustic analysis. Courts in England and Wales have since distanced themselves somewhat from the O'Doherty ruling, however, such that the expert witness guidance in the UK still prioritises the individual over the method.

13.3 Principles and regulation

In most jurisdictions there are general principles that all expert witnesses should follow. It is essential that anyone conducting forensic work make themselves aware of these principles, and any other forms of regulation that apply to their field in the relevant jurisdiction. In short, the duty of the expert is to tell 'the truth, the whole truth, and nothing but the truth'. Rhodes & Cambier-Langeveld (2025) discuss the requirements for forensic practitioners in more detail. Their focus is on forensic phonetics, but the points they raise apply to all disciplines. They identify four general principles, as follows.

Impartiality: Experts have a duty to the court and should not be biased toward any particular conclusion. Analysis and reporting must happen impartially. In inquisitorial jurisdictions, which are common in Europe, expert witnesses are instructed by the court and are thus by definition impartial (see Margot 1998; detailed accounts of how forensic language evidence is handled in Germany are given by Ehrhardt 2021 and Wagner 2019, focusing on linguistics and phonetics, respectively). By contrast, in adversarial legal systems such as those in the US, UK, and Australia, experts are engaged by either the prosecution or defence. The same principles of objectivity and impartiality should apply in all cases, however. The expert's duty is always to the court, not to the party instructing them. This means in practice that an expert witness might deliver an opinion that is not helpful to the client who solicited it, and indeed it might be helpful to the opposing party.

Transparency: Analysis and reporting must be transparent. All analyses must be documented in detail and are ideally reproducible by an external party or expert. For example, records of data management must be tracked in detail. The chain of custody – that is, the sequence of who handed over which material to whom and when, how the material was transferred, who analysed it and when – must be documented. Analysis notes must also be dated. If the chain of custody is not fully documented, an expert report may not be admissible in court because materials may have been contaminated or tampered with. Below is an example of a how one procedural step might be documented in a chain of custody:

Dr Parker – 01/01/2021 – opened sealed exhibit bag M5738276; copied interview audio from data-format CD with reference 'Disc/01'; converted to PCM WAV 44.1 kHz, 16 bit, 2-channel stereo recording using [SoftwareX] – file duration 01:30:00 hh:mm:ss.

Validity: Analyses must be valid, meaning that conclusions must be well-founded and tests must be conducted on appropriate sets of data.

Effectiveness: Practitioners often work under tough deadlines, and reports have short turnaround times (in the case of a kidnapping call, for example, authorities prioritise finding out swiftly who the caller is). Evidence must thus be produced in such a way that it is appropriate for the case at hand, given the case's time constraints and budget. It is not helpful for a report to be extremely detailed if it is submitted too late, for example. Reports should also be framed in terms that the client will understand.

Many jurisdictions offer detailed guidance for expert witnesses and/or for courts to assess expert credentials. Examples that can be consulted online include documents for jurisdictions in Australia, Canada, Germany, the Netherlands, Switzerland, the UK, and the European Union.

Several specific points are included in these protocols. For example, expert witnesses are expected to make it clear when a particular question or issue falls outside their expertise, and they should not attempt to answer questions that do. In the Ghana case, for example, UK-based experts worked in collaboration with a respected linguist from the University of Ghana, Professor Kofi Agyekum. It was agreed in advance that any questions about Ghanaian languages would be answered by Agyekum, whereas the UK experts would handle questions about forensic phonetics in general and the methodologies employed in the case. Another issue raised in guidance for expert witnesses is that they should notify the instructing party if something causes their view to change. This could be, for example, if new evidence emerges or if another expert's testimony raises issues that have not been considered.

The principle of impartiality, however, is perhaps the most important. Expert witnesses should avoid bias as far as possible. One way to limit bias is for the analyst to be shielded from any contextual information about the case. All the analyst needs to know is what question is being asked: for example, you have two recordings, X and Y, and the question is whether the speaker in X is the same person in Y. In larger labs it is possible for one member of staff to receive materials and handle communications with the client, and thus to limit what information is given to the analyst and when. Contextual information can be withheld altogether or revealed at agreed stages of the analysis. That was done, for example, in the David Bain case (see Chapter 6), where several analysts were asked to transcribe the recording with no knowledge that it contained a questioned utterance. That fact was revealed after an initial transcription had been submitted, at which point they were asked to examine the recording again and assess the QU in light of the versions that had been offered by different parties. This approach is not always possible, however, for analysts who work alone. Instructing police officers and lawyers are often keen to reveal the full details of the case.

Above all, experts should never assume the role of 'hired guns' who seek to assist the party employing them. Unfortunately, there are cases reported where specialist witnesses have done just that (see e.g., Butters 2009). Experts should also consider ethical issues in accepting and conducting casework. Some experts refuse to take on particular types of cases (e.g., relating to abuse of children), or to work for jurisdictions where a conviction might lead to the death penalty. It is, of course, the right of each expert to make their own decisions on such issues. However, if an expert does accept a case it is vital to put moral judgement to one side. Even in cases involving the most heinous crimes, the expert must focus on the question at stake and provide a thorough and truthful opinion. For instance, if engaged by the prosecution in a speaker comparison case, the expert must analyse the voices in the recordings and opine on the likelihood that the same speaker is involved. If there is doubt, or negative evidence, this must be revealed even if other information about the defendant appears damning.

To ensure public confidence in forensic sciences, some countries have now imposed regulation on laboratories, which must show that they follow approved formal procedures. In the UK, the post of Forensic Science Regulator was established in 2008 to oversee all forensic disciplines in this way. The Regulator has published Codes of Practice and Conduct for Forensic Science Providers.

The work includes specific guidance for each discipline, including speech and audio analysis (first published in 2016). A formal accreditation procedure for forensic practitioners is likely to be introduced in the near future. At present, forensic linguistics is not included in the list of the Forensic Science Regulator's defined activities. In the US there is also a serious concern over standards in forensic science (Servick 2016). Calls have been made to establish more consistent practices in forensic sciences in the US, in part to resolve the variation in standards that are applied to evaluate expert testimony.

Scientific disciplines also lay down guidance for their practitioners. For example, the International Association of Forensic Phonetics and Acoustics (IAFPA) has a code of practice for its members, as does the International Association for Forensic and Legal Linguistics (IAFLL). Note that supporting public confidence also involves countering the so-called CSI effect: unrealistic expectations of forensic sciences generated by fictional accounts in television and movie dramas.

13.4 Expert reports

Let us now devote a few words to report writing in forensic cases. The most common type of case involving language experts is forensic speaker comparison (FSC), and we therefore focus on that topic to illustrate how reports are produced. Such reports are essential because they form the basis of the evidence submitted by the expert witness. The reports inform police investigations and defence cases, and may be presented at trial.

Most importantly, reports should be understandable – in such a way that experts as well as non-experts (e.g., police officers or lawyers) can understand them. They need to be succinct and as non-technical as possible. Key terms and observations need to be explained to the non-expert. Explaining likelihood ratios is particularly difficult, and some courts have unfortunately rejected numerical LRs on the basis that juries will not understand them (see the ruling in the case *R. v. T* 2010 – the defendant is referred to as T to shield his identity, as he was a minor at the time the crime was committed – and discussion in Berger et al. 2011).

Sections to be included in the report include:

Instructions: A clear statement of the instructions received.

Materials: A description of the specific recordings analysed, e.g., phone calls, intercepts, duration of recordings, technical format of the material, accompanying written materials such as police transcripts, etc. The file names must also be included to ensure that the correct materials have been analysed.

Tools: A description of the tools used, e.g., Praat, computer and headphone models, key literature consulted, conducting additional field recordings with a phone, etc.

Methods: A description of which methods were applied to examine the materials, e.g., acoustic analysis, auditory analysis, automatic analysis; a description of which features of language were analysed (consonants, vowels, prosody, etc.). Some laboratories apply a process of peer review, where another expert checks a sample of data analysed, and the overall report. Such a procedure should also be listed if used, identifying the personnel involved.

Conclusions: A general description of the results, written for a lay audience. Particular attention is given to features in which the known and questioned samples exhibit high similarity; in these cases, information is presented regarding how typical these similar features are in the relevant population (if population data exists – if not, an estimate of how frequent these features are based on the expert's experience).

A more detailed description is usually provided as an appendix. Here the observations will be grouped by phonetic parameters, e.g., what was discovered in terms of consonant and vowel features.

Discussion: A discussion of how useful the parameters investigated are. Experts provide a statement about the likelihood that the questioned and known samples come from the same speaker. If numerical likelihood ratios are applied (see Chapter 4), experts should be transparent about how they calculated the probability of the different-speaker hypothesis (i.e., how they established typicality) – whether this was based on subjective estimation, primary database testing, or background statistics that happen to be available for these features. The scale of opinion that the expert uses should also be included, so that readers can judge the strength of the conclusion. This might, for example, be a version of the conclusion scale illustrated in Figure 4.7.

Appendices: A summary CV outlining the qualifications and experience of the analyst(s) who worked on the case, a detailed listing of equipment used, and reference to any key literature consulted.

Expert reports should also contain a statement that the expert understands their duty to the court, and that they have complied with that duty. Members of IAFPA attach a note warning the courts that the evidence provided in their reports should in most circumstances only be used corroboratively, because (in most circumstances) it is not possible to establish the identity of a speaker with absolute certainty based on voice features alone. A typical standard caveat is as follows:

Evidence from forensic speaker comparison analyses is not comparable to fingerprints or DNA. It is recognised that there could be people in the population who are indistinguishable in respect of voice and speech patterns. Speaker comparison analysis produces an opinion, supported by reference to phonetic and acoustic features of the material examined.

In addition to providing a report, the expert must also ensure that all working notes and data analysed are organised in a coherent way. The court might ask for detailed information. For example, if a report is submitted on behalf of the prosecution, the defence lawyers might appoint their own expert and ask them to scrutinise the analysis. This could involve checking the specific measurements made. In the David Bain case, addressing the substance of a questioned utterance, one expert was asked to provide all draft versions of their transcription. The final transcription submitted in the official report had left the questioned utterance untranscribed (because it was deemed too difficult to produce a reliable version of the words spoken). It emerged that earlier versions, however, had contained some words that were later removed, and these words were in line with versions submitted by other experts.

Some experts provide examples of their reports on their websites (sometimes in more complex form than might be ideal for the client's purposes). See, for instance, Rose (2009), which describes questioned utterance analysis for the Bain case, and Morrison (2014), which is a critique of a Canadian practitioner's report in a forensic speaker comparison case.

13.5 The expert in the courtroom

Although many cases are conducted by forensic speech and language experts, few result in court appearances. Rhodes & Cambier-Langeveld (2025) suggest the rate is as low as 2–3% in forensic phonetics, which accords with our experience. Shuy (2002) notes he has given evidence in around 10% of his forensic linguistics cases.

The rarity of court appearances is due to several reasons. First, a lot of work takes place at the investigation stage, assisting the police to further their understanding of what happened in a given event (especially in speaker profiling and linguistic profiling; Chapters 3 and 11). This can also be in aiding access to rights (see, for example, the work in ensuring the comprehensibility of the caution, Chapter 9). Forensic linguists in particular do the majority of their work before a case reaches trial, and some types of work are not undertaken as evidence (for example, transcripts might be to assist the court in listening to a recording). Second, the case might not reach trial at all. Even if it does, expert reports might be accepted by all parties in the case, and thus there is no need for the expert to be questioned. Third, if the report is unhelpful or prejudicial to the instructing party (remember the duty of impartiality), this line of evidence or defence might be dropped if the case can continue without it. Fourth, cases may end in a guilty plea, meaning a trial is not required. Defendants often change their plea to guilty at the last minute, when they arrive at court and realise the bleakness of the situation given the evidence against them. The expert is sometimes already at court, or travelling to attend, when this news emerges.

Finally, while the work might have been done, it might not be admitted in the trial. As we have already seen, there are various rules for judges to consider when it comes to admitting expert evidence. While most courts these days would readily accept expert testimony from 'hard sciences', for example relating to DNA analysis, speech and language are sometimes judged to be non-expert matters. Some judges take the view that listening to people speak, or reading a written text, are everyday matters that members of a jury can do for themselves. This is what happened, for instance, in the retrial of David Bain. In a pre-trial *voir dire* hearing, held to consider the evidence that would be put before the jury, the judge ruled that expert evidence was not needed because it was simply a matter of listening to the material. An appeal court subsequently overturned that decision. In the murder trial of George Zimmerman in Florida (see Chapter 10), the prosecution sought to bring expert evidence in which ASR was used to analyse screams, amounting to two seconds in duration, extracted from a telephone call. The judge refused to admit the evidence after hearing from a number of experts who argued that ASR could not be used reliably to analyse screams, or material of such short duration. A summary of some of the expert testimony is available online, as are full recordings of the experts giving testimony (Tom Owen and Alan Reich for the prosecution, Hirotaka Nakasone, Peter French, and George Doddington for the defence).

Similarly, the more qualitative fields of discourse analysis and testimony on meaning in contract and trademark disputes are not always admitted. The growing use of corpora to aid the linguist in discourse analytic findings appears to be helpful in illustrating scientific validity, but much needs to be done to improve the public perception of qualitative analysis in forensic linguistics on the stand.

When the expert witness is called to give evidence, the court normally follows a standard routine. The expert will be asked to confirm their credentials, and an outline of their work and findings will be summarised. This is often led by the barrister (advocate), based on the written report, with the expert witness merely confirming what the barrister says. This is designed to keep information to a helpful minimum for the sake of a jury or judge, and to avoid straying from what is documented in the report. Detailed accounts of expert testimony procedure include Ehrhardt (2021, focusing on Germany) and Finegan (2021, US).

Inquisitorial courts have the mission to establish facts. In this regard, the expert might then be questioned further by the judge in order to clarify their findings and thus to further the court's understanding of the facts of the case. In an adversarial court, by contrast, the expert witness might be cross-examined by the opposition barrister. Adversarial courts pit a prosecution team against a defence team. The prosecution has what is called the burden of proof: they must establish beyond reasonable doubt that the defendant is guilty of the charge. The defence team do not have to prove innocence; they merely have to undermine the prosecution case and leave the jury or judge with sufficient doubt. They are, by definition, *adversaries*. Their job is to discredit the testimony of witnesses, and they can do this by any means necessary. Sometimes this is done in a subtle way, to reveal weaknesses in a witness's account of events. Most common of these discrediting techniques is to find and exploit the witness's inconsistencies in testimony (or expertise), or to reveal a lack of expertise. For example, in the Ghana case, the defence barristers repeatedly pressed the UK experts' lack of knowledge about Ghana and its languages in order to try to undermine their evidence. (The experts held their ground by acknowledging the point and deferring such questions to their Ghanaian colleague, who had been recruited precisely for his expertise in Ghanaian linguistics.) The adversarial courtroom can present a particularly frustrating environment for expert witnesses if the adversarial lawyers stray into personal attack. In one UK case, for instance, barristers scrutinised an expert witness's CV in great detail in order to demonstrate to the court that this expert – in contrast to their own – lacked any recent publications and had not attended academic conferences for many years. The lengthy attack on the CV served to undermine confidence in the expert's testimony. In a US case, a young female academic working on her first case sought advice from an eminent and experienced male expert. When she arrived at court to give her testimony she found that the senior colleague was also present, employed as an expert witness by the opposing legal team. His testimony consisted largely of outlining his years of experience, and explaining that he had advised the junior colleague, given that it was her first case. The outcome was to emphasise in the eyes of the jury his experience and her lack of it (no doubt compounded by age- and gender-related prejudice). The actual phonetic analysis was largely sidelined.

In matters where there are multiple opposing expert witnesses, the witnesses are usually asked to discuss differences between their opinions in order to reach an agreed position. They would then jointly produce a summary document to outline their areas of agreement, and reasons for any continued disagreement. Doing so is hugely beneficial to the court, which otherwise has to evaluate competing versions of expert testimony in a complex scientific field.

Experts often end their role in a case without ever knowing whether their evidence made any difference to the outcome. It is important to note, though, that forensic scientists do not – and should not – judge their work in relation to the number of convictions they secure or 'wins' in cases they work on. Legal cases are decided on many grounds, not only the forensic evidence. It is furthermore ethically inappropriate to judge expert evidence in terms of the value it has to one party in a case. As we have explained, expert witnesses have a duty to the court, and to deliver fair justice.

13.6 Conclusion

This chapter has provided an overview of how expert witnesses are defined, the principles they should follow, how forensic sciences are regulated, and how expert testimony is handled in courts. Forensic speech and language analysis takes many forms. Not all types of work are regularly accepted as expert evidence, and the degree of understanding varies from court to court and jurisdiction to jurisdiction. It remains a key duty of speech and language experts to educate parties in legal systems, and the public in general, about their fields.

Further reading

For discussions of how forensic speech and language analysis is used in court:

Coulthard, M. (2020). Experts and opinions: In my opinion. In M. Coulthard, A. May, & R. Sousa-Silva (eds.), *The Routledge Handbook of Forensic Linguistics*. 2nd edition. Routledge, pp. 523–538.

Finegan, E. (2021). Expert testimony by linguists in US courts: An illustrative case of practices. *Language and Law/Linguagem e Direito*, 8(1): 22–42.

French, J. P. (2017). A developmental history of forensic speaker comparison in the UK. *English Phonetics*, 21: 271–286.

Tiersma, P., & Solan, L. M. (2002). The linguist on the witness stand: Forensic linguistics in American courts. *Language*, 78: 221–239.

For a discussion of protocols and regulations for forensic speech and language analysts:

Rhodes, R. & Cambier-Langeveld, T. (2025). Guidance for practitioners. In F. Nolan, K. McDougall, & T. Hudson (eds.), *Oxford Handbook of Forensic Phonetics*. Oxford University Press.

For more on considerations on what it means to be a forensic linguist:

Bowen, A., & Eades, D. (2022). Forensic linguistics and pseudoscience: How to recognise the difference. *Precedent*, 172: 35–39.

Clarke, I., & Kredens, K. (2018). I consider myself to be a service provider: Discursive identity construction of the forensic linguistic expert. *International Journal of Speech, Language and the Law*, 25(1): 79–107.

Grant, T. (2022). *The Idea of Progress in Forensic Authorship Analysis*. Cambridge University Press.

For a more general discussion of expert witnesses and legal systems:

Milroy, C. M. (2017). A brief history of the expert witness. *Academic Forensic Pathology*, 7(4): 516–526.

Servick, K. (2016). Reversing the legacy of junk science in the courtroom: Statisticians are on a mission to bring rigor to fingerprints, ballistics, and other "pattern" evidence. *Science*, 7 March.

The Secret Barrister (2018). *Stories of the Law and How It's Broken*. Picador.

References

Ash, S. (1988). Speaker identification in sociolinguistics and criminal law. In K. Ferrara, B. Brown, K. Walters, & J. Baugh (eds.), *Linguistic Change and Contact*. University of Texas, pp. 25–33.

Berger, C. E., Buckleton, J., Champod, C., Evett, I. W., & Jackson, G. (2011). Evidence evaluation: A response to the court of appeal judgment in R. v T. *Science & Justice*, 51(2): 43–49.

Butters, R. R. (2009). The forensic linguist's professional credentials. *International Journal of Speech, Language and the Law*, 16(2): 237–252.

Ehrhardt, S. (2021). Forensic linguistics in German law enforcement. *Language and Law/Linguagem e Direito*, 8(1): 6–21.

Hollien, H. (2016). An approach to speaker identification. *Journal of Forensic Sciences*, 61(2): 334–344.

Keierleber, J. A., & Bohan, T. L. (2005). Ten years after *Daubert*: The status of the States. *Journal of Forensic Sciences*, 50: 1154–1163.

Labov, W. (1988). The judicial testing of linguistic theory. In D. Tannen (ed.), *Linguistics in Context: Connecting Observation and Understanding*. Ablex, pp. 159–182.

Margot, P. (1998). The role of the forensic scientist in an inquisitorial system of justice. *Science & Justice*, 38(2): 71–73.

Matthiesen, Wickert & Lehrer, S. C. (2022). Admissibility of expert testimony in all 50 States. Online document.

Morrison, G. S. (2014). *Critique of a Forensic Voice Comparison Report Submitted by Mr Edward J Primeau in Relation to a Section of Audio Recording Which Is Alleged to Be a Recording of the Voice of Dr Marlo Raynolds*. Unpublished report.

Rodman, R. (2002). Linguistics and the law: How knowledge of, or ignorance of, elementary linguistics may affect the dispensing of justice. *International Journal of Speech, Language and the Law*, 9(1): 94–103.

Rose, P. (2009). *Evaluation of Disputed Utterance Evidence in the Matter of David Bain's Retrial*. Unpublished report.

Shuy, R. W. (2002). To testify or not to testify? In J. Cotterill (ed.) *Language in the Legal Process*. Palgrave, pp. 3–18.

Wagner, I. (2019). Examples of casework in forensic speaker comparison. In S. Calhoun, P. Escudero, M. Tabain, & P. Warren (eds.), *Proceedings of the 19th International Congress of Phonetic Sciences*. Australasian Speech Science and Technology Association, pp. 721–725.

Cases cited

UK cases
R. v. O'Doherty [2002] NICB 3173
R. v. Robb [1991] 93 Cr App R 161
R. v. Silverlock [1894] 2 Q.B. 766
R. v. T [2010] EWCA Crim 2439

US cases
Daubert v. Merrell Dow Pharmaceuticals, Inc., 509 U.S. 579 (1993)
Frye v. United States, 293 F. 1013 (D.C. Cir. 1923)
General Electric Co. v. Joiner, 522 U.S. 136 (1997)
Kumho Tire Company vs. Carmichael, 526 U.S. 137 (1999)

 Several other cases that involved forensic linguistic analysis, mostly from the US, are listed on Roger Shuy's website.

Index